Management for Professionals

For further volumes:
http://www.springer.com/series/10101

Alexander Maedche · Achim Botzenhardt · Ludwig Neer
Editors

Software for People

Fundamentals, Trends and Best Practices

 Springer

Editors
Alexander Maedche
Achim Botzenhardt
Chair of Information Systems IV
University of Mannheim
Mannheim
Germany

Ludwig Neer
CAS Software AG
Karlsruhe
Germany

ISSN 2192-8096   ISSN 2192-810X (electronic)
ISBN 978-3-642-31370-7   ISBN 978-3-642-31371-4 (eBook)
DOI 10.1007/978-3-642-31371-4
Springer Heidelberg New York Dordrecht London

Library of Congress Control Number: 2012948154

Printed on acid-free paper

Springer is part of Springer-Science+Business Media (www.springer.com)

Contents

Part II   Best Practices

Software for People: A Paradigm Change in the Software Industry

Alexander Maedche, Achim Botzenhardt, and Ludwig Neer

Abstract

The highly competitive and globalized software market is creating pressure on software companies. Given the current boundary conditions, it is critical to continuously increase time-to-market and reduce development costs. In parallel, driven by private life experiences with mobile computing devices, the World Wide Web and software-based services, peoples' general expectations with regards to software are growing. They expect software that is simple and joyful to use. Given these boundary conditions, software companies need to fundamentally reconsider the way they develop and deliver software to their customers. This editorial article motivates the paradigm change towards "software for people". We first illustrate in more detail the two important categories of challenges software companies are currently faced with. Building on a short review of the historic evolution of software, we explain the major reasons that caused these challenges. Driven by the more mature automotive industry, we outline a set of key principles that may help software companies to tackle these challenges. Finally, we summarize the structure and content of the book, building on these key principles and providing a comprehensive overview on fundamentals, trends and best practices for building software for people.

A. Maedche • A. Botzenhardt
University of Mannheim - Chair of Information Systems IV, Mannheim, Germany
e-mail: maedche@eris.uni-mannheim.de; botzenhardt@eris.uni-mannheim.de

L. Neer
CAS Software AG, Karlsruhe, Germany
e-mail: neer@cas.de

A. Maedche et al. (eds.), *Software for People*, Management for Professionals,
DOI 10.1007/978-3-642-31371-4_1, © Springer-Verlag Berlin Heidelberg 2012

1   Challenges

Software companies are faced with two important categories of challenges: First, they need to industrialize their development and delivery processes to survive in the competitive and globalized market. Second, they need to fulfill the growing expectations of people with regards to software that is simple and joyful to use.

Even after more than 50 years of software engineering research and practice, software development project failures occur far more often than they should. There are many factors that may lead to project failure; most of them being of non-technical nature, such as a lack of understanding with respect to requirements, unrealistic goals, poor communication or weak project management. By looking at these factors more detailed, it becomes obvious that it is all about people, either as providers of input, as members of a project team or stakeholders of a project or as users of the projects result. An efficient and effective orchestration of the various human entities involved in a software development project, beyond the core engineering team, can be considered as a key challenge.

In parallel, consumer market-driven trends such as the massive adoption of mobile computing devices as well as software-based services offered on the World Wide Web have made people as business software users more demanding. People want to be able to run a trial before deciding to buy a piece of software. People look at software more and more from a non-functional viewpoint, specifically the perceived usability or more general the experience of a software product has become an important buying criterion. They expect instant consumption without requiring any installation. Software should be easy-to-use and self explanatory without a necessity to read comprehensive manuals or even attend dedicated trainings. Finally, creating a positive feeling and emotions of people using their software is becoming essential for software companies.

2   Evolution of Software

Looking back on the history of corporate computing, hardware and software originally were bundled together on mainframe-based application systems providing the necessary infrastructure for running purpose-centric calculation systems in enterprises. The development of new programming languages, standardization of operating systems together with the invention of relational database management systems and client–server computing were drivers enabling new types of application systems targeting a broader group of people in companies. In the 1980s most large enterprises followed a tailor-based software development approach. Specialized Line of Business application systems were established either with internal resources or by contracting external service providers.

In the early 1990s, two important developments influenced the future evolution of software: First, the concept of standardized product software delivering best-practices out-of-the-box was established and successfully introduced to the market. Microsoft and SAP are two well-known companies that have consequently and successfully following the product software approach. However, it is important to understand that by following a product software approach the distance between the people using the software and the people developing the software is also increased. Second, the invention of the World Wide Web (WWW) including protocol and description language standards such as the Hypertext Transfer Protocol (HTTP) and the Hypertext Markup Language (HTML) as well as corresponding tools such as HTML editors and Web browsers simplified publishing and accessing information. Based on this new Web infrastructure, companies started to establish a first Web presence and first simple e-Business solutions in the form of B2C/B2B Web applications. In the last decade, the entire software industry was heavily impacted by three major trends driven by the consumer market:

1. The fast evolution of mobile devices connecting to networks further accelerated simplified access to information and established a new way of looking at information technology in general. Specifically, the launch of Apple's iPhone in 2007 and the iPad in 2010 represented a major milestone for mobile computing and introduced a "platform shift" from the established personal computer with its operating system Microsoft Windows towards an "app-driven" software product delivery paradigm enabled by marketplaces.
2. The WWW evolved into the Web 2.0, providing services such as Facebook.com (launched in 2004) or Twitter (launched in 2006) that have been massively adopted by people all over the world. These services enabled people to provide user-generated content on the Web. Furthermore, they were characterized from the very early beginning by highly interactive and easy-to-use interfaces not requiring any training and installation on the client.
3. Finally, the cloud-based computing infrastructure enables new ways for offering software-based services. Starting with basic services like Google's Gmail client (launched in 2004), we increasingly see comprehensive business software packages from established software product companies such as SAP's Sales-on-Demand or Microsoft's Office 365 (both launched in 2011) offered on a service basis. By doing so, software vendors become responsible for the entire software lifecycle including software development, delivery and its operation.

The result of these three trends originally driven by the consumer market is that peoples' expectations have dramatically changed, they expect reliable anytime, anywhere, any device access to applications with a seamless transition between private and business use. Given the growing importance of the Web as the future computing infrastructure the software industry becomes even more globalized and competitive, rapidly changing from a product into service business.

3   Key Principles

How can software companies tackle these challenges and build sustainable success in this new competitive environment? To find answers to these challenging questions, it may be worth looking at the evolution of more mature industries such as the automotive industry. The first automobiles were basically built around the engine with a strong engineering focus. Later, automobile development was heavily influenced by the enablement of mass production, e.g. the T-Model of Ford was at the beginning only available in black. With the growing competition in the automotive industry, the need for further differentiation was growing. The automotive industry came up with various concepts to address the challenge to trade-off between mass production and differentiation in a competitive and global environment. Well-known examples of such concepts are lean production, cross-functional integration in new product development, platform-based product development as well as horizontal and vertical integration.

The software industry has already adopted and taken over some of these well-established concepts: Inspired by lean production, lean and agile principles were introduced in software development. Looking beyond the core engineering process, another important well-established concept in the automotive industry is cross-functional integration in new product development. The idea is to combine staff with different functional expertise working towards a common goal. Automotive companies combine staff with engineering, design- and business-related skills in order to develop and manage products in a more effective and efficient way. In more detail, to develop a successful car it requires the sensibility and methods of a designer to match people's need, combined with the technical mind of a developer who knows what is technically feasible and finally a product manager who has the business perspective in mind. Within this collaborative product development process prototyping is leveraged, e.g. designers create paper-based sketches and hand it over to the developers that create computer-aided design models and physical prototypes of the envisioned car.

Today, even after the massive adoption of lean and agile principles the degree of cross-functional integration in the software industry is still relatively low. This book introduces fundamentals, trends and best practices in the software industry demonstrating how cross-functional integration can be leveraged by software companies to successfully build software for people. Specifically, this book provides a holistic and integrated view on the engineering, design and business function within a software company.

4   Content of the Book

4.1   Fundamentals and Trends

The first part of the book introduces basic knowledge of user-centered design, software product management and agile software development. Beyond providing an overview on the state-of-the-art of these dedicated domains we specifically will demonstrate cross-functional integration of these areas as a key principle. Additionally, we look at design thinking as one important trend in the software industry.

The **second chapter** provides an introduction to the user-centered design (UCD) methodology, a successful and practical approach to the design of software. *Dieter Wallach* and *Sebastian Scholz* represent why and how to look at users as first citizens in software development. After a detailed overview on the foundational principles the authors take a deep look at each of the five central categories of design activities, which are performed in UCD: Scope, Analyse, Design, Validate and Deliver. Following the theoretical foundations, they discuss the application of the design activities by using a real-life case study for illustration. The chapter also outlines the relationship of UCD and eLearning which offers a vast amount of fruitful synergies in the different stages. The presented content fosters the understanding of good software design and methods for achieving high usability of interactive systems.

Based on these insights, **chapter** 3 presents the results of an empirical study which explores the current status quo of software usability in small and medium sized enterprises in Germany. The study project team from the University of Mannheim, the University of Applied Sciences Kaiserslautern and Ergosign GmbH followed a hybrid approach including a combined qualitative and quantitative data collection strategy in order to explore the entire organizational field. This includes the most important actors and their interactions as well as the state-of-the-art of usability integration in software developing organizations. They specifically look at interactions between actors in the field and the outcomes of these interactions with a primary focus on software producers. In the light of the studies results, the researchers provide recommendations on how to increase awareness and maturity of software usability in small and medium sized enterprises in Germany.

Another key competitive factor in the software industry is the quality of software product management. In **chapter** 4, *Samuel Fricker* illustrates the foundations of software product management by providing key insights of this important discipline which aims for closing the gap between business and software engineering. Starting by an introduction of the software product concept the author characterizes the software product manager as well as company-internal and -external stakeholders and gives an overview on recent software product management references models. He describes the key software product management practices and discusses what is known about this discipline today. The understanding of this fundamental software product management knowledge paves the road for a successful implementation of SPM in software companies, as shown later in the best practices part.

Besides the growing importance of software product management we all have witnessed the triumphant upswing of agile software development, a major trend in the software industry over the past 10 years. This increasing shift to agile development processes thereby represents new challenges for all parties involved. Especially the relationship between product management and development moves into the center of attention. In **chapter** 5, *Hans-Bernd Kittlaus* addresses the question which many companies are faced with, namely how software product management and agile development can work together in an optimal way. He describes potential conflict areas and presents a set of developed solutions leading to an efficient and effective cooperation between the two parties.

Requirements Engineering, as a part of software product management, also faces new challenges resulting from an agile environment. In **chapter** 6, *Rainer Grau* provides an intensive introduction on Requirements Engineering in agile software development. He starts with a division of the application area of Requirements Engineering into two context levels: in the context of the product or service portfolio and in the context of projects. While agile methods and techniques are often successfully established on the project context, they are hardly at the portfolio context and thus leading to a culture clash between the portfolio and the project context. The author presents how active knowledge work can serve as the key to agile Requirements Engineering and shows how agile principles can be emerged on the product level. By taking a tour through fundamental concepts of Requirements Engineering, the ecosystem of product development, complex problems and the understanding of the ecosystem "project" he visualizes the forces behind agile techniques in Requirements Engineering which are capable to open up unimagined potential for the organization.

Chapter 7 is devoted to Design Thinking, an important trend in the software industry. *Anja Wölbling* and her colleagues describe the emergence of Design Thinking, an innovative concept which enables creativity, enhances personal development, and prescribes deep immersion into the topic along with empathetic user research. They provide a detailed overview on the four key elements of Design Thinking: the iterative process, multidisciplinary teams, creative space and designer's mindset. In combination, these elements form a distinctive context that enables creativity and increases the chances of generating innovative ideas. By providing hands-on recommendations on applying design thinking, they show how to leverage the potential of design thinking in the context of software development.

4.2   Best Practices

In the second part of the book we want to address the practical application of this basic knowledge in real-life industry cases. Qualified professionals report on their experiences and lessons learned which they have gained throughout their careers.

Our first best practice author is *Kostanija Petrovic,* Consumer Insight Manager at Nokia and president of the German UPA, a professional association for Usability and User Experience Professionals. In **chapter** 8, she presents best practices for integrating user experience design (UXD) into product development and how it can help companies to enhance the customer value of their products and services. The chapter outlines the relationship between UXD activities and agile development and addresses the implications which come along with this fundamental change. In a detailed illustration, the author shows how a so called "sprint zero", prior to the actual start of development, helps to define the core concepts and epic and user stories, and also to integrate user research activities. The presented set of hands-on best practices help product teams to collaborate more effectively, focus more on actual user needs, and allows for satisfying both, the users and the participating product teams.

Building on these foundations, **chapter** 9 by *Lennart Hennigs* deals with the question on how to make design tangible in software development projects. Based on his longtime expertise and the realization of numerous projects at Deutsche

Telekom AG, the author describes how user experience professionals can guide software development projects and create a common understanding of the targeted user experience. He specifically addresses the question how UX practitioners can provide value to an interdisciplinary team and points out appropriate activities and artifacts which fit perfectly in an agile software development environment. The right application of the presented activities and artifacts can make a significant contribution to achieve smooth project operation and attractive products.

Chapter 10 by *Ulf Schubert* and his colleagues provides valuable insights into the change process from technology-driven development to user-centered design at DATEV eG. Like many manufacturers of business software, DATEV eG has to face the challenge of creating better usability and a positive user experience in the light of many complex features and functions and parallel development within distributed teams. The authors present the solution for this complex problem in form of a style guide, which is used by developers across the whole development department. The wiki-based style guide provides design principles and guidelines which describe fundamental ideas about the practice of good user interface design. By making it mandatory for the design of all software products DATEV eG tries to tackle the challenge of a consistent user interface design throughout the development process. Based on their experiences from the change process, *Ulf Schubert* and his colleagues describe seven best practices for successfully establishing user centred design in software manufacturing companies.

The authors *Maik Schacht* and *Silvia Schacht* introduce a concrete instrument to create user experience, called Gamification, in **chapter** 11. The integration of game mechanisms in applications by itself is not a new idea. In particular, applications using game mechanisms such as ratings, rankings, or bonuses are already known in the private consumer sector. Famous applications are Dropbox rewarding users that recruit other users with additional storage space, or Facebook, where users can rate other members of their social network. In organizations, however, the potential of Gamification is only realized by first movers. Thus, Microsoft, for example, uses game mechanisms to incentivize their employees to participate in the testing phase of new products, or to coach end users in using their products. In order to underline the potential of Gamification in enterprise information systems, the authors also provide a set of use cases and rate them with regard to its capability to succeed on the one hand and its ease of implementation on the other hand.

Drawing on the knowledge of software product management from the fundamental part, *Christian Schlögel* is presenting a real-world industry experience report of a product management introduction project at Wincor Nixdorf International GmbH in **chapter** 12. He shows the challenging way from an existing line organization-driven to a development project-driven organization and recounts changes and achievements in the first year of the introduction. The chapter outlines a detailed description of the new model including the overall process, structure and responsibilities of the product management, marketing and development organization. The outstanding practical relevance of this chapter stems from the first-hand experience and lessoned learned during the introduction of product management. With the knowledge, gained in this chapter, companies can not only facilitate their introduction of product management, but also improve an existing product management approach.

Chapter 13 provides a concrete application of the Design Thinking concept at SAP AG, the world market leader in business software. *Tobias Hildenbrand* and *Johannes Meyer* demonstrate the power of Design Thinking, when concepts turn from theory into practice. While lean and agile principles are known very well in the software industry, many companies are still struggling with leveraging Design Thinking. The question is, does this new approach of Design Thinking take the place of Lean Thinking? On the contrary, Design Thinking is a perfect match for complementing lean and agile software development in early stages since it supports software development teams to come up with an innovative product vision and derive high-quality requirements. The authors show how companies can unleash unimagined potential by intertwining the two concepts.

In **chapter** 14, *Michail Theuns, Kevin Vlaanderen,* and *Sjaak Brinkkemper* explore the relationship of agile development methods and software product management processes, two topics which have become almost inseparable. Today's modern product software development settings demand for faster time-to-market, higher customer orientation and consideration of rapidly changing requirements. These demands have driven many companies to implement composites of agile methods in order to leverage the potential of their development. But with the implementation of agile methods new challenges arise. Many companies find themselves faced with the challenge of adjusting software product management in an agile environment. Specifically, the authors shed light on the link between release planning processes and Scrum leveraging key insights from a real-life case study. Their results constitute an important input to a knowledge infrastructure that helps product managers in incrementally improving the software product management processes in their organizations and adapting to the new demands.

The last professional and author of the **fifteenth chapter**, *Markus Bauer*, provides insights from the development of Software as a Service (SaaS) solutions which offer customers unprecedented opportunities with regard to customizability and extensibility. A good user interface design and an appropriate software architecture are considered as key success factors of a SaaS product. However, many companies are faced with the challenge of two conflicting requirements within their SaaS products: how to satisfy the growing expectation of customers concerning a smooth customization while exploiting the economy of scale principle by employing an architecture that handles all customers uniformly. Based on his extensive experience in the field of SaaS at CAS Software AG, he points out numerous lessons learned and hands-on recommendations that help vendors to tackle this challenge and fully leverage the potential the SaaS-based delivery model has to offer.

Part I

Fundamentals and Trends

User-Centered Design: Why and How to Put Users First in Software Development

Dieter Wallach and Sebastian C. Scholz

Abstract

In this chapter we provide an overview of the activities and artefacts of the user-centered design (UCD) methodology – a successful and practical approach to the design of software user interfaces. After tracing its foundational principles (early focus on users, empirical measurement using prototypes and iterative design) back to 1985s seminal paper by Gould and Lewis, we will highlight each of five central categories of design activities (Scope, Analyse, Design, Validate and Deliver) performed in UCD. Potential integration of UCD into two popular categorizations of software development (User Interface First vs. User Interface Later) will be explored and then demonstrated in a real life case study from the field of electronic engineering along with a practical takeaway regarding the relationship of UCD and eLearning.

1 Introduction

On January 9th, 2007 Apple announced three things: a widescreen iPod with touch control, a revolutionary mobile phone and a breakthrough internet communication device – all combined in a single device named iPhone. Six months, worldwide distributed photos showing long lines of staying the night customers willing to wait and buy, and massive international iPhone press coverage later, Apple's stock value had already climbed by 60 % when the iPhone finally became available on the market (and ascended by more than 600 % since then). It was not for providing new

D. Wallach
University of Applied Sciences, Kaiserslautern, Germany
e-mail: dieter.wallach@fh-kl.de

S.C. Scholz
ERGOSIGN GmbH, Munich, Germany
e-mail: scholz@ergosign.de

A. Maedche et al. (eds.), *Software for People*, Management for Professionals,
DOI 10.1007/978-3-642-31371-4_2, © Springer-Verlag Berlin Heidelberg 2012

functionality that made the iPhone a huge and still on-going success. Quite to the contrary: the iPhone even offered *less* functionality compared to many smart phones of that time. When presenting the iPhone in his now famous keynote, Steve Jobs focused on its revolutionary user interface as the distinguishing factor that was head and shoulders above competing devices: *And we have invented a new technology called multi-touch, which is phenomenal [. . .] It works like magic [. . .] It ignores unintended touches, it's super-smart* (Jobs 2007).

Performing as an external design partner for a variety of types of clients, industries, projects and artefacts over more than a decade we are repeatedly exposed to several fallacies regarding interface design - the first one starting with the notion that a high prioritization of the user interface is apparently something new and ground breaking. Although the above-mentioned iPhone is certainly the most often cited example, it was not Steve Jobs who invented good user interface design to support and delight users in their daily life and business. The understanding of good user interface design and methods for achieving high usability of interactive devices can at least be traced back to a seminal paper by Gould and Lewis (1985) that we will discuss in the second section of this chapter.

Another common fallacy is the equation of interface design with some form of visually bedaubing the screen – an activity that can be added later to an otherwise finished product. The iPhone itself is a perfect example for this assumption's fallaciousness with its *interaction design* being the primary innovative achievement. For a significant and sustainable impact a variety of interface design activities (covered in Sect. 4) needs to be conducted and deeply engrained throughout the complete development process (see Sect. 3).

Finally, a third fallacy – that interface design is subjective, neither measurable nor objectively discussable – is often heard. Though certain aspects such as the visual design of an interface bearing potential for more discussion than others, user interface design is a process based on gathering information relevant for informed decisions. By allocation of dedicated scoping and analysing activities upfront the actual design very limited room is left for bias and personal agenda (discussed in Sect. 4).

2 Key Principles

2.1 Twenty-Seven Years Later: Gould and Lewis (1985) Revisited

To prepare for subsequent sections of this chapter, a major potential terminological pitfall needs to be addressed at first. *Design* as a concept deals with the challenge of being used as a label for a single *activity* (e.g. icon design), a *process* consisting of multiple activities (e.g. user-centered design), a *deliverable* or *result* (e.g. design style guide) and as *field* (e.g. user interface design). This already bears much potential for confusion in establishing a common ground between stakeholders for example a board, designers and developers. Yet it even gets more complicated: These days *user experience (UX) design, user interface (UI) design, graphical user interface (GUI) design, user-centered design (UCD), interaction design (IxD), user interface developer (UIDev)* and additional terms and acronyms are used interchangeably – and frequently even with different connotations – leading to additional confusion. In this chapter we will refrain from using these acronyms and will refer to "design"/"designers" as a comprehensive hull for the respective nuance variants mentioned. Instead we will concentrate on a depiction of user-centered design as a process, opposed to the more artefact driven UI/GUI/IxD/UIDev connotation or the all embracing and thus very vague and result driven UX design.

Even though 27 years feel to be close to eternity in Information Technology, a still required read to understand the essence of user centered design is Gould and Lewis' (1985) paper *Designing for Usability: Key Principles and What Designers Think* in which the authors present and discuss three principles for the emerging field: (1) early focus on users, (2) empirical measurement using prototypes and (3) iterative design. Gould and Lewis explicitly differentiate between *understanding potential users, versus identifying, describing, stereotyping and ascertaining them.* Herefor the authors stress the importance of bringing designers into direct contact with potential users and mention interviews or exchanges with and observations of users as appropriate methods to be applied prior to design. Knowledge about a user's tasks can then be aligned with the knowledge about users themselves (in terms of cognition, behavioural working conditions, literacy level and exposure to previous systems). Gould and Lewis also emphasize (p. 302) the need for testing prototypes very early in the development process – an argument that we will pick up in Sect. 4.3.1.2 of this chapter. Their reference to testing is further substantiated by the use of empirical evaluation methods where *intended users should actually use simulations and prototypes to carry out real work, and their performance and reactions should be observed, recorded, and analysed.* (p. 300).

Interestingly enough the authors already make a distinction between the creation of a functional prototype to test the feasibility or stability of technical properties of a system and a non- or semi-functional prototype following the main goal of studying a user's reaction to it: *What is required is a usability test, not a selling job.* (Gould and Lewis 1985, p. 302).

Gould and Lewis strike a crucial chord regarding the necessity to separate the roles of designers and developers for a simple reason: It is cognitively impossible for developers (and other project stakeholders) to pretend to be a novice user. An insightful demonstration to justify this separation can be used to illustrate their argument. Humans often have a strong believe in their perspective-taking abilities and especially developers are fast in replying that they themselves are users – so why would they not be able to put themselves into the shoes of a user? (Mayhew 1999). Asking participants whether they are able to identify a meaningful pattern or object when exposed to the picture shown in Fig. 1 usually leaves them in a short moment of silence.

After a while, a cue to seeing the head of a cow in this picture typically emerges in some form of light bulb moment in which participants confirm that they *now* see the cow previously unheralded. If then instructed to ignore the cow, participants are

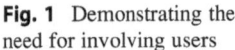
Fig. 1 Demonstrating the
need for involving users

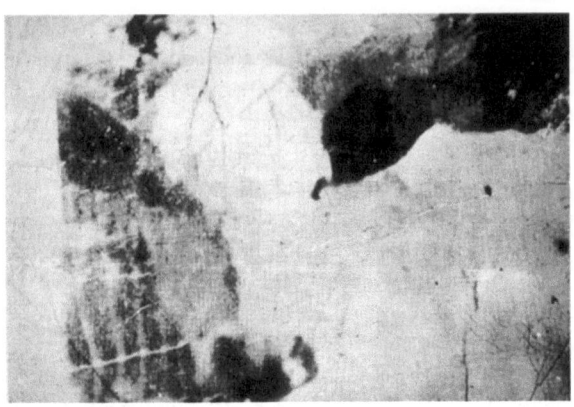

quick to point out that this impossible now. Like Heraclitus' *You could not step twice into the same river* having seen the cow once does hardly allow to switch back to the previous unknowledgeable state. In analogy to this demonstration, it is just as hard for developers, product managers, business analysts and also for designers having all the knowledge that professional life entails to go back to the unknowledgeable state attributed to a novice user. To avoid this fallacy, Gould and Lewis (1985, p. 302) recommend that *potential users become part of the design team from the very outset when their perspectives can have the most influence, rather than using them post hoc as part of an analysis team (of) end user representatives.* Isolating designers from users de facto eliminates the empathic knowledge about users as the target of design.

The final major takeaway from Gould and Lewis (1985) is their emphasis on the importance of iteration. The authors are very clear in accenting the necessity to setup a process that enables cycles of design, test, measuring (behavioural goals) and redesign frequently (p. 300) – now being a hallmark of user-centered design as discussed in section three of this chapter.

2.2   Usability

Gould and Lewis base their résumé on key principles of designing for usability on three very solid pillars: *user-centricity, empirical measurement* and *iteration.* Achieving usability then presupposes the fulfilment of the following conditions (1985, p. 307):

- *A description of the intended users must be given.*
- *The tasks to be performed, and the circumstances in which they should be performed, must be given.*
- *The measurements of interest, such as learning time, errors, number of requests for help, or attitude, and the criterion values to be achieved for each, must be given.*

While Gould and Lewis themselves do not provide an explicit definition of usability in their paper, the aforementioned conditions are in close correspondence to the widespread ISO EN 9241-11 definition of usability. The ISO EN 9241-11 defines usability as the *Extent to which a product can be used by specified users to achieve specified goals with effectiveness, efficiency and satisfaction in a specified context of use*. The metrics mentioned in the ISO definition (efficiency, effectiveness, satisfaction) can be mapped to the last condition claimed by Gould and Lewis that we will come across again in Sect. 4.4.2 when discussing the concept of *usability goals*. The mentioning of a specified user working in a specified context of use to achieve specified goals in the ISO definition have their counterparts in Gould and Lewis' description of intended users, given tasks and the circumstances in which they should be performed.

It is without doubt that Gould and Lewis laid the foundations of user-centered design by providing the key concepts on which current approaches for developing usable interactive systems are still built. It was also Gould and Lewis who came up with the memorable and often heard but rarely correctly attributed leading record that from a user's perspective *with computer systems the product is the user interface* (1985, p. 306).

Creating a truly usable interface to provide access to the functionality of an application calls for an interdisciplinary team to arrive at a comprehensive understanding of the *cognitive, behavioural, anthropometric, and attitudinal characteristics* (Gould and Lewis 1985, p. 300) of users that are to be supported by *studying the nature of the work expected to be accomplished* (Gould and Lewis 1985, p. 300). In the next section we will briefly discuss different approaches to software development in their relation to design before then providing a more detailed overview about user-centered design by differentiating its underlying core phases.

3   Development Approaches and Design

We have already adverted to the multiplicity of meanings of the term *Design*. In the context of development models the term *Design* comes with at least two different semantic references: Software Design (i.e. designing the internal structure of an application, *the aspects of the software that affect functionality and execution performance*, Biddle et al. 2007) and the design of a user interface (following the semantic scope discussed in the previous paragraph). Depending on the respective approach followed, resources devoted to the design of a user interface are concentrated at different stages of a project. For the sake of clarification we will refer to a dichotomy of *User Interface first* (UIF) versus *User Interface later* (UIL) stances to distinguish different process models of development, albeit acknowledging that actual project realities often proceed on the continuum between these semantic oppositions.

A corollary of UIF is that an entire user interface – providing interactional access to the full functionality of an application – can be completely specified before a single line of code is written. It has to be noted though, that comparable to the floor plan of an architect that presupposes a comprehensive understanding of material properties and structural analysis, user interface design (while preceding programming like floor plans precede actual building activities) requires a thorough appreciation of technical capabilities.

UIF approaches typically have a broad understanding of the concept of a user interface that is not restricted to providing a visually appealing and aesthetically pleasing wrapping of functionality and enabling efficient interaction with it. In lieu of successful interface creation, preparatory steps are required to identify the right functionality (i.e. to select the appropriate feature set) for supporting a user in achieving her working goal in a given environment. An underlying assumption in such a user-centered approach is that the cost of initially planning, validating and specifying the user interface is less than the cost of fixing implementation code due to change requests – not speaking about maintaining revised code. Due to its high amount of (formal) documentation UIF, also mitigates the risk of losing knowledge if resources leave an organization.

While the traditional waterfall model of development exemplifies a steady approach of complete specification of software before implementation, its explicit reference to a Design stage between does not necessarily imply being UIF. On the contrary: projects following the waterfall approach frequently leave the details of interface design decisions to later stages, focusing instead on the specifics of the functionality and the internal structure of the software to be engineered.

The agile approach, which can be more adequately characterized by the UIL acronym, tries to leverage small self-organizing teams working in short time boxes without long-term planning for the user interface dominating. Tasks and components are commonly broken down into sprints realizable in short periods even down to 1-week, each contributing to a successively feature-complete and sprint-wise working implementation. While agile projects might start with some initial vision of an application's user interface in an imaginary sprint zero, this clearly is not covered by UIF. The key philosophy in agile projects is the emphasis on quick adaptability with low formality thus minimal documentation. Criticizing UIF for an insufficient provision for changing requirements, the cost of overall planning is assumed to be higher than the cost of fixing.

The debate between representatives of both characterizations is a very emotional and intense one (especially with designers and developers advocating the respective oppositions involved). This is at least surprising, given that agile methodologies also refer to activities typically related to user-centered design (*Scope, Analyse, Design, Validate* and *Deliver*, outlined in Sect. 4) and both are driven by a strong interdisciplinary collaboration of different roles. Very abstractly speaking, from an interface design perspective both approaches share striking conceptual similarities, differing only with regard to granularity (UIF: analysis-design-validate cycles for the features embodied in a user interface, preceding development; agile UIL: many short design sprints, each devoted to selected feature sets, overlapping development) and maturity of deliverables (UIF: detailed top-down specification of core functionality, extensive prototyping; agile UIL: minimal bottom-up documentation of selected functionality, focus on productive (sub-)systems).

Most importantly, agile development and user-centered design are both fuelled by being highly iterative: The creation of an artefact that can be validated and refined based on feedback gathered. The shared goal is mainly deviating in the nature of the artefact: In UIF validation is usually done with lightweight prototypes; in UIL user validation is typically done with productive code. Its reliance on productive code is also the most fundamental challenge for UIL: If not carefully monitored, the risk of implicitly adjusting the design proposal to development capabilities is very high, diminishing the chance for real innovation.

The question when to follow UIF or UIL cannot be answered dogmatically. It should rather be seen as a tendency not as an either/or decision. The *placement* of design in the UIF/L continuum depends on a project's scope and setup of contributing parties. In the situation where development is outsourced, UIF makes a strong case because its output (e.g. a fully specified user interface, potentially accompanied by an illustrative interactive prototype) provides a sound base for a bid to potential contracting developers. Yet if development is done completely in-house its detailed documentation is less needed since developers can participate from start and feasibility concerns can be raised very early.

The major factor shaping the embodiment of design in a project is the question whether an evolution or a revolution of a product is targeted. If existing functionality is to be redesigned or enhanced, design-related activities are tied to the respective development specifics much more tightly. However, when more extensive new functionality is to be introduced in a product or when even an entire new application is being planned, the creation and validation of a greenfield before development is advisable. In the context of web applications, for example, a paradigm of continuous improvement is often practiced, explaining the popularity for UIL since the traditional definition of (yearly) releases is hardly applicable in this case. In the field of productivity tools for expert users, however, comparatively long release cycles (e.g.one a year) allowing unleashing the full potentials of UIF.

4   User-Centered Design Activities

Though carrying a plethora of different labels, which greatly vary through literature and agency descriptions, the activities performed in a typical user-centered design project can be assigned to the following five categories: *Scope, Analyse, Design, Validate* and *Deliver*. A structured iterative process arranged by the information needs of the corresponding phases flexibly links especially the three center categories. To perform the activities in each phase, designers base their decisions on theoretical insights and have access to practical methodologies, which – contrary to (still) popular belief – do not necessarily presuppose the *ingenious creation* of subjective art. These are rooted in the contributing disciplines of human-computer interaction that were adapted and refined to serve the goal of designing an effective, efficient and satisfying interaction for achieving a user's goal.

As outlined in the previous section, both development approaches (UIF and UIL) significantly differ in the timing of a design stage as well as in the granularity and the maturity of its deliverables. We will thus explain the activities of each phase in

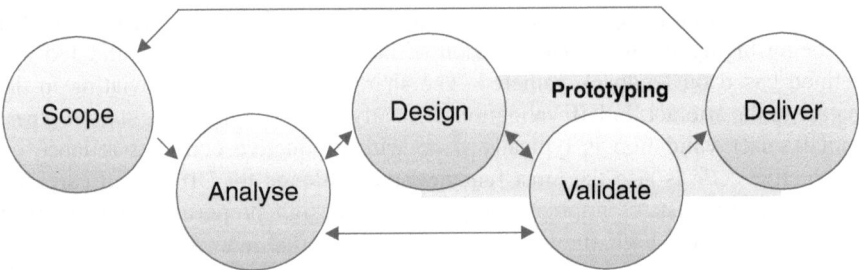

Fig. 2 User-centered design activities

their typical iterative succession – highlighting only in brief the most important supporting methods, instruments and artefacts in each phase to paint a comprehensive picture of the overall process (Fig. 2).

Deviating from common practice in usability textbooks - where methods of usability evaluation are subsumed under the umbrella of the validation phase - we are also addressing these already in our description of activities in the Analyse phase. This portrayal reflects the course of many real life projects that base their agenda on the grounds of a detailed usability inspection of the current application to arrive at a specific working goal for the upcoming application. Depending on the lapse of a project and the corresponding information needs, the corresponding activities might be applied in both, the Analyse and the Validate category.

4.1 Scope

The most crucial aspect of a user-centered design project is to initially establish a common ground (Clark and Brennan 1991) between its contributing stakeholders. This is even more challenging in the dominant situation for small/medium enterprises, where major parts or even the complete design process is often outsourced to a consulting agency with a binding offer to be delivered upfront.

Combining the product vision and the research results of a product owner's input (comprising the request for proposals, potential demos, available manuals, illustrative sketches, documented user feedback, etc.) and the output of an interdisciplinary scoping workshop (including board, product managers, developers, management, etc.), a concrete mission statement of a project should be derived during scoping that addresses two major aspects: the goals and constraints of the project. For most projects, relevant goals and constraints can typically not be established in comprehensive detail at this stage but need to be identified and discussed at a qualitative level to set the agenda for the analysis stage.

4.1.1 Goals
Since any meaningful interface exists to serve a specific purpose, the functional goals for a design project are to be addressed upfront in the light of sufficient

domain knowledge. These goals usually shift between two extremes on a continuum: from a purely visual redesign solely of existing functionality over a design for new functionality (extending or replacing current functionality) to a creation of a completely new application in a greenfield approach. Any tendency in between has to be put into perspective during scoping with the business goals of the project: Shall the new interface attract and convert new customers (in yet unclaimed markets or contexts) or will its unique selling proposition promise to yield a higher return on invest for existing users due to increased productivity, lower learning effort, higher joy of use or other goals related to product usability? The outcome of this discussion heavily plays into planning the focus of each phase in the process, especially during analysis and design.

Often the need for setting up specific interface design projects is extrinsically motivated through inquiries raised by a product's current users or by insights gathered from competing applications. Hence it is not uncommon that specific expectations regarding the usability of an artefact's new interface are already raised at this state, often in a less than organized way. It is recommendable to explicitly clarify and match these goals to defined usability metrics such as performance, learnability, error avoidance, self descriptiveness, memorability or consistency (for a full discussion of usability metrics see Tullis and Albert 2008). A stable framework has to be derived for setting up target and acceptance values for these predominantly business goals in the analysis phase and to evaluate the successful achievement of these non-functional requirements in the validation phase.

4.1.2 Constraints

Art lives from constraints and dies from freedom da Vinci once stated, which in its essence directly applies to interface design as well: Without establishing clear borders of the solution spectrum in the design space (Simon 1969), there is a latent risk of overdesigning solutions for which feasibility cannot be guaranteed. The strongest constraints are generally of technical nature; therefore it is mandatory to include development representatives right from the start in the project team. Seemingly smart design suggestions that cannot be transformed to real products within technical constraints in given time and budget can thus be quickly identified and solution spaces adjusted.

Besides technological constraints, the contextual environment of a user working with a (future) application defines another set of constraints that needs to be analysed and understood early. By referring to the context of use, we take a broad view consolidating attributes of the physical environment, involved additional tools and equipment as well as communication and workflow patterns during cooperation with other employees.

For instance if usage behaviour is characterized by mobility with customizable handheld devices utilized in exposure of multiple sources of distraction, different emphasizes in design decisions have to be considered than if the context is defined by shared large touchscreen-devices embedded in industrial manufacturing plants.

The consideration of different facets of goals and constraints generated from different perspectives (i.e. functional: product management, business: board, usability: customer service, technical: development, contextual: setup engineers) enables a shared set of expectations, a common ground for enabling an understanding between stakeholders, paving the path for planning and execution of following activities. Finally this mutual understanding also helps to generate consensus on whether the project is to be classified as a redesign or if a green field approach (generally challenging the current application) is preferred by the stakeholders.

4.2   Analyse

As the cow example showed (see section 2.1), actual users' behaviour tends to differ from the imagined behaviour assumed by product owners – especially regarding the importance of proposed features. Results from Analyse activities provide the most effective vaccination to prevent self-reference when designing an application and help to end effectively otherwise endless feature discussions. The goal of the Analyse phase is to uncover attributes of the user, her tasks and the contextual circumstances of using a future or current application. Viewed from the perspective of the project team, Analyse insights are also of central relevance when opinions of the project team drift apart (which naturally happens due to the intended interdisciplinary setup of the team).

Analyse activities take different implications for a redesign endeavour or approach to replace a current solution compared to creating an innovative solution without a direct precursor. With an existing predecessor of the application and an installed user base at hand, initial Analyse activities frequently focus on accessing its usability status quo. Inspecting the compliance of a user interface with established usability guidelines and investigating its fit to the needs and requirements of its current users provides valuable guiding information for subsequent design efforts. A thorough understanding of the actual version of an application is an especially important prerequisite for being able to appraise (and justify) the amount of relearning necessary for users when introducing significant innovations in the redesign of an application.

In order to arrive at an assessment of an application's usability status we will distinguish between methods with and without end-user involvement in the following sections.

4.2.1   Analysis Without End-Users

Sometimes time, budget or general availability of potential attendants prevents access to real end-users – especially when dealing with highly specific productivity tools for very narrow market segments. In such cases a usability inspection of an application can be approached through heuristic analysis (Nielsen and Molich 1990), often also coined expert review in practice. Heuristic analyses are carried out to identify, document and classify the usability optimization potentials of an interface. In a formative inspection these findings are generally used as input for a subsequent redesign of the system under consideration, while summative reviews are targeted at providing a précis of a system's usability.

During a heuristic analysis, reviewers, guided by a set of heuristic guidelines and established usability principles, inspect an interface to uncover usability obstacles and perceived violations to these heuristics. While this inspection step is typically carried out by two to five reviewers working individually from each other, a consolidation of their findings and an assignment of severity levels to these takes place in a joint session involving all reviewers (Nielsen 1994). In formative evaluations, solutions approaches to identified findings are finally outlined to direct subsequent design activities. Often heuristic analyses are used in comparative inspections of competitors' interfaces as well in order to generate an initial comparative benchmarking.

Heuristic analyses generally offer the advantages of being applicable even to early stages of prototypes, do not presuppose the need of specific equipment or scheduling of real users and inexpensively deliver fast results. They are, however, restricted in their scalability to more complex interfaces that presuppose broad domain knowledge and have been found to be prone to false alarms (erroneously insinuating a usability problem) and missed hits (i.e. failing to identify a usability issue). Independently of their limitations, usability reviews have the positive side effect of familiarizing the participating designers with the current functional scope (Cooper et al. 2007).

4.2.2 Analysis with End-Users

As mentioned before, people who use a product often differ significantly from the ones envisioning, designing, developing, selling and supporting applications. To gain an empathic understanding of the user of a current or future application and to acquire a comprehension of her working goals, researching actual end users in context marks the via regia in a user-centered design approach. A broad diversity of different methods have been suggested to support user research (Kuniavsky 2003), to aggregate results gathered (Holtzblatt et al. 2005) and to relate derived insights to the design stage (Meth 2012). In this section we will sketch user observation by means of a method called *job shadowing* and will exemplify *contextual interviews*, both often used in combination.

Job Shadowing

Job Shadowing provides an opportunity for the designer to observe the user performing her daily work in the actual work setting for a representative period of time, depending on the complexity of the job. Important contextual parameters of the work situation can be experienced during job shadowing including a user's technical equipment that is used (or refrained to use), physical aspects of the environment (e.g. is there enough space available for using a mouse?; to how much dirt will a touch-panel be exposed during usage?; what are the spatial relations of a control center's subsystems?) or social interactions and workflow dependencies (what communication with co-workers is required to complete the task?; what if errors are happening?). Observers receive direct insights into the importance of tasks related to a work place, their frequency and the respective steps involved, the terminology used, the appearance of incidents that are classified as critical, sources of distraction or the occurrence and repetition of assignments – factors that are of immediate influence on design decisions.

While different models of participation exist, the relationship of shadowed user and observer can adequately be characterized as a master-apprentice setting where an observer's goal is to learn as much as possible about a user's task. Dense notes are taken about the experiences, often enriched by insightful quotes, photos or even video sequences if allowed.

Contextual Interviews

To fill in gaps in the understanding of the job situation, job shadowing is often combined with contextual interviews, with different levels of structuring. Fully structured interviews, guided by a prepared list of questions come with the benefit of a high comparability across interviewees – but leave little flexibility for individually addressing specific questions that result from particular work situations encountered. Unstructured interviews, which follow the flow resulting from the interplay of questions and answers, deliver rich data but carry the danger of getting lost in the idiosyncrasies of a situation and/or a user. In practice, semi-structured interviews often turn out to be an advantageous compromise of richness, flexibility and comparability of results across different interviewees. Contextual interviews are in fact carried out at the workplace where the context serves as probes to trigger questions, and aiding a participant's memory when answering. Nielsen (2001) argues that paying attention to what users do is more important than what they say since self-reported claims are often unreliable. It is for this reason why job shadowing typically precede contextual interviews, with the later rarely being used in isolation.

Not to be neglected at this stage is the possibility to conduct an empirical usability test for getting a comprehensive picture of the usability of an application currently in use. However, since empirical testing is not applied too often as part of a status quo analysis at the beginning of a redesign project, we will cover usability testing in the section describing the Validate phase.

4.2.3 Synthesis

The outcome of Analyse activities leads to a broad stream of data that needs to be explored, classified and pre-processed to provide the required input for Design. Even the most thoroughly performed analysis can be worthless if the gained impressions cannot be consolidated into communicable objects. Specifically during job shadowing and contextual interviews it was learned which tasks are performed frequently with which functions (or even other workarounds) used in which sequence to reach which goals – either alone or in collaboration with other users. Dealing with critical incidents has also been a central topic as was the identification of exceptional situations. Potentially, findings from a heuristic analysis have contributed to understanding how well features and workflows of an existing solution are supporting the user to adequately achieve her working goals. Given these oodles of data a suitable aggregation approach is needed for synthesis.

Practitioning synthesis is a vast field (Kolko et al. 2011) so we want to concentrate on four elements in this section: affinity diagrams, Personas, Mental Models and performed scenarios.

Affinity Diagrams

Using affinity diagrams has proven to be a very effective method that can easily be applied to consolidating and structuring the various impressions gathered. Affinity diagramming is a participatory integration technique where observations, quotes, pictures and other outcomes from the analysis stage are simply written on Post-its that are then clustered and labelled to highlight signature insights. Analyse results can be integrated and relationships identified through the creation and structuring of an affinity diagram. Including different roles in the process allows not only involving those persons who conducted research data in the process, but also to inform other stakeholders and ask for their contribution.

Personas

Cooper's concept of a persona (1999) has turned out to be of eminent help in aggregating data from research to envision and substantiate the user of an interactive system. Being hypothetical archetypes of real users, Personas are defined by distinct goals and individual characteristics, helping to literally put a face to otherwise abstract target demographics. The availability of a conceivable persona with a concrete name, a credible background, documented working goals, responsibilities, challenges and pain points avoids one of the most severe risks in user-centered design project: The design for an elastic "user" who can be bent and reshaped in favour of arbitrary arguments. Instead, a persona represents a tangible incarnation of a concrete person that – based on the partial information provided in a persona description – triggers an emphatic immersion into the needs of the person to be supported by an application. With a persona in mind, a screen in question can be assessed through different lenses, fostering informed decision-making during design.

It might turn out that a single persona description is not sufficient to encompass the variety in the user information gathered, but that different Personas are necessary to adequately capture the research findings in a project. In the case study reported in a later section of this chapter we outline a situation where two very different Personas where identified as archetypes of an application's key user: a highly trained expert who is strictly focused on the efficiency and broad functional coverage of the system in daily use for complex configuration tasks, and an occasional user challenged by mastering a very restricted subset of the available functionality to fulfil comparatively simple configuration set-ups. Approaching the creation of a single user interface to find a compromise by trying to meet the requirements of both primary Personas simultaneously would necessarily result in disenthralling both. While thwarting the performance of the expert by failing to integrate all specific custom functions for immediate access, the occasional user would be overwhelmed by endless options to enhance the complexity of the user interface without being of beneficial use for her. The solution followed in this situation was to provide two distinct user interfaces, acknowledging the individual requirements of the primary Personas and reflecting different priorities in the use of functions. The example of sacrificing efficiency for learnability and memorability (and vice versa) in the two interfaces also demonstrates that Personas provide information to advise for the appraisal of usability goals that are then reflected in design decisions.

Mental Models

Persona descriptions are often also a point of origin for a discussion of the Mental Models of a user. Without the claim of being a valid or complete representation of its functioning, the concept of a Mental Model describes the sum of a user's subjective mental conceptualizations and believes of how a system works based on experience (Lidwell et al. 2010). Mental Models guide the actions of what to do next in order to arrive at specific goals and guides a user's reasoning and beliefs of what to do in unexpected situations. If there is a significant mismatch between a user's Mental Model and the conceptual model underlying the operating of a system, interaction is likely to break down. Norman (1983) refers to conceptual models as tools for the understanding and teaching of physical models. Picking up the differentiation between conceptual and Mental Models, an important prerequisite for successful user interfaces is to base the design on a coherent and graspable (but not necessarily physically correct) conceptual model to induce a stable Mental Model in congruence with a user's understanding of the task.

In the project reported in the case study later in this chapter, results from the Analyse phase revealed clear evidence that the Mental Models of users conflicted with the conceptual model underlying an application. As a result of this mismatch, using this application, determining what to do in exceptional circumstances and especially learning how to operate it was significantly impaired.

Scenarios

A missing ingredient for paving the ground for the design of a sound interface concept is to encapsulate what tasks have to be supported by an application through scenarios. These are simple narrative stories (the *what* of interaction) articulating a persona through an environmental context to achieve a specific goal (the *why* of interaction). Scenarios provide concrete descriptions but are open to how a persona is achieving a particular task goal – leaving the details of interaction to be filled in by design solutions. Scenarios do not focus on technology but are focusing on the user's view. Written in plain language and employing the terminology of users they come in different flavours ranging from simple goal statements (describing simply what the user wants to do) to elaborated user stories providing enriched contextual details. In contrast to use cases, scenario descriptions refrain from using formal notation, which simplifies their validation in discussions with users. Although we discuss the use of scenarios with reference to an analysis involving end-users, it is not uncommon to also adopt scenarios as a narrative tool without distilling actual user research.

By fleshing out the variety of scenarios that are to be supported, the underlying structure of an application begins to take shape before any design happens at all. In the context of an outsourced design process scenarios prove to be a very economic instrument for communication. Rather than enumerating feature by feature of a planned application in abstract, an analysis of scenarios allows the derivation of common features de facto needed for their realization. Depending on the project, not all scenarios are explicitly worked out, but key scenarios are identified to represent associated instances, leaving their extension to related ones to the design stage.

Having defined Personas, Mental Models and scenarios as typical outcomes from a synthesis of data, insights and potential heuristic analysis, the next section covers the anchoring of design decisions on these grounds.

4.3   Design

Designing a user interface is a process of balancing potentially conflicting requirements, considering the trade-offs of resulting solution explorations and acknowledging the constraints of the solution space. Its goal is to transform insights and findings from the Scope and Analyse phases into a tangible artefact. Having already emphasized that User Interface Design goes beyond the definition of purely visual attributes, design activities address two layers of the interface connecting users with the functionality of an application: the conceptual and the visual layer. While both layers are not independent from each other, processes for their creation ideally do not overlap too much, with conceptual design preceding its visual elaboration.

4.3.1   Conceptual Design

The conceptual layer of a user interface refers to the result of decisions regarding the layout (if graphical user interfaces are the target of the design efforts), the workflow and the underlying interaction model. Conceptual decisions comprise determinations of the spatial relationship of screen views, their approximate dimensions, the use of interface controls and the interrelation of screens. Picking up the aforementioned analogy to architecture, conceptual design renders the floor plan, the skeleton of a user interface that is further supported and enriched by appropriate visual design. Conceptual design decisions provide the answers to the *how*-questions that were deliberately left open during scenario construction when explaining *what* a persona does, concentrating on the *why* of following her task goal. Personas and scenarios thus form central ingredients for informing conceptual design about the targeted functional and non-functional requirements of the intended future application. Helpful Interface Design Guidelines (Johnson 2007; Shneiderman and Plaisant 2009; Raskin 2000) are rooted in the scientific understanding of how *people perceive, learn, reason, remember, and convert intentions into action* (Johnson 2010, p. xiii) that is provided by Cognitive Psychology. Although being abstract to allow for a broad applicability, such guidelines direct design efforts to meet elicited requirements through the creation of a user interface that takes the capabilities and limitations of the human cognitive system into account.

Scribbles

Simple scribbles are of valuable help to arrive at initial representations of conceptual design, sketching screen areas and outlining their mutual relationship without already fixing their true physical dimensions. Adding adumbrations of interface controls then provides a first coarse picture of how functionality might be wrapped by the interface. Such often hand-drawn scribbles – not although but because of their obviously unfinished and tentative nature – represent a manifest artefact for fostering communication, effectively supporting reflection to allow for the elevation of early feedback regarding the design directions taken. It is one of the insights of project experience that the more elaborate a design artefact is, the narrower will be the feedback that can be expected. E.g. when exposed to user feedback, elaborated design suggestions are mainly tweaked for incremental improvement – but rarely challenged in their essential appropriateness. It is exactly the inchoate, incomplete nature of a scribble that provokes questioning its high-level features because their typically hand-drawn effectuation spells out a disposition for revision without much effort – also evidencing that not much expense has been invested yet into their creation.

Albeit exaggerating slightly, one of the central differences in training when comparing computer scientists to designers lies in the general approach to solution finding. While computer scientists focus on selecting the most promising candidate from a (usually small) set of potential candidates for implementing an algorithmic solution, designers tend to explore and evaluate a broad range of alternatives in finally arriving at the right design. Following a process of successive elimination of candidates' branches while traveling through the solution space, the design process is described by Laseau (1980) as a symbiotic relationship between the elaboration of generated solutions and their subsequent reduction to iteratively decide on the ones worth to be further pursued (see also Greenberg et al. 2012). Scribbles are perfect tools for not committing oneself too early to a single design solution, thus avoiding the danger of getting stuck in a local maximum of the solution space. Due to their unwrought character, a set of scribbled solution candidates can be reduced to the more promising ones without the guilty conscience of having wasted valuable resources in their creation. Cutting candidate branches in the solution space can be justified, for example, by analytical considerations (for example by taking the implementation effort for a technical realization into account), or by iteratively evaluating the concepts expressed by scribbles with prospective users (see Sect. 4.4).

Wireframes and Prototypes

Pugh (1990) argues that the granularity of solution explorations is successively refined through the course of elaboration and reduction cycles, suggesting to move from the use of scribbles to so-called wireframes to reflect an increased maturity of design candidates. In contrast to scribbles, wireframes – while still being silent about the visual details of the interface – provide a consolidated view of the spatial arrangement and dimensions of an interface's layout. Wireframes communicate decisions on the selection of interface controls and navigation elements and also allow for an initial exploration of using a dedicated colour to guide a user's attention to specific interface areas. The increased concreteness of wireframes also enhances the scope of potential evaluation questions that can be addressed to also comprise, for example, validations of the appropriateness of interface controls or investigating whether the layout reflects the logical path through a screen.

Basing design activities on the use of scribbles and wireframes grants quick iterations, working out varieties of alternative solutions while subsequently moving from the bird's eye perspective of scenarios down to the specifics of interface controls. By the necessity to abstract from decorative details through the constricted expressiveness of mainly having levels of grey for conveying design decisions, wireframes focus the attention of a designer on establishing a sound logical and consistent foundation of a screen.

Again emphasizing the iterative nature of user-centered design by referring to empirical validation of early design results, valuable feedback can be gathered when involving users to inform the respective next elaboration cycle until quiescence is reached and a convincing interface solution is found. Because of their typical existence on paper (or as static digital depictions on a computer screen), neither scribbles nor wireframes are interactive – but both incarnations of potential design solutions can nevertheless be used in pseudo-interactive workflow evaluations. With a moderating facilitator in place, wireframes presented on paper can be switched in dependence of a participant's simulated *click* on the outline of a button on paper. Alternatively, simple concatenations of wireframes (or, in a slight enhancement of the setup: the use of dynamically linked areas in these) can be arranged in presentation software for simulating "interaction". Just as scribbles and wireframes instantiate different degrees of fidelity, paper prototypes are early reflections of interactivity, coarsely illustrating the intended *behaviour* of concepts under consideration. Fully interactive prototypes, created by the use of dedicated prototyping tools like SKETCHFLOW, AXURE or ANTETYPE, Java-Script frameworks or occasionally even written in the target language of an application's development framework, then excite the experience of the consecutive interplay of action and reaction spanning over time when interacting with an application. Interactive prototypes render the tangible *feel* of a future application, vividly demonstrating *the way products behave in response to the behaviour that people behave* (Saffer 2007, p. 44). Prototypes hereby also serve highly important communication purposes by allowing all stakeholders in the design process to get their hands literally on otherwise abstract emerging ideas, encouraging reflective discussions and triggering *what-if*-questions regarding future iterations.

4.3.2 Visual Design

It depends on the information needs during the design process whether to work out the appearance of an interface – its *look* – before exploring interactional aspects on the grounds of an interactive prototype.

Although mostly applied after having sanded and polished the layout and interaction details, there is, however, no reason for debating on the importance of visual design. User interface *mock-ups* are representations in which visual design decisions like colours, textures, exact font definitions, icons and decorations like the use of glossy highlights are defined on the pixel-precise layout of an interface.

Funnelling the input from the *Scope* phase regarding corporate design guidelines (if applicable), market research findings on user preferences and also technical possibilities, a range of visual styles is explored in interface mock-ups. As stated before, visual design is not independent from conceptual design, but provides the expressive means to effectively support the conceptual level. Reducing visual design to a simple bedaubing of wireframes in order to match the taste of prospective users (or the aesthetic preferences of a client) falls short of acknowledging the tight relation of conceptual and visual design. Purposeful visual design decisions help to emphasize the structure written out by conceptual design, prescinding hierarchies of interface elements and directing the attention of a user.

But of course visual design is also about the overall aesthetic impression of an interface – the appearance of it, after all, being so much more immediate to grasp than interaction. It is one of the old lessons learned from Social Psychology, known as the *Attractiveness-bias*, that humans have a tendency to perceive physically attractive people as more intelligent, competent, sociable and even taller (when asked to estimate height of people presented on portrait photographs) than less attractive ones (Dion et al. 1972). This bias has a counterpart result in the so-called *Aesthetic-Usability Effect*, describing that users *perceive more aesthetic designs as easier to use than less aesthetic designs – whether they are or not* (Litwell et al. 2003, p. 18; Kurosu and Kashimura 1995). Visual design thus clearly contributes to the acceptance of a user interface, enhancing its desirability, stimulating identification and increasing its hedonic quality (Diefenbach and Hassenzahl 2011).

Visual design efforts can range from applying standard operating system *Look & Feels* with stock icons to extensively styled applications with laborious graphical assets and custom icons. Reiterating on the architecture metaphor, a visually embellished interactive prototype of an application transcends the floor plan and can be compared to the tangible outfitted three-dimensional models that aid imagination nowadays in allowing for an interactive exploration of a house's future rooms.

A leitmotif running through the design phase – that preferably will subsequently become part of a project team's DNA in user-centered design approaches – is the appreciation of iteration, frequently validating assumptions by evaluating increasingly refined artefacts. Prototypes can be thrown away after validation or be evolutionary in the sense that they are revised and extended during validation. Especially with the advent of powerful prototyping programs it is easy to move from raw scribbles to static wireframes, fine tuning these over time to arrive at prototypes enhanced with realistic interactions and transitions vested in an elaborated visual design. The potential (and temptation) for perfection is endless, explaining why prototypes are also frequently used for convincing a product owner's board members and potential key clients before a single line of functional code being written (UIF).

4.4   Validate

As carved out in the description of the previous section, the activities in the Design and the Validate stages are strongly intertwined in practice. Independent of an artefact's fidelity the assumed progress in design efforts needs to be iteratively validated against goals to appreciate its appropriateness and maturity. This can be done by a project's team checking the current design state against the requirements derived from analysis (*Does this interface adequately support the person in achieving a scenario's goal?*), by Heuristic Analysis to inspect its usability status (see Sect. 4.2.1) or through empirical usability testing, covered in the following paragraph.

4.4.1   Usability Testing

Usability Testing is often associated with the availability of a dedicated usability lab. In such a lab setting, participants are recruited to match the profile of prospective users of a current or future application. The persona description that was established in the Analyse phase and used during design to keep the user in focus now helps to define a recruiting brief for inviting participants that are regarded to represent future users. Although usability tests are empirical studies involving human participants, they are not to be confused with experiments. Experiments serve the purpose of testing scientific hypotheses about expected causal relationships. Usability tests, on the other hand, focus on identifying the obstacles to frictionless interaction, conceptual obscurities or learning barriers of an interface. Picking up terms from the previously emphasized definition of usability, usability tests do not evaluate user interfaces as such but do so in reference to significant goal-directed tasks of a user representative working in a typical context.

The recruiting brief assures the representativeness of participants while the scenarios (representing the main task goals identified in the Analyse stage) can be reused to formulate task goals that are to be attained in testing sessions using an interface prototype. In a usability test setting, participants work through a set of task scenarios with their behaviour being monitored from an adjacent observer room. A Venetian mirror, allowing to look from the observer room to the participant room but not in the inverse direction, is a typical feature of a usability lab. Specific recording software packages like MORAE are used to capture the user-system interaction as well as behavioural indicators of the participant. Digital cameras record the facial expressions of a user, while eye trackers can be used to register her visual fixations. To gather insights into the accompanying thinking processes of participants, the *thinking aloud method* (Ericsson and Simon 1980) is often used: During interaction participants are instructed to concurrently verbalize what comes into their minds, providing conclusive evidence for the reasons behind a user's action – thus helping to retrace her train of thought that is withdrawn from direct observation.

Although in some publications incorrectly coined *user testing* (Bernsen et al. 1999) it is of course not the user who is being tested – the focus of interest is to evaluate whether the interface matches the usability requirements of a task and the expectations of a user in the work context approximated in the lab. For reasons of contextual inadequacy it would thus be a violation of representativeness to conduct a usability test of a mobile surveying application in the narrow space of the participant's room of a usability laboratory.

Whenever possible it is highly commendable to invite as many stakeholders as possible to attend at least selected testing sessions. Sitting in the observation room opens up the chance for assembling a comprehensive picture of the user experience by monitoring the user in action, proximately comprehending her successes and failures – and the reasons behind these: *Arguably, the most valuable contribution of usability testing is made when programmers are forced to sit behind the one-way mirror to view typical users struggling with their programs. The programmers are shocked and incredulous, shouting sentiments like, "You are testing mental retards!" Usability testing is a useful whack on the side of the head for recalcitrant software engineers, showing them that there is indeed a problem* (Cooper 1999, p. 207). While we endorse Cooper's statement, invitations to stakeholders for attending testing sessions are not restricted to developers – we can confirm on the empirical grounds of many projects that all stakeholders greatly benefit from the shared experience of jointly monitoring the course of interaction, rendering many otherwise vivid future discussions obsolete.

Usability testing comes in many flavours, ranging from testing in a full-fledged laboratory to informal guided walkthroughs in which participants are visited in their respective working context and questioned while being led through a (paper) prototype. Especially in the early stages of conceptual design renting a full lab often appears to be over the top while walkthroughs allow for fast and helpful feedback without much organizational effort. Worth mentioning is also the possibility to conduct remote usability tests via some screen sharing application. Although having economic and practical advantages, remote testing poses strong challenges on appropriate guiding and briefing of the participants to achieve the required quality of feedback. In addition, important capillary reactions of participants such as full body language or subtle variations in their voice might get lost in translation.

In conjunction with usability tests usability questionnaires and post-task interviews are often used to get an overview of the subjective impressions of a user regarding the usability of a system. The System Usability Scale (SUS, Brooke 1986; Sauro 2011) is an example for a compact questionnaire to elicit the perceived usability of a user judging a system (that might as well be embodied as an early prototype). Summarizing the result in a simple one-dimensional score allows for easy interpretation of the SUS and – when comparing scores over subsequent iterations – for quantifying the success (or failure) of an iteration.

4.4.2 Usability Goals

Any iterative approach needs to be informed by some termination criteria about when to stop and deliver the result of design activities – the final artefact, found to be sufficiently adequate for the targeted purpose. We need, however, a clear operationalization of this vague formulation of being *sufficiently adequate*. Simply asking designers for their impression puts us in jeopardy of iterating beyond necessity. Setting up explicit usability goals provides an appropiate solution in this situation. Usability goals are quantifiable criteria that reflect target (or acceptance) indicators on usability metrics that are found to be relevant for an application. This raises the question of when to formulate these usability goals in terms of their target or acceptance values.

The correct answer to this question is related to the type of project: When redesigning the interface for an application, discussions in the Scope phase might lead to at least comparative criteria (i.e. increasing the efficiency [operationalized as the mean time on task for the core tasks done with this application] by at least 15 % (*target value*; with the *acceptance value* being at least 10%). In such case we are not only able to quantify the usability goal by reference to experiences with the current version of an application, but we also have an understanding regarding a usability metric of relevance. This knowledge is typically not available when commissioned to design the interface for a completely new product. In this situation the Analyse stage might shed light on the metric(s) being relevant. Building on this information, contextual interviews are likely to provide initial cues for the respective target and acceptance values on this metric from a user perspective.

Usability goals are of central importance in discussions with the client, but generally need to be considered for their technical and design feasibility. Model-based analyses (John 2010) grounded on the GOMS-approach (Card et al. 1983) have been shown to be an especially powerful method for quantitatively predicting the performance using a designed interface. Although a more detailed discussion of model-based analysis is beyond the scope of this section, it should be noted, however, that this approach is to a large extent restricted to performance predictions for highly practiced routine tasks with efficiency being the metric under consideration.

After successfully meeting previously defined usability goals in empirical usability tests, model-based analyses or by the use of other inspection methods, the Validate stage comes into quiescence. The next section focuses on delivering the validated result of a user-centered design endeavour.

4.5 Deliver

In the Deliver phase the result of the Design stage, typically enhanced with explaining documentation and instructions, is handed over to development. The exact form, timing and granularity of the respective deliverables depends on the concrete project situation. Deliverables may range from mock-ups of selected key screens to comprehensive interactive prototypes, documented by brief descriptions. On the other side of the spectrum they may be extensive written specifications of an interface's structural, visual and behavioural properties. The main graphical assets like icons may be provided – or the full XAML-coding of an application's interface presentation layer, ready for integration with the business logic. Last but not least, the nature of deliverables also depends on the frame (waterfall or agile) of a project.

Certain dimensions for classifying documentation, however, always apply: Documentation can either be *static* (often lengthy text files with a dedicated owner and a strict release mechanism) or *dynamic* (typically in the form of WIKIs where different roles can edit at the same time and updating is simplified).

Documentation can be embodied in the form of a comprehensive *generic* style guide for harmonizing the interfaces of different applications of a company (ensuring overall consistently with regard to colours, measures, controls, fonts, common design patterns etc. by explicit rules for their application). On the other hand, it can be very *specific* in narrowly describing the nitty-gritty details of all core screens of a single application (often then called an *interface specification* to distinguish it from style guides). In real life projects conducting reviews at certain stages of application implementation frequently ensures compliance to such documentation provided.

Especially in the past years, technological advances provided an opportunity for designers to give developers more than just documentation and icons as reusable assets. Modern frameworks allow casting (visual) design in code for selected *Look & Feel* engines. Provided that the *Look & Feel* code is sufficiently separated from functional code, developers then do not need to care about the appearance of the elements. This approach not only allows designers and developers to communicate by reference to the very same language (instead of talking at cross-purposes by speaking in PHOTOSHOP to C# et vice versa). It also relieves the documentation effort significantly by providing developers with code ready for subsequent integration. From a designer's perspective this also comes with the advantage of preserving more control over the result of the final implementation of the validated interface concept. Although not being trivial for reasons outside the scope of this chapter, the approach outlined finally leaves open the possibility of developing and iteratively validating an evolutionary interactive prototype on a code basis that can then largely be reused during implementation.

With the differentiation of Scope, Analyse, Design, Validate and Deliver stages we have summarized the core process of user-centered design in the pervious sections. In the next section we follow the goal of briefly illustrating the course of these stages in a real life case study.

5   A Brief Case Study

Referring to the distinction between UIF and UIL introduced in the second section of this chapter, the case study sketched here exemplifies a prototypical example for a *user interface first* approach. In fact, the major deliverable of the project on which the study is based was a truly comprehensive and detailed 300 + pages user interface specification that formed the core of an invitation of tenders. The winning bidder of this tender was finally commissioned to implement the full application with the interface specification comprising the requirements stage of the waterfall model. The client mandating our company for redesigning the user interface is the owner of a worldwide standard for home and building control allowing building management components to communicate via a common bus system. The engineering tool (*ET*) is the respective configuration application to design and configure sophisticated home and building control installations. To avoid confusion, its redesigned interface will subsequently be coined *ET**.

5.1   *ET**: Scope

A comprehensive scoping workshop was conducted in which the applicant informed about already identified functional and non-functional shortcomings of *ET* that were based on an analysis of user feedback collected by the application hotline. In addition to fixing the technical framework for implementing the future *ET** solution, different stakeholders reported extensively on perceived learnability problems that they mainly associated with usability problems of the *ET* user interface, suggesting learnability as an important usability metric. A timeline for the project was fixed and a sequence of workshops to present intermediate results at selected stages was agreed upon.

5.2   *ET*: Analyse

The domain of home and building control systems covered by the *ET* application is complex. More than 250 leading manufacturers in this field provide components that can be integrated using *ET* with more than 30,000 installer companies in 110+ countries being active users of the configuration software. Over 215 partner training-centers have been established to instruct installers in courses of several days' duration on using *ET* for configuring residential and commercial buildings.

Before participating in one of these courses to gain deeper knowledge about *ET*, interface designers of the project team had to prepare themselves by studying introductory textbooks and white papers to get acquainted with the domain. By education most users of *ET* are either electrical engineers or electricians, so the designers had to master a challenging wealth of materials to come sufficiently up to par. While a project team might be split into separate roles for researchers and designers, with researchers covering the Analyse phase and then handing over (written documentations of their) insights to designers for Design, we usually involve designers directly in the analysis phase. Having the advantage of fostering unfiltered empathic knowledge about users, their task and the domain, this also eliminates the difficulty for researchers to anticipate the design importance of information and insights during documentation.

Equipped with the knowledge from having participated in the trainings, the designers were prepared for job shadowing and contextual interviews to understand how to work with the *ET* application. To consider aspects resulting from the international use of *ET*, these activities were carried out in Germany, Spain, France, the UK and Belgium.

A heuristic analysis of *ET* completed the picture to identify current usability shortcomings allowing finding an optimal trade-off between innovation and re-learning when designing *ET**. To acknowledge the space limitation of this chapter, we like to present two selected findings from the Analyse phase:

5.2.1 *ET*: Personas

When establishing Personas for ET through affinity diagramming it became clear that two primary Personas were necessary to conform the research results. One persona covered the professional user, typically trained as an electric engineer and ready to configure ET for commercial buildings as large as London Heathrow airport. The other primary persona represented an occasional user, often trained as an electrician and mostly using ET for configuring small, one-family residential buildings. Job shadowing also revealed significant differences in the technical equipment of the respective Personas: While the professional user typically had access to cutting edge laptops to run ET, the occasional user was fighting with ET's system requirements on technically rather out-dated machines.

5.2.2 *ET*: Mental Models

The Mental Models of the respective Personas were assumed to be significantly different, with the conceptual model underlying ET being up to now only in adequate correspondence with the Mental Model of the professional user. ET required users to think in terms of networks during configuration tasks. Contextual interviews with electricians revealed, however, that their Mental Model was grounded on their education of thinking in terms of switches being connected to appliances in electric circuits. This mismatch of the Mental Model of occasional users and the conceptual model of ET resulted not only in massive difficulties during learning the application, but was also hampering the user during failure detection in real life configurations.

These two findings related to Personas and Mental Models, although being more or less arbitrarily picked-out from a wealth of insights gathered in this phase, already provided very important food for thought for the design phase.

5.3   *ET**: Design

Although reported in sequence for reasons of linearity when reading from paper, the Analyse and the Design phase were substantially intertwined during actual project execution. Illustrating this overlap, scribbles and wireframes were used in selected contextual interviews mentioned above to elicit concrete feedback on early design visions. Exemplifying the descriptions in Sect. 4.3 of this paper, the design process moved through the creation and subsequent refinement of scribbles, wireframes, paper prototypes and visual design variants to the development of an interactive prototype. Starting from the key scenarios identified during the Analyse phase, the provision of two primary Personas called for the introduction of two distinct interface types to be integrated into *ET**, reflecting the differing requirements of the professional and the novice user.

While the *professional* mode allowed full and flexible access to the complex functionality provided by *ET**, the *novice* mode concentrated on offering a guided configuration process based on separate steps that matched the Mental Model of occasional users by the automatic allocation of network addresses. Albeit being restricted in the number of appliances for integration during configuration, the demonstrative visualizations offered in the *ET** novice mode not only fostered learning how to operate the interface, but also facilitated a smooth transition to the *ET** professional mode. After arriving at a mature state of the interface concept, a comprehensive interactive prototype for *ET** was developed allowing to work through the key scenarios of a representative future *ET** user.

To continuously inform all stakeholders – including the client's board – about the progress in the project, the interactive prototype (which was implemented using a JavaScript framework) was made available for inspection via password-protected web access. This procedure not only kept management up to date, but also resulted in unexpectedly vivid, helpful and often very positive feedback.

5.4   *ET**: Validate

As mentioned in the previous section, initial explorations were already conducted with early paper scribbles to consolidate the interface concept behind *ET**. In the Validate stage, a broad empirical user interface evaluation was arranged, recruiting prospective user representing professional and novice participants. Inspection of behavioural and thinking aloud data, as well as subsequent post-task interviews collected, revealed minor usability stumbling stones that were subsequently revised in an updated version of the *ET** prototype. The first half of the participants was invited to the first part of the testing sessions taking place at ERGOSIGN's usability lab. Based on their feedback and performance the *ET** prototype was refined before being exposed to the other half of participants in a second set of test sessions. Given the comprehensive input from the Analyse phase and the experiences gathered with early paper prototypes it was no surprise that the second set of testing sessions provided evidence for a quiescence of the design process, resulting in a sound and validated user interface concept.

5.5   *ET**: Deliver

As stated in the introduction to this section, the main deliverable in this project consisted of a comprehensive user interface specification used as the basis for an invitation of tenders for implementing *ET**. During the implementation process we were reviewing the state of the application with regard to the interface specification, picking up the chance for minor adjustments or – in case of emerging technical challenges – eventually discussing and providing alternative solutions for aspects of the user interface. Interestingly, the interactive user interface prototype turned out to play an unexpected role – besides providing an illustrative companion to the specification – after having fulfilled its part in empirical evaluation.

5.6   A Perspective for eLearning

Analysis brought many insights that shaped the *ET** interface in its current form. These insights also uncovered learning difficulties regarding the understanding of domain concepts as well as specific steps in the configuration process. Most of these findings were considered during Design, some of them had to remain challenges even in the final version of the user interface, mostly because they were part of the intrinsic cognitive load of understanding the complex domain of configuration in home automation. On the grounds of our experiences with making the interactive *ET** prototype available to the project's stakeholders via web access, the idea of re-using it as part of an eLearning-system to support the introduction and training of *ET** rose.

After presenting the idea to the board we were commissioned with the development of an eLearning platform. In this comprehensive eLearning-tool learners are exposed to didactically founded declarative lessons on the basics of home automation and configuration, to interactive quizzes for self-testing their learning progress, to illustrative multimedia screen-casts of user-system interaction based on the scenarios established in the analysis phase – and finally to challenging exercises with the *ET** web simulation to actively explore the actual interface without the need of installing the full application. Taking the full *ET** eLearning course requires about seven to eight hours of learning time and may – if all lessons and their corresponding tests are achieved – result in the display of a certificate to demonstrate the learning success.

This approach not only made heavy reuse of the artefacts created during the user-centered design process: Personas for focusing the eLearning content on occasional users and scenarios for setting up the storyboards of the learning lessons and the interactive prototype as the core of the *ET** web simulation. It also resulted in a highly successful multi-language web-based learning platform with almost 3,000 active users and a mere 1,300+ achieved *ET** certificates within the first 3 months of its release.

Currently conducted accompanying research is focusing on exploring and quantifying the exact learning benefits associated with the use of the eLearning platform to support training the *ET** application. Preliminary results clearly point to especially fruitful synergies of user-centered design and eLearning with the interactive prototyping being the aorta of both.

Conclusion

In this chapter we presented the methodological cornerstones of user-centered design. Using a case study for illustration, we discussed the application of these cornerstones in a real-life project and pointed to the relationship of UCD and eLearning. To put it in a nutshell: It is safe to say that Gould and Lewis' key principles from the IT stone age (1985) have survived the dynamics of time and still prove to be valid in these days. The necessity of a user-centered approach in software development is, in our opinion, beyond dispute and due to the abundance of digital interfaces in our daily lives even more crucial for sustainable differentiation than ever. User-centered design offers a great set of different tools that can easily be adjusted to fit any combination of project type, scope, timeline, budget and team setup – even without having someone like Steve Jobs on board.

References

Bernsen, N.O., & Dybkjær, H. & Dybkjær, L. (1998). Designing Interactive Speech Systems. From First Ideas to User Testing. London: Springer Verlag.

Biddle, R., Ferreira, J., & Noble, J. (2007). Agile development iterations and UI design. *Proceedings of the agile*, Washington, DC.

Brooke, J. (1986). SUS: A quick and dirty usability scale. In P. W. Jordan, B. Thomas, B. A. Weerd-meester, & A. L. McClelland (Eds.), *Usability evaluation in industry* (pp. 189–194). London, UK: Taylor & Francis.

Card, S., Moran, T., & Newell, A. (1983). *The psychology of human-computer interaction*. Hillsdale: Lawrence Erlbaum Associates.

Clark, H. H., & Brennan, S. E. (1991). Grounding in communication. In L. B. Resnick, J. M. Levine, & S. D. Teasley (Eds.), *Perspectives on socially shared cognition* (pp. 127–149). Washington, DC: American Psychological Association.

Cooper, A. (1999). *The inmates are running the asylum; Why high-tech products drive us crazy*. Indianapolis: Macmillan.

Cooper, A., Cronin, D., & Reimann, R. (2007). *About face 3: The essentials of interaction design*. Indianapolis: Wiley.

Diefenbach, S., & Hassenzahl, M. (2011). The dilemma of the hedonic – Appreciated, but hard to justify. *Interacting with Computers, 23*(5), 461–472.

Dion, K., Berscheid, E., & Walster, E. (1972). What is beautiful is good. *Journal of Personality and Social Psychology, 24*(3), 285–290.

Ericsson, K. A., & Simon, H. A. (1980). Verbal reports as data. *Psychological Review, 87*, 215–251.

Gould, J. D., & Lewis, C. (1985). Designing for usability: Key principles and what designers think. *Communications of the ACM, 28*(3), 300–311.

Greenberg, S., Carpendale, S., Marquardt, N., & Buxton, B. (2012). *Sketching user experiences: The workbook*. San Francisco: Morgan Kaufmann.

Holtzblatt, K., Wendell, J. B., & Wood, S. (2005). *Rapid contextual design: A how-to guide to key techniques for user-centered design*. San Francisco: Morgan Kaufmann.

Jobs, S. (2007). http://www.european-rhetoric.com/analyses/ikeynote-analysis-iphone/transcript-2007/. Accessed 29 April 2012.

John, B. E. (2010). Reducing the variability between novice modelers: Results of a tool for human performance modeling produced through human-centered design. *Proceedings of the 19th annual conference on behavior representation in modeling and simulation*, Charleston.

Johnson, J. (2007). *GUI bloopers 2.0: Common user interface design don'ts*. San Francisco: Morgan Kaufmann.

Johnson, J. (2010). *Designing with the mind in mind: Simple guide to understanding user interface design rules*. Burlington: Morgan Kaufmann.

Kolko, J., et al. (2011). *Exploring the magic of design: A practitioner's guide to the methods and theory of synthesis* (pp. 59–61). Oxford, UK: Oxford University Press.

Kuniavsky, M. (2003). *Observing the user experience: A practitioner's guide to user research*. San Francisco: Morgan Kaufmann.

Kurosu, M., & Kashimura, K. (1995). Apparent usability vs. inherent usability: Experimental analysis on the determinants of the apparent usability. *Conference companion on human factors in computing systems* (pp. 292–293). New York: ACM Press.

Laseau, P. (1980). *Graphical thinking for architects and designers*. Indiana: Wiley.

Lidwell, W., Holden, K., & Butler, J. (2010). *Universal principles of design, revised and updated: 125 ways to enhance usability, influence perception, increase appeal, make better design decisions and teach through design* (2nd ed.). Beverly: Rockport.

Mayhew, D. (1999). The Usability Engineering Lifecycle. San Francisco, CA: Morgan Kaufmann Publishers.

Meth, H. (2012). Reminer. http://www.youtube.com/watch?v=oavu6wX2bJc. Accessed 29 April 2012.

Nielsen, J. (1994). Heuristic evaluation. In J. Nielsen & R. L. Mack (Eds.), *Usability inspection methods*. New York: Wiley.

Nielsen, J. (2001). First rule of usability? Don't listen to users. http://www.useit.com/alertbox/20010805.html. Accessed 29 April 2012.

Nielsen, J., & Molich, R. (1990). Heuristic evaluation of user interfaces. *Proceedings of the SIGCHI conference on human factors in computing systems: Empowering people*, Seattle (pp. 249–256).

Norman, D. A. (1983). Some observations on Mental Models. In D. Gentner & A. L. Stevens (Eds.), *Mental Models*. Hillsdale: Lawrence Erlbaum Associates.

Pugh, S. (1990). *Total design: Integrated methods for successful products engineering*. Essex: Pearson.

Raskin, J. (2000). *The humane interface: New directions for designing interactive systems*. Amsterdam: Addison Wesley.

Saffer, D. (2007). *Designing for interaction: Creating innovative applications and devices*. Berkley: New Riders.

Sauro, J. (2011). *A practical guide to the system usability scale*. Denver: CreateSpace.

Shneiderman, B., & Plaisant, C. (2009). *Designing the user interface: Strategies for effective human–computer interaction*. Boston: Addison Wesley.

Simon, H.A. (1969). The Sciences of the Artifical. Cambridge, MA: The MIT Press.

Tullis, T., & Albert, B. (2008). *Measuring the user experience*. San Francisco: Morgan Kaufmann.

Software Usability in Small and Medium Sized Enterprises in Germany: An Empirical Study

Florian Scheiber, Dominika Wruk, Achim Oberg, Johannes Britsch, Michael Woywode, Alexander Maedche, Felix Kahrau, Hendrik Meth, Dieter Wallach, and Marcus Plach

Abstract

Usability has become a competitive factor in the software industry. Specifically, the software industry in the United States has recognized this important factor and successfully leverages it for achieving competitive advantage. Compared to this fast development in the US, it seems questionable whether this view is also widespread among small and medium sized software producing and client companies in Germany and whether they direct sufficient attention to usability. This article presents the results of an empirical study exploring the status quo of the importance, the knowledge and the actual use of usability concepts among small and medium sized enterprises (SMEs) in Germany. Following an organizational field perspective, we investigate how interactions between actors in the software field influence the usability awareness as well as the knowledge and

F. Scheiber • D. Wruk • A. Oberg • M. Woywode
University of Mannheim - Chair of SMEs and Entrepreneurship, Mannheim, Germany
e-mail: scheiber@ifm.uni-mannheim.de; wruk@ifm.uni-mannheim.de; oberg@ifm.uni-mannheim.de; woywode@ifm.uni-mannheim.de

J. Britsch
CAS Software AG, Karlsruhe, Germany
e-mail: johannes.britsch@cas.de

A. Maedche • F. Kahrau • H. Meth
University of Mannheim - Chair of Information Systems IV, Mannheim, Germany
e-mail: maedche@eris.uni-mannheim.de; kahrau@eris.uni-mannheim.de; meth@eris.uni-mannheim.de

D. Wallach
University of Applied Sciences, Kaiserslautern, Germany
e-mail: dieter.wallach@fh-kl.de

M. Plach
ERGOSIGN GmbH, Saarbrücken, Germany
e-mail: plach@ergosign.de

A. Maedche et al. (eds.), *Software for People*, Management for Professionals,
DOI 10.1007/978-3-642-31371-4_3, © Springer-Verlag Berlin Heidelberg 2012

actual use of usability concepts. Based on the results of our study, we provide recommendations on how to increase awareness and maturity of software usability in SMEs in Germany.

1   Introduction

Leveraging the potential of information technology (IT) has become increasingly important for small and medium sized enterprises (SMEs). Specifically, software packages such as Enterprise Resource Planning (ERP) or Customer Relationship Management (CRM) have been intensively adopted by SMEs in the recent decade. The main reasons for this development are the achievement of business objectives such as improving productivity, quality and customer satisfaction and the fulfillment of industry-specific standards for documentation and traceability of the company's activities. In parallel, large enterprises as well as SMEs are currently recognizing a change in expectations and behavior of their employees when using information technology in the business environment. This change is mainly driven by the growing intensity of IT consumption in private life in the form of Web applications such as Facebook.com and smartphones such as the iPhone. While technical decision criteria and functional aspects in the selection of software products used to be the top priorities, these criteria are no longer clear-cut due to an increasing technological flexibility and a high degree of functional convergence of competing solutions: from a user perspective, the user interface is increasingly equated with the application itself and usability issues are therefore more and more in focus. In addition to this change in priorities, it is also well-known from the literature that software usability is an important determinant positively influencing the behavioral intention of individuals to use a software (Venkatesh et al. 2003). Software clients that select and introduce a software solution with low usability may be confronted with adoption challenges.

However, it seems questionable whether this view is also widespread among SME software producing and software client companies in Germany and whether they direct sufficient attention to usability. Even if usability is seen as an important issue for individual companies, a lack of knowledge of methods, tools and know-how related to the implementation of usability concepts might lead to the production of applications that are not sufficiently usable. This may bear two serious consequences: First, there is a risk that small and medium-sized software producers in Germany may fall behind larger or more international competitors. Second, low usability negatively impacts software adoption resulting in unleveraged efficiency potential by client firms using software.

We have been tasked by the Federal Ministry of Economics and Technology in September 2010 to carry out a large scale empirical study investigating the status quo of the importance, the knowledge and the actual use of usability concepts among small and medium-sized companies in Germany. Based on these findings, problems and their causes shall be identified, so that recommendations for small and medium-sized enterprises as well as suggestions for further development of their institutional framework can be derived. This article presents selected extracts from the study's results; the entire study is available online (Usability in Germany 2011). The remainder of this article is structured as follows: Sect. 2 introduces our research design including our underlying theoretical model and the research methods that have been applied. Section 3 presents key results from a software producer, a software client and an organizational field perspective. Building on the results of our study we provide a set of recommendations in Sect. 4. Section 5 summarizes and concludes the article.

2   Study Approach and Methods

2.1   Research Model

As a foundation for our study a comprehensive research model as depicted in Fig. 1 was developed. According to this model, it is initially assumed that software producers will develop products with especially high usability, if they identify corresponding client demand and willingness to pay. It is also assumed that the establishment of favorable software producer internal structures (such as paid positions for usability experts), practices (such as the integration of end-users) and the development of knowledge (i.e. related to test procedures) help small and medium-sized software manufacturers to achieve the goal of high usability of their products. To meet the growing demands regarding the usability of their products, software producers, moreover, can rely on other organizations that provide the necessary knowledge (e.g. service providers).

All organizations involved in this knowledge exchange can be defined as being part of an "organizational field" (DiMaggio and Powell 1983). As prior research on the diffusion of organizational practices and knowledge from other sectors suggests, different relationships and interactions within the field can be of importance for the dissemination and application of knowledge on usability: graduates educated by universities are hired by producers and consulting firms and thus carry this knowledge into the firms (Palmer et al. 1993). In addition, cooperation between companies and universities lead to a transfer of relevant knowledge (Markowski et al. 2008). Producers who attentively follow specialized media probably attain innovative usability concepts faster (Hirsch 1972; Burns and Wholey 1993). Through the application of norms and standards, software producers can activate codified knowledge that would otherwise need to be developed from scratch (Human Factors International 2011; Guler et al. 2002) The more intensively software producers make use of inter-organizational exchange via relevant industry associations, the faster knowledge related to usability should flow (Swan and Newell 1995). Service organizations extend their expert knowledge to software producers in consulting projects (David and Strang 2006). Via their activities for various clients, these consulting firms are able to identify best practices and to communicate these to other companies (Kieser and Ernst 2002). Software

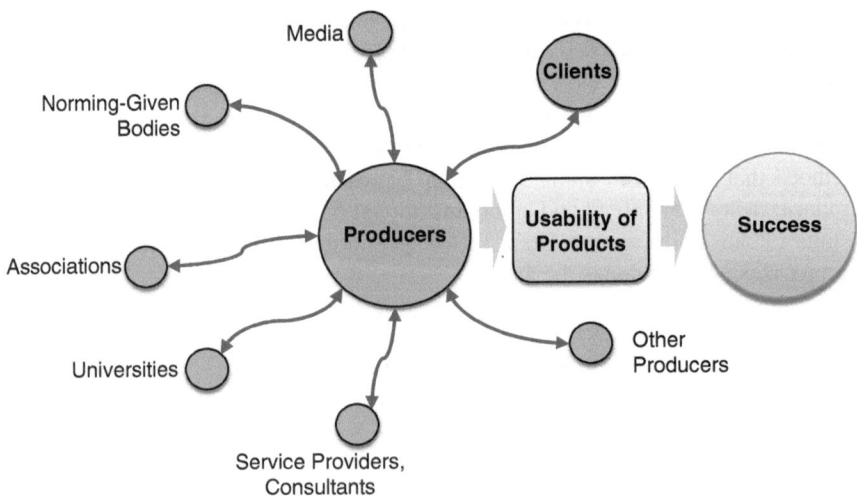

Fig. 1 Research model

producers can cooperate with each other and exchange information as well as knowledge about usability (Valente 1993; Rogers 2003). Beyond such collaborations, however, software producers can also monitor their competitors and find intelligent design solutions for their own programs (Haveman 1993).

In the analysis of the German software industry it will thus be decisive to identify actual networking connections and the amount that these are used for obtaining new knowledge. It is to be expected, for example, that a producer who holds a central position in the field and is closely linked with the other actors, can rapidly attain new knowledge, compared to a producer who is at the margin of the field (Powell et al. 1996; DiMaggio and Powell 1983). If he succeeds then to convert this knowledge into usable products that are valued by the target customers, the producer acquires a competitive advantage and above-average success from his field position when compared to other, less cross-linked or worse organized producers (4) (Yli-Renko et al. 2001).

From this research model thus result the following detailed questions which should be answered in the scope of the research project:

1. Software Client: Is usability a perceived purchasing criterion among small and medium-sized software clients?
2. Software Producer:
   (a) What practices and knowledge help small and medium-sized software companies to produce products with high usability?
   (b) How does a positive attitude about usability arise in small and medium-sized software producers and how do these discover or attain relevant knowledge?
   (c) Is usability a success factor for small and medium-sized software producers?
3. Organizational Field: Which state and which field dynamics can be observed overall?

2.2 Data Collection

We applied a hybrid approach including a combined qualitative and quantitative data collection strategy. With the qualitative part of the study we aimed to develop a thorough understanding of the knowledge and use of usability issues among software producing companies and of the importance of software usability for client companies. In addition, we aimed to identify actors in the software field who are already or potentially relevant for disseminating usability related knowledge. On this basis we refined our theoretical model. Based on the quantitative data we targeted providing statistically confirmed answers to the questions introduced above. Two surveys targeting software producers and software clients have been developed and distributed to collect corresponding data. The collected data were analyzed using various qualitative (Corbin and Strauss 2008) and quantitative methods (Backhaus et al. 2008) – especially linear regression models – and form the basis for the key results that follow as well as for the final recommendations.

Qualitative Data Collection. To gain a deeper understanding of relevant knowledge, stakeholder groups and current developments in the field, a total of 27 semi-structured qualitative expert interviews were conducted with various actors in the organizational field of the software industry with a duration of 60–120 min each. We interviewed four experts from large and eight experts from SME software producers, two SMEs that use the software, six academic representatives (in the fields of Information Systems, Media & Technology and Human Computer Interaction), two experts from usability consulting firms, two media and trade representatives and three representatives of industry associations. All interviews were recorded, transcribed and coded following established qualitative research methods (Corbin and Strauss 2008).

Quantitative Data Collection. To allow for generalization, specific emphasis was set to establish a representative sample of SMEs in Germany. As already mentioned, the quantitative study was splitted in two different surveys; one for software producers and one for software clients. The entire software producer sample covered 1.756 companies; the software client sample covered 1.873 companies. We received completed surveys by 163 producers and 182 clients (response rate of 9 %).

3 Results

This section provides an overview on selected results of the study. We first present some basic descriptive statistics of the quantitative data that has been collected. The following subsections focus on the perspective of the software client, the software producer and the entire organizational field providing answers to the questions introduced above.

3.1   Descriptive Statistics

The data describing SME software producers in Germany is characterized by the following descriptive facts: On average, SME software producers surveyed generate 300,000–1 million € annual turnover and employ 6–10 people. On average, the companies were founded 13 years ago and show an even distribution across different age classes. About 70 % of companies surveyed are limited liability companies, only about 1 % is listed on the stock market and about 50 % of companies are at least 75 % family-owned. We were thus successful in selecting truly small and medium-sized software producers.

A similar picture emerges with regard to the 182 client companies surveyed that were categorized as "SMEs using software". An average responding company employs about 20–49 people and has 5–10 million € turnover. Almost 70 % of surveyed companies generate less than 10 million € of turnover and employ fewer than 50 people. The companies are spread over various sectors (manufacturing: 25.5 %; service companies: 48.4 %; trade companies: 26.1 %) and nearly half of the companies are limited liability corporations (GmbH). As is typical in the context of SMEs, in over 70 % of the companies, more than 75 % of the shares are held in family hands.

3.2   Software Client Perspective

From a software client perspective we are specifically focusing on the question if usability is a perceived purchasing criterion among small and medium-sized software clients? Furthermore, we also target collecting baseline information on the status quo with respect to software that is currently used.

Our results thereby indicate that more than 60 % of software clients are very satisfied (6 and 7 in likert-scale) with the software that is currently used when it comes to functional and technical aspects such as reliability of the software. The degree of satisfaction is lower when it comes to actual usage aspects such as usability and flexibility of the software. Here, only approx. 40 % of the software clients express that they are very satisfied. Figure 2 visualizes the results comparing reliability against usability (mean value: 5.1) and flexibility (mean value: 4.66). In addition, 70 % of the software clients confirm that software usability issues have negative impacts on their productivity.

Based on the survey of medium-sized user companies we examined how usability is currently a decision criterion in the software procurement process. To this end, as a part of the user survey, a so-called Conjoint Analysis (Homburg and Krohmer 2005) was conducted in which a software procurement situation is simulated for respondents, allowing the identification and weighting of typical decision criteria (such as price and service). The data demonstrates that small and medium-sized user companies already emphasize usability in the software selection process. Software client firms seem to have generally adopted the issue as part of their decision making horizon. From a customer perspective, however, a discrepancy

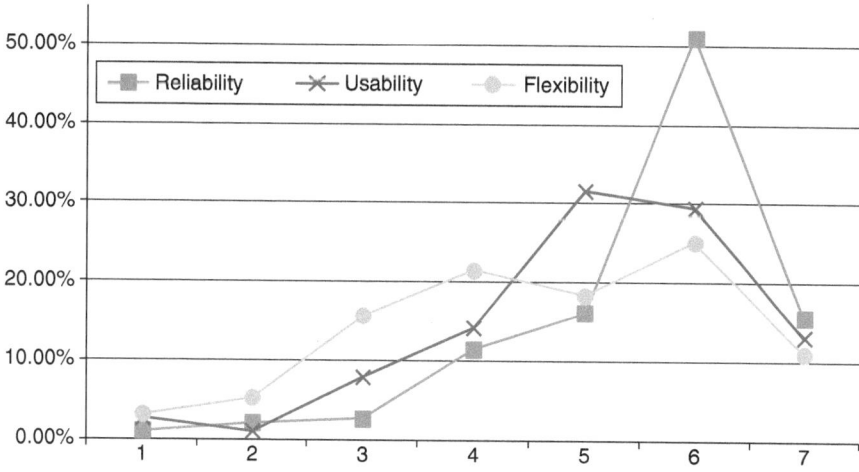

Fig. 2 Software clients' satisfaction

exists between the required usability and that currently offered by manufacturers. We thereby observe that firms that describe the usability of the software they currently use as rather low, are more likely to put high emphasis on usability in future procurement situations. In the qualitative interviews it is clear in this context that users perceive the usability of software not as a separate criterion but as part of a mix with other criteria such as service or functionality. It is thus questionable whether users and customers are currently explicitly communicating their needs regarding usability.

To summarize, we see unleveraged potential with regard to software usability from a software client perspective. The satisfaction with actual usage aspects is still lower compared to technical and functional aspects of software. Furthermore, negative experiences with currently used software have an impact on the importance of usability aspects when buying new software.

3.3   Software Producer Perspective

From a software producer point of view, we are specifically interested in the key question if software usability contributes to company success. In order to approach this general question, we first have to develop a deeper understanding of when and under which conditions companies are able to develop software with high usability. We thus ask: What practices and knowledge help small and medium-sized software companies to produce products with high usability? How does a positive attitude about usability arise in small and medium-sized software producers and how do these discover or attain relevant knowledge?

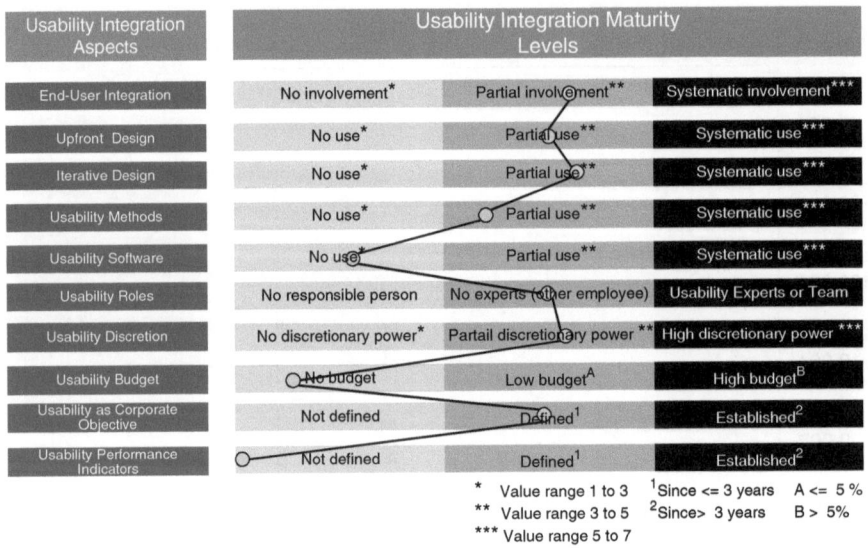

Fig. 3 Usability integration maturity model and current status quo at software producers

Looking at the status quo, we distinguish cognitive and structural aspects of usability integration and explore their effects on the perceived usability of the companies' software products and solutions. From a cognitive point of view, we look specifically at the attitude of management and availability of knowledge with regards to usability integration. Structural aspects of usability integration are based on the relevant literature and were integrated into a usability integration maturity model. This model included the following structural aspects consisting of software development practices and organizational aspects: end-user integration, iterative development, upfront design, usability methods, usability tools, usability budget, usability discretion, usability as company goal, usability measures, and explicit usability roles. The usability integration maturity model was used to visually depict the results of the collected quantitative data documenting the average status quo of German software producers. The descriptive results are visualized in Fig. 3.

Based on the data from the quantitative survey, it can be shown that among the 160 small and medium-sized software producers responding, current software development practices and organizational aspects are far from mature. End-user integration, upfront design and iterative development are development practices that are currently already leveraged. The usage of usability methods and tools is still in an early stage. From an organizational point of view, we discovered the contradiction that the respondents confirmed that usability is defined as a company goal, however, in parallel responded that the allocated budget is close to zero.

In a second step, we specifically observed which companies already have a very high degree of maturity of these practices and analyzed why this seems to be the case. Our results suggest that a positive attitude of management (Stratman and Roth 2007) towards usability in particular significantly reflected on the maturity of

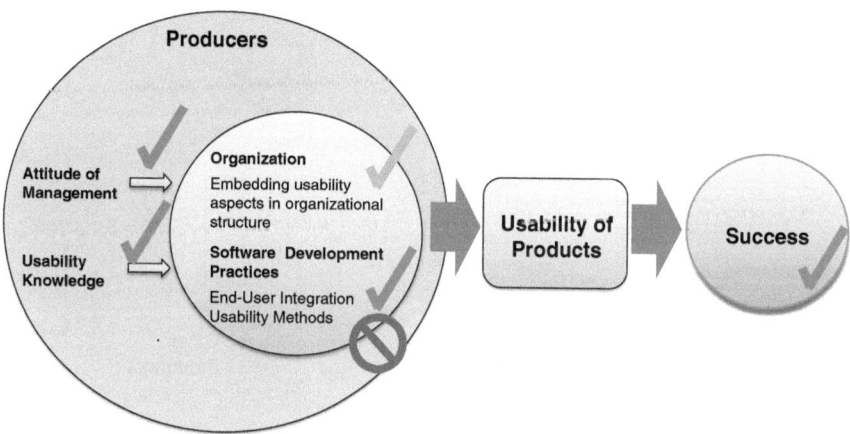

Fig. 4 Software producer perspective

relevant practices and structures. Moreover, it can be shown that existing expertise within the company has a positive influence on the intensity in which the user takes part in the development process – which in turn significantly improves the usability of the products. Because of their limited distribution as yet, the impact of the use of specific methods and tools in determining the usability of software is not yet clear. The low penetration rates can be interpreted as a sign of a perceived low suitability of these tools for the development processes in small and medium-sized software companies – potentially due to the fact that according tools and practices have not yet been "translated" (Czarniawska and Joerges 1996) for the SME context.

After systematically working out the effect of different practices on the maturity of a company regarding usability, we examine whether companies that assess the usability of their products as better than average are more successful. This is indeed evident in our multivariate data analysis; a positive and statistically significant relationship between the self-assessed usability of software products and customer satisfaction as well as sales development of the software producers surveyed was detected – while controlling for variables such as company size and customer structure. SME software producers that, through the acquisition of knowledge in the field and application of this knowledge in their structures and processes (e.g. by integrating the user directly in the development process), achieve a higher usability of their products seem to be more successful on average in terms of customer satisfaction and sales development. Figure 4 summarizes the effects we have identified based on our quantitative data.

3.4 Organizational Field Perspective

The question of how a positive attitude about usability arises in SME software producers was met with systematic analysis of the interaction and networking of

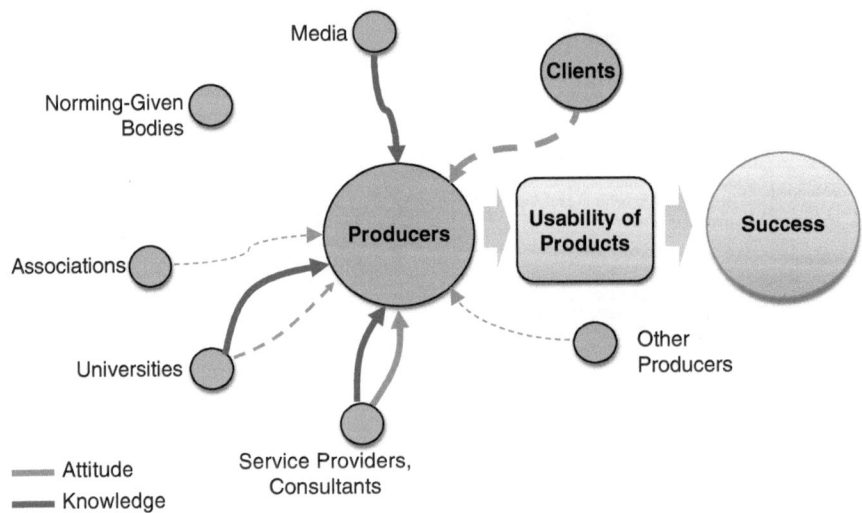

Fig. 5 Organizational field perspective

small and medium-sized software companies in the organizational field of the German software industry. Particular attention was paid to exchange relations with actors such as universities, service providers, customers, industry organizations and standardization bodies. From a theoretical point of view it was assumed that increased networking would have a positive impact on expertise in SME software producers (Powell et al. 1996). The results of the analysis support this assumption, however, the data also shows diffusion gaps in knowledge acquisition and attitude formation (see Fig. 5).

Although a high proportion of respondents indicate regular cooperation with other software producers, it was not possible based on the data to demonstrate clearly that such interactions significantly influence the attitudes and knowledge creation in relation to the issue of usability. Usability therefore rarely seems to be the main motivation behind cooperation between software manufacturers. For some producers however, universities already seem to be important sources of knowledge on the subject. However, it is not clear that universities are able to persuade regarding the issue – rather, they seem to act as pure suppliers of knowledge (also compare (Bär and Reich 2011)). It is clear that there exist specialized industry associations focused on usability, but that their activities are rarely perceived by SME software producers and, considered in isolation, do not contribute to attitude formation and knowledge dissemination. The results obtained point out that the potential of industry associations regarding usability are currently not being utilized to a significant degree. Overall, the data demonstrates that a large number of small medium-sized software producers work with external service providers and that appropriate cooperation significantly influences both attitudes towards and knowledge of usability in a positive way. At the same time, specialized usability consultants do not seem to be currently able to influence usability attitudes in SMEs. It can already be demonstrated that media are used by software producers in the acquisition of knowledge on usability. The issue of usability, however, seems not yet to have achieved significant popularity among the media, which is reflected in the lack of attitude change among software firms. The analysis further shows that the application of ISO standards serves no significant change in attitudes towards or knowledge about usability of software producers. These results suggest that strong standards both in terms of reputation as well as their potential to pool expertise and make this comparable and easy to communicate still fall short of their creator's expectations. The present results show that usability from the point of view of software producers has often been perceived as a purchasing criterion for customers. However, it seems to be the case that it is difficult for small and medium-sized software producers to react to short term customer requirements regarding usability, i.e. it is difficult to build up internal knowledge on usability. Instead, relevant knowledge gaps are frequently filled by hiring external service organizations.

To finally derive policy recommendations for government and society, it is necessary to understand the current status of the field and to observe the corresponding dynamics. It is conceivable that certain developments important for the establishment of the issue already happen on their own and are in no need of support, while other developments are blocked by factors that can be reduced or eliminated by appropriate measures. To capture the state and the dynamics of the field, theory-guided indicators were developed by which we can observe the status of the dissemination of the topic. Based on the data collected we then checked the levels of these indicators in Germany and partially compared these to those present in the United States. U.S. media and gurus are clearly perceived as role models in this regard. Corresponding usability catalysts are very scarce in the German landscape. Based on experience with products from the U.S. associated with a particularly high usability (such as the iPhone) in private life, attention regarding usability is also increasing in the professional context. Knowledge related to usability is rarely taught in Germany, however, and constitutes only a marginal area in the training of young professionals. Leading universities, professors and research are mostly associated with the U.S. The lack of specific, interdisciplinary training options is often considered a central obstacle to the spread of usability knowledge in Germany. Usability specialists today originate from different disciplines and many are newcomers to the area. A structuring of the labor market in this regard is only in the infancy stage in regards to trade fairs, initiatives, associations or standards. At the same time software producers and design agencies are desperately searching for qualified personnel. Especially for SMEs, it seems to be increasingly difficult to find appropriate candidates to occupy vacant job opportunities in usability. Software producers argue that currently no uniform professions or degrees seem to exist in Germany regarding usability.

4   Recommendations

Based on the empirically determined diffusion of usability practices we conclude with some suggestions for initiatives. These initiatives, performed by different actors could – in the short and medium term – lead to increased usability of software by German software producers. For SME software producers, based on the maturity model previously developed, a self-test is proposed on which basis individualized measures can be derived to optimize the software development process. For small and medium-sized client companies, a more professional approach to the software procurement process – i.e. using checklists or the assistance of external experts – can help make usability needs more explicit. Furthermore, based on the results obtained it can be argued that usability specialists or consultants could currently particularly benefit from increased transparency of the services offered and a more target-group focused communication with potential customers. Regarding existing associations it would make sense to extend the radius of activities to specialized industry and professional associations of small and medium-sized corporate users. To strengthen the dissemination of the topic in the media, personalization of the issue and a link to existing success stories could lead to wider attention and stronger resonance. Finally, measures with medium to long-lasting effects can be identified. In this context, on the basis of the results obtained, it is argued that a greater integration of usability into the curricula of universities and a long-term focus on the establishment of norms and standards can have a positive effect on small and medium-sized software producers and client firms. In terms of policy, pilot projects in the form of "usability vouchers" could be established to provide monetary incentives to engage in professional usability practices. These could enable small and medium-sized companies despite their limited resources to obtain expertise on usability and to gain practical experience in the implementation of basic practices together with specialists.

5   Summary

In this article we presented the results of our empirical study exploring the current status quo of software usability in small and medium sized enterprises in Germany. From a software client perspective, we identified unleveraged potential with regard to software usability. Today, the satisfaction with actual usage aspects is still lower compared to the technical and functional aspects of software used in SMEs. However, in parallel we have seen that usability is considered as equally important as technical and functional aspects. We could identify a cluster of software clients that explicitly emphasizes the importance of usability as a software buying decision criteria. Interestingly, firms in this cluster are characterized by negative experiences with regard to usability of software used in the past. From a software producer perspective, we identified that current software development practices and organizational aspects with regard to usability integration are far from mature.

Software producing companies in which executives have a positive attitude towards usability and which have been able to accumulate a usability specific knowledge, are more likely to implement usability-specific practices and to adapt their organizational structures respectively – which in turn significantly improves the usability of the products. In addition, we were able to detect a positive and statistically significant relationship between self-assessed usability of software products and customer satisfaction as well as sales development. This gives a clear indication for software producers that it is worth investing in usability practices as part of the development processes. Finally, from a field perspective, our data demonstrates that a large number of small and medium-sized software producers work with external service providers and that appropriate cooperation significantly influences both attitudes towards and knowledge of usability in a positive way. Furthermore, our study also demonstrates that there is still a lot of unleveraged potential within the field, e.g. there is a growing demand for usability professionals which currently cannot be satisfied.

Building on the results of our study, we plan to establish a usability competence center focusing on two main topics: First, we will develop a management concept for people-driven development of software and its implementation and use in the form of information systems. The management concept will embed a procedure model helping SME software producers to integrate usability into the entire development lifecycle. Second, we will establish a network of software producers, service providers, and software clients to disseminate our management concept. Further information on the study and our future activities will be accessible via the Web site http://www.usability-in-germany.de/.

References

Backhaus, K., Plinke, W., Erichson, B., & Weiber, R. (2008). *Multivariate Analysemethoden (12 Ausg.).* Berlin/Heidelberg: Springer.

Bär, N., & Reich, D. (2011). *Was Firmen wollen: eine Umfrage zu Usability Dienstleistungen für klein- und mittelständische Unternehmen.* S. 250ff.: Jahresband Usability Professionals.

Burns, L. R., & Wholey, D. R. (1993). Adaption and abandonment of matrix management programs: Effects of organizational characteristics and interorganizational networks. *Academy of Management Journal, 36*(1), 105–138.

Corbin, J., & Strauss, A. (2008). *Basics of qualitative research: Techniques and procedures for developing grounded theory* (Vol. 3). Thousand Oaks/London: Sage.

Czarniawska, B., & Joerges, B. (1996). Travel of ideas. In B. Czarniawska & G. Sévon (Eds.), *Translating organizational change* (pp. 13–48). Berlin: deGruyter.

David, R. J., & Strang, D. (2006). When fashion is fleeting: Transitory collective beliefs and the dynamics of TQM consulting. *Academy of Management Journal, 49*(2), 215–233.

DiMaggio, P. J., & Powell, W. W. (1983). The iron cage revisited: Institutional isomorphism and collective rationality in organizational fields. *American Sociological Review, 48*(2), 147–160.

Guler, I., Guillén, M. F., & Macpherson, J. M. (2002). Global competition, institutions, and the diffusion of organizational practices: The International Spread of ISO 9000 Quality Certificates. *Administrative Science Quarterly, 47*, 207–232.

Haveman, H. A. (1993). Follow the leader: Mimetic isomorphism and entry into new markets. *Administrative Science Quarterly, 38*, 593–627.

Hirsch, P. (1972). Processing fads and fashions: An organization-set analysis of cultural industy systems. *American Journal of Sociology, 77*(4), 639–659.

Homburg, C., & Krohmer, H. (2005). *Marketing management*. Wiesbaden: Gabler.

Human Factors International (2011). Certification. Abgerufen am 14. Februar 2011 von http://www.humanfactors.com/certification/default.asp

Kieser, A., & Ernst, B. (2002). In search of explanations for the consulting explosion. In K. Sahlin-Andresson & L. Engwall (Eds.), *The expansion of management knowledge: Carriers, flows, and sources* (pp. 47–73). Stanford: Stanford University Press.

Markowski, N., Grosser, K., & Kuhl, R. (2008). Analyse von Barrieren und Hemmnissen beim Wissenstransfer zwischen Hochschulen und KMU. Düsseldorf: Forschungsberichte des Fachbereichs Wirtschaft der Fachhochschule Düsseldorf.

Palmer, D. A., Jennings, P. D., & Zhou, X. (1993). Late adoption of the multidivisional form by large U.S. corporations: Institutional, political, and economic accounts. *Administrative Science Quarterly, 38*, 100–131.

Powell, W. W., Koput, K. W., & Smith-Doerr, L. (1996). Interorganizational collaboration and the locus of innovation: Networks of learning in biotechnology. *Administrative Science Quarterly, 46*, 116–145.

Rogers, E. M. (2003). *Diffusion of innovations* (5th ed.). New York: Free Press.

Stratman, J. K., & Roth, A. V. (2007). Enterprise resource planning (ERP) competence constructs: Two-stage multi-item scale development and validation. *Decision Sciences, 33*(4), 601–628.

Swan, J. A., & Newell, S. (1995). The role of professional associations in technology diffusion. *Organization Studies, 16*(5), 847–874.

Usability in Germany (2011). Abschlussbericht zum Projekt "Gebrauchstauglichkeit von Anwendungssoftware als Wettbewerbsfaktor für KMU". www.usability-in-germany.de: Bundesministerium für Wirtschaft und Technologie.

Valente, T. (1993). Diffusion of innovations and policy decision-making. *Journal of Communication, 43*(1), 30–45. Winter.

Venkatesh, V., Morris, M., Davis, G., & Davis, F. (2003). User acceptance of information technology: Toward a unified view. *MIS Quarterly, 27*(3), 425–478.

Yli-Renko, H., Autio, E., & Sapienza, H. J. (2001). Social capital, knowledge acquisition, and knowledge exploitation in young technology-based firms. *Strategic Management Journal, 22*(6–7), 587–613.

Software Product Management

Samuel A. Fricker

Abstract

Software organizations evolve and maintain software solutions with more than a single development project. The delta specifications and artifacts that result from each project make reuse difficult and challenge a company's ability to innovate. Software product management is a growing discipline for understanding how to productize and align software with company strategy, how to evolve software, and how to coordinate product stakeholders. With product focus, in addition to project focus, planning accuracy can be improved, time-to-market reduced, product quality enhanced, and economic success sustained. This chapter provides an overview on software product management and discusses what today is known about this discipline.

1   Introduction

In modern economy the companies that succeed and survive are those able to develop and market winning products. Products like phones, cars, and airplanes are increasingly software-based, rather than being electro-mechanical devices. Services like banking, information provision, and entertainment and infrastructure like telecommunications and power networks gradually tend to be run more by software products than by humans. Software is an increasingly important enabler and driver of innovation because of its adaptability and flexibility. At the same time, software allows cutting cost, reducing time, and increasing reliability of services that earlier were performed by humans, enabling humans to focus on complex and little repetitive tasks.

S.A. Fricker
Blekinge Institute of Technology - School of Computing, Karlskrona, Sweden
e-mail: samuel.fricker@bth.se

A. Maedche et al. (eds.), *Software for People*, Management for Professionals,
DOI 10.1007/978-3-642-31371-4_4, © Springer-Verlag Berlin Heidelberg 2012

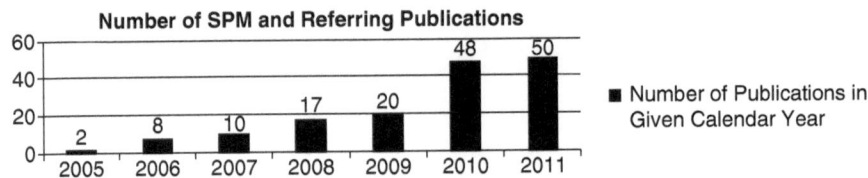

Fig. 1 Growth of the number of scientific publications that have the term "software product management" in the title, abstract, or keywords or that refer to such publications (Source: Scopus (February 26, 2012))

Software organizations see themselves confronted with software solutions evolved and maintained with more than a single development project. They incur a majority of cost not with that first development project, but afterwards (Sneed et al. 2005). The delta specifications and artifacts that result from each project make reuse difficult and challenge a company's ability to innovate. In addition, the ever increasing strategic importance of software requires that solutions are not only technically sound, but are aligned with business strategy.

In 1997, the term *software product management* was coined (Kilpi 1997). Procter & Gamble's idea of letting an individual manager championing and taking responsibility for a product (Gorchels 2006) was applied to a software organization. The software product managers extended configuration management of code and software artifacts with delivery data, customer data, and change requests. An integrated software product management process was established that covered marketing, release planning, software production, sales, customer delivery, and product support in addition to the release projects.

Today software product management is a young, growing discipline that bridges software engineering with business. The first book on software product management appeared in 2002 (Condon 2002). The first workshop of the International Workshop on Software Product Management (IWSPM) series took place in 2006. The first conference on the International Conference on Software Business (ICSOB) series took place in 2010. Figure 1 shows that an increasing number of publications are written on software product management or refer to such publications. These figures are very defensive estimates of the actual amount of activity in the field of software product management.

The aim of this chapter is to provide an up-to-date overview on software product management. It does so by characterizing software products, describing the profile of a software product manager, and introducing software product management practices and interfaces to other company functions. The characterization covers product management both for commercial software and for software solutions used to provide commercial services. The overview gives selected entry points to academic literature and to books about the topic and concludes with a short discussion of the state of knowledge.

The remainder of the chapter is structured as follows. Section 2 introduces the software product concept. Section 3 characterizes the software product manager and company-internal stakeholders. Section 3.2 surveys software product management references models and describes software product management practices. Section 5 discusses state of knowledge. Section 6 summarizes and concludes.

2   Software as a Product

2.1   Software Products

The term *product* is a central concept in marketing. It designates *anything that can be offered to a market for attention, acquisition, use, or consumption that might satisfy a want or need* (Kotler et al. 2010). The intention behind a product is the satisfaction of a set of people or organizations with comparable needs against some form of compensation. Products can be physical objects, services, people, places, organizations, ideas, or mixes of these entities.

The set of people or organizations the product is made available for is called a *market*. The market-orientation where one product may be instantiated many times differentiates product development with bespoke development where one software instance is developed for one specific customer. Characteristic for something to qualify as a product is its offering to a market, and not the concluded compensation. Even a thing that is made available for potential sales but never sold is called product. The compensation can be, but does not necessarily need to be of commercial or financial nature. Attention, use, or consumption suffices for the thing to be a product.

A "software product" is a *product whose primary component is software* (Kittlaus and Clough 2009). Software is an information good that manifests human know-how in bits and bytes. This characteristic makes a software product special in comparison to other goods.

Software becomes whatever function or application it addresses (Cusumano 2004). The utility of a software product is determined by the functionality it provides at its interfaces. Value is generated as a result of such functionality. For example, an online-banking solution may offer the possibility to enter a payment. The banking solution then generates value by initiating an account movement. The generic character of software makes businesses in many industries depend on software products, provided that the generated value is understood by those targeted by these software products.

An information good like software can be easily copied, shared, resold, or rented (Variant 2000). Production and distribution of copies require little cost in comparison to the development of the software product. This characteristic allows software product sales to achieve fascinating profit margins (Cusumano 2004). The duplication and spreading of commercial software needs to be managed, however. Defined rights need to be licensed (Kittlaus and Clough 2009). Such rights include the right to use, the right to own, and the right to resell the software.

Software can be changed or updated relatively easily by using patches or release updates (van de Weerd et al. 2006b). This flexibility make incremental product development possible, where a rapid break-even can be reached and a high return of investment achieved (Denne and Cleland-Huang 2003). The high release frequency, however, makes requirements organization highly complex, especially for large and complex software products that offer integration with other software.

The software business has also its dark sides when compared to other kinds of product businesses (Cusumano 2004; Xu and Brinkkemper 2007). Many developers consider themselves to be artists, rather than engineers or scientists. Their productivity differs up to a factor 20. Software product development, hence, is highly unpredictable and risky. Seventy-five to eighty percent of the projects routinely are late and over budget. Planning accuracy of 20 % is considered best practice. However, a successful software product has the potential be considered a "license to print money" with marginal production cost and customers locked in to the vendor. The product business model can be maintained as long as the software company succeeds to sell new products to new customers, rather than selling services and upgrades to their existing customer base.

Three types of software products are often differentiated: packaged software, software as a service, and embedded software (Kittlaus and Clough 2009). These types mainly differentiate themselves in how the product is duplicated and made available to the customer.

Packaged software is commercial software that comes ready-made (Xu and Brinkkemper 2007). Packaged software is often customized when deployed. The larger such software is the more significant customization and deployment effort can be. A typical large-scale example is an Enterprise Resource Planning (ERP) system whose adaptation cost usually outweighs the product cost. Packaged software may be offered in a standardized format as commercial off-the-shelf software, as shrink-wrapped software, or as an app. *Commercial off-the-shelf (COTS) software* is packaged software with limited configurability offered to a whole market. COTS is often integrated into other software (Basili and Boehm 2001; Jaccheri and Torchiano 2002). *Shrink-wrapped software* is COTS software that can be bought in stores or downloaded from the web (Flammia and McCandless 1997). An *app* is a form of shrink-wrapped software that typically is of small size and offered through a market place, an *app store*, dedicated for a given operating system (Miller 2010).

Software products may be offered as a service instead of being offered as packaged software (Hayes 2008). Such software is called *Software as a Service (SaaS)*. SaaS is not installed on a user's local PC, but run at a distant server managed by the supplier. The user typically accesses the software through a web browser. One of the benefits of SaaS is runtime binding, where the software decides ad-hoc to access other software services to deliver its functionality to the user (Turner et al. 2003). The SaaS software development model is likely to lead to higher software quality, greater profits, and higher social welfare than traditional forms of software (Choudhary 2007). On-demand software provision through the Internet, also called *cloud computing*, is a new paradigm shift in the software industry (Buyya et al. 2009) that can change the way software is developed and composed (Gold et al. 2004).

A third important form of software products is software embedded in microcontroller-based systems (Lee 2000; Ebert and Salecker 2009). Examples of embedded systems include home appliances (Edwards and Grinter 2001), mobile phones (Roussos et al. 2005), cars (Broy et al. 2007), and power systems (Wu et al. 2005). The end user usually doesn't recognize *embedded software*, but perceives it as a set of functions that the system provides. Embedded software produced by one supplier can be prepared for use in the products of another company that usually is called Original Equipment Manufacturer, OEM (Kittlaus and Clough 2009).

Software companies often do not sell one single product but offer *portfolios* of products tailored for different market segments (Kittlaus and Clough 2009). Quality concerns, total cost of portfolio ownership, and time-to-market of product development drives these companies towards developing platforms and *product lines* that enable planned reuse of software artifacts (Clements and Northrop 2001; Pohl et al. 2005). Usually, higher-level or senior product management is responsible for a product line, the product manager for one or a few of the products, and analysts or requirements engineers for product features or releases.

2.2   Parts of Software Products

A product is a combination of goods and services (Kotler et al. 2010). The *core product* corresponds to the problem-solving services or benefits that customers buy when they obtain a product. The *actual product* consists of various parts, functional and quality features, styling, brand name, and packaging combined to deliver the core product's benefits. The *augmented product*, finally, delivers additional services and benefits such as delivery, installation, after-sales service, and warranty.

The software domain knows engineering, business, and legal interpretations of what a software product consist of. These interpretations characterize the concerns the respective viewpoints are concerned with.

The engineering perspective focuses on the core product. Here, a software product consists of the *complete set of computer programs, procedures, and associated documentation and data designated for delivery to users* (IEEE 1990). These artifacts support planning, design, construction, and quality assurance of the product artifacts, including code development and configuration control (Bersoff 1984). A product repository is used to manage these artifacts across development projects (Kilpi 1997). It contains baselines of consistent product development plans, requirements, architecture, design, code, configuration data, test plans, test cases, test data, and user documentation (Clements and Northrop 2001; Sneed et al. 2005).

The business interpretation focuses on the actual and augmented products. Here, a software product is a *packaged configuration of software components or a software-based service, with auxiliary materials, which is released for and traded in a specific market* (Xu and Brinkkemper 2007). The packaged components refer to the software delivered to users. The software-based services cover infrastructure, software environment, and application service provision (Yourseff et al. 2008). These components and services form the actual product. The augmented product consists of auxiliary materials and the activities that support software distribution and trading. The auxiliary materials comprise software documentation, web pages, user manuals, training material, and brochures. Supporting activities include distribution, customer projects that deliver customization and integration for customers, user training, and maintenance.

The legal interpretation adds a set of rights to the services and artifacts of an augmented software product. Right management and transfer are extensively researched in the context of open source software (Lerner and Tirole 2002). The GNU General Public License GPL (GNU 2007) is one well-known open source license model among many others (Open Source Initiative 2012). These license models allow free use, modification, or distribution of software provided that restrictions with respect to copyright and open source status protection are observed (Ruffin and Ebert 2004). Affected by these restrictions is the right to integrate the open source software into other products that then are reproduced or sold (Alspaugh et al. 2010). A bypassed licensor is entitled to force an integrator to end the affected product's production, delivery, and sale and to claim for damages.

2.3   Classification of Software Products

Products can be classified based on their role for the customers (Kotler et al. 2010). Each product class has a particular customer buying and use behaviors that are addressed with a specific pricing, distribution approach, and promotion tactic. Similar differences can be observed between each type of software product: packaged software, embedded software, and SaaS. Table 1 provides an overview and examples of products.

Consumer products target end consumers for personal consumption. Convenience goods are bought relatively frequently with a little comparison and buying effort. Shopping goods are less frequently bought with significant comparison effort to alternatives. Specialty goods have unique characteristics and high brand identification. Here the customer is willing to make a special purchase effort.

Industrial products target other companies or in-house business units. These products are used to again build and offer value added products or services (Jansen et al. 2007). Materials and parts enter the customer's products completely. These products are sold directly to the industrial users who mostly look on price and service. These customers are, in the case of embedded materials and parts usually called Original Equipment Manufacturers, OEMs (Kittlaus and Clough 2009). Capital items help in the customer's production or operations and partly enter the customer's products. Capital items tend to be sold through intermediaries or integrated to the customer's environment with dedicated projects. Supplies and services are needed in the customer's production or operations, but do not enter the customer's products. Supplies are usually purchased with minimal comparison. Services are usually purchased under contract.

Predominantly in the context of SaaS, the term software product is not limited to the world of software vendors, but also encompasses the world of corporate IT

Table 1 Product classifications (Adapted from Kotler et al. 2010), and product types with examples

Software Product Type / Product Classification		Non-Software	Packaged Software	Embedded Software	SaaS
Consumer Products	Convenience Goods	Food	Web browser	Memory stick	Web-based e-mail
	Shopping Goods	Furniture	PDF reader	Smart phone	Music streaming service
	Specialty Goods	Housing	Office suite	Car	Online banking
Industrial Products	Materials and Parts	Cement	Development libraries and components	Specialized chipsets	Web services
	Capital items	Factory	Development environment (tools)	Server farm	Billing system (e.g. in telecom)
	Supplies and services	Management consulting	Enterprise resource planning system	Copier machine	Web-based CRM system

organizations (Kittlaus and Clough 2009; Cabinet Office 2011b). Corporate IT organizations deliver and operate software products in-house that enable business units to deliver business services to customers (Ward and Peppard 2002). The corporate IT organizations establish software products usually as *standard software* that is routinely installed on most computers within the business unit.

3   The Software Product Roles

Procter & Gamble has introduced product management to improve the performance of one their product lines (Gorchels 2006). Their key idea was to let an individual manager assigned responsibility for these products compete with others. This system was so successful that it was copied over again since then.

3.1   The Software Product Manager

The *software product manager*, often called *solution owner* in the context of information systems, is a *mini Chief Executive Officer* with full business responsibility of a software (Ebert 2006). A software product manager is a middle manager responsible for developing new products and managing and marketing existing ones (Gorchels 2006; Cabinet Office 2011). He defines strategy of these products, aligns them with company strategy and markets needs, and executes the strategy-implementing plans by coordinating product development, marketing, sales, distribution, service, and support.

Job descriptions for software product managers usually cover the following responsibilities. He participates in innovation and takes leadership for new product ideas. He develops the product strategy that aims at achieving sustainable economic product success in line with corporate strategy (Kittlaus and Clough 2009). In the context of commercial software, he plans the marketing mix and monitors product success in collaboration with marketing. He plans product scope and monitors product evolution in collaboration with development. He represents the product inside and outside the company and coordinates product operations with company units including sales, distribution, service, and support.

A software product manager has at least a Masters title in informatics or business administration and has developed broad knowledge of relevant technologies and markets. He has proven ability to communicate and negotiate successfully with all important product stakeholders inside and outside the company. He has excellent self-management abilities that allow him to work on a broad spectrum of tasks with changing priorities.

To summarize, the software product manager stands for what the product does, what it is, who it serves, and what it means to the company and customers (Gorchels 2006). He is a champion and driver for successful evolution and revolution of the company's portfolio.

3.2   External and Internal Stakeholders of Software Product Management

Each company acts in an industry, where it is embedded in an ecosystem suppliers, customers, system integrators, partners, competitors, suppliers of substitute products or services, and potential new entrants (Porter 1998; Messerschmitt and Szyperski 2003; Popp and Meyer 2010). *Suppliers* deliver components, platforms, and systems that enable development and running of software products (Jansen et al. 2007). *System integrators* design and implement software-based systems that are used by customers and into which software products are integrated. *Partners* may resell software products, provide referrals, integrate software products into their products, cooperate in product development, and provide certification services (Popp and Meyer 2010). *Competitors, suppliers of substitute products or services, and potential new entrants* are perceived to be threats for a product that are addressed by protecting intellectual property and by innovating continuously (Hyland and Beckett 1994; Pech 2006).

A product cuts across the company's value chain (Porter 1998). To align the product with the company's processes and activities, the product manager coordinates company-internal stakeholders (Lehmann and Winer 2005; Gorchels 2006; van de Weerd et al. 2006; Kittlaus and Clough 2009; Bekkers et al. 2010). Product management ensures that the product and the stakeholders' activities are aligned with company strategy, the market situation, and the stakeholders' interests.

The organizational structure, the position of product management, and the naming and scope of the various company functions differ from company to company and over time (Lehmann and Winer 2005). This limits the validity of any global definition of product management stakeholders. The following stakeholder characterizations, hence, need to be interpreted and adapted to each organization under consideration.

The interface between a company's marketing and development functions is the most critical in terms of challenges and criticality for product success (Griffin and Hauser 1996). The product manager bridges two these functions while planning and aligning the product with corporate strategy. The product management responsibilities and activities ensure that product-related knowledge and information are adequately shared and that product-related activities are coordinated.

The product manager closely cooperates with *marketing management* that is responsible for market and customer success. Marketing management *builds and maintains beneficial exchanges with target buyers* and *manages demand and customer relationships* (Kotler et al. 2010). The product manager is the company-internal supplier who delivers new and improved products to marketing. Marketing represents the voice of the customer, for example by providing access to marketing research and customers. Marketing also ensures that the products address the needs of target markets. Upon successful implementation of a product release, marketing undertakes promotion and selling efforts for bringing the released products to the customers and satisfy their needs.

For defining the product strategy and planning product evolution, the product manager collaborates with the following additional functions and roles. He collaborates with *research and development* to identify opportunities for product and technology innovation (Garcia and Calantone 2002). He performs triage and aligns the product with corporate strategy whose owner is *higher-level management* (Davis 2005). Higher-level management balances the overall portfolio, prepares and executes measurement and analysis, defines a consistent marketing and sales strategy, and provides funding and resources for product development and operations (Ebert 2006).

The product manager closely cooperates with product development *project managers*. Such a project manager is responsible for successfully executing a project that leads to a product release. A project, in contrast to a product, is characterized by *having a definite beginning and a definite end* and by *creating unique deliverables in a sequence of steps* (Project Management Institute 2004). The product manager is the company-internal customer who contracts each product development project by setting priorities for the targeted product release. A project manager is responsible for one such project. He ensures feasibility of the project scope, implements the agreed scope, and hands the implemented product release over to the product manager.

For launching and delivering an implemented product release, the product manager collaborates with the following additional functions and roles. These roles mostly address operational concerns on a tactical level.

He collaborates with *distribution* who make the software product ready for consumption. In the case of software-as-a-service, distribution may be called *production* and is responsible for operating and hosting the software (Cabinet Office 2011). In the case of packaged software, distribution is responsible for creating the product package and shipping it to the points-of-sales or the customers. Distribution interfaces with inbound and outbound logistics.

The product manager collaborates with *sales* and with *customer projects* that enable the customers to take advantage of the values delivered by the product. Such customer projects can involve system engineering projects, such as building a substation for power distribution, or organizational and process changes, such as in the deployment of an enterprise resource planning system. He collaborates with *customer service and support* who deliver user training, consultancy, maintenance service, and upgrades (Goffin and New 2001).

The product manager collaborates with *finance* who ensure a sufficient revenue stream for the company (Konig 2009). He collaborates with *legal* who provide advice regarding license use and who protect and defend the product against competitors and potential new market entrants.

4   Software Product Management

A software organization faces a highly competitive environment. A good product idea and a well-executed new product development project are not enough to be successful. Usefulness of a software product in accordance with the organization's strategy can only be achieved and sustained with an interrelated set of competences, practices, and processes for planning, building, marketing, distributing, evolving, and maintaining a software product.

Software product management is the *discipline, which governs a software product from its inception to its close-down to generate as large value as possible for the business.* This definition, adapted from Alcatel (Ebert 2006), encompasses three important facets: governance of a software, coverage of the full software lifecycle, and business value generation.

Software product management encompasses the practices needed for governing a software product. Governance refers to structures, processes, and relational mechanisms implemented to ensure that business goals are achieved, resources responsibly utilized, and risks adequately managed (Meyer et al. 2003; De Haes and Van Grembergen 2004). A software product manager, the mini-CEO, is responsible and accountable for the success of the software product (Ebert 2006). The product manager plans the scope and evolution of the software product and aligns it with user, market, and company needs (Gorchels 2006). To obtain commitment from the organization and to reduce risks, the product manager actively involves important stakeholders from development, marketing, sales, distribution, service, and support (Aurum and Wohlin 2003; van de Weerd et al. 2006).

A software that is used undergoes continual change or becomes progressively less useful (Lehman 1980). This law applies not only for software use, but also for the product's position in the market and its utility for the company. The product needs to be adjusted to changing customer preferences and moves by competitors (Porter 1998). A software product is adapted differently based on its current lifecycle stage (Raijlich and Bennet 2000). Initially the product is evolved to extend its capabilities and functionalities. Later when changes become difficult, it is serviced with defect repairs and simple functional changes to maintain its usefulness. The ensuing phase-out stage stops servicing, but continues revenue generation until the product is closed down. Each phase requires specific expertise, employs particular architectural tactics, and pursues own economic goals.

Every investment requires return of investment to be generated. Return can be generated with a broad variety of values, including values perceived by customer and users, market value for the company, shareholder value, production value, product differentiation, intellectual capital, value of technology, and innovation value (Khurum et al. 2011). The software product manager is responsible for prioritizing value generation and aligning the software product with company strategy. Strategic management instruments (Kaplan and Norton 1992), business cases (Reifer 2002), and goals and requirements (Gorschek and Wohlin 2006) are means to plan and manage the implementation of such value generation.

4.1   Software Product Management Reference Models

Software product management stands for a broad variety of practices for aligning the product business with corporate strategy, steering software development, obtaining customer interest, generating revenue, and supporting product use. The scope of product management can be derived from textbooks (Lehman 1980; Condon 2002; Gorchels 2006; Dver 2007; Lawley 2007; Cagan 2008; Haines 2009; Kittlaus and Clough 2009). A systematic overview, however, can be gained by studying reference models that describe software product management practices. They have been developed based on empirical research (van de Weerd et al. 2006; Bekkers et al. 2010), personal experience in large-scale companies (Ebert 2006, 2009; Kittlaus and Clough 2009), as a result of industry consultancy and training (Pragmatic Marketing 2012; Steinhardt 2012), and by seeking consensus between academic and industrial opinion leaders (ISPMA 2012).

The software product management reference models are used to benchmark, improve processes, and train practitioners. They refer to 28–68 capabilities, processes, activities, or competencies and are structured according to product lifecycle phases, functional areas, interfaces to company function, abstraction levels, or impact of decision making. Figure 2 shows an overlay of the reference models' structuring mechanisms.

A product artifact hierarchy consisting of portfolio, products, releases, and requirements, is used to structure *van de Weerd's reference framework for software product management* (van de Weerd et al. 2006; Bekkers et al. 2010). Each level in the artifact hierarchy refers to groups of three or six focus areas: portfolio management, product planning, release planning, and requirements management. The total of 15 focus areas again structure 68 capabilities of a software product organization that are implemented in collaboration with company-external and internal stakeholders.

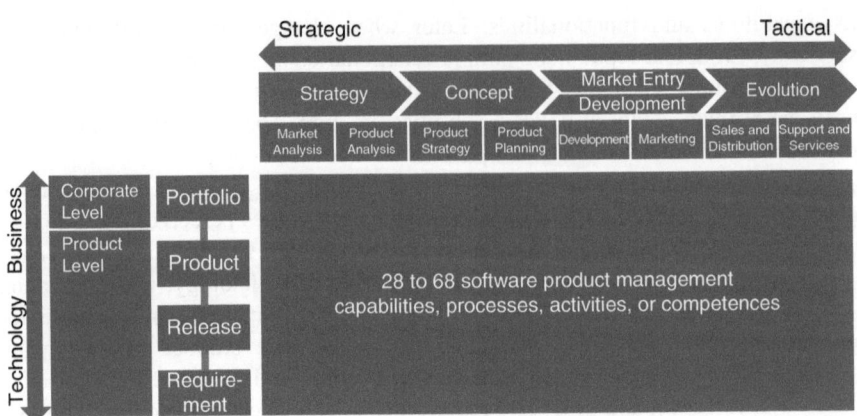

Fig. 2 Overlay of software product management reference models (Ebert 2006; Kittlaus and Clough 2009; Bekkers et al. 2010; Pragmatic Marketing 2012)

Lifecycle phases are the structuring mechanism used in *Ebert's software product management framework* (Ebert 2006, 2009). The phases strategy, concept, market entry and development, and evolution follow the major milestones of a new product development effort (Cooper 2001) and are used to order 18 product management processes and 10 competencies.

Eight functional areas, visualized as columns, are used to structure 49 activities in *Kittlaus's software product management framework* (Kittlaus and Clough 2009). The areas are market and product analysis, product strategy and planning, and collaboration with development, marketing, sales and distribution, and support and services. The framework also differentiates two abstraction levels that distinguish activities performed at the corporate and the product levels.

A well-known reference model for software product management that emerged from industry consultancy and training is the *Pragmatic Marketing framework* (Pragmatic Marketing 2012). It delineates management and marketing practices for technology products on a continuum of concerns from strategic to tactical: market, strategy, business, planning, programs, readiness, and support. Pragmatic Marketing tailors the framework to characterize special kinds of product managers. The director of product strategy is responsible for strategic business-oriented practices like market definition, product portfolio management, and business planning. The technical product manager is responsible for strategic technology-oriented practices like technology assessment, product roadmapping, and requirements management. The product marketing manager, finally, is responsible for tactical practices like customer acquisition, product sales, and support.

The *software product management body of knowledge (SPMBoK)* of the International Software Product Management Association (ISPMA) is a consensus between academic and industrial opinion leaders (ISPMA 2012). It integrates Van de Weerd's, Ebert's, and Kittlaus's frameworks for product management education purposes. In contrast to other reference models, the scope and contents of the SPMBoK continues to evolve by being discussed and adjusted by any product

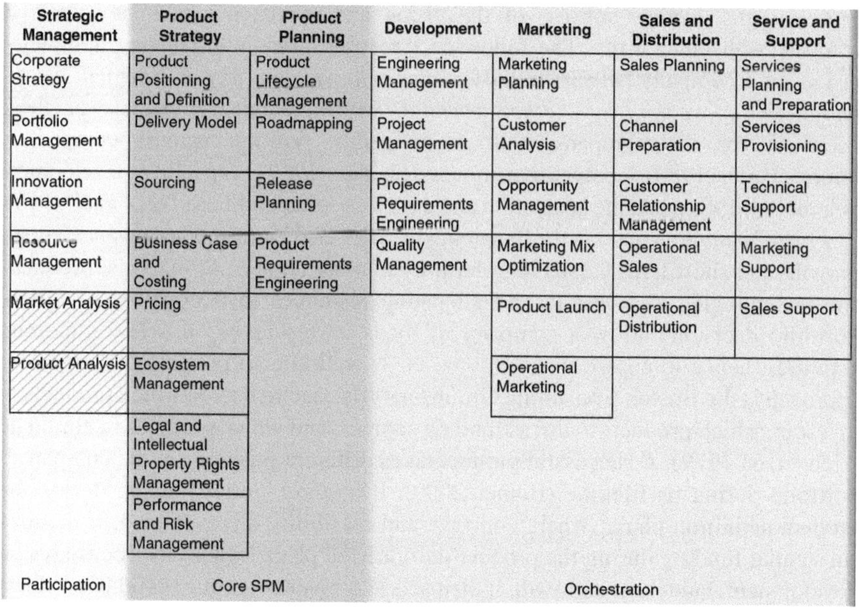

Strategic Management	Product Strategy	Product Planning	Development	Marketing	Sales and Distribution	Service and Support
Corporate Strategy	Product Positioning and Definition	Product Lifecycle Management	Engineering Management	Marketing Planning	Sales Planning	Services Planning and Preparation
Portfolio Management	Delivery Model	Roadmapping	Project Management	Customer Analysis	Channel Preparation	Services Provisioning
Innovation Management	Sourcing	Release Planning	Project Requirements Engineering	Opportunity Management	Customer Relationship Management	Technical Support
Resource Management	Business Case and Costing	Product Requirements Engineering	Quality Management	Marketing Mix Optimization	Operational Sales	Marketing Support
Market Analysis	Pricing			Product Launch	Operational Distribution	Sales Support
Product Analysis	Ecosystem Management			Operational Marketing		
	Legal and Intellectual Property Rights Management					
	Performance and Risk Management					
Participation	Core SPM			Orchestration		

Fig. 3 The software product management body of knowledge (SPMBoK) (ISPMA 2012)

management expert that joins the ISPMA knowledge network. It hence adapts to the evolving understanding of the discipline.

The SPMBoK structures 38 practices again along functional areas. The product manager participates in strategic management, is directly responsible for product strategy and planning, and orchestrates development, market, sales, distribution, service, and support. In small companies, market and product analysis are performed as core activities by the product manager. Figure 3 provides an overview of the SPMBoK.

The various structuring approaches and naming of product management practices make it difficult to provide a single, globally accepted view of software product management. The SPMBoK provides the broadest consensus of software product management opinion leaders and is used here to structure the overview of the various practices.

4.2 Strategic Management

Strategic management is concerned of the question how a company achieves and sustains competitive advantage (Teece et al. 1997). This SPMBoK pillar represents the interface between software product management and the company's higher-level management. The latter sets goals and constraints for the portfolio of company offerings, and the product manager influences and adjusts the company's strategy. The product manager participates but does not take leadership or responsibility.

Corporate strategy consists of the vision and approach a company takes to compete with other firms. The following three questions help creating a strategic vision for a company (McGrath 2001): *Where do we want to go? How will we get there? Why do we think we will be successful?* Executive management answers these questions for the company with a defensible position against competitive forces (Porter 1980), competitive moves (Shapiro 1989), capability development (Wernerfelt 1984), and the adaptation and use of these capabilities (Teece et al. 1997).

Portfolio management is the balancing of risk versus return, maintenance versus growth, and short term versus long term by making choices of markets, products, and technologies to invest in and allocating resources to (Cooper et al. 1999). Portfolio decisions allow a company to focus its resources on a few important activities, hence to ensure its ability to act. A well-known portfolio management approach is the Boston Consulting Group analysis used to decide which products to invest in, which products to use as funding sources, and which products to eliminate (Henderson 1979). A successful product takes different positions in the company's portfolio during its lifetime (Haines 2009). It requires initial funding during the product definition phase, where concepts and feasibility are evaluated. It requires substantial funding during the product introduction phase, where the focus lays on development, launch, and growth. It then acts as a revenue source for other products during maturity and decline before it is eliminated. Each phase requires dedicated product management activities.

Innovation management in a product context refers to the continuous renewal of technologies and product offerings (Trott 2011). Innovation is crucial for a company to achieve competitive advantage and long-term success. The innovation process includes the discovery of new possibilities, the choice and combination of potential innovations, and the delivery of value (Hyland and Beckett 1994; Gorschek and Fricker 2010). Appropriate organizational structure, funding and resources, and an innovation-encouraging climate provide the necessary context for innovation. The degree of desired innovativeness (Garcia and Calantone 2002) determines how product management is involved in innovation. A product manager may be a champion and leader for a radical or really new innovation. A product manager may oversee the whole innovation process in the case of incremental innovations.

Resource management is closely related to corporate strategy and portfolio management. The resources managed by a company include factors of production such as unskilled labor and capital, include firm-specific assets that are difficult to imitate such as trade secrets, specialized production facilities, business knowledge, and engineering experience, and include organizational routines and competences (Teece et al. 1997; Gold et al. 2001). Resources are scarce, hence are increasingly sought outside the boundaries of the company (Chesbrough 2003). If resources are adapted to business needs and utilized in a focused manner, they can be a source for competitive advantage.

Market analysis delivers key inputs to positioning the company and its products in the industry. Market analysis is a basis to determine a company's opportunities and threats. A well-known market approach is PEST analysis, the analysis of political, economic, social or societal, and technological factors (Ward and Peppard 2002) usually enhanced into the PRESTO analysis with regulatory and other factors (Haines 2009). Porter's five forces analysis represents a complementary analysis approach focused on customers, suppliers, existing and future competitors, and product substitutes (Porter 1998). Inputs for market analysis can be found by studying industry-specific journals and periodicals, attending fairs and conferences, scanning the Internet, or procuring market research reports from commercial analysts such as Gartner (Fenn and Raskino 2011), IDC, and Forrester Research.

Product analysis delivers information about current product performance. Product analysis is one of the inputs to determine a company's strengths and weaknesses. Many data for product analysis can be provided by finance controllers (Kittlaus and Clough 2009). Typical quantitative data are product revenue, development and operations cost, profit, sales, and support requests. Qualitative data are feedback from customers (Anderson and Sullivan 1993; Johnson and Gustafsson 2000), sales channels, and market analysts, and opinions from trade press in articles. Market analysis and product analysis provide inputs for the analysis of strengths, weaknesses, opportunities, and threats (SWOT) that can be used as a basis for defining competitive moves (Piercy and Giles 1989).

4.3   Product Strategy and Planning

Product strategy and *product planning* describe what the software product will be and how and when it will be developed and used. These two SPMBoK pillars represent the core areas of software product management. The product manager here defines the software product, sets goals and constraints for its evolution, enables business, and obtains support and commitment from stakeholders. The product manager takes leadership and responsibility for the decisions taken. The kind of software product, commercial software or in-house information system, determines how much product strategy and planning cover marketing aspects.

4.3.1   Product Strategy

Product positioning and product definition refers to the product vision and characterization of targeted markets, product use, and product scope (Kittlaus and Clough 2009). A product vision answers the three vision questions for the software product (McGrath 2001): *Where do we want to go? How will we get there? Why do we think we will be successful?* The first question can be answered with the target markets (Haines 2009), the intended differentiation with competitive products, and the planned support of company strategy (Gorschek and Wohlin 2006). The second question can be answered with the intended product use, characterized with user personas (Pruitt and Grudin 2003), use scenarios (Cockburn 2001; Cohn 2004), and value (Khurum et al. 2011), and the intended product scope, characterized with a catalogue of product features (Classen et al. 2008). The third question can be answered with the process for developing, evolving, marketing, delivering, and supporting the software product (Cooper 2001) and with a risk management plan

(Miller 1992; Carr et al. 1993). A vision is a short and concise statement with the product's key ideas and is elaborated with supporting documentation. An understood and accepted vision is important for success and short time-to-market (Lynn and Akgün 2001; Tessarolo 2007), but is surprisingly difficult to establish. It hence should be developed in collaboration with stakeholders and peers and be evolved based on results of other product strategy and planning activities (McGrath 2001).

Ecosystem management refers to building or integrating into the product's industry, the business network (Iansiti and Levien 2004). A company becomes part of a value chain in that business network by offering products and services to customers that build on products and services from suppliers (Jansen et al. 2007). The value chain structure and the company's position in that value chain affects the organization's business model (Popp and Meyer 2010). Typical players in the software industry, differentiated by their business model, are vendors, distributors, resellers, OEMs, integrators, and technological alliances (Kittlaus and Clough 2009). Software architecture, services, and competitive moves help disrupting an ecosystem and sustaining the thus obtained position (Iansiti and Levien 2004).

The *delivery model* refers to the approach chosen for delivering the software and the software's services to the users (Kittlaus and Clough 2009). The choice of the delivery model affects the licensing and pricing model and the distribution of activities between the company and the customers. Packaged software implies a sales contract, delivery of the software to the customer, installation of the solution in the premises of the customer, and potentially a customer project for tailoring and integrating the solution. Software-as-a-Service implies hosting the solution, a service level agreement with the customer, application service provision, and on-demand delivery of the software-enabled services to the user through the internet or intranet (Gold et al. 2004).

Pricing refers to the process of setting prices to market offerings. Pricing is a key instrument to generate profitable growth opportunities for the company (Nagle and Hogan 2006). A comprehensive pricing strategy captures the value offered by the product, adapts the price structure to the customer segments, ensures that price and value can be communicated, manages customer and employee expectations with an accepted price policy, and sets price levels to maximize profitability. Pricing models for software are adapted to product lifecycle stage, distribution channels, geographic location, customer importance, and delivery model (Kittlaus and Clough 2009). The pricing approach of a corporate IT product is similar to commercial software, except that the customers are the company's business units and that the price should equal cost.

Sourcing refers to the decisions of making or buying parts of the software solution (Kittlaus and Clough 2009). Buying software can lead to faster time to market, reduced development cost, reduced knowledge and resources needs for development, and increased software quality. At the same time, it can lead to reduced ability to adapt the software, generate integration problems, and build a dependency on a supplier (Boehm and Abts 1999). Sourcing software-as-a-service enables run-time binding of sourced software, but is perceived to be afflicted with security risks (Benlian and Hess 2010).

A *business case* is a scenario for economic evaluation of an investment. It is used by management to project likely financial results and other business consequences (Brugger 2009). A business case refines the product vision with economic information based on cost, price, competition, and market estimates (Gorchels 2006). *Costing* refers to the development of cost estimates. A business case describes a timeline of expected cash flows, explains the estimation methods and assumptions that were used, characterizes quantifiable business impact and non-quantifiable benefits, and discusses critical success factors and risks (Schmidt 2002). Typical software business cases discuss investments based on contributions to business objectives such as sales and financial performance (Schmidt 2002), efficiency and productivity increases and quality improvements (Reifer 2002), and avoidance of non-compliance problems.

Legal and intellectual property rights management refers to the practices and artifacts for performing business transactions and protecting the business. License or service level agreements are established and used to resolve conflicts between the vendor and the customer about the software product's functionality and quality, permitted amount and kind of product use, and handling of unused but paid product instances (Kittlaus and Clough 2009). Trademarks, trade secrets, copyrights, and patents can at many places be used to protect a software product against piracy. This implies that a software product needs to be free from legal problems before it is released, requiring lawful engineering practices (German et al. 2010) such as auditing its licensing structure (Alspaugh et al. 2010).

Performance and risk management refers to measuring the success of the software product and reacting to problems and risks. The typically monitored performance factors differ between the product lifecycle stages (Anderson and Zeithaml 1984). During the product's inception phase, innovation metrics help to benchmark, diagnose, allocated resources, compensate employees, inform markets, and setting future goals (Kuczmarski 2000). The focus changes towards monitoring buyers, advertising, and purchase frequency during the introduction stage; towards segmentation, production and marketing efficiency, and customer need satisfaction during the growth stage; towards process efficiency, marketing and distribution cost reduction, and product differentiation during the maturity stage; and towards competitive strength during the decline stage (Anderson and Zeithaml 1984). Performance measurements help identifying problems and risks that are addressed with avoidance and mitigation actions (Miller 1992; Carr et al. 1993).

4.3.2 Product Planning

Product lifecycle management in the context of a software product relates to planning the product lifecycle. A software product's initial release requires different expertise, architectural decisions, and economics than its subsequent evolution, servicing, phase-out, and close-down (Raijlich and Bennet 2000). The initial focus on learning the application domain and technology changes towards retaining expertise and understanding the interfaces and operation of the software. The architecture that initially balanced flexibility with time-to-market is continuously adapted and decays until it becomes too hard to change (Lehman 1980). The initially heavy investments start to generate revenue that is extended as long as possible (Henderson 1979). Similarly the focus of product management collaboration with company functions changes from research and development towards marketing, sales and distribution, and service and support.

Roadmapping refers to planning the evolution of a product. A roadmap shows how product features, technologies, and resource needs evolve (Albright and Kappel 2003; Phaal et al. 2003; Lehtola et al. 2005). Roadmaps are used to translate product strategy into long-term plans for research, development, marketing, sales, distribution, service, and support by capturing on best knowledge of the corresponding company functions and obtaining their commitment and support (Phaal et al. 2007). Roadmapping is adaptable to the needs of small to large-scale companies (Vähäniitty et al. 2002; Phaal and Muller 2009).

Release planning refers to the selection and assignment of requirements to projects for implementing sequences of product releases (Svahnberg et al. 2009). Implementing a product in incremental releases, rather than implementing the full product scope at once, allows reaching earlier break-even and a higher return of investment (Denne and Cleland-Huang 2003). Incremental development requires prioritization of functionality and quality levels (Berander and Andrews 2005; Lehtola and Kauppinen 2006). Release decisions aim at achieving usefulness and competitiveness (Regnell et al. 2008), satisfying capacity, schedule, business, and stakeholder needs (Cohn 2004; Wohlin and Aurum 2005), and accounting for requirements interdependencies (Carlshamre et al. 2001).

Product requirements engineering, also called *market-driven requirements engineering*, refers to the process of collecting stakeholder needs, expectations, and ideas for guiding the implementation of the software product (Regnell and Brinkkemper 2005). The product manager performs triage to reduce the large amount of inputs and to ensure the inputs' relevance and feasibility (Davis 2005; Gorschek and Wohlin 2006). These inputs are translated into product features that represent options for product evolution (Fricker and Schumacher 2012) with understood implications on architecture and implementation (Fricker and Gorschek 2010).

4.4   Orchestration of Company Functions

The software product manager depends on various company functions to realize the product vision and to accomplish the plans defined and agreed during roadmapping. These remaining four SPMBoK pillars represent the interfaces between software product management and these company functions. Development implements the software, marketing identifies and wins customers, sales and distribution generate revenue, and service and support facilitate product use. The product manager acts as company-internal customer and orchestrates the company functions, but delegates responsibility.

4.4.1 Development

Software product management orchestrates development by jointly innovating, communicating functional and quality requirements, procuring and developing technologies, planning and steering software implementation, and accepting the achieved results.

Engineering management refers to managing knowledge and staff and structuring software development to achieve development efficiency at an acceptable level of quality. A software organization needs to develop expertise and enable knowledge sharing and collaboration even when employees come and go (Rus and Lindvall 2002; Bosch 2009). Tapping into knowledge and developer networks and establishing culture and reward systems are common means. Platforms and software product lines enable planned reuse of software artifacts, hence increase development efficiency and software quality (Clements and Northrop 2001; Pohl et al. 2005). Software release management allows maintaining an overview on the many different versions of software artifacts (van der Hoek and Wolf 2003; Jansen and Brinkkemper 2006).

Project management refers to the process and activities for developing a software release (Carmel and Becker 1995). Stage-gates (Cooper 2001), a software development lifecycle model (Wallin et al. 2002), and project management practices (Project Management Institute 2004) are used to structure and control a development project. Agile approaches are increasingly employed to manage the uncertainties inherent in a new product development environment (Pichler 2010). Dedicated practices help acquiring and integrating software components (Brownsword et al. 2000) or outsourcing development (Krishna et al. 2004).

Project requirements engineering refers to the project team's inquiry process of eliciting requirements, specifying the software system the team intends to implement, and validating that specification with stakeholders (Potts et al. 1994). A rich body of techniques can be used to reach a shared understanding of requirements and to manage requirements changes (Pohl and Rupp 2011). Product management plays a key role in the communication of requirements (Fricker et al. 2010), controlling progress, and accepting the developed solution (Martin and Meinik 2008).

Quality management refers to the practices a development organization implements to meet its critical success factors and to mitigate business-critical problems (Kitchenham and Pfleeger 1996). Software quality is achieved and maintained by measuring quality (Ebert and Dumke 2007; Jones 2008) and establishing practices and responsibility for quality management (El Emam 2005). Many organizations implement process improvement programs to improve their engineering and management practices in software product management (Bekkers et al. 2010), software development (CMMI Product Team 2010), and IT-based service provision (Spalding and Case 2007).

4.4.2 Marketing

Software product management orchestrates marketing by jointly analyzing the market, customers, and opportunities, launching products and analyzing their performance, and winning customers.

Marketing planning refers to refining the *product positioning and definition* by defining the marketing goals, the marketing mix, and the approach, budget, and controls for reaching the marketing goals (Kotler et al. 2010). Marketing planning characterizes the current marketing situation by building on market, product, and customer analysis. From the identified strengths, weaknesses, opportunities, and threats are derived target sales, market share, and profits and the broad approach to achieve these objectives. Action programs, budget, and controls describe how that marketing strategy is implemented.

Customer analysis refers to the first part of marketing planning: determining and prioritizing market segments, understanding customer needs, and matching these needs with unique selling points. A company chooses between different levels of market segmentation, ranging from one offering for all customers to segment-specific offerings to tailored offerings for each individual customer (Kotler et al. 2010). Similarity of customer needs and characteristics such as geography, demography, psychography, and behavior are a basis for such market segmentation. Analysis of segments attractiveness and business strengths are a basis for prioritizing segments and for identifying actions needed to serve them (Gorchels 2006; Haines 2009). Segments are often represented with personas (Pruitt and Grudin 2003) whose key needs are matched with a suitable marketing mix differentiated from competitive offerings (Hauser and Clausing 1988).

Opportunity management refers to refining the product positioning by narrowing the market (Haines 2009). Criteria such as resource availability and capability, strategic significance, financial viability, and potential customer satisfaction are used to choose among opportunities. The resulting priorities help optimizing the marketing mix, inform the product launch and operational marketing, and guide sales.

Marketing mix optimization refers to the definition and improvement of product, price, place, and promotion to influence demand (Kotler et al. 2010). The marketing mix is what customers actually see in the marketplace. The product defines what the customer will get: functionality, quality, design, brand name, packaging, services, and warranties that address the customer's needs and wants (Boatwright and Cagan 2010). The price determines the cost to the customer. The place refers to the channels and distribution practices that make the product more or less conveniently available. Promotion refers to activities that communicate the product's merits to persuade customers to buy it. The interplay between the elements of the marketing mix affects the success of a marketing campaign (Haines 2009). Marketing mixes of competitive products can be used to analyze competitors as part of market analysis (Lehmann and Winer 2005).

Product launch refers to the process of preparing the public release of the product (Gorchels 2006; Lawley 2007; Haines 2009). The product launch makes the product visible to the markets, hence initiates the company's interaction with channels and customers and generates competitive responses. Launches are prepared by stabilizing and assuring the quality of the software (Galen 2004), by determining product viability (Kaulio 1998), by evaluating the marketing strategy, by timing and planning the market entry sequence, and by introducing the sales force, channels, and customer service (Gorchels 2006). The launch is accompanied with measurements to evaluate the new product and to improve the new product development process.

Operational marketing refers to marketing communication and analyzing the effectiveness of that communication (Gorchels 2006). A marketing communications system is established with intermediaries and the public to influence the customers with messages and word of mouth (Kotler et al. 2010). Public relations, press kits, articles, demonstrations at trade shows, press releases, and advertising are used to communication the product's unique selling proposition or most critical benefits for the most critical markets (Gorchels 2006). Measurements are established to determine customer awareness, knowledge, liking, preference, conviction, and purchase (Kotler et al. 2010).

4.4.3 Sales and Distribution

Software product management orchestrates sales and distribution by planning the sales, preparing sales channels, and supporting sales operations and product distribution.

Sales planning refers to defining the market and product profiles, preparing sales channels, and training sales in how to sell the software supporting (Haines 2009). A software company's sales channels include direct sales, telesales, internet sales, sales through partners such as integrators, and sales through resellers (Kittlaus and Clough 2009). Sales materials describe customers, their rational and emotional reasons for buying the product, decision and purchase processes, and the role of influencers (Gorchels 2006). A similar approach is taken for *channel preparation*, with the exception that channels usually do not receive company-internal information (Gorchels 2006). Sales and distribution channels need to be coordinated and position the product favorably compared with alternatives (Kittlaus and Clough 2009).

Customer relationship management refers to managing interactions with customers and sales prospects along the customer lifecycle (Buttle 2008). *Operational sales* refers to setting adequate incentives for salespeople, forecasting and planning customer interactions, and monitoring sales progress and success (Calvin 2004). Consolidated results of the customer interactions are fed back to marketing and software product management to support market and product analysis.

Operational product distribution refers in the case of packaged software to production and shipment, online download, or automated deployment (Humble and Farley 2010) and in the case of software-as-a-service to operating servers and the software that offers services to customers (Rhoton 2010; Cannon and Wheeldon 2011). Software distribution includes updating of existing software installations with updates and patches (Ballintijn 2005).

4.4.4 Service and Support

Software product management has to support users, marketing, sales, and customer projects to facilitate product use and the product's business operations.

Services planning and preparation and *services provisioning* refer to facilitating product deployment and use. Services include bespoke projects are performed to customize, enhance, install, and integrate software (Kittlaus and Clough 2009). Large-scale packaged software or products for complex systems are often performed by consultants or integrators. Other forms of services targeted at users include the provision of helpdesks to provide *technical support* (Bruton 2002).

Marketing support and *sales support* refer to providing sales and customer service trainings, performing events and promotions, and producing brochures and other materials of publicity and sales (Gorchels 2006).

5   State of Knowledge

Software product management is a young discipline that aims at closing the gap between business and software engineering. Much of the discipline has its roots in the corresponding established bodies of knowledge. Nonetheless, a growing part of the discipline, especially in the area of product planning, contributes with research results specific to the management of software products.

Software product management has not succeeded yet to establish a sharp differentiation, neither to traditional product management nor to software engineering. The implications of the special characteristics of software, for example its flexibility, intangibility, and ease of duplication and distribution, on product management are not fully understood yet. Conversely, many software engineering practitioners and scholars think that software product management is too far away from the technical artifact to really affect the domain of software.

Software, however, has the potential to change product management. For example, new software technologies such as cloud and app stores establish new communication paths between the company and the so far anonymous mass of customers and users. The utilization of these channels would allow moving away from imagined stakeholders (Karlsson et al. 2007) towards integrating real people in the market-driven requirements engineering process. Such a change can reduce product development risks by basing product decision-making on facts rather than opinion. Early applications of this concept are emerging: social media complement traditional media for eliciting and communicating information (Mangold and Faulds 2009). Analytics are used to study in user behavior in real-time for building user segments, evaluating feature attractiveness, monitoring product performance, and understanding the impact of marketing campaigns and channels (Phippen et al. 2004). App stores simplify software distribution and allow identifying product and service offering gaps (Kim and Park 2010). The field, however, is still far away from providing an understanding of software-enabled and software-specific product management.

Product management also has the potential to change software engineering. The product manager is the central hub for information exchange and focal point for decision making for a long-lasting software solution. Aligning software product management practice with software architecture can increase overall engineering efficiency and the value of product ownership (Helferich et al. 2006). Companies have started to align management practices with software architecture by moving from software development projects to software product management (Artz et al. 2010). Unclear, however, is still how effective business-socio-technical congruence is achieved and what its empirically grounded business case is.

A third knowledge issue is software product manager education. Most university curricula focus on project-level software engineering and do not teach management and engineering disciplines such as software product management, evolution, and maintenance that cut across development projects. One of the hindering factors is the lacking understanding of educational needs of software product managers. His scope of responsibilities is initially not as broad as the discussed reference models suggest and changes throughout his career when moving from junior to senior positions. Empirically grounded models of the learning process and of how the learning process can be supported effectively are missing today.

6 Summary and Conclusion

Software solutions undergo continuing adaptation or become progressively less useful. Software product management is the discipline that puts attention on the concepts and approaches for achieving long-term usefulness of software for users, customers, and the software organization. A software product manager, armed with the right competences and responsibilities, is able to position and plan software as a product and lead development, marketing, sales, distribution, service, and support towards developing and sustaining a business aligned with company objectives.

This chapter has provided an overview of the current knowledge landscape of software product management. It has introduced software as a product in the contexts of commercial markets and in-house information systems. It has given an overview on reference models of software product management practices. It has discussed the various elements of software product management based on the ISPMA SPMBoK that represents a consensus between software product management industry and academia. It has highlighted limitations of current software product management knowledge and posed some of the most pressing research questions whose answers are needed for developing the field.

Software product management is still in its infancy. Business and software knowledge need to be further consolidated to provide an integrated and clearly differentiated understanding of the peculiarities of product management for software. This requires even more collaboration between industry and academia than has been seen until now. The results will allow tapping into the value of the technology that has become a driver for innovation and growth.

References

Albright, R. E., & Kappel, T. A. (2003). Roadmapping in the corporation. *IEEE Engineering Management Review, 31*(3), 31–40.

Alspaugh, T. A., Scacchi, W., et al. (2010). Software licenses in context: The challenge of heterogeneously-licensed systems. *Journal of the Association for Information Systems, 11*(11), 730–755.

Anderson, E. W., & Sullivan, M. W. (1993). Antecedents and consequences of customer satisfaction. *Marketing Science, 12*(2), 125–143.

Anderson, C. R., & Zeithaml, C. P. (1984). Stage of the product lifecycle, business strategy, and business performance. *Academy of Management Journal, 27*(1), 5–24.

Artz, P., van de Weed, I., et al. (2010). Productization: Transforming from developing customer-specific software to product software. *1st international conference on software business*, Jyväskylä.

Aurum, A., & Wohlin, C. (2003). The fundamental nature of requirements engineering activities as a decision-making process. *Information and Software Technology, 45*, 945–954.

Ballintijn, G. (2005). A case study of the release management of a health-care information system. *IEEE international conference on software maintenance (ICSM 2005, Industry Track)*, Budapest, Hungary.

Basili, V. R., & Boehm, B. (2001). COTS-based systems top 10 list. *Computer, 34*(5), 91–95.

Bekkers, W., van de Weed, I., et al. (2010). A framework for process improvement in software product management. *European systems & software process improvement and innovation (EuroSPI 2010)*, Grenoble, France.

Benlian, A., & Hess, T. (2010). The risks of sourcing software as a service – An empirical analysis of adopters and non-adopters. *18th European conference on information systems (ECIS 2010)*, Pretoria, South Africa.

Berander, P., & Andrews, A. (2005). Requirements prioritization. In A. Aurum & C. Wohlin (Eds.), *Engineering and managing software requirements*. Berlin: Springer.

Bersoff, E. (1984). Elements of software configuration management. *IEEE Transactions on Software Engineering, 10*(1), 79–87.

Boatwright, P., & Cagan, J. (2010). *Build to love: Creating products that captivate customers*. San Francisco, CA: Berrett Koehler.

Boehm, B., & Abts, C. (1999). COTS integration: Plug and pray? *Computer, 32*(1), 135–138.

Bosch, J. (2009). From software product lines to software ecosystems. *13th international software product line conference (SPLC 2009)*, San Francisco.

Brownsword, L., Oberndorf, T., et al. (2000). Developing new processes for COTS-based systems. *IEEE Software, 17*(4), 48–55.

Broy, M., Krüger, I. H., et al. (2007). Engineering automotive software. *Proceedings of the IEEE, 95*(2), 356–373.

Brugger, R. (2009). *Der IT business case*. Heidelberg: Springer.

Bruton, N. (2002). *How to manage the IT helpdesk*. Routledge: Chapman & Hall.

Buttle, F. (2008). *Customer relationship management*. Routledge: Taylor & Francis.

Buyya, R., Yeo, C. S., et al. (2009). Cloud computing and emerging IT platforms: Vision, hype, and reality for delivering computing as the 5th utility. *Future Generation Computer Systems, 25*(6), 599–616.

Cannon, D., & Wheeldon, D. (2011). *ITIL service operation*. The Stationery Office.

Cabinet Office. (2011). *ITIL service strategy*. The Stationery Office.

Cagan, M. (2008). *Inspired: How to create products customers love*. SVPG Press, Sunnyvale, CA, USA.

Calvin, R. J. (2004). *Sales management*. McGraw-Hill Professional, New York, NY, USA

Carlshamre, P., Sandahl, K., et al. (2001). An industrial survey of requirements interdependencies in software product release planning. *5th IEEE international symposium on requirements engineering*, Toronto.

Carmel, E., & Becker, S. (1995). A process model for packaged software development. *IEEE Transactions on Engineering Management, 42*(1), 50–61.

Carr, M. J., Konda, S. L., et al. (1993). Taxonomy-based risk identification. Technical Report, CMU/SEI-93-TR-6, Software Engineering Institute, Carnegie Mellon University.

Chesbrough, H. W. (2003). The era of open innovation. *MIT Sloan Management Review, 44*(3), 35–41.

Choudhary, V. (2007). Software as a service: Implications for investment in software development. *40th Hawaii international conference on system sciences (HICSS'07)*, Hawaii.

Classen, A., Heymans, P., et al. (2008). What's in a feature: A requirements engineering perspective. *11th international conference on fundamental approaches to software engineering*, Budapest, Hungary.

Clements, P., & Northrop, L. (2001). *Software product lines: Practices and patterns*. Boston, MA: Addison-Wesley Professional.

CMMI Product Team. (2010). CMMI for development. Version 1.3, Carnegie Mellon University.

Cockburn, A. (2001). *Writing effective use cases*. Boston: Addison-Wesley Professional.

Cohn, M. (2004). *User stories applied*. Pearson Education, Boston, MA, USA.

Condon, D. (2002). *Software product management*. Aspatore Books, Eagan, MN, USA.

Cooper, R. (2001). *Winning at new products: Accelerating the process from idea to launch*. B&T.

Cooper, R. G., Edgett, S. J., et al. (1999). New product portfolio management: Practices and performance. *Journal of Product Innovation Management, 16*(4), 333–351.

Cusumano, M. (2004). *The business of software*. New York: Free Press.

Davis, A. (2005). *Just enough requirements management*. New York: Dorset House Publishing.

De Haes, S., & Van Grembergen W. (2004). IT governance and its mechanisms. *Information Systems Control Journal 1*. See: http://www.isaca.org/Journal/Past-Issues/2004/Volume-1/Pages/IT-Governance-and-Its-Mechanisms.aspx

Denne, M., & Cleland-Huang, J. (2003). *Software by numbers: Low-risk, high-return development*. Upper Saddle River, NJ: Prentice-Hall.

Dver, A. (2007). *Software product management essentials*. Tampa, FL: Anclote Press.

Ebert, C. (2006). The impacts of software product management. *Journal of Systems and Software, 80*, 850–861.

Ebert, C. (2009). Software product management. *Crosstalk, 22*(1), 15–19.

Ebert, C., & Salecker, J. (2009). Embedded software – Technologies and trends. *IEEE Software, 26*(3), 14–18.

Ebert, C., & Dumke, R. (2007). *Software measurement: Establish – extract – evaluate – execute*. Berlin: Springer.

Edwards, K., & Grinter, R. (2001). *At home with ubiquitous computing: Seven challenges*. Atlanta: Ubiquitous Computing (UBICOMP).

El Emam, K. (2005). *The ROI from software quality*. Boston, MA: Auerbach Publications.

Fenn, J., & Raskino, M. (2011). *Understanding Gartner's hype cycles*. Gartner.

Flammia, G., & McCandless, M. (1997). From software to service: The transformation of shrink-wrapped software on the internet. *IEEE Expert, 12*(2), 4–6.

Fricker, S., Gorschek, T., et al. (2010). Handshaking with implementation proposals: Negotiating requirements understanding. *IEEE Software, 27*(2), 72–80.

Fricker, S., & Schumacher, S. (2012). Release planning with feature trees: Industrial case. *Requirements engineering: Foundations for software quality (RefsQ 2012)*, Essen, Germany.

Galen, R. (2004). *Software endgames: Eliminating defects, controlling changes, and the countdown to on-time delivery*. New York: Dorset House.

Garcia, R., & Calantone, R. (2002). A critical look at technological innovation typology and innovativeness terminology: A literature review. *The Journal of Product Innovation Management, 19*(2), 110–132.

German, D. M., Weber, J. H., et al. (2010). Lawful software engineering. *FSE/SDP workshop on the future of software engineering (FoSER 2010)*, Santa Fe, New Mexico.

GNU. (2007). GNU General Public License. GNU. http://www.gnu.org/licenses/gpl-3.0

Goffin, K., & New, C. (2001). Customer support and new product development – An exploratory study. *International Journal of Operations & Production Management, 21*(3), 275–301.

Gold, A. H., Malhotra, A., et al. (2001). Knowledge management: An organizational capabilities perspective. *Journal of Management Information Systems, 18*(1), 185–214.

Gold, N., Mohan, A., et al. (2004). Understanding service-oriented software. *IEEE Software, 21*(2), 71–77.

Gorchels, L. (2006). *The product manager's handbook.* New York: McGraw-Hill.

Gorschek, T., & Wohlin, C. (2006). Requirements abstraction model. *Requirements Engineering, 11*(1), 79–101.

Gorschek, T., Fricker, S., et al. (2010). A lightweight innovation process for software-intensive product development. *IEEE Software, 27*(1), 37–45.

Griffin, A., & Hauser, J. (1996). Integrating R&D and marketing: A review and analysis of the literature. *Journal of Product Innovation Management, 13*, 191–215.

Haines, S. (2009). *The product manager's desk reference.* New York: McGraw-Hill.

Hauser, J., & Clausing, D. (1988). The house of quality. *Harvard Business Review, 66*(3), 63–73.

Hayes, B. (2008). Cloud computing. *Communications of the ACM, 51*(7), 9–11.

Helferich, A., Schmid, K., et al. (2006). Product management for software product lines: An unsolved problem? *Communications of the ACM, 49*(12), 66–67.

Henderson, B. D. (1979). *Henderson on corporate strategy.* Abt Books, Cambridge, MA, USA.

Humble, J., & Farley, D. (2010). *Continuous delivery: Reliable software releases through build, test, and deployment automation.* Amsterdam: Addison-Wesley Longman.

Hyland, P., & Beckett, R. (1994). Engendering an innovative culture and maintaining operational balance. *Journal of Small Business and Enterprise Development, 12*(3), 336–352.

Iansiti, M., & Levien, R. (2004). *The keystone advantage.* Boston: Harvard Business School Press.

IEEE. (1990). IEEE Standard Glossary of Software Engineering Terminology 610.12-1990.

ISPMA, International Software Product Management Association. (2012). Software product management body of knowledge (SPMBoK). Retrieved July 1, 2012, from http://ispma.org/spmbok/

Jaccheri, L., & Torchiano, M. (2002). Classifying COTS products. *7th European conference on software quality (ECSQ 2002)*, Helsinki, Finland.

Jansen, S., Brinkkemper, S., et al. (2007). *Providing transparency in the business of software: A modeling technique for software supply networks.* Virtual Enterprises and Collaborative Networks.

Jansen, S., & Brinkkemper S. (2006). Ten misconceptions about product software release management explained using update cost/value functions. *1st international workshop on software product management (IWSPM'06)*, Minneapolis, MS, USA.

Johnson, M. D., & Gustafsson, A. (2000). *Improving customer satisfaction, loyalty, and profit: An integrated measurement and management system.* New York: Wiley.

Jones, C. (2008). *Applied software measurement: Global analysis of productivity and quality.* New York: McGraw Hill.

Kaplan, R. S., & Norton, D. P. (1992). The balanced scorecard: Measures that drive performance. *Harvard Business Review, 70*(1), 172–180.

Karlsson, L., Dahlstedt, Å., et al. (2007). Requirements engineering challenges in market-driven software development – An interview study with practitioners. *Information and Software Technology, 49*, 588–604.

Kaulio, M. A. (1998). Customer, consumer and user involvement in product development: A framework and a review of selected methods. *Total Quality Management, 9*(1), 141–149.

Khurum, M., Gorschek, T., et al. (2011). *A homogeneous and consolidated view of software value. Decision support for product management of software intensive products.* M. Khurum, Blekinge Institute of Technology, Doctoral Dissertations Series (Vol. 12), 2011.

Kilpi, T. (1997). Product management challenge to software change process: Preliminary results from three SMEs experiment. *Software Process Improvement and Practice, 3*(3), 165–175.

Kim, J. & Park, Y. (2010). Identifying a new service opportunity from potential needs: User-centric service map. *IEEE international conference on industrial engineering and engineering management (IEEM 2010)*, Macao.

Kitchenham, B., & Pfleeger, S. L. (1996). Software quality: The elusive target. *IEEE Software, 13*(1), 12–21.

Kittlaus, H.-B., & Clough, P. (2009). *Software product management and pricing*. New York: Springer.

Konig, S. J. (2009). Finance as a stakeholder in product management. *Third international workshop on software product management (IWSPM 2009)*, Atlanta, GA.

Kotler, P., Armstrong, G. (2011). *Principles of marketing*. Pearson Prentice Hall. Upper Saddle River, NJ, USA.

Krishna, S., Sahay, S., et al. (2004). Managing cross-cultural issues in global software outsourcing. *Communications of the ACM, 47*(4), 62–66.

Kuczmarski, T. D. (2000). Measuring your return on innovation. *Marketing Management, 9*(1), 24–32.

Lawley, B. (2007). *Expert product management*. HappyAbout.info.

Lee, E. (2000). What's ahead for embedded software? *Computer, 33*(9), 18–26.

Lehman, M. M. (1980). Programs, life cycles, and laws of software evolution. *Proceedings of the IEEE, 68*(9), 1060–1076.

Lehmann, D., & Winer, R. (2005). *Product management*. Burr Ridge, IL: McGraw-Hill.

Lehtola, L., & Kauppinen, M. (2006). Suitability of requirements prioritization methods for market-driven software product development. *Software Process Improvement and Practice, 11*, 7–19.

Lehtola, L., Kauppinen, M., et al. (2005). Linking the business view to requirements engineering: Long-term product planning by roadmapping. *13th IEEE international conference on requirements engineering (RE'05)*, Paris, France.

Lerner, J., & Tirole, J. (2002). Some simple economics of open source. *The Journal of Industrial Economics, 50*(2), 197–234.

Lynn, G. S., & Akgün, A. E. (2001). Project visioning: Its components and impact on new product success. *Journal of Product Innovation Management, 18*(6), 374–387.

Mangold, W. G., & Faulds, D. J. (2009). Social media: The new hybrid element of the promotion mix. *Business Horizons, 52*(4), 357–365.

Martin, R. C., & Meinik, G. (2008). Tests and requirements, requirements and tests: A möbius strip. *IEEE Software, 25*(1), 54–59.

McGrath, M. E. (2001). *Product strategy for high technology companies: Accelerating your business to web speed*. New York: McGraw-Hill.

Messerschmitt, D., & Szyperski, C. (2003). *Software ecosystem: Understanding an indispensable technology and industry*. London: The MIT Press.

Meyer, M., Zarnekow, R., et al. (2003). IT-governance: Begriff, Status quo und Bedeutung. *Wirtschaftsinformatik, 45*(4), 445–448.

Miller, K. D. (1992). A framework for integrated risk management in international business. *Journal of International Business Studies, 23*(2), 311–331.

Miller, R. (2010). Apps: Exploring the next content frontier. *EContent, 33*(5), 18–22.

Nagle, T. T., & Hogan, J. E. (2006). *The strategy and tactics of pricing: A guide to growing more profitably*. Upper Saddle River: Pearson Prentice Hall.

Open Source Initiative. (2012). Open source licenses by category. Retrieved February 12, 2012, from http://www.opensource.org/licenses/category

Pech, E. (2006). Making innovation happen. *Annual Review of Communications, 59*, 169–172.

Phaal, R., & Muller, G. (2009). An architectural framework for roadmapping: Towards visual strategy. *Technological Forecasting & Social Chane, 76*(1), 39–49.

Phaal, R., Farrukh, C., et al. (2003). Technology roadmapping – A planning framework for evolution and revolution. *Technological Forecasting and Social Change, 71*, 5–26.

Phaal, R., Farrukh, C., et al. (2007). Strategic roadmapping: A workshop-based approach for identifying and exploring strategic issues and opportunities. *Engineering Management Journal, 19*(1), 3–12.

Phippen, A., Sheppard, L., et al. (2004). A practical evaluation of web analytics. *Internet Research, 14*(4), 284–293.

Pichler, R. (2010). *Agile product management with scrum.* Addison-Wesley Pearson Education, Boston, MA, USA.

Piercy, N., & Giles, W. (1989). Making SWOT analysis work. *Marketing Intelligence & Planning, 7*(5/6), 5–7.

Pohl, K., Böckle, G., et al. (2005). *Software product line engineering: Foundations, principles and techniques.* Berlin: Springer.

Pohl, K., & Rupp, C. (2011). *Requirements engineering fundamentals: A study guide for the certified professional for requirements engineering exam – Foundation level – IREB compliant.* Rocky Nook Computing.

Popp, K. M., & Meyer, R. (2010). *Profit from software ecosystems.* Books on Demand.

Porter, M. E. (1980). *Competitive strategy.* New York: Free Press.

Porter, M. (1998). *Competitive advantage: Creating and sustaining superior performance.* New York: Free Press.

Potts, C., Takahashi, K., et al. (1994). Inquiry-based requirements analysis. *IEEE Software, 11*(2), 21–32.

Pragmatic Marketing. (2012). Pragmatic marketing framework. Retrieved February 26, 2012, from http://www.pragmaticmarketing.com/pragmatic-marketing-framework

Project Management Institute. (2004). A guide to the project management body of knowledge. PMBOK Guide. ANSI/PMI 99-001-2004.

Pruitt, J., & Grudin, J. (2003). Personas: Practice and theory. *2003 conference on designing for user experience (DUX'03),* New York.

Raijlich, V. T., & Bennet, K. H. (2000). A staged model for the software life cycle. *Computer, 33*(7), 66–71.

Regnell, B., & Brinkkemper, S. (2005). Market-driven requirements engineering for software products. In A. Aurum & C. Wohlin (Eds.), *Engineering and managing software requirements* (pp. 287–308). Berlin: Springer.

Regnell, B., Svensson, R. B., et al. (2008). Supporting roadmapping of quality requirements. *IEEE Software, 25*(2), 42–47.

Reifer, D. J. (2002). *Making the software business case: Improvement by the numbers.* New York: Addison-Wesley.

Rhoton, J. (2010). *Cloud computing explained: Implementation handbook for enterprises.* Recursive Press, Kent, United Kingdom

Roussos, G., Marsh, A. J., et al. (2005). Enabling pervasive computing with smart phones. *Pervasive Computing, 4*(2), 20–27.

Ruffin, M., & Ebert, C. (2004). Using open source software in product development: A primer. *IEEE Software, 21*(1), 82–86.

Rus, I., & Lindvall, M. (2002). Knowledge management in software engineering. *IEEE Software, 19*(3), 26–38.

Schmidt, M. (2002). *The business case guide.* Boston: Solution Matrix.

Shapiro, C. (1989). The theory of business strategy. *The RAND Journal of Economics, 20*(1), 125–137.

Sneed, H., Hasitschka, M., et al. (2005). *Software-Produktmanagement: Wartung und Weiterentwicklung bestehender Anwendungssysteme,* dpunkt.verlag.

Spalding, G., & Case, G. (2007). *ITIL continual service improvement.* The Stationery Office.

Steinhardt, G. (2012). *PTMK action model.* Retrieved February 26, 2012, from http://www.blackblot.com/pmtk-action-model/

Svahnberg, M., Gorschek, T., et al. (2009). A systematic review on strategic release planning models. *Information and Software Technology, 52,* 237–248.

Teece, D. J., Pisano, G., et al. (1997). Dynamic capabilities and strategic management. *Strategic Management Journal, 18*(7), 509–533.

Tessarolo, P. (2007). Is integration enough for fast product development? An empirical investigation of the contextual effects of product vision. *Journal of Product Innovation Management, 24*(1), 69–82.

Trott, P. (2011). *Innovation management and new product development.* London: Prentice Hall Financial Times.

Turner, M., Budgen, D., et al. (2003). Turning software into a service. *Computer, 36*(10), 38–44.

Vähäniitty, J., Lassenius, C., et al. (2002). An approach to product roadmapping in small software product businesses. *7th international conference on software quality (ECSQ 2002)*, Helsinki, Finland, Portland, Oregon, USA.

van de Weerd, I., Brinkkemper, S., et al. (2006). On the creation of a reference framework for software product management: Validation and tool support. *International workshop on software product management*, Minneapolis.

van de Weerd, Inge, S. B., et al. (2006). Towards a reference framework for software product management. *14th IEEE international requirements engineering conference (RE'06)*. Minneapolis: IEEE Computer Society.

van der Hoek, A., & Wolf, A. (2003). Software release management for component-based software. *Software: Practice and Experience, 33*(1), 77–98.

Variant, H. (2000). Buying, sharing and renting information goods. *The Journal of Industrial Economics, 48*(4), 473–488.

Wallin, C., Ekdahl, F., et al. (2002). Integrating business and software development models. *IEEE Software, 19*(6), 28–33.

Ward, J. L., & Peppard, J. (2002). *Strategic planning for information systems.* Chichester: Wiley.

Wernerfelt, B. (1984). A resource-based view of the firm. *Strategic Management Journal, 5*(2), 171–180.

Wohlin, C., & Aurum, A. (2005). What is important when deciding to include a software requirement into a project or release. *International symposium on empirical software engineering (ISESE 2005)*, Noosa Heads, Australia.

Wu, F. F., Moslehi, K., et al. (2005). Power system control centers: Past, present, and future. *Proceedings of the IEEE, 93*(11), 1890–1908.

Xu, L., & Brinkkemper, S. (2007). Concepts of product software. *European Journal of Information Systems, 16*(5), 531–541.

Yourseff, L., Butrico, M., et al. (2008). Toward a unified ontology of cloud computing. *Grid computing environments workshop (GCE'08)*, Santa Barbara.

Software Product Management and Agile Software Development: Conflicts and Solutions

Hans-Bernd Kittlaus

Abstract

Agile software development has been established over the last 15 years as a popular development approach. In a time when speed of change is of utmost importance, agile approaches are often the most appropriate roads to success. They do not only change the way development is performed, but they also impact other parties involved in development projects, in particular the software product manager. Software companies are faced with the question how software product management and agile development can work together in an optimal way. Who is responsible for requirements? Is the software product manager automatically the designated "product owner" (Scrum)? Or is "product owner" a new and separate role? Does he/she replace the software product manager?

The Software Product Management Framework which has been developed by the *International Software Product Management Association* (ISPMA e.V., www.ispma.org) provides orientation. It can be used as a helpful tool to make the change process towards agile development successful.

1 Introduction

Agile – what a wonderful word! Everybody wants to be agile. Marketing people rejoice! Amazing that some presumably nerdy software people came up with the idea to use that term in relation to a new approach for software development and set the fundamentals of that new approach in stone with the "Agile Manifesto"

Special thanks to Gerald Heller for inspiring discussions in the preparation of our joint invited talk on "Software Product Management and Agility" at the International Workshop on Software Product Management (IWSPM) 2012 in Essen, Germany.

H.-B. Kittlaus
InnoTivum Consulting, Rheinbreitbach, Germany
e-mail: hbk@innotivum.de

A. Maedche et al. (eds.), *Software for People*, Management for Professionals,
DOI 10.1007/978-3-642-31371-4_5, © Springer-Verlag Berlin Heidelberg 2012

(Beck et al. 2001). Over the last 15 years this approach has changed the landscape of software development methodology in a significant way.

Agile – as opposed to slow, bureaucratic, old-fashioned, complicated, hindering. Both the Agile Manifesto and the Scrum Guide (Schwaber and Sutherland 2011) are clearly focused on software development only. But it must have been too tempting to extend the scope of that word to other areas. Roman Pichler uses it in "Agile Product Management with Scrum" (Pichler 2010) which deals with the role of "Product Owner" in Scrum without explaining that the spectrum of activities and responsibilities of a product manager is much larger than this product owner role. Dean Leffingwell writes about "Agile Software Requirements" (Leffingwell 2011) – oops, not just people, process, or methodology are agile, the requirements themselves are. This semantic mismatch should not keep anybody from reading the book since it provides a rather balanced approach how Software Product Management and agile methodologies can be combined. The Requirements Engineering (RE) community wants to be agile as well (see Rainer Grau's article in this book on "Agile RE").

Agile Software Product Management – from a marketing perspective, we should use that as the title of this article. But we do not – for several reasons. First of all, a software product manager being responsible for the economic success of a product has always had to be "agile" if he or she wanted to be successful. That is nothing new, but has been part of the job description long before the term "agile" was applied to a software development approach (see Kittlaus and Clough 2009). Secondly, the success of agile approaches to software development does not mean that one size fits all. There can still be development projects where due to contents, people and other conditions different methodological approaches like iterative development or even the good old waterfall model may be appropriate (see Figs. 1 and 2). A mature software development organization should be able to choose the optimal method for each individual project, and the software product manager should be able to cooperate with the project teams whatever the chosen development method is. Thirdly, the agile approaches were originally intended for and focused on software development. Then the agile community, in particular Jeff Sutherland and Ken Schwaber started to apply the agile ideas to enterprises (Schwaber 2007), even outside of the IT industry, be it in church (Sutherland et al. 2009) or in sales (de Waard et al. 2011). There are certainly concepts in agile approaches like Scrum that can be helpful for other organizational units of a company or other industries. However, the idea to fundamentally change the way a whole enterprise is run modeled after a software development methodology seems to be rather challenging from a marketing perspective, given the reputation that a lot of corporate IT organizations enjoy in their respective corporations.

So for the purpose of this article let us restrict "Agile" to software development and analyze how software product management can cooperate and interact with an agile software development project. The history and status of software product management are described in this book by Samuel Fricker (2012), so we will not repeat that here. A short history of agile development approaches and a description of the key concepts of Scrum as the market leader can be found in chapter 2. In

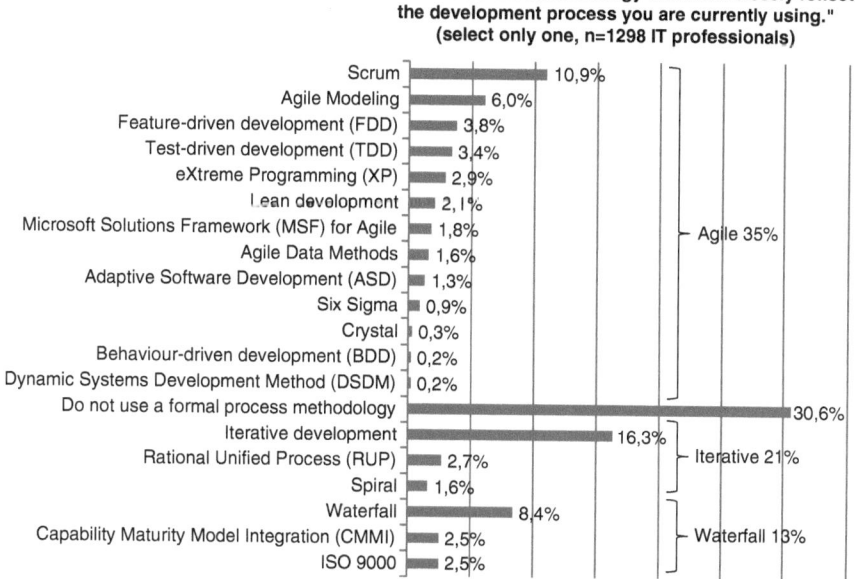

"Please select the methodology that most closely reflects the development process you are currently using." (select only one, n=1298 IT professionals)

Fig. 1 Agile methodologies (Source: Forrester/Dr. Dobb's Global Developer Technographics® Survey, Q3 2009)

Percentage of a company's development projects using agile methodologies	0 - 25	26 - 50	51 - 75	76 - 100
Percentage of respondents	39	21	12	27

Fig. 2 Percentage of companies' projects using agile (VersionOne 2011)

chapter 3 we will analyze the areas of conflict between Software Product Management and Scrum and show how to solve these conflicts and cooperate and interact in a productive way. Chapter 4 looks at the management implications of chapter 3's findings.

2 Agile Development

2.1 Short History

Ever since software started to be created in the 1950s, it has had an unprecedented track record of amazing impact on business and society, of being the source of incredible wealth and disastrous failure, of triumphant success and deep frustration.

The more important software became from a business perspective, the stronger became the desire to make the process of creating software more manageable, more reliable, more "engineering"-like or more manufacturing-like. So it reflected more wishful thinking than reality when the term "software engineering" was coined in 1968 or the term "software factory" in the 1980s (Kittlaus 2003). And there are good arguments why these terms do still not describe reality (Davis 2011; White and Simons 2002).

Nevertheless, in order to improve a rather unsatisfying situation, the industry turned more and more to methodology based on practical experience. For software development, the waterfall model had been dominant since the 1970s which is a phase model in which one phase needs to be finished before the next can begin. Bigger real world software development projects have never really worked like that, but that model found its correspondence in project management methods which started to be standardized in the 1980s. Examples are PMI or PRINCE2 which come with training, certification and consulting. The move to methodologies was a push from management and consultants, not a pull from developers who typically viewed them as restrictions of their freedom, their creativity and their productivity. The next wave of software development methodology was iterative development which took into account that cutting a piece of work into smaller chunks which could be developed one after the other increased the probability of success and gave management a better feeling for progress. Fowler refers to all these approaches as "engineering methodologies" (or plan-driven methodologies). In the mid-1990s agile methods started to become popular as Martin Fowler describes in (Fowler (2005): "Engineering methodologies have been around for a long time. They've not been noticeable for being terribly successful. They are even less noted for being popular. The most frequent criticism of these methodologies is that they are bureaucratic. There's so much stuff to do to follow the methodology that the whole pace of development slows down."

To some degree, agile methodologies can be seen as a reaction to these engineering methodologies, providing "just enough" process. That means a smaller amount of documentation and more code-orientation. Fowler sees deeper differences (Fowler 2005):

- "*Agile methods are adaptive rather than predictive.* Engineering methods tend to try to plan out a large part of the software process in great detail for a long span of time, this works well until things change. So their nature is to resist change. The agile methods, however, welcome change. They try to be processes that adapt and thrive on change, even to the point of changing themselves.
- *Agile methods are people-oriented rather than process-oriented.* The goal of engineering methods is to define a process that will work well whoever happens to be using it. Agile methods assert that no process will ever make up the skill of the development team, so the role of a process is to support the development team in their work."

The term "agile" was agreed upon in a workshop in 2001 that was attended by 17 method gurus including Fowler (Fowler 2005). It resulted in the *Manifesto for Agile Software Development* (Beck et al. 2001) which gained a lot of attention and is worth citing here in full:

"We are uncovering better ways of developing software by doing it and helping others do it. Through this work we have come to value:

- Individuals and interactions over processes and tools
- Working software over comprehensive documentation
- Customer collaboration over contract negotiation
- Responding to change over following a plan

That is, while there is value in the items on the right, we value the items on the left more."

Advocates of the established methodologies, be it in software development or in project management, considered this manifesto as a declaration of war. Some tried to associate "agile" with the old hacking, i.e. software development without plan or documentation, but to no avail. The community of software developers striked back, the term stuck, and agile approaches have become more and more popular over time.

In the late 1990s eXtreme Programming (XP) developed by Kent Beck and others (Beck 1999, 2004) got the most attention of all agile approaches. It is not only a framework and philosophy, but gives very practical advice in the form of concrete techniques, so called practices. Crystal was developed by Alistair Cockburn and is more light-weight. It comes in a number of variations for different sizes of projects, but not all variations are as properly documented as Crystal Clear (Cockburn 2004). There have been a number of other approaches, the most popular of which has been Scrum developed by Jeff Sutherland and Ken Schwaber (Schwaber 2004; Schwaber and Beedle 2001).

There are some statistics available that make quantitative statements about the adoption of agile methods in general and Scrum in particular. Forrester Research (West and Grant 2010) published Fig. 1.

Based on this research conducted in 2009 agile methodologies had a market share of 35 % with Scrum being the agile market leader at 10.9 %.

The results of VersionOne's 2011 State of Agile Survey (VersionOne 2011) show even higher adoption rates (Fig. 2 and 3).

Since VersionOne is a vendor of tools for agile development, it is not clear if the 6,042 international participants in the study are really representative of the total worldwide software development community. So the numbers regarding the adoption rate may be a bit too high. Even with these numbers, it is obvious that the majority of companies has not moved to agile development fully, i.e. software product management has to cooperate with both agile and non-agile development teams. Given Scrum's high market share of 52 %, or 66 % when Scrum Hybrids are included, for agile development this article focuses on Scrum (Fig. 3).

Fig. 3 Agile methodology
most closely followed in agile
projects (VersionOne 2011)

Agile Methodology	Market Share (in %)
Scrum	52
Scrum / XP Hybrid	14
Custom Hybrid	9
Kanban	3
Scumban	3
Feature-Driven Development	2
Extreme Programming XP	2
Lean	2
Other	5
Don't Know	8

2.2   Scrum: Key Concepts

Scrum is not a fully elaborated method, but rather a framework based on a philosophy that values self-organization and the individual skills and abilities of the team members highly. The guiding document for Scrum is the Scrum Guide published by the creators of Scrum, Jeff Sutherland and Ken Schwaber. In its 2011 edition it has just 13 pages with contents (Schwaber and Sutherland 2011). Compared to the 2010 edition, the authors removed and changed some concepts. So Scrum is a moving target which may contribute to its success. Even though Schwaber and Sutherland state that "A common language referring to the process must be shared by all participants.", the Scrum Guide does not define fundamental terms like "product" or "release".

A project is organized in iterations called Sprints that must not last more than a month each. Other Scrum Events are Sprint Planning Meeting, Daily Scrum, Sprint Review, and Sprint Retrospective.

Additional key elements of Scrum are the following roles in a so-called Scrum Team:

Product Owner
- Responsible for maximizing the value of the product and the work of the Development Team.

- The sole person responsible and accountable for managing the Product Backlog and deciding what the Development Team works on. Work can be delegated to Development Team.
- One person that is respected by the entire organization, not a committee.
- With regard to the Product Owner role the Scrum Guide says "How this is done may vary widely across organizations, Scrum Teams, and individuals" (Schwaber and Sutherland 2011, p. 5).

Development Team

- Responsible for delivering potentially shippable product increments at the end of each Sprint.
- 3–7 people with cross-functional skills who do the actual work.
- Self-organizing.

Scrum Master

- Responsible for ensuring Scrum is understood and enacted.
- Servant-leader for the Scrum Team.
- Protects the Development Team and keeps it focused on the tasks at hand.

The Scrum Guide lists a number of relevant artefacts:

Product Backlog

- Single source of requirements for any changes to be made to the product.
- Lists all features, functions, requirements, enhancements, and fixes that constitute the changes to be made to the product in future releases.
- Product Backlog items have the attributes of a description, order, and estimate.
- Dynamic and evolving
- Grooming, i.e. the act of adding detail, estimates, and order to items in the Product Backlog, is an ongoing process in which the Product Owner and the Development Team collaborate. Estimates are only done by the Development Team.

Sprint Backlog

- Set of Product Backlog items selected for the Sprint plus a plan for delivering; forecast by the Development Team about what functionality will be in the next Increment and the work needed to deliver that functionality.
- Owned and updated by the Development Team.

Increment

- The sum of all the Product Backlog items completed during a Sprint and all previous Sprints.
- Product Owner responsible for the decision if increment is released.

The Scrum Guide states explicitly that Scrum does not define a process or a technique (Schwaber and Sutherland 2011).

3   Areas of Conflict and Solutions

Given the rather rudimentary specification of Scrum which has been changing over time, there are different interpretations and different views on how Scrum can or should be positioned and implemented in an organization. In contrast to traditional development methods, Scrum demands changes not only in development, but also in other parts of the enterprise. The interfaces of the Scrum Team to the rest of the enterprise are embodied in the roles of "Product Owner" and "Scrum Master" which are new with Scrum.

3.1 The Naming

The product owner role is central to Scrum, and with the success of Scrum it has found wide-spread use. It had its origins in the start phase of Scrum when the focus was only on a development project and the implicit understanding of the term "product" was "that what was produced in the development project". Up to this day, the term "product" has not been explicitly defined in Scrum, but its meaning has shifted towards a broader understanding that is more in line with ISPMA's definitions (ISPMA 2012b):

- A product is a combination of goods and services, which a supplier/development organization combines in support of its commercial interests to transfer defined rights to a customer.
- A software product is one whose primary component is software.

In a lot of software product companies, the term "product owner" is used for a business executive who has the full P&L responsibility for a product. There are cases where the software product manager is called "product owner". Both situations are in conflict with the Scrum definition of the term. So we suggest that in those environments a different term is used for the Scrum role, e.g. business systems analyst or requirements analyst (see Leffingwell 2011, p. 206).

For the remainder of this article, we use the Scrum role name "product owner".

3.2 The Roles of Product Owner and Software Product Manager

While the Scrum Master is supposed to shield off the Development Team from the outside world, the Product Owner is to represent the outside world within the Scrum Team. Since the Product Owner is supposed to be an individual, not a group or a committee, this is a daunting task.

Practical experiences and reports in Scrum-related blogs show that these requirements towards the Product Owner can very often not be fulfilled. Schwaber writes in (Schwaber 2007, p. 85): "Until recently, I viewed this relationship (between Product Management/Customer and the Development Team) as one of many changes in a Scrum adoption. I now view it as the most critical change, the lynchpin of the adoption." For Schwaber it goes without saying that the Product Owner and the Product Manager are the same. In his rather drastic way of phrasing, Schwaber says (Schwaber 2007, p. 83): "Almost all the product management and development work is done in a hierarchy of Scrum teams. Unless remaining staff and managers have other solid work to do, their idle hands are the devil's workshop. They interfere with the Scrum teams." So the Product Owner does the product

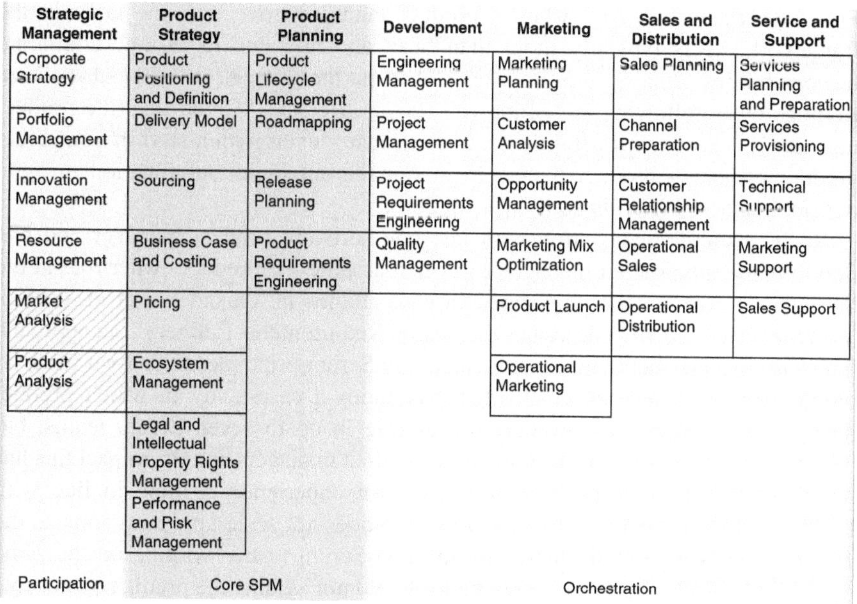

Strategic Management	Product Strategy	Product Planning	Development	Marketing	Sales and Distribution	Service and Support
Corporate Strategy	Product Positioning and Definition	Product Lifecycle Management	Engineering Management	Marketing Planning	Sales Planning	Services Planning and Preparation
Portfolio Management	Delivery Model	Roadmapping	Project Management	Customer Analysis	Channel Preparation	Services Provisioning
Innovation Management	Sourcing	Release Planning	Project Requirements Engineering	Opportunity Management	Customer Relationship Management	Technical Support
Resource Management	Business Case and Costing	Product Requirements Engineering	Quality Management	Marketing Mix Optimization	Operational Sales	Marketing Support
Market Analysis	Pricing			Product Launch	Operational Distribution	Sales Support
Product Analysis	Ecosystem Management			Operational Marketing		
	Legal and Intellectual Property Rights Management					
	Performance and Risk Management					
Participation	Core SPM			Orchestration		

Fig. 4 ISPMA software product management reference framework V.1.1 (ISPMA 2012a)

management work, and if an employee is not part of a Scrum team, he/she is not only superfluous, but dangerous. Roman Pichler is not as drastic, but works from the same assumption in (Pichler 2010), i.e. the Product Owner does the product management.

In Fig. 4 the ISPMA's SPM Reference Framework is illustrated. It is structured in the following way:

- The horizontal structure (columns) is based on the functional areas of a software organization.
- Vertically, i.e. within the columns, the structure is based on a top-down approach, i.e. from more strategic and long-term to more operational and short-term.
- There is an additional overlay structure with "Core SPM" (grey shading), "Participation" and "Orchestration". For Market Analysis and Product Analysis in the Strategic Management column the responsibility is typically with corporate functions in larger companies with the product manager participating, in smaller companies the product manager may be responsible. In any case, getting reliable information on market and product on a frequent basis is part of the core SPM responsibilities.

A more detailed explanation of the framework and its elements can be found in ISPMA (2012b).

When looking at the detailed description of the tasks a Product Owner is responsible for, some of them can be found in the SPM framework (Fig. 4), in particular product vision and requirements engineering. However, there are so many additional tasks listed in that framework that are not part of the Scrum

Product Owner role. And when a product manager covers all the tasks in the framework, he is typically more than busy and not able to assume additional responsibilities that Scrum imposes. That is the line of thought that Dean Leffingwell is following in Leffingwell (2011). He says "Given this (the product manager's) set of responsibilities, it is clear that – even with a staff of competent product owners – product management remains an important function in agile development . . ." (Leffingwell 2011, p. 280).

So in a small organization with just one software product manager and one Scrum team, the product manager will often assume the product owner role in the Scrum team. This is also described in case studies in Vlaanderen et al. (2012). Vlaanderen et al. (2011) describes the "Agile Requirements Refinery", an approach how software product management can apply Scrum principles to its own work on requirements. Vlaanderen et al. (2012) contains a case study in which product management assumes the product owner role in up to seven Scrum teams, but does not give details about the number of product managers and the impact this has on the rest of their responsibilities. Our own experience is more in line with Leffingwell (2011, p. 205) that that approach does not scale up, i.e. as soon as the organization is bigger and there are multiple Scrum teams working on the same product, the product manager cannot and should not assume the product owner role in all these teams. Plus product managers may neither be willing nor able to work on a very technical level close to development due to their individual backgrounds.

The solution is a split of responsibilities between product manager and product owner that needs to be clearly defined. The ISPMA SPM Framework (Fig. 4) turns out to be very helpful in determining this definition in detail. In general, the product owner is closer to development, technology and the project aspects of the product, i.e. in the Development column of the framework. The product manager is closer to the business, the customers, the life cycle aspects of the product, i.e. in the Product Planning and Product Strategy columns of the framework. This is very much in line with Leffingwell's view (Leffingwell 2011, p. 288).

Basically the product owner is a member of the Scrum team and the development organization, with a strong dotted line to Software Product Management, i.e. it is some kind of matrix organization. The product owner is responsible for (see Leffingwell 2011, pp. 51 and 207–208):

- Managing the backlog (project requirements engineering),
- Performing just-in-time story elaboration (detailed requirement specifications), and accepting new stories,
- Participating in sprint planning meetings and progress reviews,
- Driving the iteration,
- Collaborating with product management, e.g. on release planning.

The product manager has to adapt his/her activities in a number of aspects (see also Leffingwell 2011, p. 283 ff.) if development utilizes agile methodologies:

- Product Requirements Engineering: Analysis and specification more high-level since details will be determined in the product owner's story elaboration; tight and ongoing cooperation with product owner regarding synchronization of product and project RE. Vlaanderen et al. (2011) describes how Scrum principles can be applied on the SPM side.

- Release Planning: More flexibility regarding changes during development phase, i.e. contents and prioritization of requirements and addition of new requirements; release dates more reliable, scope more flexible which impacts expectation management (see also Leffingwell 2011, pp. 299 ff.). In this book, Theuns et al. (2012) describe a case study on the impact of the adoption of Scrum on release planning in the case that the product manager assumes the product owner role.
- Roadmapping: Higher change rate due to increased flexibility in release planning.

With this split of responsibilities, the roles of product owner and software product manager can be adequately defined and positioned so that productive cooperation is facilitated. Company-specific details can be defined based on the SPM Framework. The success of an implementation is highly dependent on the availability of people who have the skills and abilities to convincingly fill these positions.

3.3   The Timing Considerations

The agile methodologies, and Scrum in particular, are focused on creating a work environment for the developers that enables high productivity by ensuring a continuous flow of elaborated user stories in a sequence governed by value assessments. This puts a lot of pressure on the product owner who is responsible for the timely availability of these user stories. In cases where a software product manager assumes the product owner role, these demands can easily lead to overload situations and/or to neglection of other product management responsibilities. Vlaanderen et al. (2011) proposes the agile requirements refinery as an approach to meet these demands by applying Scrum principles within software product management. The corresponding Sprint cycles can be overlapping.

When the product owner role is not assumed by software product management, the work of the software product manager is less directly triggered by the Scrum rhythm. This enables the product manager to synchronize his work more with the frequencies of other important processes that require his involvement, like corporate planning processes (e.g. portfolio management, marketing plan, sales plan) or his own processes like roadmapping. In short, he can focus more on the important than the urgent (Kittlaus and Clough 2009, p. 42) while he is still sufficiently involved in project requirements decisions through the dotted line from the product owner to software product management.

4   Management Implications

From a management perspective, agile methodologies like Scrum in software development promise a number of significant advantages like higher productivity and faster reaction to changing requirements. The adoption, however, means a significant change process and takes a longer period of time (see the case study in

Theuns et al. 2012). It requires a champion on the executive level and guidance from experienced consultants. In most companies this is not a black-or-white issue, i.e. there may be development projects that will continue to be better served by more traditional development methodologies.

If Scrum is used in a development project this has significant implications for other organizational units within the company, in particular software product management. These SPM implications result from the relationship between the software product manager and the Scrum product owner roles and are described in 3.2.

The ISPMA SPM Framework (Fig. 4) helps to resolve any conflicts. We suggest using it as a basis for the following steps:
– Analyze as-is situation
– Identify current owners of tasks
– Identify tasks not taken by anyone
– Clarify and communicate definitions of relevant terms across company
– Establish company-wide roles and responsibilities
– Find the optimal balance and cooperation between SPM and agile development teams

As above, this requires a champion on the executive level and guidance from experienced consultants.

Though we do not recommend the adoption of a vanilla Scrum approach to all units of a company, there are a number of elements in Scrum that can be very useful in improving productivity and time-to-market in units other than development, in particular:
– Team approach
  • With small teams (5–9 people)
  • Dedicated not only in terms of mindset, but also in terms of time allocation
  • Leaving room for self-organization, but with some key roles and responsibilities.
– Appreciation of the individual skills and abilities of the team members.
– Organization of work in time-boxed iterations with frequent "success" points (Sprints).
– Team communication structured and organized in a way that enforces sufficient communication and learning without sacrificing productivity (Sprint Planning Meeting, Daily Scrum, Sprint Review, and Sprint Retrospective).

If and how this can be implemented in the other units including SPM needs to be determined by the responsible management. Again, a guided change management process is required.

5   Summary

Scrum as the market leader in agile methodologies for software development projects contains terminology and the role definition of "product owner" including its demands regarding timing which are in conflict with the state of the art of software product management. In this article we have described the conflicts and developed solutions how to deal with these conflicts in a way that enables and ensures productive cooperation. The ISPMA Book of Knowledge, in particular the SPM Framework prove to be very helpful in analyzing a given situation in an organization and define specific solutions in detail. Some elements of agile approaches may also be helpful and applicable in a company's units outside of development in order to improve productivity and time-to-market.

So far there has been very little scientific work and publications on the relationship of Software Product Management and agile methodologies. Progress has primarily been driven by consultants and companies adopting agile methodologies. There is a lot of room for research in the areas of software product management, software development methodology, and economic sciences.

References

Beck, K. (1999). *eXtreme programming explained – Embrace change*. Upper Saddle River: Addison-Wesley.

Beck, K. (2004). *eXtreme programming explained – Embrace change* (2nd ed.). Upper Saddle River: Addison-Wesley.

Beck, K., et al. (2001). Manifesto for agile software development. http://agilemanifesto.org/

Cockburn, A. (2004). *Crystal clear*. Upper Saddle River: Addison-Wesley.

Davis, M. (2011). Will software engineering ever be engineering? *CACM, 54*(11), 32–34.

de Waard, D., van Solingen, R., & Sutherland, J. (2011). Scrum in sales: How to improve account management and sales processes. *Agile conference 2011*, Salt Lake City.

Fowler, M. (2005). The new methodology. http://martinfowler.com/articles/newMethodology.html

Fricker, S. A. (2012). *Software product management*, in this book.

ISPMA. (2012a). Software product management reference framework V.1.1. www.ispma.org

ISPMA. (2012b). Software product management – Foundation level syllabus V.1.1. www.ispma.org

Kittlaus, H.-B. (2003). Software Engineering und Software Fabrik – vom Nutzen und Schaden der Metapher in der Informatik. In: Informatik-Spektrum 26: pp. 8–12 and 291–292.

Kittlaus, H.-B., & Clough, P. C. (2009). *Software product management and pricing – Key success factors for all software organizations*. Heidelberg: Springer.

Leffingwell, D. (2011). *Agile software requirements*. Upper Saddle River: Addison-Wesley.

Pichler, R. (2010). *Agile product management with scrum*. Upper Saddle River: Addison-Wesley.

Schwaber, K. (2004). *Agile project management with scrum*. Redmond: Microsoft Press.

Schwaber, K. (2007). *The enterprise and scrum*. Redmond: Microsoft Press.

Schwaber, K., & Beedle, M. (2001). *Agile software development with scrum*. Upper Saddle River: Prentice Hall.

Schwaber, K., & Sutherland, J. (2011). The scrum guide. http://www.scrum.org/storage/scrumguides/Scrum_Guide.pdf

Sutherland, A., Sutherland, J., & Hegarty, C. (2009). Scrum in church: Saving the world one team at a time. *Agile conference 2009*, Chicago.

Theuns, M., Vlaanderen, K., & Brinkkemper, S. (2012). *Exploring the relationship between scrum and release planning activities*, in this book.

VersionOne. (2011). State of agile survey 2011. http://www.versionone.com/state_of_agile_development_survey/11/

Vlaanderen, K., Jansen, S., Brinkkemper, S., & Jaspers, E. (2011). The agile requirements refinery: Applying SCRUM principles to software product management. *Information and Software Technology, 53*(2011), 58–70.

Vlaanderen, K., van Steen, P., Brinkkemper, S., & van de Weerd, I. (2012). Growing into agility: Process implementation paths for SCRUM from an SPM perspective. *Proceedings of the 13th International Conference on Product-Focused Software Process Improvement*, Heidelberg/New York, NY: Springer.

West, D., & Grant, T. (2010). *Agile development: Mainstream adoption has changed agility*. Cambridge, MA: Forrester Research.

White, J., & Simons, B. (2002). ACM's position on the licencing of software engineers. *CACM, 45*(11), 91.

Requirements Engineering in Agile Software Development

Rainer Grau

Abstract

In all organization requirements engineering is applied at two different context levels: in the context of the product or service portfolio and in the context of projects. At the project context agile methods and techniques are often successfully established, although the discipline of requirements engineering often still is unattended. At the portfolio context agile techniques are hardly ever established thus leading to a culture clash between the portfolio and the project context. As requirements are the most important link of the chain from portfolios to projects, a solid and continuous agile approach in the discipline of requirements engineering from portfolio management level down into every single project is a key to open up unimagined potential for the organization. This article visualizes the forces behind agile techniques in requirements engineering, the "root causes" that interact and open up this potential. The understanding of these root causes enables individuals to implement the optimal version of agility in the organization.

1   Introduction

Agility is relevant. Many success stories and serious reports as the Chaos Manifest of the Standish Group[1] prove that agile methods and techniques fundamental increase project success. However, the aim of any organization cannot just be the efficient completion of projects. Projects are organizational units with time

---

[1] See www.standishgroup.com – CHAOS MANIFESTO, the Laws of CHAOS and the CHAOS 100 Best PM Practices, Copyright 2011, Standish Group.

R. Grau
Zühlke Engineering AG, Schlieren (Zuerich), Schweiz
e-mail: rainer.grau@zuehlke.com

A. Maedche et al. (eds.), *Software for People*, Management for Professionals,
DOI 10.1007/978-3-642-31371-4_6, © Springer-Verlag Berlin Heidelberg 2012

limitations which aim to achieve the organization's targets. This might be an innovation designed to secure the future, produce SOMETHING to earn money or simply a plan to optimize the organization. So what really is requirements engineering in this context? Asking a 100 experts delivers 200 answers. The answer of this article is very simple: Requirements engineering is one out of many activities we need to create the SOMETHING. In the commercial world, this SOMETHING is typically a PRODUCT (such as a mobile phone, a car or commercial software), a benefit (such as a bank account, internet connection or Cloud service), a service (property management, consulting or customer services) or a mixture of all these things. The PRODUCT – I will use this term in what follows to refer to all of these options – is the subject of our actual endeavor. This is how we will make our money. So rather than simply creating a product, it is even better to create it with the lowest possible total cost of ownership (TCO). To be more precise now, requirements engineering is a TOOL which is used to create a product required by the market in a WAY that ensures that the brainstorming, production and distribution, i.e. the TCO, costs less than the proceeds.

On closer examination, the Chaos Manifest reveals two interesting aspects. First, it states in every single issue that defects in requirements engineering are one of the root causes of projects failures. Second, in discussions about agile methods and techniques, the discipline of requirements engineering is somewhat neglected, especially the techniques to work with stakeholders in elicitation, consolidation and conflict resolution. It is about time to fill this gap. This article highlights opportunities and undreamt potential which can be unlocked by a smart combination of best practices in requirements engineering with agile techniques and knowledge management. Unlocking this potential in our organization enables us to outperform our competition by developing and offering products and services that delight the user in an efficient mode of production.

The remainder of this article is organized into six chapters. First, we discuss basic concepts, drivers and structures of product or service development in organizations in chapter "Fundamental Concepts". This chapter visualizes that product or service development implicates solving a complex problem. Efficient teams of high potential knowledge workers are identified as the key of successful problem solving. Chapter "Knowledge Work as Key to Agile Re" focuses on knowledge and knowledge work and its correlation with efficiency and the discipline of requirements engineering. With these essentials chapter "Investigations on Life Cycle Models" reflects on work organization in teams. The transfer of this discussion into real world scenarios shows that limiting constraints of an existing organization influence the potential degree of efficiency. Chapter "Emerging Agile Principles on the Product Level" applies the findings on product and service development. All teams working on all context levels in the organization must comply with the identified concepts in an aligned and synchronized way. The last chapter offers a set of thesis and guidelines and reflects on typical obstructions in real life. It strongly encourages invest into the identified most important factors of modern and innovative organizations: the knowledge workers, the teams and the collaboration of the teams at different context levels of the organization; able to combine best practices from requirements engineering with agile techniques and knowledge management; empowered to develop outperforming products and service in dynamic changing markets.

2   Fundamental Concepts

2.1   Requirements Engineering and the Ecosystem of Product Development

OUTPERFOMING PRODUCTs are those which are launched in the market with the right features and at the right time. Let's assume we already have a set of products in our organization, which we are currently offering on the market. It is clear that tomorrow, the products have to look different; we will need to alter or develop some products so that they remain attractive. We need to create a new product to replace an existing one. So far it is obvious. Now typically, products are created or developed within projects. According to the definition, a project is a temporary form of organization to transfer an existing condition, in this case the condition of the product, into a new condition. We therefore have one or more projects to create a new version of one or more products or to develop new products.

I would like to repeat at this point: an "OUTPERFOMING PRODUCT" brings the right features to the market at the right time. A successful organization actively focuses on these two very abstract concepts "RIGHT FEATURES" and "RIGHT TIME". Important cornerstones involve the identification of the products right at the beginning of the innovation process, followed by the definition of our product portfolio and the release planning coordinated with it. Release planning results in the management of the project portfolio as the operative level below the product portfolio. From the point of view of the organization, the definition of the product portfolio represents the strategic level. Management and release management represent the tactical implementation of the strategy and projects are the operative execution of the strategy and tactics (see Fig. 1).

At some point in this process we will use the tool "requirements engineering". The responsibilities of requirements engineering are:

- To work with the marketing department, customers and/or customer services and care for the needs of these stakeholders.
- To manage the characteristics which existing products possess, along with the framework conditions under which they are produced and used, such as regulatory requirements.
- To incorporate result from an innovation process, dealing with new ideas which are implemented as new requirements for upcoming product versions.
- To assesses the boundary conditions of technology and the production process to take economic aspects into consideration and optimize the TCO.

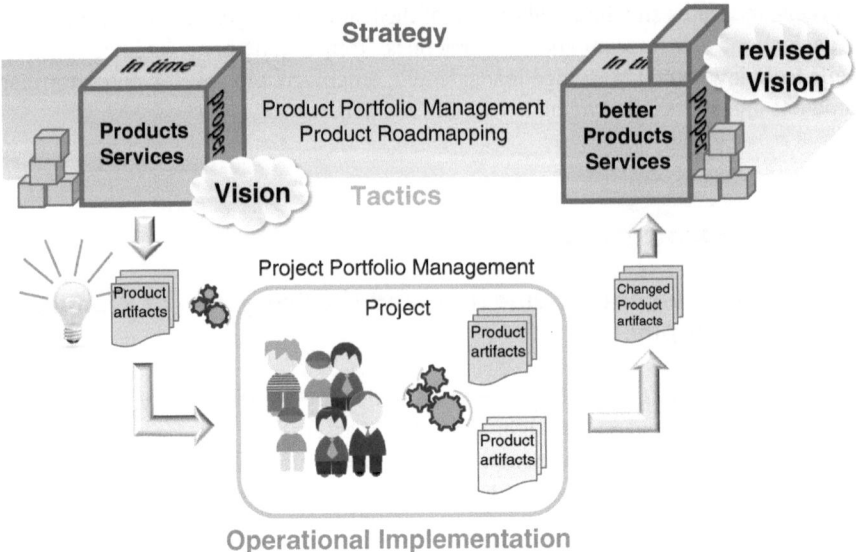

Fig. 1 The ecosystem of PRODUCT development

We now have a picture of where requirements engineering is located within the context of our considerations. If we look at the ecosystem of product development (see Fig. 1), two things particularly stand out:

1. There is a working context above project level, the product portfolio level (even if there is only one single product managed). Tactical decisions about the evolution of products are at this level. The release roadmap and the derived project portfolio are the implementation of the product portfolio decisions. The management of the product portfolio is an ongoing process with input variables as there are: market requirements, innovation pressure, constraints of the organization and available budget. To prepare these input variables a fair amount of requirements engineering is required to ensure that the organization will sell the RIGHT product on the market at the RIGHT time. At this stage it could be argued whether this is requirements engineering, or business analysis or another concept. If we consider the skills required and the activities carried out by individuals involved, we can clearly state, to a large extent, this is requirements engineering. I will therefore simply refer to these activities as requirements engineering.

2. The projects are the operative implementation level of the product release map. This level, the project portfolio level, needs to be synchronized in close collaboration with the process level of portfolio management. A significant aspect immediately becomes evident here: the tactical level and operative level use

information and knowledge which may result from both levels and which must be able to move transparently between the levels. At this stage, there is no doubt that this is requirements engineering.

Requirements engineering is involved at the tactical level and the operative level. Both levels need to work closely with each other. Requirements engineering is an important link with regard to the communication between these two levels. It is a key discipline and therefore one of the truly important tools in product development. The success or failure of the organization is closely associated with the question of whether requirements engineering can be efficiently organized in each context level and subsequently facilitate an efficient implementation of the organization's strategy.

2.2 Complex Problems and the Understanding of the Ecosystem "Project"

The concept of "agile" has not come up in any sentence yet. To understand this concept we first have to understand very important and fundamental concepts behind agility related with knowledge management. The organizational unit of a project is perfectly suited to make these fundamental concepts visible. Let's start from the following situation: a product already exists. A project will transform the existing version of the product into the new version of the product which is the RIGHT PRODUCT at the RELEASE POINT IN TIME at the end of the project.

A project is an ecosystem with time limitations. A team of people work on the new product version which, when deployed or sold, will create value to one or more user groups. In the social context, the team which creates the product is influenced by and integrated into the environments in which the product is used and created. There is close interaction between the social context of these environments and the team. In a nutshell: the team, the integration of the team into the context of the organization, and the interaction with the usage context of the new products version plays a major role in successful project work.

Requirements engineering plays a key role in all of this, works with stakeholders, and identifies the interactions between the product to be created and the context. These activities capture and work with the RIGHT characteristics of the product in detail and – taking the constraints of the organization into consideration – increase the TCO of the product. Requirements engineering also brings stakeholders on board, connects to other sources of information and links all of these things together. The fact that the vision of the new products version might change during the project must also be dealt with.

According to the general conclusions of research (Dirbach et al. 2011), these features (many stakeholders, sources of information and connections, moving target) correspond to the definition of a complex problem. In abstract terms,

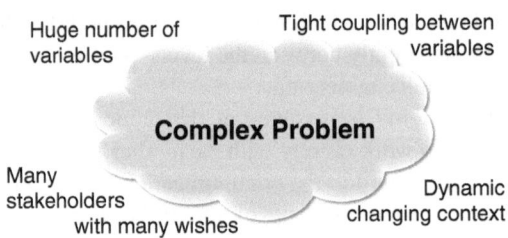

Huge number of variables   Tight coupling between variables

Complex Problem

Many stakeholders with many wishes   Dynamic changing context

Fig. 2 A project is a container to solve a complex problem

a project deals with the solution to a complex problem (see Fig. 2). For this purpose, the generally recognized view in research (Dirbach et al. 2011) is: no mechanical production process can be implemented to solve a complex problem in the manner of, e.g. the preparation of hamburgers (rolls, beef, mince, mayonnaise, ketchup, pickles, salad assembled in well-defined working steps). In order to solve complex problems knowledge workers are required. These workers need to collaborate as efficiently as possible. In addition they need to work with, process and create further knowledge.

For the transformation of the product from one version to the next version, knowledge is required. There are two significant aspects of this knowledge:

1. Knowledge about the features of the current version of the product and knowledge about the features which the new product should possess in the future, i.e. product knowledge.
2. Knowledge and skills regarding the way in which the new version of the product will be implemented and put into production, i.e. process knowledge.

A significant characteristic of knowledge when solving a complex problem is the fact that at the beginning of a project, the knowledge often is quite rudimentary. This is why a problem becomes a complex problem. In any event, the project team does not have access to complete knowledge about the features of the new version of the product, merely a more or less well-defined idea of these characteristics. It is precisely the role of requirements engineering to define these within the project. The project team, however, has equally little information about how to develop the product, as the stakeholders may still be unknown: so how can we work with them? The same applies to testing: what part of testing can we automate and where do we still need people to carry out tests? Not to mention the deployment process and many other details. Furthermore, all of these things will change during the course of the project work (Fig. 3).

In very general terms, knowledge is not sufficient at the beginning of a project. The team must learn as it goes on by experience. The knowledge required to solve the projects complex problem has significant gaps in all aspects. An important task to be completed by a project team is to fill these knowledge gaps. This applies to gaps in the domain knowledge, as well as to those relating to technical and process knowledge.

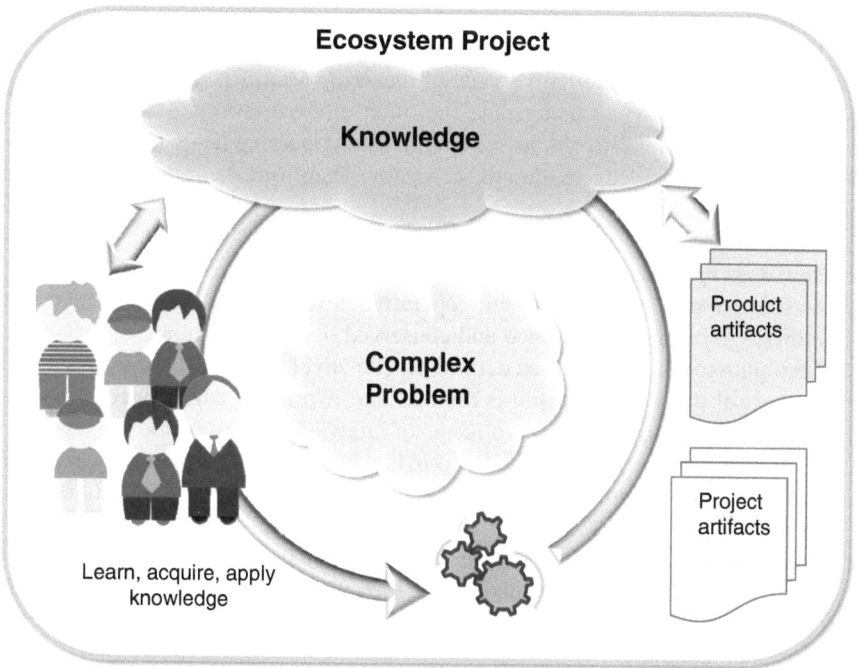

Fig. 3 The ecosystem project: solving complex problems

3   Knowledge Work as the Key to Agile Re

Now that we understand fundamental concepts it is time to talk about agility. Under the catchword of "agility", organizations typically follow the targets of a shortened time to market and improved flexibility with regards to changes to the business model due to external or internal influences (Poppendieck and Poppendieck 2003). If we reflect on what we have gained so far, the acquisition of knowledge and the efficient retention of knowledge are important measures. The Agile Manifesto,[2] available on the internet for over 15 years now, specifies – not surprisingly – such measures. To remind us:

- Individuals and interactions over processes and tools
- Working software over comprehensive documentation
- Customer collaboration over contract negotiation
- Response to change over following a plan

    In addition to other aims (the Agile Manifesto originated from the idea of placing the central focus on the team rather than the processes and documentation),

---

[2] http://agilemanifesto.org/

these measures precisely address the aim of optimizing the learning process within the team to work on and fill knowledge gaps regarding the complex problem. This gives us an interesting alternative view of the Agile Manifesto.

Now it is necessary to understand the often referred term "knowledge" in the context of the working world, as requirements engineering deals mainly with the development of knowledge within the company. Therefore, the following questions need to be considered:

- What is knowledge exactly?
- How does knowledge manifest itself within an organization?
- And to support the tactical and operative level within the company: Can knowledge be created, retained and conserved – and if yes, how?

According to current accepted definitions (Polanyi and Sen 2009), knowledge in the context of the working world is divided into two forms and defined as having three main characteristics. The two forms of knowledge are:

1. *Explicit knowledge*: If a person can provide an answer to a question or problem in a clear and structured way, as in a formula or in evidence, this is explicit knowledge.
2. *Implicit or tacit knowledge*: If a person carries out an action or makes a (usually correct) decision, the determination of which they are unable to specifically and clearly describe, and is perhaps not even able to explain the background for the performed action.

Tacit knowledge is often also described as a gut feeling or intuition. The term "tacit knowledge" is recognized and documented (Polanyi and Sen 2009). Significantly, more decisions and actions are based on tacit knowledge than one would expect. This is a good thing; this is a cornerstone of efficiency. Correct implicit actions and decisions based on tacit knowledge increase efficiency. Information does not need to be gathered and analyzed first so that conclusions can be drawn using explicit knowledge. An explicit process would often work as well, but much less efficient. In many cases, the explicit process would not even work, as it may not be possible to describe the reasons for making a decision or the motivation for taking a specific action, because even an expert is not always aware of all of the implicit criteria.

Let's look at a concrete example from requirements engineering to see how efficient tacit knowledge can be: making a decision about the classification of requirements, for example which abstraction level a requirement will be allocated to (business level, product level, user level or technical level).

It would be difficult for anyone to write criteria and the "algorithm to use" to make this abstraction level decision explicit. Imagine creating a catalogue of criteria and the algorithm with a group of experts. Ignoring the question of whether this makes sense, the effort of an entire person year might be spend to gain just consensus about the criteria. Engineers who have mastered requirements engineering at expert level are able to make these kind of decisions highly efficiently, quickly and with a high hit rate. Decisions of this nature are common in projects – and not only when it comes to requirements.

The three characteristics of knowledge are:

1. It is used to link **pieces of information** with each other to form knowledge content and to make them accessible.
2. **Benefit** can be gained from the knowledge, meaning the knowledge can be **applied**.
3. Knowledge only has meaning in the **social context** in which it is made available. The knowledge is therefore only relevant to a group of people who are together in a shared context, such as in a project.

In the following we will have a closer look at these specific characteristics of knowledge.

3.1   Knowledge Is About Linking Information and Making It Accessible

The first characteristic of knowledge was *linking information and making it accessible*. Now we could state that qualitatively good documentation, the requirements specification for example, accomplishes these things. A high-quality requirements specification ideally contains the right requirements and describes these in the correct way. The traceability between the requirements assures that the information is linked. If the documentation is then made accessible to everyone, in a project share or tool, it is available as well.

I would like to focus on this. Let's consider Project X and imagine a truly perfect requirements specification (I had a dream):

- Does the requirements specification contain ALL information required to process ALL necessary product knowledge to progress with the project, solely on the basis of this requirements specification?
- Does it include ALL information links, in the form of traces that are required to successfully complete the project?
- Is this true not only for the documentation related with the discipline of requirements engineering but with ALL other disciplines as well required to complete the project?
- Is it possible to pour ALL knowledge within a project as information into documents, i.e. not only necessary but also adequate knowledge?
- Is it possible to document ALL required and sufficient links in the form of traces?

The answer is a clear NO. The following thought experiment confirms this clear NO. Picture two teams; each receives this perfect requirements specification and, completely independently of each other, creates the product. If you are completely convinced that the products created independently by each of the teams will be COMPLETELY IDENTICAL, then this "NO" does not apply …

Reasonably, documentation should be limited to cost justifications. Writing, reviewing and updating documentation is effort. Documentation shall contain only by the organization required information to successfully solve the complex problem associated with the project.

And additionally and most important: Documentation contains no knowledge, only the information elements which can be used to create knowledge.

The intriguing questions are: Where is knowledge created and where resides the knowledge? Where does all the rest of the information, which a project requires, come from? How is all this information, i.e. the information contained in the documentation and the "remaining" information which is not in the documentation, converted into knowledge to successfully complete a project?

The answer is simple: In the heads of the team working on the project. This leads us to the next intriguing question: How did the knowledge get into their heads? According to the principle in the movie MATRIX: We strap down the team member on a chair, a plug is inserted into the head and we load the two programs "The product knowledge is like this" and "the process knowledge to implement the product is like that"!!

In reality, other methods apply: Either people explicitly take part in training, or they develop their knowledge explicitly (by coaching) or implicitly (by learning on the job). Training is a good way of introducing missing knowledge into the organization. Coaching and learning on the job work well if the knowledge is already in the heads of others in the organization and "only" needs to be transmitted or developed. Common to both methods is that to build knowledge requires learning. Modern forms of learning in the professional environment are based on self-motivated learning in learning groups with teachers as coaches. Direct communicating, obtaining fast feedback from experts based on the results of applying knowledge in daily work are the keys to bringing knowledge which cannot be acquired through documentation into the heads of employees and anchoring it there.

In conclusion, communication and feedback are significant and fundamental principles when it comes to distributing and anchoring knowledge within the project team. If we are able to optimize communication and feedback in a project, then we can accelerate the acquisition of knowledge, especially of tacit knowledge and therefore increase efficiency. Daily stand-ups, reviews and retrospectives, as in Scrum, for example, gain a completely unexpected and extended meaning, as well as the daily team morning coffee break at 10:30 and the (alcohol-free;-) end-of-day beer. The end-of-day beer as a means of increasing efficiency – wow!

3.2   Knowledge Work Is Applying Knowledge

The second characteristic of knowledge was *gaining benefits from knowledge*. Gaining benefits from knowledge means applying the knowledge. Applying knowledge automatically means following a process. A process in turn is defined by roles, activities and artifacts as results of the activity processed by the persons acting in the context of a role. A process places the activities in a chronological order through the definition of workflows.

Simple example: Fred Flintstone comes into the office and picks up the notes made at yesterday's interview with a stakeholder. He uses them to analyze and document use cases or user stories. Fred Flintstone is working in the role of the requirements engineer and is producing part of the requirements specification as the result artifact of this activity.

The interesting thing in this "story" is: how did he learn this activity? What learning process did Fred Flintstone undergo so that he knows how to carry out this activity as requirements engineer. Where did he get the interview notes from, how did he convert these notes into use cases and how did he know the procedure and the individual steps required to transform an interview into a use case or user story?

Two example scenarios:

Scenario 1: The company follows a well-developed and documented process model (e.g. V Model according to CMMI Maturity Level 3). The detailed process is documented, with full details on all roles, all activities together with their sequence and dependencies, the incoming and produced artifacts including the to-be-used templates. Fred Flintstone received 20 days of training, which taught him the theory of this process. In his projects he learned the real life version of how to apply the process – either in some areas or completely. His colleagues acted as his coaches. The regular process reviews ensure that the process is adhered to – at least formally. At any rate, process compliance is always indicated to the companies Quality Control department. This is said to have led to black economies and underhand dealing in companies in the past …

It is interesting to track how Fred Flintstone gained the knowledge in Scenario 1. The process was initially created by others, typically the experts of a method group. These others do not necessarily have the knowledge to create an optimal process, not having experienced the process themselves and informed about it only indirectly. These method experts document process information into documents. This information is again extracted from documents by a trainer and converted to theoretical knowledge in Fred Flintstone's head during training. This is a form of Chinese whispers (we know the game from our childhood, where one word is whispered from ear to ear in a circle). What the process group created in the context of process definition is different to what the trainer interprets during the training and how it is understood by Fred Flintstone. This difference evens out the reality of the project, i.e. the trial and error of daily life and the concrete project work with colleagues. So once again, coaching and learning in context and in a team.

Scenario 2: Fred Flintstone picks up the notes from yesterday, to continue processing the user stories which were discussed in the meeting with the product owner and experts from the specialist area. Part of this is done in discussion with a team member as peer. The team decided during the last retrospective that it is reasonable to initially design a low-fidelity paper-based GUI prototype and check the procedure and acceptance criteria with the specialist area using this prototype, so this is what Fred Flintstone and his peer are working on now before writing new user stories with acceptance criteria. GUI prototype, user stories and acceptance criteria are carried out to the team and confirmed by the product owner within the requirements workshop in this sprint. The company's only process framework constraints are: user stories must be complemented with acceptance criteria; a subset of the done criteria defines general acceptance criteria for product documentation and quality; well defined synchronization points between projects (internal releases) are defined to steer deployment procedures.

At this point, we have come to the topic of efficient working in an agile context. The feedback loops (daily standup, peer reviews, pair working) and retrospectives (indispensable part of each agile life cycle), which are fixed anchors of agile work, create precisely the right learning environment to support the acquisition of knowledge, to enable an efficient application of knowledge through consistent and permanent improvement of the process currently being used. Plenty of the knowledge – both the product knowledge and process knowledge – is thereby anchored as implicit knowledge, i.e. in the efficient form of knowledge. The required flexibility is also taken into consideration, as the adjustment of knowledge to a changing context has been integrated into the continuous learning process as a basic value.

This creates the bridge between requirements engineering and agile work – at this point only discussed at the context level of the project. Agile techniques foster the team's knowledge acquisition process and anchor the knowledge as efficient tacit knowledge. A project team solving a complex problem is as well a self-learning and self-improving team when acting with an agile mindset and techniques.

3.3   Knowledge Is Valid in its Specific Context Only

A team member as part of a learning environment named project learns through interaction within a particular context – his peers in the same context. The application of knowledge and closure of new identified knowledge gaps which is a measure that takes effect within the context of the learning group only. An implicit conclusion here is that the acquired knowledge only has meaning within this social context. Now, various contextual levels exist within a company, as mentioned at the beginning of this article: the context of project work; the context of a single product with its roadmap; the context of managing a product portfolio; the context of defining the strategy of a company.

We discover that different "learning groups" exist within a company and each of these carry out knowledge work and acquire knowledge. These teams work at different contextual levels in the organization: the project teams, the steering committee, which makes decisions about the product roadmap at a tactical level, the management, which deals with the strategy, an R&D department, a specific testing group, operations and others. An interesting task is to identify these contextual levels, and therefore also the learning groups, in your company and the context they work in. These context levels and learning groups are not automatically in line with the organizational structure of the company! It is also interesting to note that many people work in more than one context within the company. This often leads to personal conflicts for these people, as the targets and working techniques (including the culture) can differ at the various contextual levels.

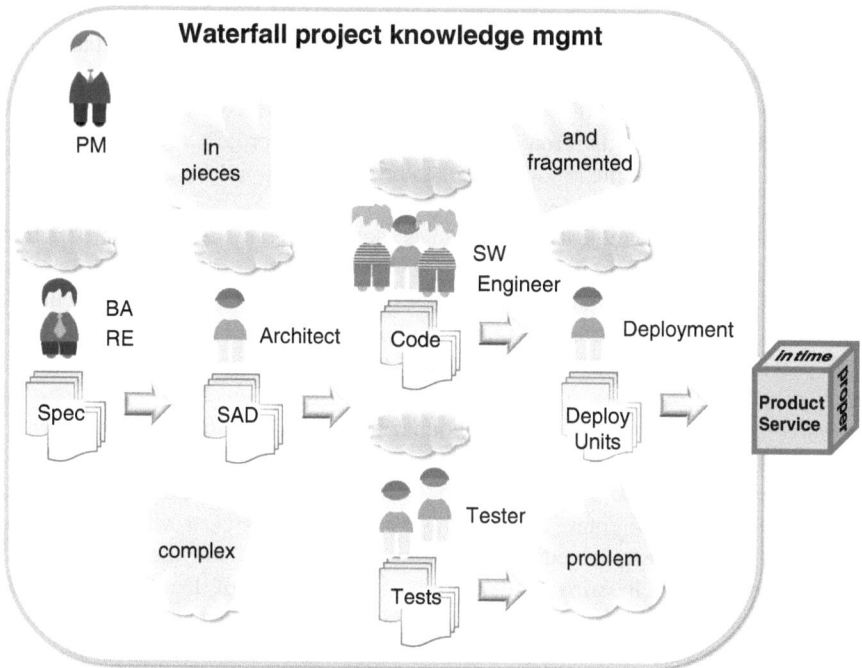

Fig. 4 The document-oriented working model

4 Investigations on Life Cycle Models

On basis of the previous considerations we can derive important conclusions. Two theoretical experiments shall demonstrate these conclusions as extreme examples.

4.1 Extreme 1: The Pure Document-Orientated Working Model

Picture this: A company has decided to record all of its knowledge in the form of information in documents. This applies to both procedural and product knowledge. An appropriate corresponding quality assurance procedure checks that the recorded information is complete in both areas. Beginning with the strategy process at a product level, moving on to the development of the product portfolio and finishing with the definition and execution of projects, all information has to be stored in the form of documents.

4.1.1 Consequences of the Document-Orientated Working Model

A member of staff can be replaced at any time (this is an attractive aspect for management, isn't it?). A new member of staff can use the documentation and appropriate training to become familiar with the process and product knowledge in order to ultimately become productive in accordance with the standards (Fig. 4).

4.1.2 Advantages of the Document-Orientated Working Model

One advantage plays a role if a product is not developed on a permanent basis. For example, it may be sold or in production for 2 years without any changes. No one develops the product in this period; it is simply "produced". The team which developed the product therefore no longer exists. If a project is then reinitiated when a new version of the product needs to be created, the information is available to create a new project team.

Another advantage (at least often cited as such) is that any part of the production chain can be transferred offshore; it is "easy" to move the process and production documentation offshore. This corresponds to the often mentioned arguments of global and distributed teams, flexibility and a "breathing workforce". I think that this pretended advantage will fortunately now, based on gained experience, be looked at differently for cost and efficiency reasons. Nevertheless, in case of resource shortcuts compared to the amount of work to be implemented this argument is sustainable.

This working model requires high standardization. It is defined clearly and explicitly in terms of roles, activities and artifacts. It is clear which incoming documents are to be received by a requirements engineer and the results which the requirements engineering needs to produce in the form of documentation. It is clear how the requirements engineer can learn more through training. The job profile is clear and can be communicated to the HRM. There are often pools of job families in large companies, such as the requirements engineering pool.

4.1.3 Disadvantages of the Document-Orientated Working Model

This approach obviously has a major impact on efficiency. At least with regard to the process side of things, information is documented by people purely on the basis of explicit knowledge. The documented status of working technique typically implemented and supported by a tool chain is always structurally outdated, as learning, documentation, releasing, teaching and application take some time to implement and therefore lag seriously behind the "state of the art".

No value is placed on tacit knowledge – in this extreme case it is deliberately avoided. This applies to the team which is disbanded after each project and then re-created. Each project team will then practically start from the beginning and must learn what the previous team left behind by studying the documents. On the other hand, the team can be installed at any time. This principle applies at a team level and also to the collaboration between the individual disciplines in the project. The business analyst passes documents to the requirements engineer, the requirements engineer to the test manager and to the architect and designer, subsequent to the developer and so on. The statements regarding problem-solving, processing with tacit knowledge and dealing with knowledge gaps which we discussed above nevertheless apply to all of these people. The completely extreme situation would be achieved if the people were not allowed to communicate with one another and were only able to interact by exchanging documentation. Every single person in the value chain of the project builds its own learning team.

The specialization of people in roles is also double-edged. Thus if a requirements engineer is trained in a specific way, he can only be used for these specific tasks. In the worst case, he will only be responsible for requirements engineering in a project. I personally provided support for a specific project at a major company, where 30 % requirements engineering capacity was allocated – as role and as person. For this purpose, a member of staff out of the requirements engineering pool was allocated, present 1.5 days per week in this project. One half day of this time was required for the weekly project meeting. The effectiveness of this employee was almost zero – although he was a good requirements engineer. He was removed from the project after 1 month and the project leader took over the role of requirements engineering. The efficiency of this expert was near zero, the motivation of all involved persons below zero.

Does this model work? Yes it does – this has been proved in practice. I know companies which tend towards this extreme and are successful. Companies which operate in this way manage inefficiency just with higher TCO than their competitors, who are likely to be a bit more inefficient.

4.2 Extreme 2: The Pure Team-Orientated and Agile Working Model

There is no documentation required as result of an implementation activity. The team only uses temporary documentation to drive the process (please keep in mind, product-related documentation will inevitably be produced, such as the handbooks for users or – if required by a legal regulation or norm – a traceability matrix). The temporary documentation helps the team with its everyday work, such as cards on Scrum or Kanban boards or whatever the team decides to use. All of the process knowledge and as many details as possible of the product knowledge are in the heads of the team members and will be permanently developed there. This working model is naturally highly efficient in a local and small team which works together constantly.

4.2.1 Consequences of a Purely Agile Working Model

An agile working model in its extreme form has clear consequences for the organization of work. In each team, the project specific skills set must be available; every team member is ideally qualified in more than one discipline. This has consequences for the role of the requirements engineer, the test manager, architect and all other roles. The Mr. requirements engineer, the Mr. chief architect, no longer exists. Job profiles restricted to one role disappear. The ideal team member is a professional and self-directed software engineer with ideally two or three areas of special interest (requirements engineering, SW architecture, testing, deployment, usability, security, . . .).

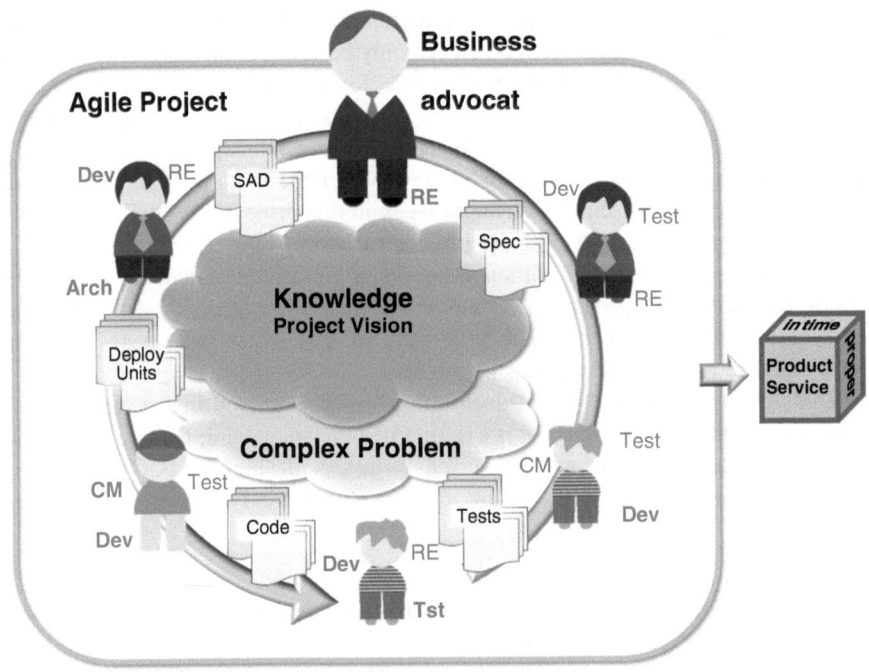

Fig. 5 The team-oriented and agile working model

The product owner (to use Scrum jargon at this point) for sure must be a requirements engineering expert. This brings us to one difficulty of the Scrum approach: the product owner needs to be available in the project team; as well he needs to be active dealing with stakeholders outside of the team; he is bound into the project context and into the product context at the same time; he carries a significant amount of implicit knowledge. This person carries a tremendous responsibility and potentially is in a conflict situation (Fig. 5).

4.2.2 Advantages of the Team-Orientated and Agile Working Model

Clearly, the advantage of an agile team is its high level of effectiveness and efficiency. The shared tacit knowledge reduces the number of defects, as misinterpretations become immediately obvious thanks to permanent feedback and no defects are caused as a result; or, if they do occur, they are immediately identifiable and can be suitably addressed.

In a living agile organization the project team members who feel responsible for requirements engineering, including the product owner, receive continuous feedback from business and stakeholders. This is the ideal setup to ensure that business requirements are optimally met (effectiveness). The agile project team can develop, optimize and apply the process leading to high level of efficiency through this continuous learning process. Overall, this results in an individual and team-orientated increase in productivity and therefore a huge competitive advantage.

A further benefit is the avoidance of specialist roles. Generalist would be the wrong expression, but employees in agile projects typically master a broader skill set than employees in companies organized according to roles. When we look at agility in this context, we may well wonder why to work in any other way. Well, this form of work organization also has some disadvantages.

4.2.3 Disadvantages of the Team-Orientated and Agile Working Model

One disadvantage of the extreme form of agile working is that the product typically dies when the project team has disbanded. The company must keep its teams "alive" to keep the product alive. The team carries the product and process knowledge to implement the next version of the product. If the team is disbanded, the knowledge is gone. No documentation except the system itself and its test harness exists to recreate knowledge from any information. A permanent investment needs to be made in the team in form of highlighting vision, maintaining motivation and developing skills, so that social cohesion is maintained and the right skills are available.

The next important question is: What is a good combination of disciplines for a project employee to cope with? In general terms, this thoroughly real problem for a company is: How can I find this multi-disciplinary staff member in the market and how do I develop this person's skills? How do I assess performance? The agile type of employee is more difficult to "manage" and "develop" than a role restricted specialist.

A further disadvantage comes into play if a product does not need to be continuously developed; there is a "break" in development. Let's consider a major company with a large service platform, such as a bank or an insurance company, where several hundred applications provide the service platform. It will not be necessary to constantly work on all of these applications. In fact, only a subset the applications are under development in a given period of time. Additionally, the term "product" cannot be trivially defined for a complex service platform. The appropriate identification of the product portfolio and, aligned to incoming customer request, the derived optimal project portfolio to establish are complex and demanding responsibilities. Product and project portfolio management under these constraints of the organization are not trivial either the traditional or agile way.

There is an often listed risk that an organization with a completely agile structure would completely evade standardization because of local optimization and thinking "inside the project box", thus damaging the overall organization. Although I am unable to provide any evidence besides pointing to companies like Google and Amazon, in my experience, TRULY agile organizations subject themselves to voluntary very strict self-discipline. Organizations which appear to be agile, but operate in an extremely blinkered way lack the basic principle of transparency and consequently the culture of healthy self-discipline.

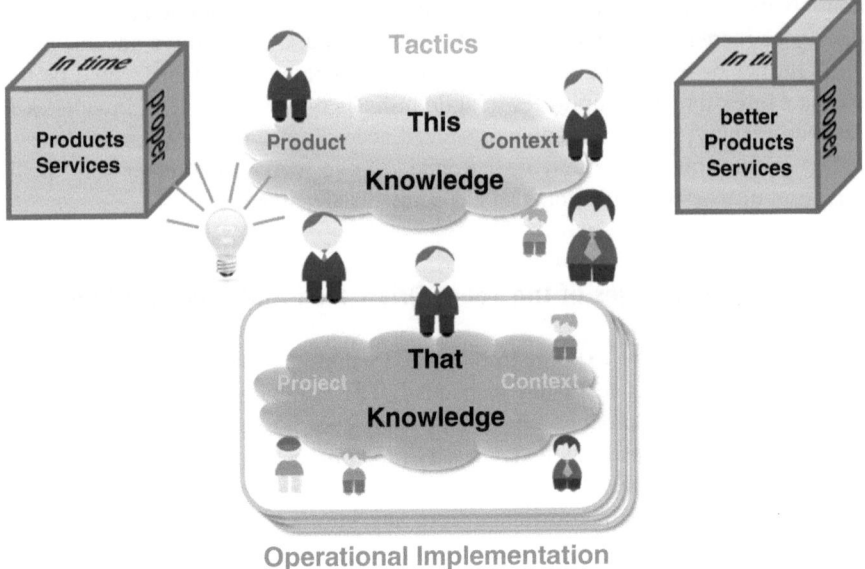

Fig. 6 Project and product portfolio management are two different context areas

5   Emerging Agile Principles on the Product Level

We now know a lot about fundamental concepts with regard to agility. We reflected these concepts on context level of the project and discovered that agility opens the door to efficiency and productivity. We also know that we have to care about the product portfolio context. Will agility improve efficiency and productivity on product portfolio context as well?

The ideal situation, as in agile projects, is that in the product portfolio context a constant team will work together continuously for most of the time is yet not given (Fig. 6).

The individuals working at this level do not typically work together continuously. The individuals on that level are involved in many different initiatives and processes. There daily life is a constant context switch. It is significantly more difficult to build up shared knowledge on that level. The amount of time communicating with peers each week is very limited. Building up a shared and tacit knowledge, closing knowledge gaps, constant collaboration, is significantly harder at the product portfolio level. This is a serious drawback; a change to more agile working methods is significantly harder.

Furthermore, the protagonists at the product portfolio level are typically unable to see any advantages in the agile working style – this is particularly the case for middle management. This is often due to the personal situation of middle management. Middle managers are under high pressure to perform, have to succeed with low budgets, of course there is a focus on the personal career and each day is driven by a high workload. Under such circumstances, any new working model is a risk. This will lead to an even higher workload combined with an incalculable risk for the managers own career. What is evident for any improvement program at this level is the protection of the top management.

It is important to recognize that some individuals, for example the product owner, are also simultaneously involved in both contextual levels. Of course this is the ideal way to align the knowledge in both teams. These individuals are, however, now in a conflicting situation if they need to work in different working styles in each context.

Even more serious is that a non-agile culture at product portfolio level can also effectively prevent agile working within the context of the projects, for example when certain requirements are not fulfilled or welcome, such as feedback from on-site customers.

In summary: Agile working at the product level – and therefore also requirements engineering at this level – is a challenge. Companies which success-fully work agile on product portfolio level and in definition of product roadmaps, heavily work with the concept of product visions. A vision is a future picture of a product which is easy to understand and remember, ideally visualized under inclusion of prototypes or samples. These visions are constantly revised and defined for a set of permanent moving milestones: the 3 months, 6 months, 1 year or 3 years milestone from today on. Visions are created with a substantial share in require-ments engineering. The typical stakeholders working on these visions are product owners, representatives from marketing, research, sponsors, customers, architects, customer services and others.

6   Summary and Conclusion

The article started with the statement that requirements engineering is only a tool used to create a product. By taking a detour to discuss knowledge work in the project, we saw that the agile form of requirements engineering deals primarily with the recognition and closure of knowledge gaps in product knowledge and process knowledge. The optimization of the specific process in each context is left to be dealt through the use of agile ideas. In summary, I would like to put forward four theses about requirements engineering:

First thesis: Agile requirements engineering does not exist in isolation. All
disciplines are equally agile or not agile, i.e. development, testing, architecture, simply everything.

Second thesis: If an organization or part of an organization is agile, this part will
work significantly more effectively and efficiently, so more productively, than working in a document-orientated, knowledge isolated way – as long as the framework conditions allow this, of course (thesis three).

Third thesis: The potential degree of agility depends on framework conditions,
on constraints and on the culture of the organization. This means, if certain framework conditions exist, that the advantages of agility can be overshadowed by the disadvantages.

Fourth thesis: There are two context levels of requirements engineering in organizations: the operative requirements engineering at project level and tactical requirements engineering at product level. The operative requirements engineering at a project level can always work in an agile way without it being compulsory for the product level to be agile. The organization must, however, act in an agile way at the project level if it also wants the product level to be agile.

The first and second thesis has become clear from our discussion so far. Agility means efficiency in knowledge work and this requires another working model which must involve all disciplines.

The third thesis is visible when reflecting the extreme cases in chapter "Investigations on Life Cycle Models" into reality. In order to be completely agile at all levels, operatively within the project, tactically at the product level and possibly even strategically, teams must work together constantly. They must work in a well-integrated way, which is both very disciplined and self-organized. Management must permanently invest in the teams, the collaboration between the teams and the topic of self-discipline. Self-discipline, in turn, is a feature of well-trained and motivated staff.

If we are – for example – in organizations where a specific product development is abandoned for a period of time longer than half a year, an agile approach has to deal with constraints. Without rules about additional measures like the creation of additional documentation on product level then the agile project would create on its own, a product which is not developed ongoing will die when the team is disbanded. To define and manage an "as lean as possible" product repository and information base represents an example for a state of the art measure. Real documents, models, source and testing code, handbook, risk profile, . . .; each organization defines, deriving from its business model, what will be part of the repository. Another important role of management must be to constantly maintain a comprehensive vision of the future on the product portfolio level and ensure that highly motivated teams are always in a state of self-renewal and consistently review every product. This is no easy task and might not be possible under certain circumstances or given a particular history. Successful companies master the permanent process of re-invention.

Only in rare cases existing major organizations (500, 1,000, more employees) successfully make the change to this working model and become completely agile when producing their products or services. The third and fourth of my theses are tightly bound to the existing culture and structure of organizations and their limiting framework conditions which determine whether an agile approach is possible on all context level in the organization and whether it will lead to success. My personal experience places the following limiting framework conditions on the top of the list:

- Specification of top-down targets with no creation of vision and buy-in from peers, i.e. a classic top-down strategy process with no integration of customers or even middle management and knowledge carriers within the company itself.
- The creation of knowledge work with the fundamental misinterpretations that knowledge work can be managed with the factory image of production as general principle, which may happen and based on – fundamental misinterpreted – style of standardization and specialization.

- Inflexible and annual budgeting. I recognized that many missed chances and shadow projects on account of this.
- Knowledge at a tactical level is completely separate from knowledge at an operative level in organizational and personnel terms – the much-discussed gap between business and IT.
- The customer (including an internal one) is an external stakeholder which is only involved at selective times.
- An organization which, for unhealthy corporate policy reasons, changes too quickly and constantly, involving a replacement of most valuable knowledge carriers.
- Middle management is under high pressure, created by the organization and career driven self-caused. Any improvement engagement is just dead if seen as no personal value but additional risk to surpass expectations.

Agile working also requires, to a large extent, the organization's orientation according to agile principles. The idea of having a pool of specialists in resourcing, a pool of requirements engineers, architects, testers, etc. conflicts with agile working. The work force within the company must be structured, trained and allocated to the skills needed in projects and processes. Projects must be tailored and established in different ways. This is a significant change for traditional companies. This is demanding for management and human resources.

In this article two extremes are discussed: the completely document-orientated, inefficient yet secure and standardized – almost "factory-like" working model – on the one side and the completely agile, highly efficient working model of collaboration on the other side. Any person who has a good understanding of human nature can recognize that extremes in their purest form are often unhealthy. Extremes often fail in real life. Real-life sustainable and successful constructs are located somewhere in the middle. When we talk about requirements engineering, the task of the management is to position itself and the organism of its organization consciously between these two extremes (see Fig. 7). Their task is to decide how their company will work at the operative project level and at the tactical product level.

As a representative, manager or employee of a company, have you ever asked yourself WHERE your company stands between the two extremes? Take a few moments at this point to think about where you personally would position the company which you manage or where you work. Have you ever asked yourself WHY your company is in this position? Is this chance, strategy, corporate culture or a boss simply stating "this is how it is"? What are the reasons? And above all, this: In your company, is the culture identical everywhere or does a different position need to be taken between the two extremes in each area of the company?

Personally, I do not know any complex organization with history which has completed the transfer to an agile working style, i.e. has achieved agile requirements engineering at all levels and in all areas. In my personal opinion, this is not even the aim. The aim of an organization should be to look at every area of the company to assess whether the agile working model is appropriate and

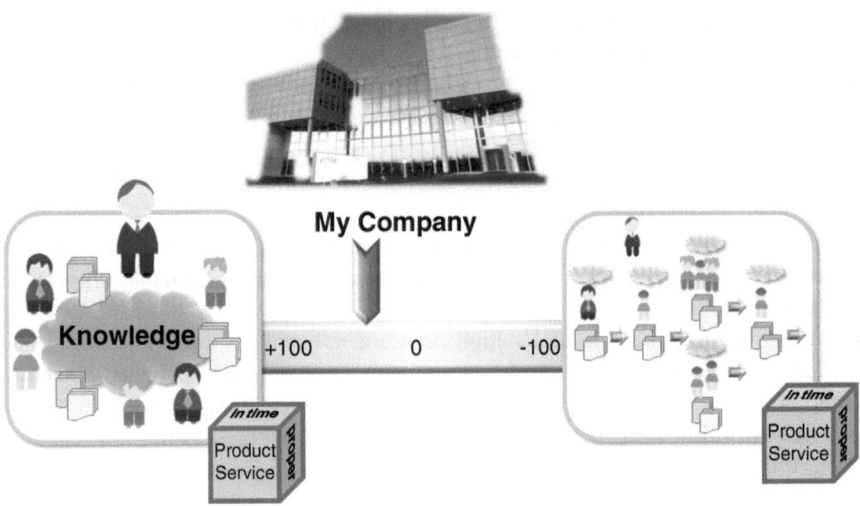

Fig. 7 Place your organization appropriately between the extremes

whether it will increase efficiency and productivity. The goal must be to achieve more efficiency with at least the same degree of effectiveness. Reaching a certain level of agility is easily possible in many areas of organizations. That would be a significant step towards efficiency and effectiveness. In business terms – for top management, the benefits are "time 2 market" and "flexibility", i.e. the RIGHT product at the RIGHT time. The way to get there, as I suggested, is typically a bottom-up approach. The reason is that agile work on an operative level is significantly easier and possible in most organizations and the consequences are much smaller in the event of failure than if initiated at a tactical level.

The discussion in this article demonstrates that an agile method of working can be an efficiency booster. This efficiency booster can be effective on two closely interweaved contextual levels within an organization, tactically at the product level and operatively at the project level. In minimum this should always be possible at the project level. Every organization should aim for this. At the product level, the framework conditions and constraints of the organization have a significant influence on whether investment in agility will achieve a competitive advantage. A bottom-up approach, ideal under the protection of top management, enables at least a review of these framework conditions. It is important to recognize that there will be no agile requirements engineer in the sense of a traditional requirements engineer, i.e. a specialist who (only) takes on the role of a requirements engineer. Instead, requirements engineering is one of many disciplines which an employee needs to master, along with others such as architecture, testing and writing the handbook. Bearing this in mind we can finally conclude, that yes, agile requirements engineering does exist – and no, there is no such thing as an agile requirements engineer. The future demands and requires the multi-disciplinary employees who are able to work in an agile way and master requirements.

References

Dirbach, J., Flückiger, M., & Lentz, S. (2011). *Software entwickeln mit Verstand*. Dpunkt: Verlag GmbH.
Polanyi, M., & Sen, A. (2009). *The tacit dimension*. Chicago: University of Chicago Press.
Poppendieck, M., & Poppendieck, T. (2003). *Lean software development: An agile toolkit*. Boston: Addison-Wesley Professional.

Design Thinking: An Innovative Concept for Developing User-Centered Software

Anja Wölbling, Kira Krämer, Clemens N. Buss, Katrin Dribbisch, Peter LoBue, and Abraham Taherivand

Abstract

In times of economic crisis and rapid technological change, innovation is necessary for competitive advantage and successful business. Design processes and tools are one way to create innovative solutions. This article describes the emergence of design thinking in business and focuses on the four key elements of design thinking in detail: the iterative process, multidisciplinary teams, creative space and designer's mindset. The limitations and potentials of design thinking are also discussed. While design thinking enables creativity, enhances personal development, and prescribes deep immersion into the topic along with empathetic user research, it does not include a business model or blueprint for the implementation. Still, design thinking is a large step toward identifying user-centered solutions. The software industry can benefit from the powerful approach in order to create innovative software products.

1 Emergence of Design Thinking

1.1 Innovation in Today's World

In recent years, innovation has become a buzz-word that has spread into various areas of politics and business. It is used extensively in entrepreneurship, business consulting, at conferences, in university lectures and management literature.

The first two authors were the main contributors. The other four contributed equally.

A. Wölbling • K. Krämer • C.N. Buss • K. Dribbisch • A. Taherivand
Entrepreneur, Germany
e-mail: anja.woelbling@googlemail.com; kira.kraemer@gmx.de; cebuzz@gmail.com; katrin.dribbisch@googlemail.com; info@taherivand.com

P. LoBue
NTT DATA Americas, Philadelphia, PA, USA
e-mail: pejalo@gmail.com

A. Maedche et al. (eds.), *Software for People*, Management for Professionals,
DOI 10.1007/978-3-642-31371-4_7, © Springer-Verlag Berlin Heidelberg 2012

Innovation is considered key to unlocking the answers to the economic and social problems of the twenty-first century. It is only through constant innovation that an organization can survive in the long run, regardless of its size. Companies that do not develop the skills to generate innovative products and also innovate their internal processes will inevitably fail to compete in their industry (Vahs and Burmester 2005). But how exactly can organizations become more innovative?

It has been widely acknowledged that employees will only come up with break-through ideas in the right organizational environment with a corporate culture that encourages creativity. Yet even those companies that do have innovation-friendly processes and structures in place often fail to generate innovative ideas (Von Stamm 2003). There seems to be something more to good ideas than just the right culture. There must be tools and methods that enable some organizations to create many innovative ideas while others appear to remain stuck.

Why is innovation so difficult to achieve? First, it is hard to change an organization's internal structure and procedures. Innovation means change: creation of the new and letting go of the old. In daily business routines, there is little room for such reform. Without leadership or a role model for innovation, it is hard to bring about the necessary change and establish an innovation-friendly culture in any organization. Second, innovation cannot be forced upon an organization. An underlying openness toward unexpected events and results is needed in order to create something radically new. This uncertainty threatens most businesses' principles that naturally favor an adherence to tradition and the status quo. Third, innovation is often associated with creativity, and the notion that only artists can be creative keeps people from realizing their own creativity. And fourth, businesses often mistake technological novelty or economic profit for innovation. While innovative products or services need to be both technically feasible and economically viable, they must also satisfy user needs. Innovation is about creating meaningful and relevant solutions to human problems.

1.2   Thinking like Designers

Apart from creating an innovative organizational culture, organizations need to know how to proceed: how to fully understand a problem and then solve it by creating something relevant for their customers, or users. The "designer's way of thinking" has been identified as a fruitful approach to user-centered innovation (Dunne and Martin 2006). The designer's role is to identify an existing need, generate ideas that cater to that need, and then prototype and refine the ideas so that they can later be converted into products and services. Creativity and unconventional thinking are characteristics associated with designers and also considered key to innovation.

As far back as the 1950s, designers identified the user as the key element of their processes (Hestad 2009). They acknowledged that users provided valuable insights and that focusing on the users enabled them to come up with more relevant products. In the late 1960s a new definition of design emerged, namely as an activity "aimed at changing existing situations into preferred ones" (Simon 1969, pp. 55–56). This extended far beyond the roles commonly assigned to professional designers. In the following decades the idea spread that design might be of tremendous importance to organizations' never-ending search for sustainable competitive advantage (Kotler and Rath 1984). From the designer's way of thinking (Dunne and Martin 2006), the concept of design thinking emerged and gained more prominence as an approach whose application might be valuable in other fields (Kimbell 2009). Schools of business, education, law and medicine have begun to concern themselves with processes of design.

Business managers are now not only considering the design of products, but also the design of the business itself (Martin 2004, 2009). In The Art of Innovation (2001) Tom Kelley, general manager of the design and innovation consultancy IDEO, provided deep insights into the application of design thinking to business practices, which has fueled the interest in design thinking in the business sphere (Bell 2008). As industry markets turn from supply-driven to demand-driven, the importance of providing meaningful products increases dramatically. The focus has expanded from asking what people need in a product to why they need it (Verganti 2009). Design thinking promises to deliver some of these answers.

Business managers are traditionally taught to choose the best course of action from an existing set of alternatives. On the contrary, designers never assume that the right solution is already available (Boland and Collopy 2004). They seek to create entirely new alternatives by realizing opportunities that were previously unthinkable. They face the challenge of conceiving and planning something that does not exist yet, even in the context of the vagueness and uncertainty of wicked problems (Buchanan 1992). Wicked problems can be described as a "class of social system problems which are ill-formulated, where the information is confusing, where there are many clients and decision makers with conflicting values, and where the ramifications in the whole system are thoroughly confusing" (Churchman 1967, pp. 141–142).

Often the true problem, also referred to as the latent need or the key insight, is deeply hidden within a complex system. Designers allow themselves to become immersed in this system, to become inspired by exploration in search of the true problem. Businesses, on the other hand, are quick to assume that they already understand the problem and the needs of their customers. Unsurprisingly, many solutions fail because they are designed for the wrong problem. In order to create meaningful products and services, it is necessary to search for hidden insights and to shed light on a field of uncertainty that includes incomplete or confusing information or differing interests of various stakeholders. This lies in stark contrast to the linear approaches and need for certainty desired by businesses. By nature of their definitions, creativity and innovation cannot be planned in detail. However one can still increase the chances of producing innovative ideas. Design thinking as an innovation method incorporates this uncertainty while at the same time offering a grounded process to follow.

1.3   Design Thinking Elements

The term design itself can be understood and interpreted very differently. In the context of design thinking, design can include any "creative and innovative activity" (Verganti 2009, p. 20). Based on this broad definition, design thinking may be simply described as an enabler for the creation of innovative ideas. Design thinking as it is presented here is about user-centered innovation with a focus on desirability. It revolves around the human needs of those who are using a product or a service or the underlying infrastructure (Brown and Wyatt 2010).

Design thinking is a framework that allows people to collaboratively engage in the creative and playful processes of problem solving and out-of-the-box thinking commonly used by designers. It thus makes use of the design process, which is perhaps best conceived as a "system of overlapping spaces rather than a sequence of orderly steps" (Brown and Wyatt 2010, p. 33). Two additional elements that support the process are multidisciplinary teams and creative working spaces. The combination of these three allows a fourth, overarching element to arise: the design thinking mindset. All four elements are described in detail below.

The user plays a crucial role in design thinking and is integrated into the process at various points. There are two general approaches to integrating users into design processes: the expert mindset and the participatory mindset (Sanders 2006, 2008). In an expert mindset users are interviewed and give feedback to ideas and prototypes developed by a design thinking team, or the experts. In this case, they are not part of the team and do not create the solutions themselves. In the participatory mindset users are seen as partners in the design process. They take on the role of active co-creators. Obviously, the choice of either approach, expert or participatory, heavily influences the design process. The description of design thinking presented here focuses on the expert mindset.

The various components and methods of design thinking have existed for generations. The value of design thinking lies in combining these parts to create a new, more generalized and accessible process and mindset. Design thinking also remains open for countless other methods and approaches, including other tools to be used directly within its framework, whose discussion extends far beyond the scope of this article.

2   Design Thinking

2.1   Iterative Process

Design thinking consists of various interdependent elements. At the core is the design thinking process. For simplicity the process follows consecutive phases, however they must be regarded as iterative and interconnected, allowing the design thinker to jump back and forth whenever necessary. There are many variations of design processes that use different terminology. Figure 1 illustrates the phases of the design thinking process described below.

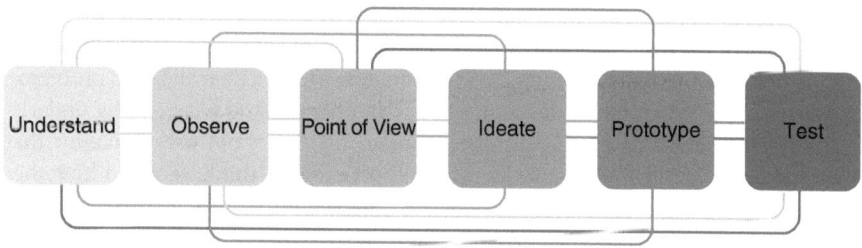

Fig. 1 Design thinking process (terminology adopted from the Stanford d.school)

2.1.1   Understand

The design thinking process always starts with an initial definition of the problem, also known as a design brief, which gives a broad outline of the subject matter. The first two phases of the process are committed to fully understanding the problem and possibly identifying a deeper root cause of that problem, described above as the true problem. Solution finding is intentionally reserved for the second half of the process. No judgment should take place during this initial phase of exploration and inspiration. In order to understand the problem, it is necessary to first become an expert on the topic.

Here, *understand* means to familiarize oneself with the topic, identify the main stakeholders, and define the context of the challenge or problem. The goal is to gain a deep understanding as quickly as possible. To do this, team members can create a plan to perform research individually and then reconvene and share insights. Desk research refers to reviewing literature, performing online searches, and other forms of information gathering. Looking for analogies in other fields or contexts can also reveal new insights (Rowe 1987). Collecting unanswered questions will be helpful in the next phase of the process. Any initial ideas that emerge to solve the problem during this phase should be written down and set aside to refer to later, if still relevant.

Experimenting directly with related products and services is essential to developing an initial perspective of the problem's context. Through testing out attempted solutions one begins to empathize with the users' pains and gains.

2.1.2   Observe

No clear boundary exists between the first and second phase of design thinking, and often they are combined. This *observation* phase is about understanding and empathizing with the user, which is the key to creating desirable products and services. There are a multitude of user research methods available.

Quantitative surveys, like street surveys and online surveys, allow researchers to interview large groups of people and collect standardized data. The data can be compared to analyze answers to given questions, like the ones collected in the previous phase. Contrarily, qualitative interviews with open-ended questions expand the breadth of possible insights. They lead to a better understanding of users' needs, preferences, thoughts, and routines regarding the future product or service. Users are encouraged to express themselves openly in the hopes of revealing deeper, unanticipated insights, leading the team to discover the true problem.

Observing people in their daily routines is another method of revealing underlying needs. Observation provides more detailed insights about user behavior than one might gain by just talking to them. What people say, think, feel and how they behave are often not as closely aligned as one would expect. One should also consider non-users who resist using a product or service (Beckman and Barry 2007), extreme users who are extremely excited about a product or service (Brown 2009), as well as stakeholders who are indirectly affected by the product, service or situation.

It is important to document research properly during these initial phases, because the insights gained will be the basis for the problem solving phase that follows. When talking to users, it is useful to collect pictures, artifacts and quotes in addition to taking notes. All insights should be shared with the rest of the team using storytelling techniques. Storytelling is a narrative method by which explicit and tacit knowledge is conveyed through verbal and non-verbal communication. A team member will take on the role of someone he or she interviewed to relay the key insights discovered during an interview. Role-playing is a helpful method of communicating empathy.

Research results that have been visualized will inspire team members and keep them focused during the next phases of the design thinking process. Once everything has been shared the team needs to synthesize all the information, notes, pictures, and stories.

2.1.3 Point of View

Team members may be overwhelmed by the magnitude of information gained during the research phases. However, patterns or themes in the gathered information emerge naturally and should be visualized by clustering the information. It is important to frame a shared perspective that will guide the team through the following phases. By condensing the information from the research phase into a clear definition, the team develops a *point of view*. A good point of view captures the essence of many of the observations made during the research phase. It should answer the questions: What problem must be solved, and for whom? There are various types of point of views and methods of forming them, and more than one point of view can be created.

A one-sentence point of view condenses research results into three general components: the user, the need, and the insight gained, and merges them into a one-sentence summary. For example: Marisa, an ambitious young business woman (user), loves to relax at her favorite coffee shop in the morning (need), because it is the only time of day she has all to herself (insight).

Along the same idea, but much more comprehensive, personas are collections of gained information and insights from all those observed and interviewed. A persona is fictional because it does not exist as a real person, yet it comes to life as a fusion of many people to represent an archetypical user. Compared to a more general description of a target group that might include an estimated age range and a few very high-level characteristics, a persona is given a name, age, hobbies, interests, dislikes, and even memories and dreams. These details allow the team to empathize. The persona can serve as a reference point when making decisions regarding the solutions and features developed during the next phases of the design thinking process.

Other frameworks can also be helpful to synthesize the information gathered during the research phase. User scenarios or storyboards illustrate stories with a specific setting and actors that can be used to describe a user's routine involving a specific product or service (Cooper 1999). User journeys and maps help illustrate the points of interaction between the user and a service or product, as well as show the process it takes to acquire, use, store, re-use, and dispose of a product or leave a service. Venn diagrams and two-by-two matrices help visualize key challenges by showing the relationships between multiple associated factors (Beckman and Barry 2007).

2.1.4   Ideate

The point of view acts as a reference point for the second half of the design thinking process. It can be formed into a brainstorming question, such as "How might we take aspects of Marisa's morning coffee shop experience to help her relax more throughout the day?" The question helps the team generate user-centered ideas. It can also help to think up new metaphors or visual descriptions to inspire the team.

Brainstorming requires a certain attitude and atmosphere that is accomplished by following some basic guidelines. Everyone must be able to voice their opinion and suggest ideas without being criticized or judged (Ambrose and Harris 2010). The evaluation of ideas is initially deferred in preference of coming up with as many as possible. It is not important at this point whether the ideas are realistic or feasible, because by encouraging wild ideas the solution space grows rapidly. It is easier to tone down a wild idea than to make a realistic one more radical. Allowing crazy ideas inspires everyone to think beyond the obvious. Building on the ideas of others is very much encouraged and generates ideas within ideas that can end up in a completely unanticipated context. Using visual illustrations supports the inspirational atmosphere. Additionally, as many sessions should be held as necessary until the whole team feels confident that some potential solutions exist among the suggestions. It can help to bring in external people during this phase who offer new perspectives and can contribute with a clear mind.

After generating many ideas the team must cluster them. The method used to choose from the pool of generated ideas depends on the priorities of the project and the scope of the original design problem. One way to filter ideas is to consider the viability of implementation: Can or should the idea be realized work in the next week, year or five years? Another possibility is to judge an idea according to its value for the user: What is the most relevant solution to the problem of the user? An idea might be evaluated according to the degree of risk involved with implementing it. It is important that the team reaches a joint decision. Ideas that are neglected in this phase are not necessarily lost, as all ideas are documented and can be recycled at a later point in the process.

2.1.5 Prototype

Even if the team agrees on one idea (or a combination of multiple ideas) from the ideation phase, not everyone in the group may have the same understanding of the idea at this point. An almost overwhelming number of questions begin to arise: How will the product or service work? How comfortable does it need to be? What will it look like? It is therefore necessary to find a common language and method of answering those questions. *Prototyping* helps by making an idea tangible.

A prototype can be described as "any representation of a design idea, regardless of medium" (Houde and Hill 1997, p. 369). Rather than representing the whole idea, prototypes can be designed to represent one's thoughts on a specific aspect of it. They are an important means of communication in order to collaborate, exchange information, and interact with clients, users, fellow designers and stakeholders. Prototypes help "define an idea's role, implementation, and look and feel" and create empathy for users (Dow et al. 2009, p. 165).

Prototyping can also be described as the act of thinking with one's hands in order to solve a problem (Kelley and Littman 2001). In design thinking, rapid prototyping is used to quickly create cheap abstractions that help test an idea as early as possible in order to receive valuable feedback. This keeps team members from discussing superfluous details about the prototype that are not relevant at this phase of the process. Any available materials can be used to build physical prototypes, from Lego, paper and modeling clay to fabric, furniture and office supplies. However, prototypes do not necessarily have to be physical objects. Role-playing, videos and storyboards can also work as prototypes as long as they communicate some aspect of the idea.

Different kinds of prototypes can serve divergent purposes. Those intended to work like the future service or product focus on the functionality. Prototypes meant to feel like the envisioned product or service emphasize the user experience with it. Those that should look like it are concerned with outer appearances. During the process, prototypes must be refined, changed and improved. A team may also want to create prototypes for multiple ideas to explore alternatives. Parallel prototyping uncovers new opportunities and constraints and result in more diverse solutions (Dow et al. 2010).

2.1.6 Test

As mentioned, the purpose of prototypes is to gain feedback from potential users on the team's ideas. Testers should resemble the user group for which the solution is intended. The obtained feedback needs to be interpreted with care, because not all feedback is useful. Seemingly poignant comments can distract the team from the original problem. It is important however to defer judgment toward feedback as it is coming in.

One method to gather information in usability testing is the think-aloud protocol. Participants think out loud as they perform a set of specified tasks while interacting with the prototype, expressing their thoughts, asking questions, and verbalizing what they are doing, seeing and feeling. Again, just like in the observe phase, it is important to remember that what a user says and actually feels and thinks are often not the same.

A useful tool to organize feedback when testing prototypes is the validation grid. The validation grid consists of four fields to capture users' comments on the prototype: positive aspects, negative aspects, new questions and new ideas. The grid helps determine how well users understand the idea and what questions are still unresolved.

After the testing sessions, the team must go back to the prototype phase to upgrade and make changes based on the gathered user feedback. During testing, the team might realize that they focused on the wrong idea or that they even addressed the wrong problem or overlooked an essential aspect during research. This is the point when the team can take advantage of design thinking's iterative nature, to go back to the phase where things were missed and gain a deeper understanding.

2.2   Multidisciplinary Teams

Design thinking relies on radical collaboration. Every team member contributes a unique thinking and working style. This promotes a diversity of thought and provides multiple perspectives on the given problem (Garcia 2008). Working in a small team, consisting of four to six people with diverse backgrounds, expertise and experiences can foster team discussions and create a broader range of ideas and solutions than a team of people with similar expertise. A homogeneous team is more likely to view a problem only from one perspective. The complexity of reality can only be captured through the synthesis of varying perspectives.

Multidisciplinary teams require higher levels of communication skills and coordination. Team members with different backgrounds need to learn how to express their views and communicate their knowledge in a way that other team members will understand (Adams et al. 2011). A high degree of empathy is also required. Intense communication is therefore a core aspect of design thinking culture. Communication skills and empathy are also needed to interact with users in any phase of the process (Owen 2006).

Having multiple teams work on the same challenge simultaneously increases variations and possible outcomes. Competition fuels creativity. Sharing status reports and presentations among the teams motivates the exchange of thoughts, inspiration and critical discussion. Coordinating additional teams obviously requires much more effort.

2.3   Creative Space

The space in which design thinking takes place is an integral part of creating an innovation-friendly atmosphere. Surroundings should be creatively inspiring, engage the team members, encourage the exchange of thoughts and ideas, and foster a playful atmosphere where everyone feels comfortable and free to express themselves.

To enable these characteristics one must consider the infrastructure, facilities and furnishing of the environment. Typical office interiors stifle creativity, but they can be re-designed. One can start with a designated space for design thinking activities. Setting up areas that support informal conversations separate from team working spaces will allow team members to regularly breathe and acquire new inspiration. A flexible environment facilitates inventive thinking and promotes creativity. Freely movable furniture allows teams to create their own space according to what they need in any particular situation. Not only can the pieces of furniture be used, but all surfaces offer a usable area for making thoughts and ideas visible.

An additional consideration is the physical stance of team members. Standing while working encourages a positive and more active workflow. When people receive visual signs that their team members are working they are more encouraged to participate themselves (Doorley et al. 2012). The possibility to move around while working creates a participatory and social atmosphere and prevents team members from loosing motivation. Physical activity can be enhanced through warm-ups, or quick games that cause team members to move, play, laugh and gain energy. A flexible and inspiring space supports the creative culture and atmosphere of an organization by strongly influencing the people who work in it.

2.4   Collaborative Mindset

The process is the core element of design thinking that provides direction. Supported by a multidisciplinary team setup and an inspiring, flexible space, a certain creative atmosphere is formed that captivates participants. Through practice in this environment the most valuable element of design thinking emerges: the *mindset* of a design thinker.

The mindset includes of a set of tacit knowledge on how to collaborate successfully. By going through the process one becomes mindful of where the team stands and what they should be focusing on. Through active engagement and contribution to the team one develops a bias toward action rather than over-planning and thinking about what to do. The user-centered approach builds empathy skills and the ability to immerse oneself in a new environment. Visualizing thoughts and ideas contributes to the ability to communicate effectively and form a common language with others. The act of prototyping results in creative confidence, skills to build with one's hands and awareness to take full advantage of one's surroundings. Practicing design thinking is even said to increase enthusiasm and optimism (Owen 2007).

Another sentiment of design thinkers is the ability to recognize the value of failure during projects. Failing early and often allows one to learn quickly by understanding why certain paths are unfeasible. Every failure is seen as a chance to learn and to improve. To fail during the process takes on new meaning: to recognize a potential problem that was previously overlooked, to discover new opportunities and to dismiss ideas that could have wasted valuable time.

The above competencies enable a new attitude toward problem solving that is inseparable from everyday life. The design thinking mindset helps establish an atmosphere that naturally enables creative collaboration. Of course, a certain working attitude is required for collaboration to begin with. When teaching design thinking it is helpful to include team coaches or moderators who have already achieved the mindset to guide them through the process and mitigate team conflicts.

In summary, design thinking takes a problem solving approach to identifying and satisfying user needs. It is a starting point to create meaningful products and services with a focus on desirability. However, other factors, namely technical feasibility and business viability, are necessary for true innovation (Brown 2009).

3   Discussion on Applying Design Thinking

3.1   Implementing Ideas

Design thinking is a great approach to generating novel ideas. The ideas that come out of the process have been challenged, tested and communicated through prototypes. By the end they can seem deceivingly close to instigating real change. But in fact the road to realization is barely in sight. Even the most innovative idea does not make a business case on its own. Without the knowledge necessary to launch them into marketplace, ideas are relatively worthless.

Throughout the design thinking process, the aspects of technical feasibility and economic viability are set aside in favor of desirability. During brainstorming teams are encouraged to produce wild, even unrealistic ideas. This approach produces ideas that nobody has thought of before, ideas that might be the key to the next groundbreaking innovation. However, for an idea to have value, knowing that it will satisfy a user need is not enough. If an organization wants to assess the probability of the idea becoming a reality, it needs to integrate technical and economic factors into the process as the idea becomes refined.

The next challenges to consider are creating a business model that reflects the value created by the idea, as well as the revenue and cost mechanisms, marketing concept and resource strategy. A truly innovative idea often needs an innovative business model, for example to handle the high complexity resulting from the interconnectedness of many stakeholders. Obviously this requires a team or team members experienced in business model creation and deep organizational and strategic knowledge. Ground-breaking ideas that arise within an existing organization that are not consistent with their values, routines and overall strategy will be more difficult, if not impossible to implement. A spin-off that brings an idea into the market is a possible approach, but that in turn requires further expertise in start-up creation, financing and growth strategy.

Technological factors act as their own barriers to an idea's implementation. The creation, testing and refining of a product requires tight collaboration between departments like IT, product design and engineering. The production of a new product might depend on a special material or an innovative production process or technique that may need to be identified or even invented. Collaborations with new suppliers or researchers might become necessary as well as the involvement of relevant expertise in a new process. Without the knowledge of all relevant disciplines, the implementation of the product will inevitably fail along the way or deliver unsatisfying results.

3.2   Organizational Change

If an organization desires to work with design thinking in the long-run, rather than hiring design thinking consultants for a certain project or time period, it needs to carefully evaluate its existing structure. Organizations are traditionally structured in departments according to areas of expertise. For example, the marketing department will handle the marketing for all products across the organization. Likewise, there are software divisions, sales forces, design departments, and so on. This segregation often causes a problematic lack of exchange among departments.

A powerful form of organizational structure groups individuals into teams around products or projects rather than knowledge expertise. In a so-called product – or project-centered organization, people who are involved with the product or project tend to have higher self-identification with it and are thus more motivated. This obviously requires radical managerial effort and strong communication between the departments and individuals within an organization. Start-up ventures in the IT world are typically single-product businesses that deliver a specific service. Every employee works toward reaching the same goal. In these start-ups people use strong communication skills to work together intensively across disciplines.

In general, traditional and hierarchical structures may inhibit an organization's adoption of design thinking culture. In order to form teams for design thinking, departments, schedules and procedures need to be re-organized. The entire mindset might conflict with the existing organizational mindset, concerning the methods of communication, collaboration, processes, values, routines, level of openness and many more aspects. For example, an organization might be very risk-averse. Outcomes of the design thinking process are by nature highly uncertain, as innovation cannot be planned or managed in a predictable way. This can create a divide between people who recognize idea generation as an early investment to later be linked to monetary return, and those who refuse to finance a business activity without accurate sounding return-on-investment predictions.

Another obstacle to consider is the not-invented-here syndrome. It refers to a culture that rejects innovative solutions, products, standards and methods not developed within the organization, department or team. Caught up in their own expertise, employees lack the will to integrate solutions generated from outside perspectives. External design thinking consultants may bring new ideas into a company only to see them phased out after their project is finished. Prevalence of the not-invented-here syndrome between departments within the same company or institution can be equally detrimental. In these cases, information flow within an organization is blocked, hindering the exchange of ideas. Knowledge stays locked in people's minds instead of being shared. This is especially problematic when the implementation of an idea is not handled by the same group that developed it. The approach of mixed teams championed by design thinking is a good method to avoid counterproductive, self-centered thinking, yet it requires strengthening the ability to cooperate internally, as well as inter-departmental training and enhanced communication through constant effort.

In addition, organizations face the constant risk of their structures becoming too rigid, or their focus or expertise becoming too specific, thereby overlooking important opportunities for innovation. These organizations might be shocked by the disruptions by innovators who approach a market very differently. These innovators often disregard well-established standards recognized by the players in a market, possibly causing drastic alterations to the rules, products, methods or entire market.

A good example is the often-cited case of Apple's iPhone. Breaking paradigms, such as the notion that a smartphone must have a keyboard, was a large part of the iPhone's success. The decision symbolized the point of view that a smartphone is more than just a telephone. It became a device that runs software, of which telephony is just one piece. In hindsight perhaps it is not so surprising that a company that builds its own software and hardware was able to envision combining them on a handheld device.

3.3   Leadership

Even if design thinking is accepted and incorporated into an organization, it cannot sustain on its own without constant leadership effort, reconsideration of market situations and continuous refocus on ever-changing customer preferences. Constant attention is needed to maintain an innovation-friendly environment. Initial inspiration may fade when design thinking projects that are unsuccessful or not realized result in demotivation or frustration. The leading figures of an organization must be truly dedicated to this approach of working and need to actively encourage it.

Companies like Deutsche Bank and SAP successfully work with design thinking by creating internal design thinking teams or realizing design thinking projects with external consultants. For example, the mission of the Design Services Team at SAP is to continuously challenge internal developments in the company and to provide other departments with insights from users (Holloway 2009).

Leaders must be aware of the constant efforts needed to keep a business open to new ideas from inside and outside. Whether design thinking is implemented and executed by external consultancies or brought into a team from within the organization, leadership is needed to overcome skepticism as well as structural and communication barriers.

4   Design Thinking in Software Development

As described above, design thinking focuses on what is desirable by users in order to create relevant products and services. This distinguishes the approach from common software development methods where technical feasibility is given priority. Aspects of design thinking can be applied to software development to help understand the needs of users for whom the software is being designed.

To understand the potential that design thinking may have for software development one must first consider the conventional methods of operation. For example, the waterfall model of software development is relatively inflexible. Users are generally not actively involved in the development process; rather they are brought in at the end to provide feedback. There is little consideration for the user's needs or preferences during most stages. Team members working with this approach tend to have similar academic or professional backgrounds, sharing a technologically-oriented mindset further encouraged by their organizational structure.

In the 1990s, agile development methods like scrum and extreme programming evolved out of traditional methods. These processes strive to be leaner and more flexible. By progressing in shorter, iterative steps, users are much more involved, for instance to provide feedback early on. This active user participation demands strengthened communication between team members and a more collaborative atmosphere. Agile methods have much more in common with design thinking than traditional ones. However, agile development methods focus on incremental improvements, while design thinking explores entirely new solutions. And although collaboration is enhanced, team members generally still come from the same technical discipline, thereby only realizing a single homogeneous perspective.

Some components of design thinking may contribute to a better working atmosphere for software developers and potentially result in more innovative software products. For example, the diversity of design thinking teams promotes out-of-the-box thinking and encourages creativity. While software developers obviously need programming skills to write code, teams could consider other aspects of the programmers' backgrounds that may provide diverse perspectives.

Adopting the attitude of solving for user needs is crucial for the future of software development. Through empathetic research, like in the initial phases of design thinking, user needs are discovered, along with important insights for the subsequent stages of the development process. By integrating the user as early as possible, the likelihood of expensive succeeding adaptations is reduced. This is facilitated by clarifying visions of the intended future software product through rapidly and roughly developed prototypes. Fast iteration loops and a fail-early-and-often attitude help mitigate risk.

Design thinking can supplement traditional software development approaches by being implemented either at the beginning of a development process or as an overall culture for enabling user-centered innovation in software organizations (Lindberg et al. 2011). In order to achieve adoption, fundamental rethinking of development processes and cultural aspects is necessary.

The risk that design thinking will not be accepted is ubiquitous. Reluctance and fear are the natural enemies of the mindset's permanent openness to drastic change.

Even though design thinking may not be the Holy Grail to solve all problems, it approaches challenges through a compelling perspective that can be leveraged to help create more relevant and valuable software solutions.

5   Summary

Design thinking is a powerful approach to user-centered innovation. It makes use of the design process and methods to develop relevant products and services based on user needs. This article focused on the emergence of design thinking and gave an overview of the four key elements: the iterative process, multidisciplinary teams, creative space and designer's mindset. Together these elements form a distinctive context that enables creativity and increases the chances of generating innovative ideas. Through deep immersion into the topic and thorough empathetic user research, underlying needs are identified and catered to.

Implementation is not necessarily part of the design thinking process. While design thinking does not provide a business model to realize the generated ideas, it does explore the value proposition. Design thinking is just one step toward identifying meaningful solutions. They must then be evaluated based on their technical feasibility and economic viability at a later stage. Expert knowledge rather than creative thinking is required to develop a business model.

Design thinking offers a new mindset regarding innovation. It promotes learning within organizations and fosters an open-minded organizational culture that embraces failure as a learning opportunity. The approach is harder to implement in large corporate environments as it requires clear leadership commitment from top management.

Similar to agile processes, design thinking builds on fast iteration loops to incorporate user feedback throughout the entire process. Traditional software development team members have similar skill sets and approaches to their work, so there is potential to diversify teams and introduce new perspectives into the process, thereby encouraging creativity. Other aspects of the design thinking mindset such as creative confidence and prototyping skills can be applied to software development to produce more relevant and desired solutions.

References

Adams, R. S., Daly, S. R., Mann, L. M., & Dall'Alba, G. (2011). Being a professional: Three lenses into design thinking, acting, and being. *Design Studies, 32*(6), 588–607.

Ambrose, G., & Harris, P. (2010). *Design Thinking, Fragestellung, Recherche, Ideenfindung, Prototyping, Auswahl, Ausführung, Feedback*. München: Stiebner.

Beckman, S. L., & Barry, M. (2007). Innovation as a learning process: Embedding design thinking. *California Management Review, 50*(1), 25–56.

Bell, S. J. (2008). Design thinking. *American Libraries, 39*(1/2), 44–49.

Boland, R. J., Jr., & Collopy, F. (2004). Design matters for management. In R. J. Boland Jr. & F. Collopy (Eds.), *Managing as designing* (pp. 3–18). Stanford: Stanford University Press.

Brown, T. (2009). *Change by design: How design thinking transforms organizations and inspires innovation.* New York: Harper Collins.

Brown, T., & Wyatt, J. (2010). Design thinking for social innovation. *Stanford Social Innovation Review, 8*(1), 30–35.

Buchanan, R. (1992). Wicked problems in design thinking. *Design Issues, 8*(2), 5–21.

Churchman, C. W. (1967). Wicked problems. *Management Science, 4*(14), 141–142.

Cooper, A. (1999). *The inmates are running the asylum: Why high-tech products drive us crazy and how to restore the sanity.* Indianapolis: Sams.

Doorley, S., Witthoft, S., & Hasso Plattner Institute of Design at Stanford University. (2012). *Make space: How to set the stage for creative collaboration.* Hoboken: John Wiley & Sons.

Dow, S. P., Heddleston, K., & Klemmer, S. R. (2009). The efficacy of prototyping under time constraints. *Proceeding of the 7th ACM conference on creativity and cognition* (pp. 165–174). Berkeley: ACM.

Dow, S. P., Glassco, A., Kass, J., Schwarz, M., Schwartz, D. L., & Klemmer, S. R. (2010). Parallel prototyping leads to better design results, more divergence, and increased self-efficacy. *ACM Transactions on Computer-Human Interaction, 17*(4), 1–24.

Dunne, R., & Martin, R. (2006). Design thinking and how it will change management education: An interview and discussion. *The Academy of Management Learning and Education, 5*(4), 512–523.

Garcia, R. (2008). *Understanding the creative process: A systematic approach to effective project management* (2nd ed.). Madison: Ennovation Press.

Hestad, M. (2009). Changing assumption for the design process: New roles of the active end user. *FORMakademisk, 2*(2), 16–25.

Holloway, M. (2009). How tangible is your strategy? How design thinking can turn you strategy into reality. *Journal of Business Strategy, 30*(2/3), 50–56.

Houde, S., & Hill, C. (1997). What do prototypes prototype? In M. Helander, T. E. Landauer, & P. Prabhu (Eds.), *Handbook of human-computer interaction* (2nd ed., pp. 367–381). Amsterdam: Elsevier Science B. V.

Kelley, T., & Littman, J. (2001). *The art of innovation: Lessons in creativity from IDEO, America's leading design firm.* London: Crown Business.

Kimbell, L. (2009). Beyond design thinking: Design-as-practice and designs-in-practice. *CRESC conference* (pp. 1–15), Manchester, September.

Kotler, P., & Rath, A. (1984). Design: A powerful but neglected strategic tool. *Journal of Business Strategy, 5*(2), 16–21.

Lindberg, T., Meinel, C., & Wagner, R. (2011). Design thinking: A fruitful concept for IT development? In H. Plattner, C. Meinel, & L. Leifer (Eds.), *Design thinking – understand – improve – apply* (pp. 3–18). Berlin/Heidelberg: Springer.

Martin, R. L. (2004). The design of business. *Rotman Management, Winter,* 7–17

Martin, R. L. (2009). *The design of business. Why design thinking is the next competitive advantage.* Boston: Harvard Business Press.

Owen, C. L. (2006). Design thinking: Driving innovation. *The Business Process Management Institute,* September, 1–5.

Owen, C. L. (2007). Design thinking: Notes on its nature and use. *Design Research Quarterly, 2*(1), 16–27.

Rowe, P. (1987). *Design thinking.* Cambridge: MIT Press.

Sanders, E. B.-N. (2006). Design research in 2006. *Design Research Quarterly, 1*(1), 1–8.

Sanders, E. B.-N. (2008). On modeling: An evolving map of design practice and design research. *Interactions – Designing games: Why and How, 15*(6), 13–17.

Simon, H. A. (1969). *The sciences of the artificial.* Cambridge: MIT Press.

Vahs, D., & Burmester, R. (2005). *Innovationsmanagement. Von der Produktidee zur erfolgreichen Vermarktung.* Stuttgart: Schäffer & Poeschel.

Verganti, R. (2009). *Design-driven innovation: Changing the rules of competition by radically innovating what things mean.* Boston: Harvard Business Press.

Von Stamm, B. (2003). *Managing innovation, design and creativity.* London: John Wiley & Sons.

Part II

Best Practices

Best Practices for Successful Deployment of User Experience Design

Kostanija Petrovic

Abstract

The pervasive use of technology in everyday life, at work, at home and while on the go increases the demand for easy to use systems, irrespective of platform or domain. Many companies recognize the need for successful deployment of user experience design (UXD) but still struggle to bring it to life in their product development. Best practices for integrating UXD into product development can help companies enhance the customer value of their products and services. They help product teams to collaborate more effectively and focus more on actual user needs. A set of simple, hands-on best practices can help UXD teams deliver their services more efficiently, effectively and to the satisfaction of not only the users, but also the participating product teams.

1 The Importance of User Experience Design

Companies like Apple® and Braun® build their success on good user experience (UX) and product design. Their brands are associated with "design" and "innovation". Apple's success in consumer products, driven by user experience design (UXD), has raised user expectations in application development to an extent where a hard to use piece of software is considered a failure. Forrester Analyst Mike Gualtieri (2011) succinctly sums this up by stating, "if you get the user experience [of your product] wrong, nothing else matters". Now you might be thinking that Apple and Braun are in the consumer business so why should I care? Consider this: have you ever been part of a huge software implementation project that failed to be successfully embraced by its users? Poor user experience design is one of the biggest adoption obstacles when introducing new software to an organization

K. Petrovic
Nokia gate5 GmbH, Berlin, Germany
e-mail: kostanija.petrovic@nokia.com

A. Maedche et al. (eds.), *Software for People*, Management for Professionals,
DOI 10.1007/978-3-642-31371-4_8, © Springer-Verlag Berlin Heidelberg 2012

(Ragsdale 2004). Users expect simple effortless interaction no matter what the usage context is (Petrovic and Siegmann 2011). Despite the public attention that companies such as Apple receive, there is still little awareness in many companies, as well as the public, how this is actually achieved.

User experience (UX) is defined as *a person's perceptions and responses that result from the use or anticipated use of a product, system or service* (Law et al. 2009 see also ISO FDIS 9241-210 2009). The discipline of User Experience Design (UXD) is the application of User Centered Design (UCD) practices to generate consistent, predictable and desirable products and services based on the complete consideration of users' experiences. In short, UCD is the practice of creating and building products centered on the needs of real people (Gould and Lewis 1985; Karat 1997), while UXD is the discipline of creating these. As of today, UXD still remains the domain of experts. Ironically, in the past it was those experts who often faced a lack of appreciation and understanding when working with product teams. Although the activities and deliverables of UXD professionals have been perceived as useful, those efforts were often neither considered a substantial contribution to the product success, nor a priority.

Building products around user needs requires organizational change (Seffah and Metzker 2004). This chapter identifies aspects of organizational requirements (such as process, roles etc.) and also includes a set of everyday best practices for UXD that help to successfully apply UCD in the creation of new products and services. We have provided a list of practical activities that will help you do the right thing from a user point of view on an organizational, process and communication level. In the recommended approach, we are user centered for all our users, including those colleagues using our UXD deliverables.

2   Establishing User Experience Design

2.1   Bringing User Centered Design to Organizations

Business is not about user centered design. Business is about revenue, profit, customer satisfaction and market share (Rhodes 2009; Jokela 2000). As UX professionals we have to be cognizant of the value we bring to our organization and adapt our practice and communication to the needs of our organizational context. Below is a summary of UCD benefits (Kuniavsky 2003, for case studies see Bevan 2005):

- Decreased development cost through prioritizing features and functions based on user needs and key use cases
- Increased revenue and increased customer loyalty (Sauro and Lewis 2012) by better meeting customer and user needs, positive reviews and usability as a selling argument
- Reduced training effort means faster user adoption when introducing business software, low or no training cost when the software is self-explanatory
- Increased brand value with good usability as a key differentiator against the competition

How can you establish UXD in your company? According to Schaffer (2004) there are three essential success factors to the institutionalization of UXD in enterprises: *well-educated UX professionals* that follow *usability standards* and talk about their projects using *success stories that help illustrate the advantages of UCD*. When asked in a workshop (Anderson 2007) what holds UXD back in enterprises, the participants identified the lack of *executive support* and *sponsorship*, the need of a thorough *understanding of UXD roles and processes* as well as objectives of the respective organization in combination with an *inadequate measurement or sharing of user experience success*. The above emphasize an important and often undervalued part of best practices for UXD – communication, or using what Rhodes (2009) refers to as *selling,* usability and user experience design.

2.2   Part of the Process to Be Part of the Solution: The Development Process

All UXD related activities are useless if they are not part of the actual product development process. From a UXD standpoint, our goal is to build products that serve actual user needs by following UCD. This requires the integration of UCD methods into the development process in ways that fit the particular organizational and resourcing conditions of a company.

2.2.1   The Advantage of Agile Development and Why You Should Do a Sprint Zero

The introduction of agile product development methods such as user stories (Cohn 2007, 2009) have facilitated the refocusing on user needs when building a new product or service offering. It has also empowered UX professionals as the members of the project team with the best understanding of actual user needs (Blomkvist 2005).

The fast pace of agile development iterations has added substantial time pressure to deliver and the scheduling of activities has become much more challenging. The UX community has discussed the implications of agile product development on user centered design to a great extent (Sy and Miller 2008). There seems to be agreement that a so called "sprint zero" before actual development starts helps to define the core concepts and epic and user stories, and also to integrate user research activities. Jeff Patton (2008) summarizes agile best practices for UXD that basically follow these principles: UXD is part of the customer or product owner team; research and design begin before actual development starts; UCD activities keep pace with development; design ahead and validate as you go. For quick feedback use RITE (*Rapid Iterative Testing*) to iterate designs before development starts (Medlock et al. 2002). RITE requires quick access to end users, so establish a user panel to conduct continuous research during development. The use of a product backlog helps to document and track resulting requirements. The following Fig. 1 illustrates the relationship between UXD activities and agile development.

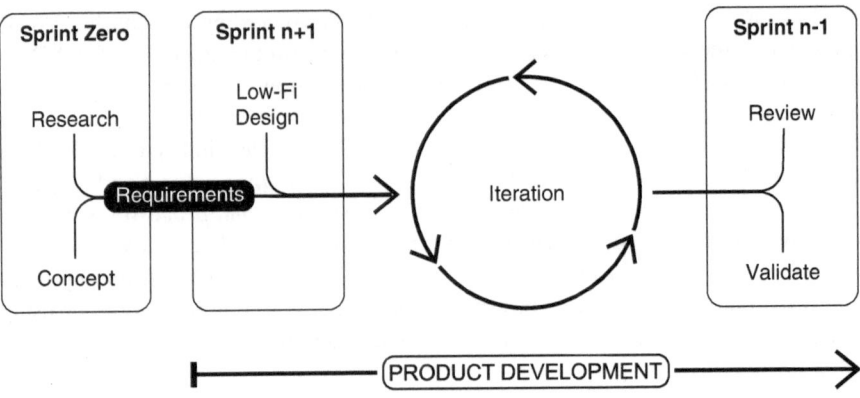

Fig. 1 UXD activities and agile development process

2.2.2   Select and Engage in the Right Project

Experience shows that most organizations do not have sufficient resources and people to cover all ongoing product development efforts. Since UX is a critical success factor for many products, UXD management has to choose its projects carefully, making sure that they put effort into the most important as well as most promising projects. Nieters (2007) gives practical advice on how to select such projects:

- Product team receptivity. The product team itself has requested support from UXD, rather than having it "pushed" upon them by management. If a product team is ambivalent, the UXD group disengages.
- Potential revenue or cost savings. The UXD group seeks projects on which they anticipate a substantial revenue increase.
- Advanced technology. A new technology that has not yet been introduced to the market is preferable, but not required, so the UXD Group can make a larger impact than on legacy products.
- Leveraging the User Experience (UX) Standards (UI guidelines and tools). If a product team does not intend to adopt the UX Standards, the UXD Group should not assign resources. These standards include component libraries to help engineers quickly create code that is accessible, usable, internationalized, and branded.
- High visibility. If a project is a "pet project" of a cross-functional or highly visible organization within the company, the UXD Group is more willing to accept it.
- Point in the product lifecycle. If design has already begun, it is often too late for the UX team to impact the product's overall experience at a fundamental level. There are times, however, when the UXD team agrees to work on a project through multiple iterations, starting late in one cycle, to impact a subsequent release.
- Realistic time-to-market demands. If project schedules make delivering a high-quality user experience impossible, the UXD group should be less likely to accept the project.

3   Putting It into Practice

So what should you do to help your company build products that serve the needs of actual people as opposed to feature monstrosities no one can use? In this section and the next we outline a set of project work and communication best practices that will help you build awareness of UCD in your organization.

3.1   How to Do It: Project Work Best Practices

Before the UXD team starts the actual project work, it should clarify expectations. Example deliverables from previous projects as well as a project brief help to establish a common ground for future collaborations with the project team. The project brief should cover project objectives, UCD activities, resources and budget. This is the basis for embedding the UCD activities into the overall product development plan. This preparation pays off during the life of the project, enabling the UX team to focus on driving the product delivery forward.

This is also a good opportunity to demonstrate the value of UCD by actively involving project team members in user research and design activities. Various surveys (Rosenbaum et al. 2000) of UX professionals show that this is one of the most successful selling activities for UXD.

While engaging in actual projects, it has proven useful to use a standardized toolkit. These materials should be not only used by the UXD teams, but also made available throughout the organization. At SAP's UX department, all process materials and templates have been published in the intranet to be available to everyone. In addition, regular training sessions give project team members the opportunity to get the baseline of UCD straight before starting the project itself. At Wells Fargo (Watson 2008), they kept real people and their stories at the center of product development by creating consumable and reusable UCD tools such as user profiles and user task models. Their UXD team also shared methods across the organization, allowing stakeholders to engage with these reusable UCD tools without recourse to the design team. Such toolkits also ensure that all results are delivered in a transparent and consistent fashion.

The following table (Table 1) maps selected project work best practices per project phase.

4   The UXD Communication Imperative

It's hard to be successful if no one knows about it (Rhodes 2009). Communicating UXD work and best practices is essential for the successful integration of UCD into the product development process. As part of the process definition and implementation activities, make sure you communicate (sell) the benefits of UCD with the people involved in building, marketing and selling your products: developers, product managers/product owners, marketing and sales.

Table 1 Overview of project work best practices by phase

Phase/Method	Deliverable	How to
Project planning	UX project brief	One page document
	Objectives	
	Activities and methods	
	People and roles	
	Resources and budget	
Sprint zero/contextual inquiry	User profile or persona	Method and participants
	Usage context	Personas and scenarios
	Task flow	Taskflow
	List of user requirements	User quotes
		Images of the user's environment
		Videos
		Example artifacts, e.g. documents users work with
Sprint zero/concept validation	Concept prototype	Method and participants
	Summary of findings including positive findings as well as issues	Videos illustrating feedback
	List of issues with frequency and severity rating	Annotated screenshots or annotated paper prototype images
	Recommendations for concept iteration	
Sprint n/usability test (e.g. Rapid Iterative Test)	Working prototype	Method and participants
	Summary of findings including positive findings as well as issues	Videos illustrating feedback
	List of issues with frequency and severity rating	Annotated screenshots
	Recommendations for iteration (for the product backlog)	Interaction flow diagrams, illustrating where the UX "breaks"
Sprint n/heuristic evaluation	List of issues with frequency and severity rating	Annotated screenshots
	Recommendations for iteration (for the product backlog)	Videos illustrating task flows
Project end/sanity check	Working prototype	Method and participants
	Summary of findings including positive findings as well as issues	Videos illustrating feedback
	List of issues with frequency and severity rating	Annotated screenshots
	Recommendations for the next version (for the product backlog)	Interaction flow diagrams, illustrating where the UX "breaks"

4.1   Getting the Most Value Out of Face to Face Communication

Just sending a report of user research findings is the best way to ensure no one will read it. When planning your projects, allow time for preparing a presentation and running presentation sessions. Be mindful that people are usually already booked for the next 2 weeks so plan some time ahead when setting up the presentation sessions. Be sensitive to your target audiences information needs and follow communication design best practices. You're basically sharing your findings with a lay audience, so avoid "UXD speech". If your findings are presented in a confusing, badly structured and hard to read document, you lose credibility. This loss of credibility applies both to the presented results as well as to you as a UX professional. It is also recommended to not give in to the temptation of "developer bashing". It does not help. Let developers know that you appreciate the work they do and also what users appreciate. This approach will increase the acceptance of your work results.

Make sure that you adjust your communication to your target audiences. The value of UCD differs from department to department. It is imperative that you know what to sell to each group.

4.1.1   Developers

Surprisingly, in the age of touchscreen computers and smartphones, there are still developers who think that good usability and a good product experience is a "question of personal taste" and that UXD "decorates the UI". And there is of course the dispute that everything related to UCD (process, methods, research, design) takes too long. Developers are the ones who are actually building the application. If they get it right, you have succeeded and your company will be offering more usable, more attractive, and more appealing products and services. The following are things to consider when selling UCD to developers:

- Better decision making. UCD makes it easier to make good product decisions when users and usage context are considered. The knowledge from UCD activities helps developers prioritize features and take the right architectural decisions ahead of time.
- First-hand knowledge. Include developers as observers when running usability tests. Make sure to run the tests in a professional and consistent fashion and following best practices (cf. Table 1). If developers can't observe a test, show highlight videos from a test so they can see first-hand how users interact with the application.
- Improved efficiency. UCD best practices such as re-usable user interface patterns and modular interfaces help to reduce overall development effort and also emphasize the importance of concept definition.

4.1.2 Product Manager/Product Owner

Depending on their background and prior experience, some product managers believe they already know everything there is to know about users and usage context as well as customer and end user needs. (Customer and end user needs might not always be the same, especially in business software). User research findings, such as usability test reports, help to validate correct assumptions and revisit wrong ones. All materials gained in user research activities can help market products better. The value of UCD to Product Management/Product Marketing includes:

- UCD identified user objectives align with the overall business objectives of the application.
- From the customer perspective: well designed applications reduce training cost, and total cost of ownership.
- From the internal business perspective: well designed applications can result in fewer support calls, and lower maintenance cost (maintenance fees being one of the major revenue drivers in business software).

4.1.3 Marketing

There is sometimes confusion between market research and user research. Frequent contact and enhanced communication between the UX team and the consumer intelligence departments help to clarify roles and also shows that combining insights leads to more valid findings. UX professionals can give detailed qualitative insights into the target user audience, describing it with deliverables such as personas, which can be also be used for campaign design and delivery. Things you should talk about with Marketing:

- Personas and scenarios for the target audiences (e.g. key market segments)
- Application sweet spots and how the enhanced designs provide value to users

4.1.4 Sales

Good UX is not only a convincing sales argument but, as recent developments show, good UX is a strategic key differentiator in the market. Engaging with customers in UCD activities is not only helpful for gaining insights. It shows the customers that their needs are recognized and appreciated, which helps build lasting customer relationships. Things you should focus on when communicating with Sales:

- Projected revenue expectations based on UXD driven feature improvements
- Customer needs and benefits: total cost of ownership, reduced training costs, better user adoption

4.2 Communication Best Practices

So, now we have finished our project. We have built good relationships throughout the organization and we have an application we are proud of. The only thing left to do is to let others know.

There is a wide variety of means available to UX professionals when communicating about their work. There are, for instance, newsletters and the earlier mentioned intranet pages. Project deliverables are also a good means of communication if they are well done and appropriate for the target audience. By now you probably have guessed that a full blown user research report is not for everyone, but an article summarizing the findings or well-designed poster are good alternatives. When reporting insights focus on the "why?" and "what for?" instead of the "how?." Save method discussions for an expert audience. When planning your communication strategy, consider:

- Audience – not everyone needs all the details.
- Language – use friendly, simple language. Ask a helpful copy writer to have a look before publishing.
- Communication design – consider principles like visual hierarchy, simplicity, proximity, contrast and legibility.
- Format – HTML newsletters don't display very well on mobile devices and no one reads long newsletters.
- Amount of information – be concise, tell a story. Real projects are the best success stories. Use a few strong visuals to emphasize information.

In the 2011 annual member survey of the German Usability Professionals Association (305 participants), 77 % of the participants said that communicating and explaining UX is the biggest challenge they face as UX professionals (Diefenbach and Ullrich 2011).

The German Usability Professionals Association e. V. (German UPA) is the biggest German speaking professional association for usability and user experience professionals with more than 1,000 members, mainly in Germany. The association offers usability and user experience professionals a network of like-minded people and gathers the community in the biggest German speaking conference in the field (Mensch und Computer/Usability Professionals).

The members of the German UPA In-house section, a group of in-house UX professionals, have run several conference workshops and subsequently surveyed workshop participants about communication best practices (Meurer et al. 2009). Table 2 summarizes the survey responses (13 participants):

Table 2 Overview of communication methods and related implementation efforts

Method	Example	Effort	To consider
Intranet page	Team page, get in touch, projects	Varies according to contents and complexity	The content depends on your team size, you have to keep the page up to date
	Process information, templates		
	Guidelines, styleguides, icon library, persona library		
Newsletter	Team newsletter	One to two person days	Newsletters should be short and sweet
	Section in internal newsletter		Focus on highlights from current projects
			Include links to further information
Piece in the in-house magazine	Success Story based on a recent project	One to two person days	Make sure you have defined your main communication objectives ahead of time
	Features about UCD, design thinking		
	Team profile		Include pointers to more information, such as links to your team page
Poster	Persona posters in projects	One person day	The poster should be self-explanatory
	Poster about UX maturity		
	"Living wall" about current projects		
Training, workshops	Workshops about UCD, accessibility, guidelines etc.	High	Avoid making the impression that UCD is something that does not require skilled personnel
		Covers the creation of training material, training set up and delivery, up to person weeks and months	
Internal talks	Brown-bag sessions during lunch time	Two to three person days	You can re-use the materials
	Internal world usability day events		
Networks	Formal networks for UX interested folks	Low	Networks are a good way to keep in touch with project and product team members, go across department boundaries, include marketing, consulting, sales
	Informal networks e.g. a UX round table		

5 Summary

Dan Rosenberg, SAP Senior Vice President User Experience, once famously stated that it takes an entire company to build a great user experience. Thus UX is not only the responsibility of those people with "UX" in their job title. We have seen that UX is a strategic differentiator that requires organizational change. Key success factors for implementing UCD in product development are professional conduct by the UX team, following standards and best practices and good communication with project teams and departments. If you are reading this as a UX professional, I hope it gave you some hands-on advice on how you can facilitate the building of the great user experiences Dan mentioned. If you are reading this as a product manager or an executive, I hope you understand a bit more about the actual business of everyday UX. Great user experiences don't just happen. You have to keep employing best practices every day.

References

Anderson, R. (2007). *What is holding user experience back where you work?* Online Retrieved on 19 March 2012 from http://www.uxmag.com/articles/what-is-holding-user-experience-back-where-you-work.

Bevan, N. (2005). Cost benefits evidence and case studies. In R. G. Bias & D. J. Mayhew (Eds.), *Cost-justifying usability: An update for the internet age*. San Francisco: Morgan Kaufmann.

Blomkvist, S. (2005). Towards a model for bridging agile development and user-centered design. In A. Seffah, J. Gulliksen, & M. C. Desmarais (Eds.), *Human-centered software engineering – integrating usability in the software development lifecycle* (Human–computer interaction series, Vol. 8(4), pp. 219–244). Netherlands: Springer.

Cohn, M. (2007). *Succeeding with agile: Software development using Scrum*. Boston: Addison-Wesley.

Cohn, M. (2009). *User stories applied: For agile software development*. Boston: Addison-Wesley.

Diefenbach, S., & Ullrich, D. (2011). Branchenreport usability 2011: Ergebnisse einer Befragung unter usability professionals in Deutschland. In H. Brau et al. (Eds.), *Usability professionals 2011* (pp. 52–57). Stuttgart: German UPA.

Gould, J. D., & Lewis, C. (1985). Designing for usability: Key principles and what designers think. *Communications of the ACM, 28*(3), 300–311.

Gualtieri, M. (2011). *Three megatrends to master for application development*. Posted on 6 April 2011, online retrieved on 19 March 2012 from http://blogs.forrester.com/mike_gualtieri/11-04-06-three_megatrends_to_master_for_application_development.

ISO FDIS 9241-210 (2009). *Ergonomics of human system interaction – Part 210: Human-centered design for interactive systems (formerly known as 13407)*. International Organization for Standardization (ISO), Switzerland.

Jokela, T. (2000). Making user centered design usable to managers. In J. Gulliksen et al. (Eds.), *How to make user centered design usable*. Stockholm: CID.

Karat, J. (1997). Evolving the scope of user-centered design. *Communications of the ACM, 40*(7), 33–38.

Kuniavsky, M. (2003). *Observing the user experience: A practitioner's guide to user research*. San Francisco: Morgan Kaufmann.

Law, E., Roto, V., Hassenzahl, M., Vermeeren, A., & Kort, J. (2009). Understanding, scoping and defining user experience: a survey approach. In *Proceedings of the 27th international conference on human factors in computing systems (CHI'09)* (pp. 719–728). New York: ACM.

Medlock, M., Terrano, M., & Wixon, D. (2002). Using the RITE method to improve products: A definition and a case study. *Proceedings of UPA 2002*. Orlando: Usability Professionals' Association.

Meurer, A., Kälble, H., Kowallik, P., Leidermann, F., Petrovic, K., & Zimmermann, D. (2009). Arbeitskreis in-house usability: Workshops. In H. Brau et al. (Eds.), *Usabilty professionals 2009*. Stuttgart: German UPA.

Nieters, J. E., Ivaturi, S., & Dworman, G. (2007). The internal consultancy model for strategic UxD relevance. *CHI 2007*, San Jose.

Patton, J. (2008). *Twelve emerging best practices for adding UX work to Agile development*. Retrieved online on 19 March 2012 from http://agileproductdesign.com/blog/emerging_best_agile_ux_practice.html.

Petrovic, K., & Siegmann, M. (2011). Make space for the customer: The shift towards customer centricity. *HCI* (9). (2011), 485–490.

Ragsdale, J.; Kinkin, E.; Herbert, L.; Temkin, B. D. (2004). Put Enterprise Applications To The Usability Test – Usability Drives Adoption, Productivity, And Project ROI. *Forrester Research Report*. MA: Cambridge.

Rhodes, J. (2009). *Selling usability: User experience infiltration tactics*. Lakeland: Create Space Publishing.

Rosenbaum, S., et al. (2000). A toolkit for strategic usability: Results from workshops, panels and surveys. In *Proceedings of the SIGCHI conference on human factors in computing systems*, New York.

Sauro, J., & Lewis, J. R. (2012). *Quantifying the user experience: Practical statistics for user research*. San Francisco: Morgan Kaufmann.

Schaffer, E. (2004). *Institutionalization of usability: A step-by-step guide*. Redwood City: Addison Wesley Longman.

Seffah, A., & Metzker, E. (2004). The obstacles and myths of usability and software engineering. *Communications of ACM, 47*(12), 71–76.

Sy, D., & Miller, L. (2008). Optimizing agile user-centered design. In *Extended abstracts, workshops proceedings CHI 2008* (pp. 3897–3900), 5–10 April 2008, Florence.

Watson, S. (2008). The business of customer experience: Lessons learned at Wells Fargo. *ACM Interactions, 15*(1), 38–43.

Making Design Tangible in Software Development Projects

Lennart Hennigs

Abstract

User Experience (UX) Professionals often face the problem that their role and their contribution to software development projects are misunderstood. They are confronted with new challenges when they join agile or lean project teams. Over the following pages I will explain how UX professionals can make design tangible. I will describe how they can guide software development projects, how they can create a common understanding of the targeted User Experience and how they can involve others in the shaping of the design. After outlining the current challenges, I will explain how activities such as *Design Studios, Sketching* and *Prototyping* can be used to foster an understanding of the design rationale, and how artifacts like *Product Vision Statements, Design Tenets, Personas, User Scenarios, Wireframes* and *UI Flows* help to frame the design problem and document the design solution. Using these activities and artifacts will lead to smoother project operations and better results.

1   Introduction

User-Centered Design (UCD) and User Experience (UX) practices focus on creating products and services with a high level of usability. In the 'early days' of our discipline the main challenges were to create an understanding of UCD within companies and 'fight' to be included in the existing software development processes.

As our discipline matured, we moved away from simply recommending usability testing at the end of the product development cycle, when the product was almost done and we started to develop full User-Centered Design process models

L. Hennigs
Deutsche Telekom AG, Bonn, Germany
e-mail: Lennart.Hennigs@telekom.de

A. Maedche et al. (eds.), *Software for People*, Management for Professionals,
DOI 10.1007/978-3-642-31371-4_9, © Springer-Verlag Berlin Heidelberg 2012

that describe the various activities and documents needed to ensure user-centricity throughout software development projects (Mayhew 1999, Constantine & Lockwood 1999 and ISO 2011). It was during this time that our view of how usable products ought to be created was shaped, along with our view of our role of within software development. Simply focusing on *ease of use* it not sufficient, we need to think 'outside our own box'. Don Norman (1999) used the metaphor of the *three-legged stool* to describe the three factors (or 'legs') a successful product needs: Technology, Business and User Needs. He states that a product can only be successful if these three factors are equally taken into account. Cut short on one of them and a product will 'fall'.

Nowadays, most of the software development industry has a general understanding of the concept of usability. The term is known and UX practitioners don't need to explain their value every time they join a project. However our challenges did not diminish – they merely shifted.

Where we previously had to find our place within software development projects, we now have to rethink our way of working in line with new software development methodologies. The waterfall approach to software development[1] is less frequently used and more agile and lean software projects (Schwaber & Sutherland (2011); Poppendieck 2004) are carried out. Agile and lean development provides less time for upfront conception and design work. They are less structured and put more emphasis on self-organized, interdisciplinary teams that work autonomously. They suggest short development cycles and quick iterations, in which parts of the final product are being designed, developed, tested and deployed. We have to adjust our current practice to meet these new challenges. A step-by-step approach will not work. We need to offer a toolbox of activities and documents to meet the demands of agile software development approaches.

Questions we need to answer are:
- How can UX practitioners provide value to an interdisciplinary team?
- What activities are the best fit in an agile software development environment?
- How can you involve your team members in describing the targeted User Experience?
- What is the right document to communicate the design to your team?

Being able to work with and to provide value to an interdisciplinary team becomes even more important in an agile environment. We need to understand what the other people involved are contributing and how we can best support them. We need a set of activities and artifacts that can create and document the common understanding of the targeted user experience. And last but not least we need the other team members to contribute to our own activities.

Artifacts that allow different disciplines to share their knowledge are called *boundary objects*, first described by Susan Leigh Star & James R. Griesemer (1989). They are "scientific objects which both inhabit several intersecting social worlds [...] and satisfy the informational requirements of each of them." They are

---

[1] http://en.wikipedia.org/wiki/Waterfall_model

"both plastic enough to adapt the local needs and constraints of the several parties employing them, yet robust enough to maintain a common identity across sites."

The good news is I strongly believe that we already have the documents available that can serve as boundary objects for interdisciplinary teams communicating the design. We also have the skills to support and guide interdisciplinary teams. We are able to establish a common mindset for the problem domain. We can capture the design rationale in such a way that it can offer guidance throughout the software development process. With our focus on the user, on their tasks and on the context of use, we have a broader perspective of the problem domain than most other disciplines involved. Our discipline strongly embraces the idea of a designed user experience – an experience tailored to the user's needs and expectations. This is more than just addressing usability and ease-of-use issues: we are trying to delight our users with the products and service we design.

Activities like *Design Studios, Sketching* and *Prototyping* are easy to explain to and carry out with non-UX professionals. They are low-fidelity approaches, fast paced and allow members of a development team to contribute to the design of the product. Artifacts like *Product Vision Statements, Design Tenets, Personas, User Scenarios, Wireframes* and *UI Flows* are fairly easy to read and understand for non-UX professionals. They are more compact than typical software development documents (such as Requirement Specifications or Product Definition documents), but they capture the essence of the problem domain and the solution and foster a common understanding.

2 The Situation Today

Software development and design projects are *Wicked Problems* (Poppendieck 2002; Dorst 2003). They belong to a family of problems that share certain attributes that makes them hard (or wicked) to solve. Wicked problems are typically characterized by the involvement of different stakeholder with different views and priorities. Furthermore, the requirements of such a project are complex and interlinked. The problem is hard to describe and keeps changing while we are trying to solve it. Its solution will be unique – there is no precedent for it. There is no prior indication as to what an optimal solution will look like – there are no 'boxes to tick' while developing our solution. Only the end product will show how well it is suited solving the problem. However, there are some best practices that can ease the problem's 'wickedness'. John C. Camillus (2008) who analyzed company strategy creation recommends the following steps when faced with a wicked problem:
1. Define a common vision.
2. Document ideas and communicate.
3. Involve stakeholders.
4. Take small steps forward and evaluate and iterate.

As UX professionals we are already are doing these steps (to some degree) in our projects and day-to-day work. The following sections will discuss methods and documents fitting these recommendations and the benefit they provide during software development.

2.1   Define a Common Vision

There are two aspects of design relevant to software development projects: problem setting and problem solving. In other words, defining what it is we want to solve and how we approach it.

Since software development projects are wicked problems, agreeing what is to be achieved (setting the problem) is key. Here, the problem space is being explored: what constraints does the team want to place on themselves; what are their working assumptions, etc.?

2.1.1   The Product Vision Statement

To create a common goal you first need to establish a common understanding of the expectations and the requirements of the different parties involved in your project. You need to come to some form of agreement on the project scope and its targets. You need to define the criteria for the projects' success. You need to understand what the other parties can contribute and how you will be able to support each other. This is typically done in some form of kick-off meeting. One key artifact that should be created during a kick-off meeting is the *Product Vision Statement*. It describes the characteristics of the final product in a few sentences and explains the targeted user experience. It needs to be brief and to the point in order to make the statement easy to remember, easy to communicate and relate to.

A good example is the product vision statement of Metro, the design language of Windows Phone 7 shown in Fig. 1: "Metro is our design language. We call it Metro because it's modern and clean. It's fast and in motion. It's about content and typography. And it's entirely authentic." (Shum 2010)

Another way to create a vision statement is to use the elements described by Geoffrey Moore (2002) in his book "Crossing the Chasm": the target audience for the product, their needs, the product category, the key functionality and the major benefits, current practice/competition and key differentiators. These can be used to fill in the blanks in the following sentences "For _____ who are dissatisfied with_____. Our product is a _____ that provides _____ unlike_____, we have assembled_____."

2.1.2   Design Tenets

Ideally, after you have created the *Product Vision Statement* you should create a short set of guidelines (less than 10) describing the Product Vision in more depth. These guidelines are often referred to as *Design Principles* or *Design Tenets*. "Design principles are short, insightful phrases that act as guiding lights and support the development of great product experiences. Design principles enable you to be true to your users and true to your strategy over the long term." (Buley 2009)

The goal is to have a set of principles that can help when faced with design decisions. They should inspire the team and guide their decisions. They function as a beacon, highlighting how the user experience of the finished product ought to be. Good principles are specific to your project, concrete and non-ambiguous, catchy

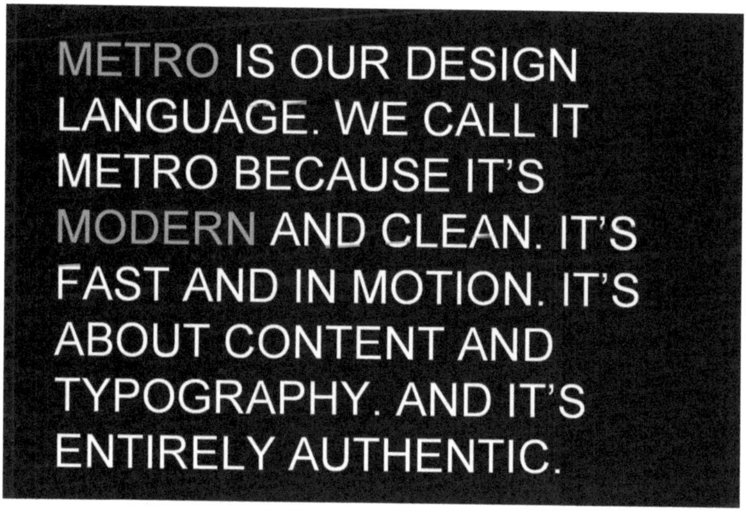

METRO IS OUR DESIGN LANGUAGE. WE CALL IT METRO BECAUSE IT'S **MODERN** AND CLEAN. IT'S FAST AND IN MOTION. IT'S ABOUT CONTENT AND TYPOGRAPHY. AND IT'S ENTIRELY AUTHENTIC.

Fig. 1 Product Vision Statement of Windows Metro (Copyright by Microsoft)

and describe differentiating properties (and not only a single feature) of your product (Saffer 2009; Anderson 2011; Spool 2001).

Good examples of design tenets are the principles behind the HTC Sense User Interface (UI) that was introduced on the HTC Hero mobile phone in 2009. With this HTC was the first company to offer a customized version of Google's Android mobile operating system and the first company to create a more user-centric and visually pleasing version of Android. Their Sense user interface was based on the following principles.[2]

- **Make it Mine**: Personalization needs to reach a level never before possible.
- **Stay Close**: Staying in touch with the people in your life means managing a variety of communication channels and applications.
- **Discover the Unexpected**: Many of the most memorable moments in your life are experienced, not explained.

These principles not only offer insights on the targeted user experience. They are also an example of how well defined design principles can be implemented and utilized because HTC used them to explain its product and features (see Fig. 2).

A frequent point of discussion is whether design tenets should be general statements like 'easy to use' or if they should be tailored to your project. I recommend the latter. If your design tenets are too general they become 'boilerplate phrases'. Of course, everyone wants to create a product that is 'easy to use'; no one would try to design something that didn't meet this criterion. Try to make your tenets specific to your product, so that they help you with the design decision you will face.

---

[2] http://www.youtube.com/watch?v=Kax24GN1458

Fig. 2 Screenshot from the HTC Hero Product Tour Video (Copyright by HTC, http://www. youtube.com/watch?v=kshGq8COSiM)

You can use general principles as a starting point to create your own, project-specific design tenets. Good examples of general design principles are the "10 Principles of Good Design" by Dieter Rams (1993). In addition, Human Interface Guidelines (HIG) contain general statements about the user experience for a specific platform, e.g. for iOS or Windows Phone 7 (Microsoft 2011; Apple 2011). For each general principle you need to ask yourself what it means for your product, your users, your context of use, your business, etc. By doing so you can extract specific rules tailored to your problem.

A frequently asked question is whether the product vision and the design tenets should be created prior to user research, or afterwards. The answer is: there is no best way. Usually it is advisable to do research first, before establishing your design idea but Don Norman (2011) states that reversing the sequence will also work: Create the design tenets and validate them afterwards.

2.2 Document Ideas and Communicate

Another recommended activity to solve a wicked problem is to document your ideas and communicate them frequently to your team and the involved stakeholders. These are the two key tasks for creating a consistent user experience – but also the key success factors. As Bill Buxton (2007) states: "Successful execution of a design depends on communication, and capturing the design rationale is an important component in this."

Why are these two factors so important? Because design (as an activity) consists of a large set of small decision that results in how the product or service that we create looks, feels and behaves. Thus these design decisions make up the product experience – the perceived effect your product or service will have on the user. Being consistent in these small decisions creates a certain style that will be reflected in the product's experience. However, creating a consistent user experience is easier for a single individual than for a team: "The solo designer or artist produces works with this integrity subconsciously; he tends to make each micro decision the same way every time he encounters it." (Brooks 2010) That is why it is of utmost importance that a team has an agreed common vision and documents and communicates their ideas so that all team members consciously or unconsciously shape, share and adapt a common style in their design work.

2.2.1 Sketching

We commonly use diagrams and sketches for different purposes when working on a design. It can be said that sketching out our ideas and thoughts serves as a means for (visual) conversations we have with the problem, ourselves and others. We use it to frame the problem and to solve it. While sketching our thoughts, new ideas will emerge – that is why sketching is *generative*: sketching sparks new ideas in us as well as capturing the ideas we already have.

Another strength of sketching is that it is done on paper. As Sellen and Harper (2003) point out: "[Paper] will continue to predominate in activities that involve knowledge work, including browsing through information, reading and make sense of information; organizing and structuring and reminding of ideas; [...] and activities that involve showing and demonstrating ideas and actions to others." This is due to the *affordance* of paper (for details on the concept of affordance see Soegard 2008) – i.e. paper can easily be used for these types of human activity, more so than digital media.

Another advantage of sketches is that they are low-fidelity. Sketches are quick and easy to make, inexpensive and easy to dispose of (so you won't grow too attached to them), they suggest new ideas due to their ambiguity and don't offer too much detail. "Learning from sketches is based largely on the ambiguous nature of their representation. That is, they do not specify everything and lend themselves to, and encourage, various interpretations that were not consciously integrated into them by their creator." (Buxton 2007)

The following best practices are suggested by Brown (2011) to create better sketches: Initially list the information you have and you want to capture, make a first set of sketches, get some feedback, iterate your concepts and sketch out a different angle to the problem. Re-order elements to see where it leads, review your results with the input you started with and use conventions in your sketches to make the consistent and easier to understand. Use color sparingly and label your sketches to make them easy to read for others.

What do we sketch? We sketch the problem domain: We picture our understanding of the current situation – how things relate to each other, what steps the user currently needs to take with the current solution, etc. But we also sketch the solution: We picture the situation as we plan it to be. Our solution can be depicted in *Information Architecture* Diagrams, *Wireframes* or *User Interface Flows*. These different types of diagrams will be described later on.

While sketches encourage the discussion a designer has "with himself" they also foster the discussion among team members. Whether you use them in structured meetings such as *Design Studios*, which will be introduced later, or used 'ad-hoc' to discuss ideas, sketches often 'say' more than 1,000 words.

Depending on the concept you are trying to capture and how you sketch it (i.e. the type of diagram you use) your sketches will vary in fidelity. One dimension of fidelity is the level of granularity. A sketch could describe things from a 30,000 ft point of view or provide a micro view of a specific detail. An *Information Architecture Diagram*, for example, provides a high level view of the elements of an application or web site. The other dimension is sketching is the level of abstraction used. A sketch can roughly lay out an idea or be very detailed. Sometimes *Wireframes* contain only the general content of a page, and sometimes they are very specific and show the visual design and the interface elements to be used. Of course, this depends what you want to document in or communicate with your sketch.

2.2.2   Wireframes and User Interface Flows

Wireframes depict the layout of a user interface. They describe the structure, navigation, content and behavior of a single screen (or parts of it); its visual design is not shown. "The aim is to focus the team's attention and encourage conversation about what a screen does, not what it looks like." (Brown 2011) Wireframes are one of the key deliverables of UX professionals because they "are a means of documenting the features of a product, as well as the technical and business logic that went into those features, with only a veneer of visual design [...]. They are the blueprints of a product." (Saffer 2009)

A *User Interface Flow* is a set of wireframes visualizing an 'interaction path'; highlighting what interface elements were used through the flow (e.g. a mouse click or gesture on a touch interface) and how the system responded (e.g. with animations, transitions, pop-up dialogs, the next screen) while working with the system. Sometimes conditions are visualized as well (e.g. error cases) to showcase important variations of the user interface.

A wireframe shows the relationship and the hierarchy of the page elements. Questions a wireframe should answer are: What are the main components of the user interface? How is it organized? What information is important? What information is secondary?

A wireframe highlights the navigational structure of a UI. It should explain the navigational elements that are used, how the user knows where he is, how he can he navigate away from the current screen and what his options are.

A wireframe explains the content of a user interface. Related questions include: What type of content is needed? How is it displayed? Can the user interact with it? What content is important and how is this communicated?

A wireframe showcases the behavior of a UI. It highlights the interactive elements, their relationship to each other and how the user gets feedback from the product.

Wireframes usually contain annotations to explain certain details. They sometime highlight a design decision, explain how to interact with an element, explain its

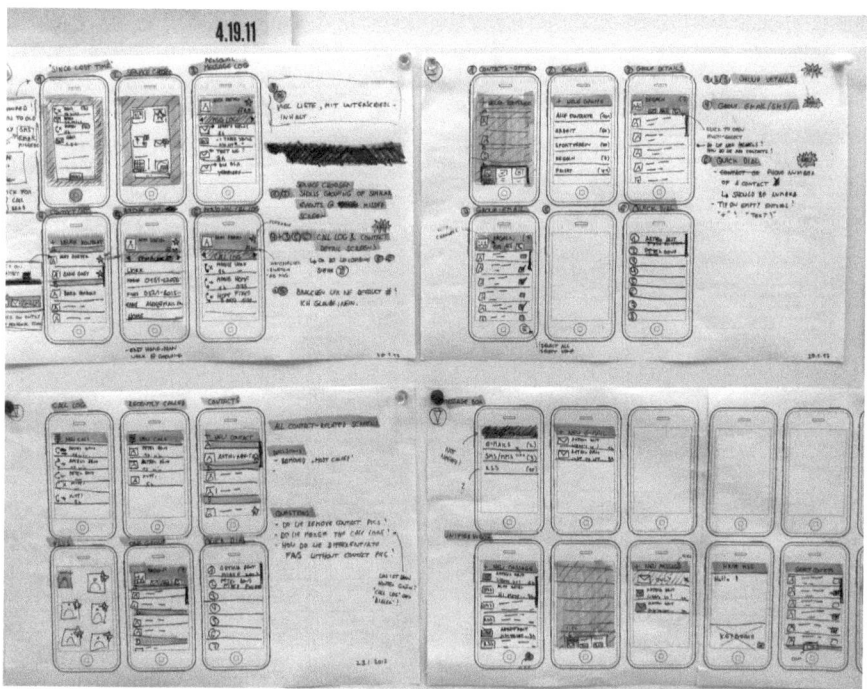

Fig. 3 Low-fidelity wireframes (of a mobile application). Copyright by the author

content, and point out a special case or an open issue in the wireframe. Points of interest are numbered and explained in a sidebar or highlighted by arrows, depending on personal preference.

Wireframes can be created with different levels of fidelity. Their visual, functional and content fidelity can be differentiated.[3] The simplest wireframes are typically sketches (as shown in Fig. 3) done on paper. Low-fidelity wireframes are fast to create and to discard. UX professionals create them to try out different variations of the user interface and to see if an idea could work (Boersma 2010; Johnson 2011). If a set of sketches is 'stable' enough (i.e. they correctly answer the questions the UX practitioners created them for) they are transferred into higher fidelity wireframes. These are usually created with dedicated wireframing tools and will be closer to the final design of the product. Ward (2008) showcases wireframes of the same screen in different stages of completion and different levels of fidelity.

2.2.3 Information Architecture Diagrams

Information Architecture Diagrams (IA diagrams) provide the 30,000 ft point of view of an application or web site. They visualize the different areas of a product

---

[3] Different styles of wireframes can be viewed at http://wireframes.tumblr.com/

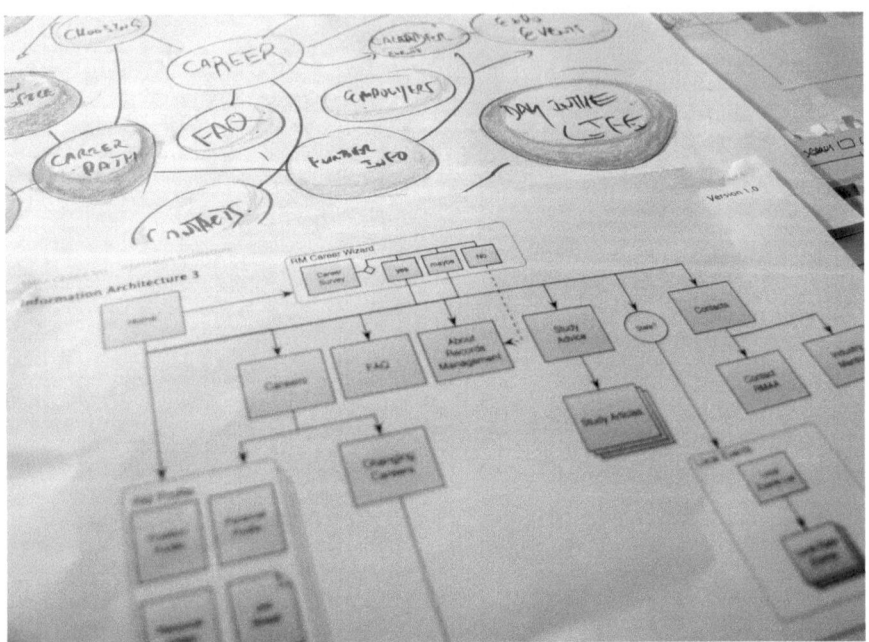

Fig. 4 Information architecture diagram (Photo by Gary Barber, http://www.flickr.com/photos/cannedtuna/4853380320/in/photostream/)

and how they are connected to each other. They provide an overview of the scale of the overall solution and indicate what paths a user can take within the product. They are the 'floor plan' of your solution. For web sites IA diagrams are often called *Sitemaps*.

Together with wireframes they are also a key deliverable of UX professionals because IA diagrams provide a high-level view of the solution, while wireframes show the content of the different areas (Fig. 4).

Different notations exist for IA diagrams, such as Jesse James Garrett's "Visual Vocabulary" (2002) or Jacob Linowski's "Interactive Sketching Notation" (2011).

Information Architecture diagrams consist of a set of nodes connected to each other via arrows showing the possible navigation paths. Sometimes different types of nodes are used (e.g. for different types of content) and similar items belonging together (e.g. part of the same page or area) are grouped. Nodes are labeled to explain their purpose and make them distinct. Sometimes flowchart elements (such as diamonds visualizing decision points) are also added for clarification.

2.2.4 Personas

Personas are an established means of documenting knowledge about the targeted user groups, first described by Alan Cooper (1999) in his book "The Inmates are running the Asylum" (see also Pruitt and Adlin 2010; Mulder and Yaar 2006).

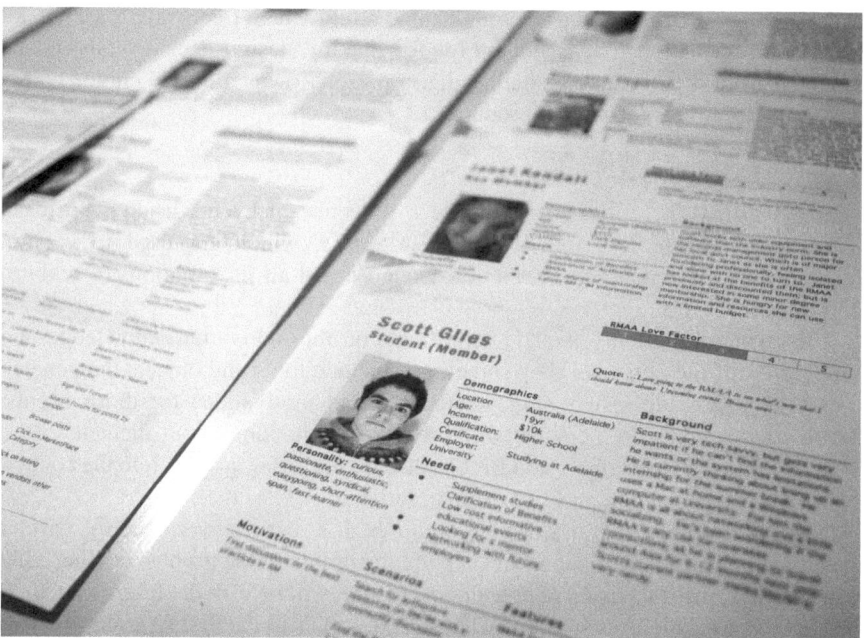

Fig. 5 Persona descriptions (Photo by Gary Barber, http://www.flickr.com/photos/cannedtuna/4852756417/in/photostream/)

A persona is a human-friendly format for user-research related facts. It is a description of an intended user of the solution to be designed. It distills the information about a specific user group into a fictitious user profile.

Persona descriptions usually include some background information about the persona (name, a picture showing the person, age, gender, and a product-related quote), the persona's needs and requirements and often a scenario describing the persona's typical day or an event where the solution we are trying to design would benefit them. These are called User Scenarios, which will be described in the next section (Fig. 5).

The strength of personas is that they offer a tangible and accessible format for user research findings – they literally give mere facts 'a human face.' People will relate to them as if they were real people, and when discussing design decisions they will, for example, say: "If we do it this way we won't help Peter." Personas leave a longer lasting impression than a simple bullet-point list stating facts.

That's why it is essential that the persona is based on user-research findings. If it is not, it is a work of fiction and it will not provide value. A persona needs to capture the real needs and requirements of your intended users. Otherwise the persona will not be of any use in guiding your design decisions. If you create a persona based on assumptions, you need to validate them, similar to design tenets.

The format and layout of personas are also very important. Sometimes personas are printed on posters, or poster boards are created of the personas to make them visible and accessible to people. The documents should be easy to read, understand

and remember, because you want your team to refer to them frequently. Last but not least, all information that is not useful for making design decisions should be removed from a persona, e.g. stating that a persona owns a dog is clutter unless you are designing a pet-related product.

2.2.5 User Scenarios

User Scenarios are stories that describe a sequence of events leading up to an outcome. They are less formal than *Use Cases*, which are used to capture requirements, describing an interaction sequence and all its variations (Cockburn 2000).

User scenarios usually include some hints on the motivation, knowledge and capabilities of the persona. They sometimes include tools and objects the persona uses. They "provide insight into the reasons and motivations for those events. Stories that accompany personas often describe something about their activities or experiences." (Quesenbery and Brooks 2010) They offer insights into the context of use as well as the personas' goals and motivations.[4]

Scenarios can be used for different purposes. If a scenario describes the current situation, they are used to define and capture the problem (the problem setting). If a scenario describes the vision of how the interaction will be with the future system, it describes the solution. Rosson and Carrol (2002) refer to the first type as scenarios as *Problem Scenarios* and to the second as *Design Scenarios*. In addition, scenarios can be used to describe a specific context of use or illustrate a current shortcoming or a pain-point of the existing solution. Scenarios should be only about one or two paragraphs long and describe a single topic.

Just like *Design Tenets* and *Personas, User Scenarios* require input and verification through user research because they are tools for capturing user insights and design decisions.

2.3 Involve Stakeholders

Due to their role UX practitioners are always 'caught in the middle' between the different stakeholders involved in a software development project. We negotiate with Product Managers about features and priorities, we discuss how the solution should look and behave with Developers, we talk to Marketing to understand their targeted customers, and we join System Analysts on site visits, etc. We therefore often have a broader view of the various complexities and interdependencies of a project.

Interdisciplinary work poses the following challenges to UCD practitioners:

- We are always under-represented within projects. Close cooperation with the other stakeholders and involving them in our own work is therefore a necessity for UCD practitioners.

---

[4] An example of a user scenario combined with some persona information can be found at: http://www.flickr.com/photos/rosenfeldmedia/4459979060/

- Usability is known as a term, its value is understood but its place within the project (not only after the development is complete) within the project is often misunderstood as is the impact it will have on the project (UX practitioners will discuss requirements, challenge design decisions, etc.)

That is why we need to make the other parties involved aware of the consequences of design decisions being taken during the development of a product.

2.3.1 Design Studio

A well-suited method of involving the other parties in the creation of a product is the *Design Studio* (Ungar 2008; Evans 2011; Lindstrom 2011). This approach is borrowed from Industrial Design and Architecture and offers a structured approach to problem solving and innovating. It essentially involves a meeting in which the participants sketch different design options, discuss their sketches and agree on a direction to move forward. It is independent of the software development model used – it works both for waterfall or agile processes. As Ungar (2008) states: "The design studio is a collaborative workshop that fits well within the timeframes Agile software development practices while incorporating the benefits of UCD research." It is an iterative design and critique process where non-UX professionals can participate. Design Studio sessions are usually hosted by a moderator who keeps track of the time, as each activity is intended to be completed quickly, within a rather short time frame. The critique sessions are also moderated.

A typical design studio session comprises of the following steps: First, the problem you want to solve is briefly described. Then, each participant is given some time to brainstorm ideas and sketch them out – e.g. several screens of a product or website or steps of a process. Afterwards, each participant presents their ideas and gets feedback from their peers. The feedback needs to point out the strengths of the presented concepts and highlight areas that still need improvement. The participants are then given time to improve their concepts. At the end, the best elements of each concept are selected and combined into a final concept (Fig. 6).

A Design Studio session combines several techniques to rapidly create and evaluate design alternatives. The result of (individual) brainstorming sessions are visualized and criticized by the team. This is the idea generation phase. Individuals then improve their best idea, which is ultimately combined into the best-fitting solution. This is the idea refinement phase.

The session allows non-UX practitioners to participate in concept creation, offering them first-hand experience of design. It facilitates the knowledge transfer among the participants. Non-UX professionals gain a better understanding of how UX practitioners work, and in return they have the chance to the other participants' points of view. It creates a common understanding of the design decisions taken by the team and the implications of these, and last but not least it supports the team's commitment to the design.

A variant of a Design Studio session uses sketchboards to showcase the concepts created during the session, and was introduced by Adaptive Path, a design consultancy firm. It puts a strong focus on idea generation and refinement and suggests a

Fig. 6 A design studio sketchboard. Copyright by the author

structured approach for the critique session. (For details see Schauer 2007; Harrelson and Buley 2008; Downes 2010.)

2.4 Take Small Steps and Evaluate and Iterate

As explained before, *Sketching* and *Design Studio* are inherent iterative activities. Artifacts such as *Wireframes* and *Information Architecture Diagrams* can be created as low-fidelity paper versions before recreating them in a high-fidelity digital format. "Sketches and prototypes are both instantiations of the design concept however they serve different purposes, and therefore are concentrated at different stages of the design process. Sketches are dominant the early ideation stages, whereas prototypes are more concentrated at the later stages where things are converging within the design funnel." (Buxton 2007)

2.4.1 Prototyping

Prototyping is the practice of creating something to test your assumptions and learning from its results. "Prototyping is practice for people who design and make things. It's not simply another tool for your design toolkit – it's a design philosophy." (Warfel 2009)

Prototyping needs to be iterative, because each prototype shapes and improves your understanding of the problem and the solution domain. With prototypes you refine your design step by step. Unlike written requirements prototypes are able to *show* and not only *tell* how parts of the solution behave. You can create prototypes to evaluate only a small aspect of the problem, or to look at the broad picture instead.

In their simplest forms, your wireframe sketches can serve as paper prototypes you evaluate by yourself, with colleagues or even with users (Snyder 2003). You want to get feedback and new ideas about the design problem you are facing. If your project is more advanced you might create high fidelity wireframes and prototypes of the user interface to gather more feedback on different aspects of your design.

Just as with wireframes you can choose different levels of fidelity for your prototypes. Again the dimensions are: visual, functional and content fidelity. Prototypes with a low level of visual fidelity contain sketches of the user interface, not showing the visual design. Prototypes with a low level functional fidelity will consist of a set of still screens; higher fidelity prototypes will offer interactive elements. Prototypes with a low level content fidelity can contain blind text ('Lorem ipsum'); higher fidelity version should showcase real content.

Prototypes should be created for the more complex aspects of your solution. "Good candidates for prototyping include complex interactions, new functionality and changes in workflow, technology or design." (Cerejo 2010) The most used functionality should also be prototyped – a good rule of thumb offers the Pareto Principle: What is 20 % of the functionality that is going to be used 80 % of the time?

Since prototyping is supposed to be done repeatedly and happen quickly you should try not to spend too much time on polishing the details of your prototypes. Your peers and test-users will understand that the prototype is not the real solution. Last but not least don't try to prototype the full solution. Prototypes are there to demonstrate a behavior or functionality you want to explore. Keeping this in mind will keep your prototypes' scope smaller and you'll be able to create them faster.

3   Summary

The previous sections described a set of low-fidelity activities and artifacts to capture the User Experience of a product. As these are easy to do and create by UX professionals, they also foster collaboration with non-UX people and create a shared understanding of and responsibility for the design and the User Experience of the product.

But the interesting question is: why do they work?

One reason is that they are people-friendly. Humans are visual creatures. *Sketching* lets us explore the problem and the solution space visually; it allows us to generate new ideas and see new connections. The same is true for *Prototyping*. We can show and see how we envision the solution (or parts of it), and test it out to gather feedback. We can show our sketches and prototypes to colleagues and team members to foster a shared understanding and learn their point of view. We are able to validate our assumptions and learn from our prototypes. We can later discard them easily because creating them did not cost too much effort. Humans are also social creatures. *Design Studio* sessions foster teamwork and collaboration and create a common understanding of the design.

Another reason can be found in the book "Made to Stick" (2007) by Chip and Dan Heath. It describes six key characteristics to make ideas and concepts understandable and memorable. 'Sticky' ideas are simple, unexpected, concrete, credible, emotional and they tell a story. All of the techniques and artifacts described above share some of these traits. The *Product Vision Statement* and the *Design Tenets* are 'simple', in the sense that they describe the core design rationale of the solution. They are concrete and often emotional. *Personas* give a 'human face' to user research data, they become credible, while *User Scenarios* use stories to communicate and frame the design problem and the solution.

References

Anderson, S. (2011). Principles to build by. *IA Summit 2010*. Available online at http://www.slideshare.net/stephenpa/design-principles-to-build-by. Accessed 29 Jan 2012.

Apple Inc. (2011). *iOS human interface guidelines*. Available online at https://developer.apple.com/library/ios/documentation/UserExperience/Conceptual/MobileHIG/MobileHIG.pdf. Accessed 29 Jan 2012.

Boersma, P. (2010). *Good design faster*. Available online at http://www.slideshare.net/pboersma/good-design-faster-at-design-by-fire-2010. Accessed 29 Jan 2012.

Brooks, F. P. (2010). *The design of design*. Boston: Pearson Education.

Brown, D. M. (2011). *Communicating design: Developing web site documentation for design and planning* (2nd ed.). Berkeley: New Riders.

Buley, L. (2009). *Design principles in a nutshell*. Available online at http://www.adaptivepath.com/ideas/d120209. Accessed 29 Jan 2012.

Buxton, B. (2007). *Sketching user experiences*. San Francisco: Morgan Kaufmann.

Camillus, J. C. (2008). Strategy as a wicked problem. *Harvard Business Review*, May 2008.

Cerejo, L. (2010). *Design better and faster with rapid prototyping*. Available online at http://www.smashingmagazine.com/2010/06/16/design-better-faster-with-rapid-prototyping/. Accessed 29 Jan 2012.

Cockburn, A. (2000). *Writing effective use cases*. Boston: Addison-Wesley.

Constantine, L. L., Lockwood, L. (1999). Software for Use: A Practical Guide to the Models and Methods of Usage-Centered Design, Reading, MA: Addison-Wesley.

Cooper, A. (1999). *The inmates are running the asylum*. Indianapolis: Sams.

Dorst, K. (2003). The problem of design problems. In N. Cross & E. Edmonds (Eds.), *Expertise in design* (pp. 135–147). Sydney: Creativity and Cognition Studio Press.

Downes, J. (2010). *Using sketchboards to design great user interfaces quickly*. Available online at http://www.boxuk.com/blog/using-sketchboards-to-design-great-user-interfaces. Accessed 29 Jan 2012.

Evans, W. (2011). *Introduction to design studio methodology*. Available online at http://uxmag.com/articles/introduction-to-design-studio-methodology. Accessed 29 Jan 2011.

Garrett, J. J. (2002). *A visual vocabulary for describing information architecture and interaction design*. Available online at http://www.jjg.net/ia/visvocab/. Accessed 29 Jan 2012.

Harrelson, D., & Buley, L. (2008). *Sketchboards and prototypes*. Available online at http://www.slideshare.net/ugleah/sketchboards-prototypes-presentation. Accessed 29 Jan 2012.

Heath, C., & Heath, D. (2007). *Made to stick: Why some ideas survive and others die*. New York: Random House.

ISO (2010). *ISO 9241–210:2010: Ergonomics of human-system interaction – Part 210: Human-centred design for interactive systems*, Switzerland.

Johnson, J. (2011). *Close photoshop and grab a pencil: The lost art of thumbnail sketches.* Available online at http://designshack.net/articles/inspiration/close-photoshop-and-grab-a-pencil-the-lost-art-of-thumbnail-sketches/. Accessed 29 Jan 2011.

Lindstrom, J. (2011). *Design studio: The good, the bad and the science.* Available online at http://www.uxbooth.com/blog/design-studios-the-good-the-bad-and-the-science/. Accessed 29 Jan 2012.

Linowski, J. (2011). *Interactive sketching notation.* Available online at http://www.linowski.ca/sketching. Accessed 29 Jan 2012.

Mayhew, D. (1999). *The usability engineering lifecycle.* San Francisco, CA: Morgan Kaufmann.

Microsoft (2011). *Windows user experience interaction guidelines.* Available online at http://msdn.microsoft.com/en-us/library/windows/desktop/aa511258.aspx. Accessed 29 Jan 2011.

Moore, G. A. (2002). *Crossing the chasm (Revised Edition).* New York: Harper Business.

Mulder, S., & Yaar, Z. (2006). *The user is always right: A practical guide to creating and using personas for the web.* Berkeley: New Riders.

Norman, D. A. (1999). *The invisible computer: Why good products can fail, the personal computer is so complex, and information appliances are the solution.* Cambridge, MA: MIT Press.

Norman, D. A. (2011). *Act first, do the research later.* Available online at http://www.core77.com/blog/columns/act_first_do_the_research_later_20051.asp. Accessed 29 Jan 2012.

Poppendieck, M. (2002). Wicked projects. In *Software Development Magazine.* Available online at http://drdobbs.com/184414851. Accessed 29 Jan 2012.

Poppendieck, M. (2004). An introduction to lean software development. Available online at http://www.leanessays.com/2004/06/introduction-to-lean-software.html. Accessed 29 Jan 2012.

Pruitt, J., & Adlin, T. (2010). *The essential persona lifecycle: Your guide to building and using personas.* San Francisco, CA: Morgan Kaufmann.

Quesenbery, W., & Brooks, K. (2010). *Storytelling for user experience.* Brooklyn: Rosenfeld Media.

Rams, D. (1993). Ten principles for good design. Available online at http://www.vitsoe.com/en/gb/about/dieterrams/gooddesign. Accessed 29 Jan 2012.

Rosson, J. M. & Carroll J. M. (2002). Usability Engineering: Scenario-Based Development of Human-Computer Interaction, San Francisco , CA: Morgan Kaufmann.

Saffer, D. (2009). *Design for interaction* (2nd ed.). Berkeley: New Riders.

Schauer, B. (2007). Sketchboards: discover better + faster UX solutions. Available online at http://www.adaptivepath.com/ideas/sketchboards-discover-better-faster-ux-solutions. Accessed 29 Jan 2012.

Schwaber, K., & Sutherland, J. (2011). The scrum guide. Available online at http://www.scrum.org/scrumguides/. Accessed 29 Jan 2012.

Sellen, A. J., & Harper, R. (2003). *The myth of the paperless office.* Cambridge, MA: MIT Press.

Shum, A. (2010). Designing windows phone 7 series. *MIX 10, Las Vegas.* Available online at http://channel9.msdn.com/events/MIX/MIX10/CL14. Accessed 29 Jan 2012.

Soegard. (2008). Affordances. Available online at http://www.interaction-design.org/encyclopedia/affordances.html. Accessed 29 Jan 2012.

Spool, J. (2001). Creating great design principles: 6 counter-intuitive tests. Available online at http://www.uie.com/articles/creating-design-principles. Accessed 29 Jan 2012.

Star, S. L., & Griesemer, J. R. (1989). Institutional ecology, 'translations' and boundary objects. *Social Studies of Sciences, 19*(3), 387–420.

Synder, C. (2003). *Paper prototyping: The fast and easy way to define and refine user interfaces.* San Francisco: Morgan Kaufmann.

Ungar, J. (2008). The design studio: Interface design for agile teams. *Agile 2008 conference*, IEEE Computer Society, Washington.

Ward, J. (2008). Sketches, wireframes and CSS. Available online at http://jeff.io/posts/user-interface-wireframes. Accessed 29 Jan 2012.

Warfel, T. Z. (2009). *Prototyping: A practitioner's guide.* Brooklyn: Rosenfeld Media.

User Experience and User-Centered Design at DATEV eG

Ulf Schubert, Martin Groß, and Stefanie Pötzsch

Abstract

DATEV eG products are not only convincing with technical and professional perfection, but also with a design that turns simple usage into a positive experience. In order to achieve the objective of a positive *user experience*, DATEV eG has long been focused on user-oriented development and user centered design respectively.

The following article offers you an insight into user experience and user centered design at DATEV eG today and points out important milestones on the way from technology-driven development to user centered design. We describe different challenges that needed to be addressed during the change and demonstrate our practical solutions. These solutions encompass methods and tools on the one hand and organizational and personal prerequisites on the other hand. All these measures facilitate enhanced design quality and efficient development of excellent software products with a positive user experience.

1 Introducing DATEV eG

DATEV eG stands for high quality software solutions and IT services for auditors, tax consultants, and lawyers as well as entrepreneurs. The headquarters are located in Nuremberg (Germany) and further offices and associated companies are distributed across Europe. DATEV eG is a cooperative with about 40,000 members and more than 6,000 employees. About 1,000 of them work in the development department.

The DATEV eG portfolio offers about 200 business software products ranging from business accounting via tax calculation, personnel accounting and management until auditing. Software products mean classic desktop applications, cloud

U. Schubert • M. Groß • S. Pötzsch
DATEV eG, Nuremberg, Germany
e-mail: ulf.schubert@datev.de; martin.gross@datev.de@datev.de;
stefanie.poetzsch@datev.de

A. Maedche et al. (eds.), *Software for People*, Management for Professionals,
DOI 10.1007/978-3-642-31371-4_10, © Springer-Verlag Berlin Heidelberg 2012

services and mobile apps. The probably best known product is from personnel accounting, because DATEV eG delivers more than 10 million payrolls in Germany every month.

2   User Experience and Design in Business Software

2.1   Challenges

In the business software area design is often misunderstood as adding colors, icons and something with a "wow-effect." Designers are expected to make products look nice at the end of the development process. However, "wow-effects" and optically overloaded user interfaces are inappropriate as revenue drivers in the business area. They do not create a positive user experience, but arbitrary product design that has no impact on your business objectives.

The big challenge for software companies today is to understand and apply user interface design as a strategic instrument. Usually, customers cannot evaluate the technical quality of a software product and its detailed professional features at first sight, but they judge what they can see. This implies that design plays a highly important role in the buying decision and customer loyalty.

In order to make excellent user experience design a solid competitive differentiator, it is not sufficient to follow the latest design trends. Primarily, the design of your products needs to fulfill your brand's promises and match customers' expectations. That means, user interface and interaction design should be based on business objectives and it should be measurable by the extent to which it reaches these objectives.

2.2   Attractiveness of Software

Whether customers find a software product attractive or not depends on several pragmatic and hedonic factors (Hassenzahl et al. 2000). In order to describe and measure the attractiveness of our software products, DATEV eG applies a model which is based on the user-experience questionnaire (Laugwitz et al. 2008) and combines both, pragmatic and hedonic factors as shown in Fig. 1. As *pragmatic factors* the model considers efficiency, perspicuity, dependability and up-to-dateness. *Hedonic factors* are aesthetic, stimulation and novelty.

The overall importance of a single factor depends on the specific product and its target group. For instance, a well-designed mp3-player primarily aims for high scores at hedonic factors, whereas business software addresses pragmatic factors first. However, also in the business software area the importance of hedonic factors is growing. From DATEV eG user studies we know that – besides pragmatic factors – especially the hedonic factor *aesthetic* contributes to customers' overall satisfaction with business software products.

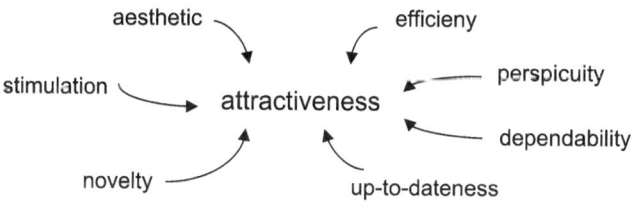

Fig. 1 Model of attractiveness of software

In order to build attractive business software that meets our customers' needs, DATEV eG has introduced and improved user centered design in its development process over the last couple of years.

3 Changing the Development Process

3.1 From Technology-Driven Development to User Centered Design

DATEV eG has successfully changed its development process from a primarily technology-driven approach to user centered design. The starting point for this change goes back to the 1980s when the DATEV eG product portfolio grew more and more. With no consistent design strategy at that time, user interfaces and interaction mechanisms were different across products and this situation annoyed customers. By the same time, software ergonomics and usability were emerging topics since products became more complex and interconnected with each other.

Therefore, DATEV eG decided to found a central design team. In the beginning this team consists of three experts, who introduced different measures to promote their topics throughout the software development process. Retrospectively, three of the key measures were:

- Creating and maintaining a *style guide*
- Conducting regularly *usability inspections* and
- Providing standardized *user interface patterns*

In the following, each of these three measures is explained in more detail and evaluated with regard to practical advantages and disadvantages.

3.2 DATEV Style Guide

Business software with its many complex features and functions is developed by several development teams in parallel. Creating a positive user experience under these circumstances requires consistent and high-quality user interface design from all teams. Therefore, DATEV eG employs a style guide, which is mandatory for the design of all software products and which is used by developers across the whole development department. The wiki-based style guide fosters consistent user interface design throughout the development process by providing design principles and guidelines.

Design principles describe fundamental ideas about the practice of good user interface design. The main principles at DATEV eG are:

- Be aware of performance.
- Workflows to get tasks done have to be efficient.
- Consistent user interfaces minimize users' learning curve.
- User interfaces have to be aesthetic and visually attractive.

Design guidelines contain full documentation of the visual design and the interaction design. This includes all rules of layout, color schemes, usage of icons, etc., available templates for user interface controls and descriptions of best practices.

In order to prevent that consistency of user interfaces and interactions might be misunderstood as strict sameness, the DATEV eG style guide also explains reasons for general design decisions and points out to which extent developers have the freedom to make own design decisions which are most reasonable in the context of their special software product.

Of course, the mere availability of a style guide does not necessarily result in consistent user interfaces and continuously high ergonomic quality. Important success factors for a style guide are:

- The content of your style guide is understandable, complete, practically oriented, supported by visual examples, up-to-date and unambiguous.
- The style guide is organizationally anchored in your development process.
- The style guide is enriched with data from user centered design studies to explain design rules und user interface patterns.
- Your technical user interface developers also have a sense for appealing and consistent design.
- You have a fair amount of time for the development of your products.

At DATEV eG the acceptance of our style guide is very good and the wiki-based approach works fine. There is no misuse of the non-restrictive editing function but developers correctly use the comment area if they have any specific hint or question.

In order to keep up good adherence to a style guide, control mechanisms, e.g. usability inspections, are needed for two reasons. First, control mechanisms ensure that user interface development is consistent with current design principles and rules from the style guide. Second, control mechanisms also work the other way around and help the design team to identify missing aspects in the style guide.

3.3   Usability Inspections

The team of usability experts regularly inspects DATEV products in order to check for possible ergonomic problems and analyze inconsistencies with the style guide but also to see awesome new best practice examples. Usability inspections in this extent require a lot of time. But it is worth it. They really help to identify most of the stumbling blocks in user interface and interaction design (Nielsen and Landauer 1993).

However, usability inspections also have some drawbacks. First, for a large software product portfolio there is a multitude of different user interfaces to inspect. Even with a lot of inspections it is nearly impossible to continuously monitor all user interfaces. Second, thorough usability inspections cost time and their findings may delay the development process. Third, if inspections are conducted with almost finished software, i.e. shortly before the product should be released, all user interfaces are fully developed but it may be too late and/or too costly to change interfaces or interaction processes.

Therefore, besides design principles and rules, developers need standardized user interface templates that can be reused and modified to a certain extent. In the following, we explain how user interface patterns enable consistent software design for the comprehensive DATEV eG product portfolio.

3.4   User Interface Patterns

There are a lot of recurring user interface and interaction problems in the development process of a comprehensive software product portfolio. Centralizing the design and developing solutions to these problems as *user interface patterns* is an important step towards consistent user interfaces (Segerståhl and Jokela 2006) and development effectiveness. We consider user interface patterns as design rules documented in the style guide and translated in software components. User interface patterns are reusable and to a certain extent modifiable building blocks which comprise controls, interactive behavior and data binding mechanisms.

At DATEV eG user interface patterns are composed of simple default controls and complex controls. Simple default controls are, e.g. buttons or text boxes. These controls already have a DATEV eG-specific design and features like validation and formatting. Complex controls are a collection of simple controls enriched with data binding mechanisms or complex user interface components like a table view. User interface patterns can comprise simple controls and complex controls. All user interface patterns are deployed as part of the DATEV eG development framework which is the technical platform of all DATEV eG products. Technical developers choose from the available set of user interface patterns when implementing user interfaces for their software products and combine patterns with product specific user interface development. The information which pattern to apply for a certain interaction problem is documented and explained in the style guide.

The application of user interface patterns in the development process has advantages for all stakeholders.

Advantages from users' perspective:

• Consistent user interfaces within a software product and across multiple products

- Reduced efforts for education and training since acquired knowledge can easily be transferred to further products
  Advantages from technical developers' perspective:
- Reduction of workload since there is no need to deal with recurring interaction and design questions
- Central requirements engineering for user interface patterns instead of multiple, distributed efforts
- Central maintainability and correction in case of technical or ergonomic problems instead of multiple, distributed efforts
- Central enhancement and further development of user interface patterns instead of multiple, distributed efforts
- Central testing and quality control instead of multiple, distributed efforts
  Advantages from management perspective:
- Higher development efficiency due to reusability of user interface patterns
- Better and faster acceptance of user interface enhancements and further development among users

However, there are also a few challenges when applying user interface patterns, which should not be underestimated. Apparently, user interface patterns require efforts for requirements engineering, maintainability, further development and testing at a central pattern development team. The more complex user interface patterns become with regard to design and technical realization, the more central development effort is needed. In addition, intensive coordination and feedback between the central pattern development team on the one hand and technical product developers on the other hand is an essential success factor. User interface patterns should not lead to general decreased efforts for conception of the user interface and their workflows. If technical developers would take user interface patterns as an easy available solution for the wrong kind of interaction problems, that would be a misuse of the whole concept and finally even lead to lower design quality of your software products.

In order to decide whether a specific user interface solution should become a general user interface pattern, DATEV eG uses the following decision criteria.

Frequency of use:

- How often will the user interface pattern be used in different products?
- How generic has the solution to be to meet the requirements of all products?

Complexity:

- Is it necessary for the user interface pattern to make changes of functionality immediately available to all products?
- Do we expect new functionalities or changes in the functionality triggered by legislation amendment?
- Does a user interface pattern help to reduce the probability of implementation errors caused by high interaction and design complexity?

Figure 2 shows the decision matrix and the expected benefit of a user interface pattern. For example, if the complexity of a solution is high but the frequency of use low, it is much cheaper to develop individual user interfaces instead of trying to implement a generic and reusable pattern.

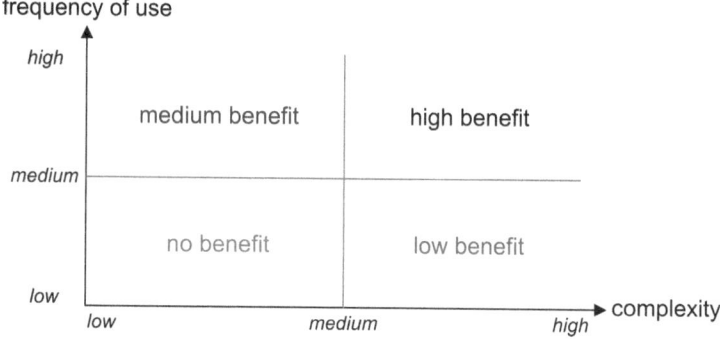

Fig. 2 Decision matrix for user interface patterns

User interface patterns are not a panacea that automatically leads to excellent user interface design. Good decision criteria, a well-established cooperation process between the pattern development team and product developers and an always up-to-date style guide are important factors for successfully working with user interface patterns in the development process.

4   Rethinking Prerequisites

4.1   Methods and Tools

The previous section pointed out how measures such as a style guide, usability inspections and user interface patterns support good user interface design. For a highly efficient and qualitative user centered design process, further methods and tools are needed. Involving users in the software development process from the beginning reduces risks of undesirable development and costly changes at later stages in the process.

Table 1 shows an overview of user centered methods for different stages of the development process. In the following, we explain two of these methods and how they are applied at DATEV eG.

The *user experience questionnaire* is a tool for qualitative evaluation of user experience objectives (Laugwitz et al. 2008). The standardized questionnaire contains 26 semantic differentials, e.g. whether users find a product attractive or boring, fast or slow, etc. For users the questionnaire is relatively easy and fast to answer and for your company it is a budget-friendly way to monitor the quality of your software.

DATEV eG regularly sends out user experience questionnaires via online survey. The results allow two kinds of analyses: First, we can compare the user experience of different versions of the same software product and conclude which one is better received. Second, we can compare the user experience of different products in order to ensure continuously high quality across the whole product

Table 1 User centered design in the development process

Stages of the development process			
1 Requirements engineering	2 System design	3 Implementation	4 Release and maintenance
Methods			
User experience questionnaire (UEQ)	Storyboards	Usability testing	User experience questionnaire
Interviews	Wireframes	Rapid prototyping	Field studies
Focus groups	User scenarios	High fidelity prototyping	Online surveys
Personas	User stories		
Field studies			
Online surveys			
Goal			
Who are our users? How do they work?	How will users interact with the system?	Do processes work and fulfill the requirements?	Has user satisfaction improved?
Which added value do our products provide?		Does user interfaces match with guidelines?	Are all errors fixed?

portfolio. Note that presenting absolute values from a user experience questionnaire without anything to compare these values with is not very meaningful. Questions from the user experience questionnaire fit to the model for software attractiveness (see Sect. 2.2). For DATEV eG products we learned from statistical analysis that especially the factors dependability, perspicuity and aesthetics increase users' overall satisfaction.

Another awesome method to gain user feedback directly is *usability testing*. Usability testing enables you to test the whole range from a first clickable prototype to a fully developed product. Usually usability testing determines all positive and negative experiences of subjects with an interface through observation and questioning. At DATEV eG it is mandatory that the whole team of developers observe test sessions in order to get a realistic impression of how their product is used by users, which user interfaces work fine and which ones still need improvement.

DATEV eG often combines both of the previously described methods. We invite selected users to test prototypes in a usability lab and ask them to fill in a user experience questionnaire afterwards. This combination allows enrichment of the qualitative results from the lab with quantitative results from the questionnaire.

4.2   Technicians Are not Designers

How difficult it is to introduce user centered design depends on your company and your established development process. At DATEV eG it was relatively easy to start with user centered design in general since there always have been feedback mechanisms between DATEV eG as a cooperative and its users who are members of DATEV eG at the same time.

The main challenge was enabling technical developers to create excellent user interfaces and interaction design. Establishing a central design team was a first important step in this direction.

Today, there are basically three roles in the DATEV eG development process:

- *Domain developers* who have very good specific knowledge in the business domain of the software and mainly develop concepts.
- *Technical developers* with excellent technical and programming skills for the implementation of concepts.
- *User experience designers* who are highly familiar with user centered design methods and support their implementation throughout the development process. As part of a development team, user experience designers are also responsible for user interface and interaction design.

Historically, DATEV eG had a lot of domain developers and technical developers but not enough designers. Therefore, the first approach was to further qualify technical developers and teach them design lessons. In the process it became clear that you cannot expect excellent technicians to become excellent designers. As a consequence, additional designers have been hired. Nowadays, the responsibility for user experience design at DATEV eG is shared between the central design team and further decentralized user experience designers who are an integral part of a product development team together with domain developers and technical developers. The decentralized designers accompany the development of a software product from requirements engineering to product release.

4.3   The Role of User Experience Designers

In the past, user interface and interaction design was characterized by a lot of transformation work by the central design team and developers. Ideas were via use cases and wireframes that finally lead to a design concept. This concept was given as bitmap image to the technical developers, who implemented the user interface design in real code. As a result, the final user interface design and the design concept were only approximately the same.

Today, the user takes the central role in the development process. User experience designers start their work by understanding users and their tasks. Based on this understanding, designers create use cases, further usable wireframes and design resources (e.g. color schemes, icons, etc.). Wireframes and user interfaces are designed by the user experience team with a technology that can be reused by technical developers. This means, designing user interfaces is not only showing graphics, but already creating code that describes key aspects of the design. Thereby, user experience designers are an integrated part of the software development process. At MIX '11 Jeff Croft explained the challenge for designers as follows (Croft 2011; Schubert 2011):

Designers: Your material is code. Code is the building block of all digital products.

Both, designers and technicians need a general understanding of design and technics in order to cooperate effectively and use modern development technologies to their full advantage. If this is working, the triad of domain-specific, technical and design-related know-how will create the best possible product.

5   Best Practices

In the course of the development of the current DATEV eG product line, more than 3,500 users were involved trough user centered design methods. As a conclusion we present best practices that we learned during the years.

5.1   The Key to Good Design is the Management

User centered design is best enforceable top down. It is essential that the management understands design as a strategic instrument that helps to reach the corporate objective and fosters innovation. Good design is not for free, but it costs time and money. These resources need to be allocated by the management.

5.2   Numbers Convince the Management

The best way to convince the management is presenting numbers. Therefore quantify the quality of the user experience your products deliver. Reasonable instruments to evaluate and benchmark the user experience of your products are, e.g., the user experience questionnaire (see Sect. 0) or the AttrakDiff questionnaire (Hassenzahl et al. 2003).

5.3   The Change from Technology-Driven Development to User Centered Design Needs a Trigger

Nobody wants to change a running system. The decision for user centered design needs a trigger. Does your company have a lack of revenue? Is the satisfaction of your users decreasing and criticism growing? Is there a new, very powerful competitive product on the market or will be released soon? Use this situation to start a change and introduce or improve the user centered design in your company.

5.4   Start Small and Promote Your Success

If you plan to introduce user centered design in general or fundamental new methods, start with a small, promising project and promote the success broadly. This will be the best motivation for other projects to follow and cooperate with your design team.

5.5   Communicate Your Design Guidelines Clearly and Effectively

To successfully establish continuously excellent design, communicating the rules and guidelines is absolutely important. Explaining the background of design decisions helps to enhance the acceptance also among technical developers. Whether you should dictate strict design rules or rather provide general principles depends on the question, how much design background and knowledge the target group has. In general, the more design know-how is already available, the less strict guidelines need to be, e.g. in a style guide (see Sect. 0).

5.6   Define Clear Responsibilities and Dependability

User centered design is not a democratic process within your company, so define and communicate responsibilities and dependability. However, access boundaries to user centered design methods should be as low as possible. Cooperate with product managers and invite not only designers but also technicians, e.g., as observers to a usability test. This will broaden the understanding and acceptance of user centered design across your company, while the final decisions are still made by the design team.

5.7   Do a Lot of User Centered Design in Early Stages of the Development Process

The earlier you collect user feedback, the cheaper it is to fix identified problems. Asking your users, e.g. via questionnaire or focus groups, does not cost much and provides you and your company's management a solid basis for further decisions.

6   Summary

This article provides insight into the change from technology-driven development to user centred design at DATEV eG. It describes our pattern-based approach, the design methods and tools we employ, and how responsibility for user centred design at DATEV eG is shared between the central design team and further decentralised user experience designers who are an integral part of a product development team. We condense our overall experiences from the change process and describe the seven best practices for successfully establishing user centred design in software manufacturing companies. The application of these measures facilitates design quality and efficient development of excellent software products with a positive user experience.

References

Croft, J. (2011). Designer and developer: A case for the hybrid. *MIX11*, Las Vegas, 12–14 April 2011. http://channel9.msdn.com/Events/MIX/MIX11/EXT07

Hassenzahl, M., Platz, A., Burmester, M., & Lehner, K. (2000). Hedonic and ergonomic quality aspects determine a software's appeal. In T. Turner, & G. Szwillus (Eds.), *Proceedings of the SIGCHI conference on human factors in computing systems (CHI'00)* (pp. 201–208). New York: ACM.

Hassenzahl, M., Burmester, M., & Koller, F. (2003). AttrakDiff: Ein Fragebogen zur Messung wahrgenommener hedonischer und pragmatischer Qualität. In J. Ziegler, & G. Szwillus (Eds.), *Mensch and Computer 2003. Interaktion in Bewegung* (pp. 187–196). Stuttgart/Leipzig: B.G. Teubner.

Laugwitz, B., Held, T., & Schrepp, M. (2008). Construction and evaluation of a user experience questionnaire. In A. Holzinger (Ed.), *HCI and usability for education and work* (Lecture notes in computer science, Vol. 5298, pp. 63–76). Berlin: Springer.

Nielsen, J., & Landauer, T. (1993). A mathematical model of the finding of usability problems. In *Proceedings of the INTERACT'93 and CHI'93 conference on human factors in computing systems (CHI'93)* (pp. 206–213). New York: ACM.

Schubert, Ulf (2011). MIX11: Designer and developer: A case for the hybrid. http://www.user-experience-blog.de/archives/2011/04/mix11-designer-and-developer-a.html

Segerståhl, K., & Jokela, T. (2006). Usability of interaction patterns. In *CHI'06 extended abstracts on human factors in computing systems (CHI EA'06)* (pp. 1301–1306). New York: ACM.

Start the Game: Increasing User Experience of Enterprise Systems Following a Gamification Mechanism

Maik Schacht and Silvia Schacht

Abstract

"Hi dear, how was your day?" In the rarest of cases the responded would answer: "I had so much fun when entering the customer data into our Enterprise Systems." However, the usage of Enterprise Systems is nowadays for many employees a key element of their working activities. Therefore, their motivation to use these systems consistently is essential for organizations to ensure transparency and process accuracy. While today most software products have a high usability, they lack in positive user experiences such as fun. One trend having the potential to solve this issue is Gamification. Using mechanisms of traditional games such as achievements or rankings is successfully implemented in private applications such as social networks (e.g. Facebook) or online traveling portals (e.g. tripadvisor). These mechanisms motivate individuals to perform certain activities they would otherwise not do. Gabe Zichermann – a visionary of Gamification – explained this phenomenon as following: *Games are the only force in the known universe that can get people to take actions against their self-interest, in a predictable way, without using force.* The principle of Gamification and its potential in organizations is presented in this book chapter.

1 Motivation

Why are accounts payable clerks entering data sets into a SAP system enthusiastically despite it is a highly seasoned and monotonous job? Why do managers fight against dragons when preparing a presentation using Microsoft's PowerPoint? The

M. Schacht

e-mail: maik.schacht@gmx.de

S. Schacht
University of Mannheim - Chair of Information Systems IV, Mannheim, Germany
e-mail: schacht@eris.uni-mannheim.de

A. Maedche et al. (eds.), *Software for People*, Management for Professionals,
DOI 10.1007/978-3-642-31371-4_11, © Springer-Verlag Berlin Heidelberg 2012

answer to these questions is as simple as unexpected. They have fun in using their job-related software products. However, this was not always the case. In the past years, software products underwent an evolution form purely "solving problems" to "make software usable" to "improve overall user experience."

With the emergence of software as a product its sheer objective focused on machine programming. Software was solely some lines of codes which could only be understood and used by developers themselves. But soon developers had to realize that instructing users in dealing with software applications became more and more difficult. In particular, the growing complexity of enterprise software has led to increased reluctance of employees. These difficulties resulted in the second stage of software evolution integrating users and designers into the software development process to create more usable products. The user-centered design paradigm was born. The paradigm focused on increasing usability of software products by moving the user into the center of any design activities instead of the software system. It became the designer's primarily role to simplify the tasks of users and to ensure that the actual use of the software system corresponds to its intended use. Today, many software products fulfill users' demands on utility and usability. Nevertheless, most of these products – especially when used in enterprises – do not motivate individuals to use them despite they are usable. Improving user experience has become to the central objective of the third stage in software product evolution.

One trend in the efforts of improving user experience is Gamification, which is defined as "the use of game design elements in non-game contexts" (Deterding 2011, p.13). According to Gartner's 2011 Hype Cycle report[1] Gamification is identified as an upcoming trend on its way to the "peak of inflated expectations", which is anticipated to be adopted by the mainstream in the next 5–10 years. Various developments in our society as well as used technology reinforce this trend. One of the most decisive developments is the change of generations. The Baby Boomer generation (1946–1964) is retiring and will be replaced more and more by members of Gen X (1965–1978) and Gen Y (1979–2000). Especially employees of the Gen Y grow up with modern technologies such as internet, mobile devices or game consoles. Because of their experiences with modern technologies, both generations (X and Y) changed significantly the way how employees interact with each other (Burke and Hiltbrand 2011). Now one might wonder why these changes in generations have an impact on enterprise software and why companies should implement games. The answer is: consumerization. While the Baby Boomer generation grew up without an early technological socialization, Gen X and Gen Y cultivate their interaction with modern technologies intensively. The difference in technological socialization between these generations led to changing behavior and working patterns. Key characteristics of this difference are the need for a constant access to new and actual information (e.g. via Google, News and Feeds), the desire for intensive networking (e.g. via Facebook and Twitter), and the multi-tasking ability (e.g. with the aid of iPad or SmartPhones). All in all, in new generations one

---

[1] http://www.gartner.com/it/page.jsp?id=1763814

can observe an increased desire for individualization. Once accustomed themselves to all these applications, the young employees prefer to use them not only in their private life but also in their everyday work. However, the IT landscape of companies is yet not prepared for this desire of individualization respectively consumerization of enterprise systems (Vogel et al. 2010). With their affinity to modern technologies, applications or games, Gamification can be a first step along the way towards the needs of young generations.

The remainder of this book chapter is structured as following: After some motivating examples of successful Gamification implementation in products of Microsoft and SAP, we provide a definition of the term Gamification and subsequently delimit this concept from other levels of gaming. We then give an insight in the world of Gamification by describing its key elements, presenting a user categorization and mapping the users to most fitting elements. Of course, it is not enough to implement Gamification applications in enterprises. Therefore, we assembled a collection of pre-conditions and pitfalls companies have to pay attention for. In the third and fourth chapter we provide some managerial implications and conclude this book chapter with a brief summary.

2 Concept of Gamification

2.1 The Cases of Microsoft and SAP

Despite Gamification is a pretty much new trend, few companies have already implemented games to improve employees' user experience. Some selected examples are Microsoft and SAP.

One of the visionaries adapted Gamification is Microsoft. Meanwhile, the software company has launched so many "gamified" applications that they categorized them in internal productivity games and productivity games for end users. The first example, we want to present, is one of Microsoft's internal productivity games called *Communicate Hope*.[2] This gaming application supported developers in the development process of Microsoft's new a communication platform Lync. *Communicate Hope* motivated thousands of employees to participate the testing process by playing the game. When testing out particular features of Lync users could collect points by providing feedback on usability as well as product design and by submitting bugs. Product testers were also able to collect points if they responded to the submitted feedback of users. Finally, the accumulated points lead to a monetary reward. All in all, thousands of dollars were spent to the participating employees. *Communicate Hope* was not only a success because thousands of users played the game, but also because the product testing team received 16× more feedback from "gamers" than non-gamers.

---

[2] http://blogs.technet.com/b/next/archive/2011/05/16/microsoft-s-ross-smith-asks-shall-we-play-a-game.aspx

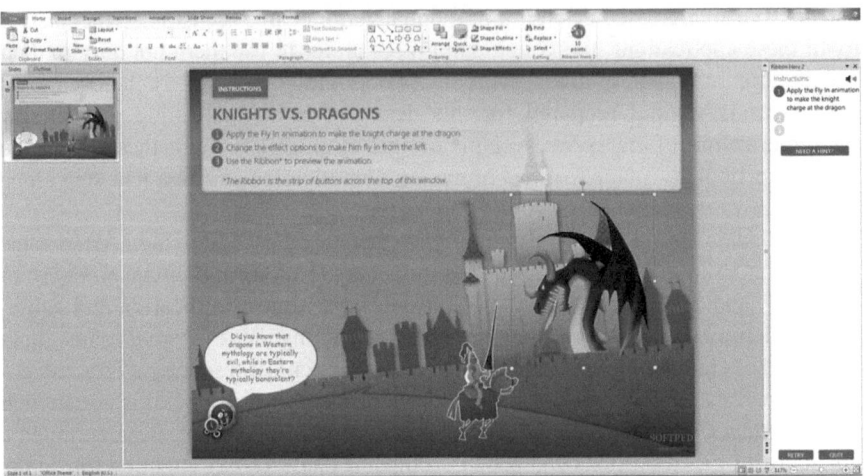

Fig. 1 Screenshot of Microsoft's *Ribbon Hero*

Our second example also comes from Microsoft. *Ribbon Hero*[3] aims to train users on Microsoft's Office Suite by incentivizing them through fun and games if they learn new skills when dealing with one of the Office products. The user gets shifted into a 2D world (see Fig. 1) and has to complete several challenges to get to the next level. The challenges introduce the users into the features of PowerPoint, Word, Excel, or OneNote. By actually using the new features, the user collects experience points and can race for a high score with colleagues. In the meantime Microsoft launched a sequel because of the success of *Ribbon Hero*.

Even though Microsoft is one of the leading companies in terms of Gamification, so it's not the only one. SAP also seeks to improve the user experience through the use of playful elements. In *SAP's Gamification Project* the company tries to breathe fresh life into a monotonous work such as maintaining vendor data. Accounts payable clerks, for example, enter thousands of invoices manually. To increase the motivation on this monotonous work, SAP integrated a reward system (see Fig. 2). When entering invoices or line items the users and their team can earn points. By collecting these points they can raise their status and participate in regular challenges.

All three examples show, employees become motivated to do work they are usually reluctant to do and thus support their colleagues. Even the most moronic task can be done enthusiastically when a playful goal is behind it. By integrating gaming elements in non-game context, users are introduced to a software product without the need of reading a bulky handbook. Summarizing, modern work can make fun. Now, one might say, that it is enough to design software products as easy to use as possible. However, there is a difference between ease of use and fun.

---

[3] http://www.ribbonhero.com/

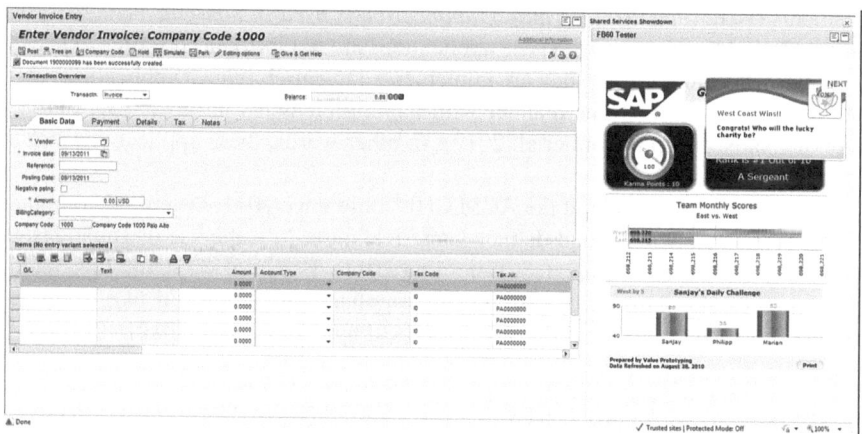

Fig. 2 Screenshot SAP's Gamification project (http://enterprise-gamification.com/index.php/de/finanzwesen/51-having-fun-with-accounts-payable)

Work that is fun is more attractive to employees. Unlike ease of use, fun has a more powerful influence on individuals with regard to their motivation to try to do something or their perseverance when doing it (Carroll and Thomas 1988). Nevertheless, playing is not equal to Gamification.

2.2   What Is Gamification?

The first time reading about Gamification, our spontaneously reaction was: "that sounds interesting" as we also like games to relax in our free time. But in the following months as we had learned more about this trend, we discovered that there are little connections to traditional games one plays on the pc, gaming consoles or on a table with family and friends. In fact, when collecting more detailed information, we realized that researchers make a clear distinction between playing a game and using Gamification mechanisms in a software application. So, what is Gamification?

Most definitions on Gamification we found in literature have three main elements. First, *Gamification is a kind of games*. It is characterized by the set of rules, a declarative content and the gameplay as well as a social context (Bree 2011). In the context of Gamification most "games" are extended by some kind of competition, where users strife to defeat others. In Gamification applications, often the game is not limited to the digital world. Real users are competing with each other and are solving tasks of the real life. Second, *Gamification is not an entire game*. Rather, Gamification is the inclusion of single game elements in software products that do not have the purpose to entertain the users. When, for example, integrating single game elements into organizations' software applications the goals and rules of the organization have to be considered and reflected by the elements (Deterding 2011). Third, *Gamification is used in non-game contexts*, but in a real world environment. These applications are not introduced for the expected purpose of playing. Rather they are implemented to enrich typical applications used at work or in other serious manner with gaming elements to create joy, fun and working satisfaction (Thom et al. 2012). In other words, these applications aim to enhance user experience.

In his conference paper at the ACM CHI Conference 2011, Deterding combines these three key elements and defines Gamification as "... the use of game design elements in non-game contexts" (Deterding 2011). Because, we think, this definition lacks on the purpose of Gamification applications, we would like to extend Deterdings definition with the words expressed by (Thom et al. 2012):

> Gamification is the use of game design elements respectively mechanisms in non-game contexts to "... create a sense of playfulness [...] so that participation becomes enjoyable and desirable."

2.3   What Is Gamification Not?

Now that we've got a fairly clear picture of what is Gamification, we still have to answer the question, what is it not. From the definition described above, we know that Gamification is not a complete game and is used in non-game environments. Generally speaking, the two dimensions of completeness and environment of usage span the domain of games displayed in Fig. 3. On the one hand there are games respectively game elements designed for entertainment characterized by purely playful interactions. Applications of this domain are more a toy than a game. On the other hand the main purpose of *serious games* and Gamification applications is not entertainment. They focus on training, education and working motivation in a playful way. However, the borders between serious games and Gamification seem to be blurred. Therefore, we also give a brief overview on various forms of serious games.

Combining entertainment and education in games became popular in the early 1990s in so-called *edutainment* games. These applications were mostly video-games with an educational objective for preschool children. However, edutainment applications were not accompanied by the desired commercial success. On the contrary, *serious games* became more successful than edutainment games despite they encompass the same objectives. The main differentiation between both game classes is the integration of all aspects of education such as teaching, training, and informing instead of focussing on mere teaching facts and memorization. The design of serious games for users of all ages is the second key difference to edutainment games which make up the largest part of its success. A branch of serious games are (digital) game-based learning applications which have a clearly defined learning outcome (Susi et al. 2007). An overview on the differences between serious games and entertainment games is summarized in Table 1.

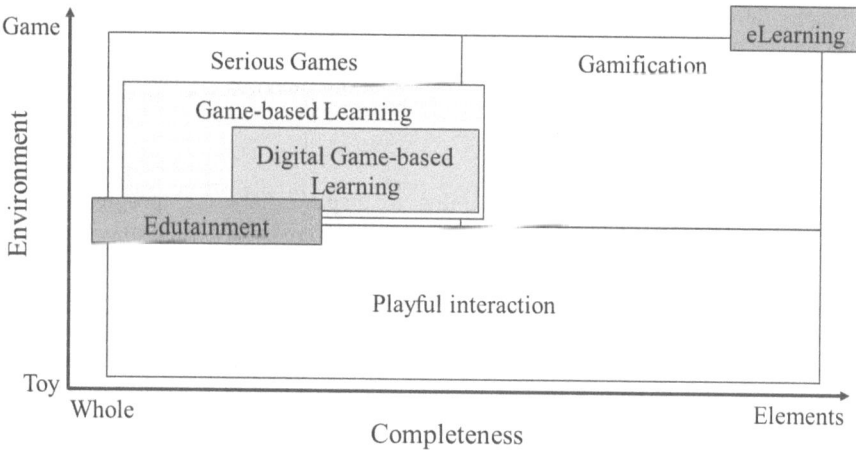

Fig. 3 Differentiation of gaming applications (Source: Based on Deterding 2011)

Table 1 Differences between serious and entertainment games (Source: Susi et al. 2007)

	Serious games	Entertainment games
Task versus rich experience	Problem solving focus	Rich experiences preferred
Focus	Important elements of learning	To have fun
Simulations	Assumption necessary for workable simulations	Simplified simulation process
Communications	Should reflect natural communication	Communication is often perfect

Another concept related to Gamification is e-learning. E-learning is a more general concept using single elements of games such as progression bars or achievements. It refers to adult learning supported by computer technology. Its spectrum ranges from computer-enhanced learning to computer-based learning to commonly, distance learning (Susi et al. 2007). Unlike Gamification applications, e-learning primarily focusses on train and teach adults, rather than increase user experience by providing more fun.

3 Framework of Gamification to Increase User Experience

3.1 Mechanics of Gamification

Gamification desires to raise users' experience when using software products. To do so Gamification has a tremendous pool of game mechanics adaptable in software applications. While some of them are components directly implementable in the software others more address users' emotions. So, we distinguished between *in-game* and *in-person mechanics*. Within these categories we clustered the mechanics by their overarching target. There are three main targets the mechanics pursue: (1) display progression, (2) provide feedback, and (3) engage a specific behavior (Source: gamification.org).

3.1.1 In-game Mechanics

Examples of in-game mechanics aiming to display the users' progression are *achievements, points, bonuses, leveling up* and *progression*. When playing, users can collect some rewards in the form of points, bonuses or achievements for carrying out their duties. For each single activity points will be allotted and cumulated to a total player score. Additionally, users can get bonuses when completing several tasks or combinations of tasks also called *combos*. If the activity is perceived as substantial and challenging, achievements are helpful motivators fostering users to tackle the task. While these types of rewarding are short-term motivators, leveling up and the display of users' progression can be seen as mid-term incentives. By collecting points, users progress consistently. This is usually displayed in numeric metrics like a progression bar. If levels are integrated in the Gamification software, the progression bar reveals the amount of points necessary to reach the next level. Leveling up unlocks new tasks and sets of challenges motivating users for playing.

Providing feedback is the second target of Gamification applications embodied by *appointments, extinction, countdown, and leader boards*. Appointments reward players when participate the game at a predetermined time or place. With such a game mechanic companies can foster team work and collaboration. It is necessary to provide a feature which enables users to tally their tasks. Therefore, the extinction mechanic refers to the concluding action and is directly associated to rewards. A forced kind of extinction is the countdown providing players a reward only if they accomplish the task in a certain amount of time. Feedback is also provided by leader boards where users are ranked in comparison to each other by their progression, achievements, levels or status.

Finally, typical examples of Gamification mechanics aiming to engage a specific behavior are *community collaboration* and *virality*. Both mechanisms engage team work among players. Community collaboration is the connection of multiple players aiming to jointly solve a specific task. Such a mechanic is only feasible if a critical mass of users exists. To reach such a critical mass, game designers developed a mechanic called virality. Virality rewards players when they invite friends or colleagues to participate in the game.

3.1.2 In-person Mechanics

While previously described mechanics are directly implementable in software products, in-person mechanics only works in combination with users' characteristics, emotions and feelings. Since it will be difficult, if not impossible, to measure these metrics, we were not able to determine any in-person mechanics displaying users' progression. Even to find an example of feedback-related game mechanics was a challenge. The one and only mechanic we have found is the

Table 2 Overview on selected Gamification mechanics

	Progression	Feedback	Behavior
In-game	Achievements	Appointments	Community collaboration
	Points and bonuses	Extinction	Virality
	Leveling up	Countdown	
	Progression	Leader boards	
In-person		Cascading information	Envy
			Epic meaning
			Loss aversion
			Free lunch

cascading information theory which refers to provide minimal snippets of information to users. These information snippets should avoid an information overflow and facilitate an appropriate level of understanding.

In contrary, we have found so many in-person mechanics targeting to engage a specific user behavior that we can only provide a small selection of them. One mechanic appealing users' behavior is *envy*. Envy is a very often used game mechanic taking advantage of users' desire to get what others already have. Thus, games provide some kind of visibility where players can compare themselves with others. This game mechanic is closely related to *loss aversion*. Since people want to retain their game rewards in possession, the introduction of punishments such as the lost of points or even status if they do not participate for a certain period of time, motivates them to persist in playing. Another game mechanic is the principle of *free lunch* where users get a reward for free because another player has done a specific task. Implementing the principle of free lunch in Gamification applications demands prudence, because it discourages those players who are doing the necessary work. The last game mechanics we are presenting is called *epic*. Epic refers to individuals' motivation to do a work because they believe that they can achieve something great, something awe-inspiring, and something bigger than themselves (Burke and Hiltbrand 2011). An overview on both categories of game mechanics is provided in Table 2.

3.2 Gamification User Categorization

Despite Gamification does not primarily focus on entertainment, the player classification of traditional entertainment games helps to understand the users' motivations to play. A well-known taxonomy of player types is drawn by Bartle in 1996. He categorized players by identifying the four most important factors in games that users enjoy when playing. These elements are (1) receiving an achievement within the game-context, (2) explore the game and its landscape, (3) socialize with others, and (4) impose upon others. Although Bartle has noted that mostly players combine all of these styles in themselves – depending on their mood or current playing style – he assumes that they prefer one single style. Thus, he labeled

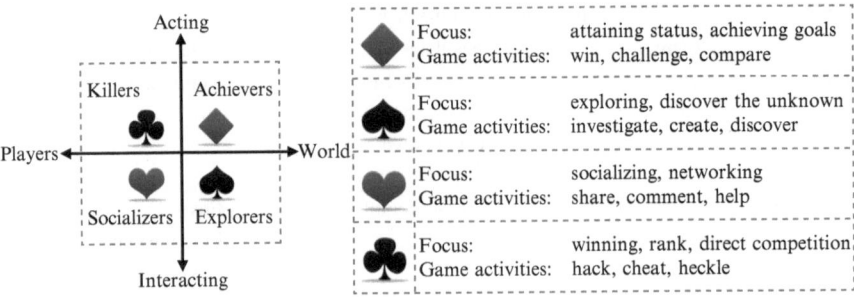

Fig. 4 Types of players, their focus and game activities

the player types according to their preferences. As an analogy to traditional game pack of cards he also assigns the four player types to the four symbols diamonds, spades, hearts and clubs (Fig. 4).

Those players who are primarily focusing on achieving specific goals or a certain status within the game he called *achievers* or diamonds, since they are always seeking for secrets and treasures. They prefer to act with the virtual world, to discover new areas, to collect points and to level up as central element of playing. Therefore, their primary game activities are geared to winning, challenging and comparing. Players striving to explore the world of the game, Bartle labeled *explorers*. In analogy to the traditional deck of cards these players are also called spades, because they always dig for more information. Explorers want the game surprising them. They favor to discover and investigate the unknown. The third type of players is the *socializer* (in analogy: hearts) using communication technologies of the game to chat and empathize with fellow players. They realize the game world as a setting, whereas the characters of other players arouse the socializer's interest. By chatting, commenting and helping others they maintain their relationships to fellow players and increase their own network. The fourth player type prefers the battle against others in direct peer-to-peer competitions. They act on other players through fighting in some way against them using game-internal tools. With their desire to win and to being listed on top of all rankings, they tend to resort to means like cheating, hacking or heckling. Therefore, Bartle called them *killers* or clubs, because they hit people with them (Bartle 1996).

Summarizing, Bartle's research starts from the premise that individuals are motivated playing games because of (1) their interest to explore its environment, (2) their desire to socialize with others, (3) their perceived satisfaction when collecting points and achieve game-related goals, or (4) their preference to compete with others. Because the motivations of users differ, various game mechanics fit more to a player type than others. Therefore, a comparison of player types and appropriate game mechanics may be helpful for design decisions of Gamification applications. Such a comparison is displayed in Table 3.

Any game mechanic listed by us is appropriate for achievers. These players do not only hoard rewards such as bonuses, points or achievements. They also strive to obtain every goal achievable including goals such as come out as winner in

Table 3 Comparison of player types and appropriate game mechanics (Source: Based on gamification.org)

	Achievements	Points	Boruses	Leveling up	Progression	Appointments	Countdown	Leader board	Extinction	Comunity Collab.	Virality	Casc. Information	Envy	Loss Aversion	Epic	Free Lunch
Achiever	●	●	●	●	●	●	●	●	●	●	●	●	●	●	●	●
Explorer	●	●	●	●		●	●		●	●		●	●	●	●	●
Socializer			●			●				●	●	●	●		●	●
Killer	●	●	●	●	●		●	●	●		●	●	●		●	●

comparison with others or win a challenge. To do so, they would take advantage of each opportunity provided by the game. If they are rewarded by inviting colleagues and friends to participate (virality), they would do so. If they see any possibility to become the top of a ranking e.g. in a leader board, they would fight for it. If they are afraid to lose some of their already earned achievements, they would do anything to avoid this. Countdowns and appointments also motivate them to catch the next reward.

Similar to achievers, explorers are satisfied by nearly every possible game mechanic. Only progression, virality and leader boards are exceptions. Explorers typically strive to discover the unknown, explore the game and its characteristics. Therefore, progression and leader boards are less important game mechanics for them. In contrast, explorers perceive leveling up as a necessary mechanic. Accomplishing the next level unlocks new challenges, tasks and skill sets facilitating them to discover new areas of the game. Whereas, they realize fellow players as additional feature to discover, interacting with others is not their primary goal. If needed explorers use other players to achieve their goals. Therefore, it is absolutely sufficient to access the aid of already active players, so that virality will not arouse their interest.

To catch socializers in Gamification application becomes more difficult. Socializers seek contacts to other individuals. Especially mechanisms focusing on displaying the progression and providing feedback are less important for most of them. Socializers' demands can be integrated by behavioral mechanics such as common collaboration or virality. In their pursuit to help others and share information, socializers prefer common collaborations and team work within the game. They persist in playing when they get the feeling their help is needed and desirable. Thus, they tend to suggest the game to colleagues and friends. To enrich the gaming community with more users of this player type, non-game related mechanics are useful. Such mechanics can be chat functionalities, news feeds or lists of friends.

If the mechanic does not addresses a generic need of individuals (e.g. extinction of tasks, cascading information, envy, epic meaning) and thus fits to all types of players, the killer is the opposite of socializers. Game mechanics motivating socializers to participate are less motivating for killers and vice versa. Killers focus on winning, rankings and the direct competition with fellow players. To satisfy their desire, mechanisms such as achievements, points, countdowns or leader boards are convenient.

3.3 Factors Organizations Should Consider

Knowing the users and the game mechanics is not enough to implement Gamification applications successfully. Thus, success is not only related to increased user experience in companies' workforce but also related to improved productivity of employees. Many factors like corporate culture, social norms within the team or leadership style influence the impact of Gamification. These factors have to be considered when designing appropriate use cases for participating in a Gamification application (Cheng et al. 2011).

One important factor companies should consider when designing Gamification applications is the concept of flow. In his work Csíkszentmihályi defines flow as "the holistic experience that people feel when they act with total involvement." The concept of flow can be adapted to many situations of individuals' life. People might enter into the flow when playing a game in their free-time. Because the game is a passion for them, players follow the rules and pursue the goals without questioning what for tasks or guidance. For this time the player immerses within his own universe of the game. Entering the state of flow can occur because of two reasons or to a certain extent their combination. Either the task to solve is challenging but the individual is aware that it can solve the task with his set of skills. Or the individual realizes that the task is not too challenging but he has to extend his existing skill set. If tasks are too challenging or too many new skills are required for solving the task, individuals either get into anxiety respectively into boredom. Thus, flow is only a small bandwidth between anxiety and boredom as displayed in Fig. 5.

Especially in the use and acceptance of information technology, many researchers examined the concept of flow. Most of this research has identified different characteristics of flow such as control, concentration or enjoyment. Because they perceive the definition of Csíkszentmihályi as too broad, Hsu and Lu (2004) define flow as ... *an extremely enjoyable experience, where an individual engages in a [...] game activity with total involvement, enjoyment, control, concentration and intrinsic interest.* (p. 857)

Following this definition it is not surprisingly that the concept of flow is not only used in games for entertainment. According to Csíkszentmihályi games and thus the concept of flow are applicable in enterprises as well, since:

> Work is much more like a game than most other things we do during the day. It usually has clear goals and rules of performance. It provides feedback either in the form of knowing that one has finished a job well done, in terms of measurable sales or through an evaluation by one's supervisor. A job tends to encourage concentration and prevent distractions, and ideally, its difficulties match the worker's skills. (Csíkszentmihályi 1997b)

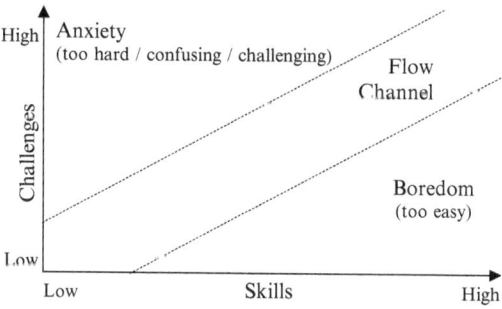

Fig. 5 State of flow between boredom and anxiety (Source: Csíkszentmihályi 1997a)

The concept of flow in combination with social norms – a further popular concept of the psychology area – result in 11 main design principles for Gamification applications introduced by Groh (2012). The clustering of the principles bases on Deci's and Ryan's "self-determination theory" which describes three innate needs of individuals for intrinsic motivation. The first need refers to relatedness – a universal need of individuals to interact with others and keep in contact with them. A second basic need is competence. Generally, individuals aspire to work effectively and to manage problems in a given environment. To have and keep control over their own lives is the third need of individuals also called autonomy. Groh's 11 design principles categorized to the basic needs are summarized in Table 4.

3.4 Threats

While we have described intensively the opportunities of Gamification in the previous chapters, we also want to provide a brief discussion on possible threats. The first and most obvious issue is the privacy of users. Leader boards, rankings and levels provide a lot of player-related information. When the corporate culture and social norms convey the feeling that participating in Gamification-based applications is viewed as wasting of time, users may refrain from participating when their playing activity is visible by achievements or leader boards. While on the one hand game mechanics publishing user interactivity can be motivating since they also display possible contacts and friends, they can on the other hand also be demotivating when users tend to hide their working actions (Burke and Hiltbrand 2011).

Another threat is the so-called "Gamepocalypse" introduced by Jesse Shell.[4] In his vision Jesse Shell sketches a "gamified" future where individuals only get

---

[4] http://fora.tv/2010/07/27/Jesse_Schell_Visions_of_the_Gamepocalypse

Table 4 Design principles for Gamification applications (Source: Groh 2012)

Relatedness	Connect to personal goals
	Connect to a meaningful community of interest
	Create a meaningful story
	Beware of social context meanings
Competence	Provide interesting challenges
	Provide clear visual varying, and well structured goals
	Provide juicy feedback
	Beware of unintended behaviors
Autonomy	Play is voluntary
	Beware of losing autonomy
	Beware of devaluating activities

motivated by earning points, achievements or bonuses. Every personal interaction will be gamified. Even when brushing their teeth, eating healthier food or visiting friends they would expect some kind of reward (Groh 2012). This also goes along with one of the pitfalls mentioned by Burke and Hiltbrand (2011). They advise against a moral hazard of game play referring to the risk that actual moral of an activity will be removed and replaced by game-based rewards. Especially in cases where the game-related rewards will be removed the original motivation of a person to take a specific action is lost, even if it was once fun for the person (Burke and Hiltbrand 2011).

When not carefully designed Gamification applications can also being perceived as unfair. Especially in situations where one leader board or ranking is applied in more than one Gamification-related application, users can get the feeling they get a raw deal. Thus, it is important to avoid a usage of same leader boards in multiple applications, when those are differing in the complexity of tasks. Otherwise, Gamification applications create a perceived inequality (Burke and Hiltbrand 2011).

4   Management Implications

In the following section we want to inspire managers implementing Gamification applications by providing a selection potential use cases supporting organizations to improve the user experience of their employees and consequently increase the overall performance. To get a first comprehensive but brief overview on possible usage scenarios we offer beside a short description some exemplarily Gamification mechanisms as well as an assessment of the use case via a star rating system. We assess the use case with regard to two aspects. First, we appreciate the usage scenario with respect to its capability to become successful in organizations. The higher we assume its capability, the more stars we assigned. Second, we assess its ease of implementation. The more stars we assigned to a use case, the lower will be its implementation effort in terms of time, costs and man power.

4.1   HR: Training of Employees

Today, many firms are using e-learning platforms to educate employees or train new, unskilled workers with little man power in periods of peak activities. However, employees have less or even no motivation to click through e-learning programs. Often they perceive the usage of such education applications as boring and waste of time. Traditional e-learning platforms only offer progression bars or multiple choice questionnaires, which can be answered by the users incorrectly without any consequences. This results in only nominal learning effects. Reasons for the low user acceptance may be its slight user experience. We suggest enriching e-learning platforms by implementing additional Gamification mechanisms.

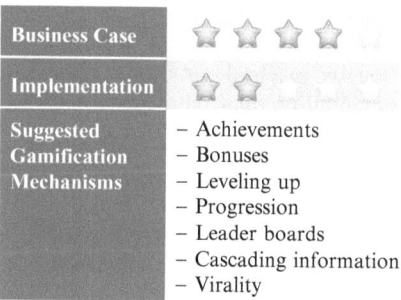

Business Case	☆ ☆ ☆ ☆
Implementation	☆ ☆
Suggested Gamification Mechanisms	– Achievements – Bonuses – Leveling up – Progression – Leader boards – Cascading information – Virality

Because knowledge of employees is today one of the most valuable assets of companies, we rate the business case of Gamification usage to train employees with four out of five stars. Only, if companies have experts in particular knowledge areas, they can remain competitive and generate revenue. Regarding the implementation effort, we assess this use case with two out of five stars. Often companies are using commercial e-learning platforms only adjustable by its vendors. Thus, we expect a high customization and synchronization effort.

4.2   HR: Recruiting of New Specialists

Employers are often faced to a tight job market. Companies have to battle for experts and the situation will be aggravated because of the demographic change. Actually, companies struggle to hire specialists and outstanding junior employees using traditional strategies of motivation and recruiting. We therefore suggest using so-called alternate reality games (ARG) that are implemented and offered by special providers. At the moment these games are mostly used to promote new products. However, ARGs are also feasible to put the player into a gaming situation, provide some challenges and thus test his or her skills. Corresponding to players' success in solving different kinds of problems the HR department is able to choose adequate potential employees.

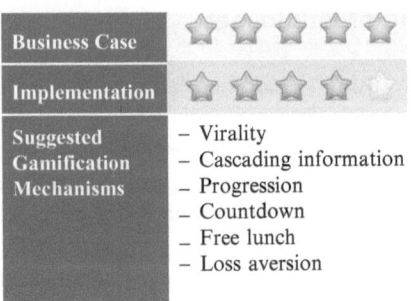

Business Case	☆ ☆ ☆ ☆ ☆
Implementation	☆ ☆ ☆ ☆
Suggested Gamification Mechanisms	– Virality – Cascading information – Progression _ Countdown _ Free lunch – Loss aversion

Since we perceive the topic of recruiting experts and young, motivated employees as a key topic in the next years, we rate this use case with five stars. The implementation effort is also relatively low, because the conception and service can be purchased by external providers. Consequently, companies only have to pay for the commercial product. Thus, we assess the implementation effort with four out of five stars.

4.3   HR: Measure Employees' Performance

Each year, managers negotiate target agreements with their employees. Often these target agreements are arranged in a cascading fashion, to bring employees' contribution in line with strategic business goals and optimize their payments. Thus, target agreements serve in nearly every company as central element for motivation and controlling. However, besides the fact that the fulfillments of these targets are very seldom measurable in an objective way, there are some other issues with this controlling element. In most cases, the target agreements are defined individually resulting in difficulties of synchronizing among the entire organization. Furthermore, the agreed targets leave only little room for adjustments to changing business needs. From our point of view Gamification can be a potential solution for future performance measurement of employees. Let us think this idea up in more detail. Imagine the following scenario: A company maintains a catalogue containing all possible targets for employees. This catalogue is managed centrally according to the business needs of the company. Each of these targets is accompanied by the corresponding points. Employees are maintaining their targets by their own including reasons for their activities. These reasons facilitate the manager to check the target against its plausibility. Finally, the system computes the actual, total points and determines the bonus payments. Even when the business targets will change the targets in the system and points can be adapted for all employees.

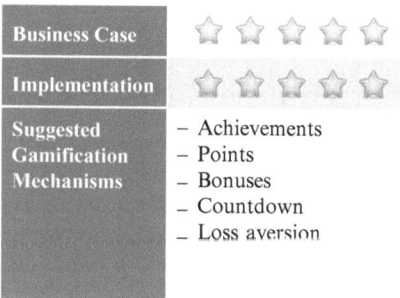

The implementation of such a target catalogue and the corresponding information systems is quite simple to implement and provides a high value, because changing business needs are easily to illustrate. The calculation of the payments will be automated. Therefore, we assigned five stars for both, high business value and low implementation effort.

4.4   IT Service Provider: Freemium Services

Virtual market places providing a number of various applications were the first who demonstrated the success of freemium services. Freemium services are those services that exist in two forms: a light version and a full version. Often the light version can be purchased at low or no costs so that the buyer can get a taste of the product. Once the customer is on the hook, he or she is more willing to buy the full service. Such Freemium services offer a great potential for internal services, because company-internal service providers often have some difficulties to compete against external services since their return on investment is not clearly visible.

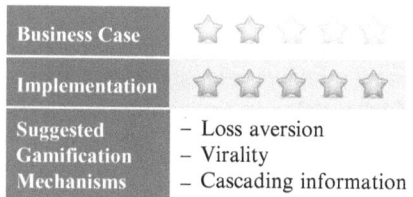

There is little experience on the application of Freemium services in businesses, but we assume that the success of these trial versions may be as successful in business contexts as in gaming background. However, we rate the business case with two out of five stars as a result of missing experiences. The implementation effort of Freemium services is assessed by us as very low, because the already offered service has simply been slimed down. Thus, we gave to this use case with respect on its implementation effort five stars.

4.5   IT Service Provider: Increase Utilization of IT Applications

IT applications are embedded in Enterprise Systems to support organizations in their day-to-day business. Often these applications are either purchased for a lot of money or implemented by an IT service provider with high effort. However, employees may be reluctant to use the applications because of a lack of qualified trainings, low user experience and motivation. Gamification mechanisms can be integrated in existing IT applications to improve users' attitude toward the software product. If the employees are more willing to use the systems, the transparency, efficiency and accuracy of processes are also increased. Thus, we rate the business case as highly promising and give it five stars. Depending on the adaptability and flexibility of the particular IT application the implementation effort of Gamification mechanisms varies. In average we assume a medium implementation effort and assess it with three out of five stars.

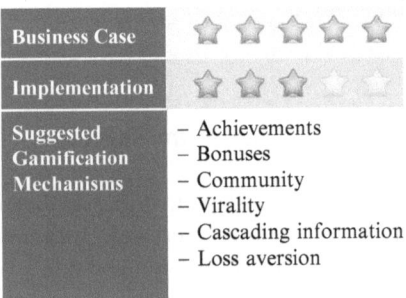

Business Case	☆ ☆ ☆ ☆ ☆
Implementation	☆ ☆ ☆ ☆ ☆
Suggested Gamification Mechanisms	– Achievements – Bonuses – Community – Virality – Cascading information – Loss aversion

5   Summary

Now you have an initial idea, how Gamification mechanics can be used to increase user experience of software products in organizations. We expect, in the near future Gamification will be widely used to motivate employees performing monotonous or disliked work. By implementing in-game mechanics such as achievements, bonuses, leader boards or community collaboration as well as in-person mechanisms like loss aversion, envy, epic and free lunch, software users may perceive their work as more enjoyable and desirable. Implementing Gamification in organizational software products is no guarantee to change the game of companies' day-to-day business. Organizations have to consider their strategic goals, corporate culture and predominant leadership style on the one hand, and the individuals' needs and preferences on the other hand.

But where can you use Gamification to generate advantages for your company? Our suggestion is to remember the last discussions with your IT users about the needs and problems. Now map the player types and appropriate game mechanics matrix to the issues you still remember to find first valid approaches. Take care of the pits when implementing the first Gamification mechanism and you can be one of the winners that change the game.

References

Bartle, R. (1996). Hearts, clubs, diamonds, spades: Players who suit MUDs. *Journal of MUD Research, 1*(1). Retrieved from http://www.mud.co nk/richard/hcds.htm

Bree, J. V. (2011). The end of the rainbow: In search of crossing points between organizations and games. In *Think Design Play DiGRA Conference,* Hilversum.

Burke, M., & Hiltbrand, T. (2011). How Gamification will change business intelligence. *Business Intelligence Journal, 16*(2), 8–17.

Carroll, J. M., & Thomas, J. C. (1988). Fun. *SIGCHI Bulletin, 19*(3), 21–24.

Cheng, L.-T., Shami, S., Casey, D., Muller, M., DiMicco, J., Patterson, J., et al. (2011). Finding moments of play at work. In *CHI 2011 Workshop* (2–5). Vancouver: Canada.

Csíkszentmihályi, M. (1997a). *Finding flow: The psychology of engagement with everyday life.* New York: Basic Books.

Csíkszentmihályi, M. (1997b). Finding flow (Book Review). In *Psychology Today.* Retrieved from http://www.psychologytoday.com/articles/199707/finding-flow

Deterding, S. (2011). Gamification: Toward a definition. *Design,* 12–15.

Gartner Report (2011). Gartner's 2011 Hype Cycle Special Report Evluates the Maturity of 1,900 Technologies. Retrived from http://www.gartner.com/it/page.jsp?id=1763814

Groh, F. (2012). Gamification: State of the art definition and utilization. In *4th seminar on research trends in media informatics* (39–46). Ulm: Germany.

Hsu, C.-L., & Lu, H.-P. (2004). Why do people play online games? An extended TAM with social influences and flow experience. *Information and Management, 41*(7), 853–868.

Susi, T., Johannesson, M., & Backlund, P. (2007). Serious games: An overview. *The American Surgeon, 73,* 1039–1063.

Thom, J., Millen, D., & DiMicco, J. (2012). Removing Gamification from an Enterprise SNS. In *CSCW 2012 Proceedings* (1067–1070). Washington: USA.

Vogel, R., Koçoğlu, T., & Berger, T. (2010). Consumerization. In R. Vogel, T. Koçoğlu, & T. Berger (Eds.), *Desktop-virtualisierung* (pp. 25–28). Wiesbaden: Vieweg + Teubner Verlag.

Introduction of Software Product Management at Wincor Nixdorf: Challenges and Lessons Learned

Christian Schloegel

Abstract

The importance of product management in the software industry is widely recognized and empirically validated. Despite its importance, the maturity level of software product management in companies is low, many companies struggle with the challenge of introducing product management. This paper describes a real-world industry experience report of a product management introduction project in a banking and retail IT Solutions Company. We illustrate the initial situation before the product management introduction project, the approach that has been pursued within the project, the challenges of the first year and the experiences that have been made.

1 Introduction

Product management has been recognized as a key success factor for any enterprise across all industries. Empirical studies such as described in Ebert (2007) have shown that also in the software industry good product management is highly relevant for the success of the individual products. Although, there are concrete guidelines about key success factors for good product management available, introduction of product management in software companies still seems rather an art than a well-defined process (Condon 2002; Gorchels 2000). Overall, the maturity level of product management in the software industry is still relatively low (van de Weerd et al. 2010). The reasons for this are manifold: First, the software industry historically has been driven by R&D and engineering today is still characterized by a technology-centric approach. Second, software is an immaterial product, with no production and logistics processes involved and changes after production are possible (Xu and Brinkkemper 2007).

C. Schloegel
Wincor Nixdorf International GmbH, Paderborn, Germany
e-mail: christian.schloegel@wincor-nixdorf.com

A. Maedche et al. (eds.), *Software for People*, Management for Professionals,
DOI 10.1007/978-3-642-31371-4_12, © Springer-Verlag Berlin Heidelberg 2012

The overall challenge of introducing product management can be approached from different angles. First, one can provide concrete artifacts such as reference frameworks or tools structuring and supporting the software product management process. Reference frameworks capture relations between key process areas, stakeholders and most important deliverables of software product management. Some well-known examples can be found in Ebert (2007, 2009), Kilpi (1998), Kittlaus and Clough (2009) and van de Weerd et al. (2006). A very comprehensive and often cited framework from the practice is Pragmatic Marketing (2012). Furthermore, tools such as requirements elicitation software support product managers in the process and target process transparency. Second, one can follow a behavioral research approach for a better understanding of the boundary conditions, the cause-effect-relationships and derive best practices for a successful introduction of product management. Introduction projects can be empirically analyzed either following a qualitative or quantitative approach. In general, there is not much empirical work published regarding product management introducing projects in the software industry. In this paper we present the results of a qualitative study in the form of an experience report at the German IT solutions company Wincor Nixdorf, which has recently introduced product management.

The paper is structured as follows. First, we give an overview on Wincor Nixdorf and the initial situation before the introduction project. Second, we provide a detailed description of the approach that has been pursued in the introduction project. Third we describe the challenges and changes in the first year. Fourth we document the experiences and lessons learned we made during the introduction process and the first year after implementation. Finally, we summarize the paper and give an outlook.

2 The Company and the Initial Situation

2.1 The Company: Wincor Nixdorf

Wincor Nixdorf is an internationally operating high-tech company focusing on delivering IT solutions for the banking, retail and postal industry. The company is providing specialized hardware and software products packaged into integrated solutions. The company has more than 9,000 employees on a global base and is market leader for cash handling and cash cycle solutions.

The business of Wincor Nixdorf can be grouped into three major pillars: First, Wincor Nixdorf is providing high-tech hardware for the banking and retail industry such as multifunctional ATMs, Automated Teller Safes (ATS), Cash Recycler, Kiosk Terminals, POS terminals, Automated Check Outs, specific PCs for thin client branch and store thin clients. In the hardware sector, Wincor Nixdorf is combining innovative technologies like RFID, digital video processing or OCR to build advanced hardware solutions.

From a software point of view as second pillar, the company is offering a complete suite of client technologies for the specialized banking and retail hardware following a multi-vendor approach. Wincor Nixdorf is offering a holistic front-office solution following a multi-channel approach for the banking market. The largest ATM net of the world with more than 50,000 ATMs is managed by a high scalable and reliable multi-cluster software solution from Wincor Nixdorf. It includes forecasting, optimization, monitoring and marketing components, which can be configured for the specific customer needs. In the retail area, the software solutions are focused on store processes, and point of sales solutions to optimize cash handling, cashless payments and general optimization of store processes. Finally, the third pillar is the service area, which includes product related services, managed services and outsourcing on a global scale. The company has a central software development organization with several development hubs. The industry specific software solutions are built by specialized teams with deep industry knowledge. The central software development is extended by country specific professional service units, which are pursuing integration, customization and individual programming to build solutions adopted for the individual customer needs.

2.2   The Initial Situation

Major pain points of the initial situation are depicted visually in Fig. 1. The situation before the introduction of software product management was characterized by powerful development managers, who decided the functional scope, selected non-functional requirements, defined the architecture, and managed release management with an integrated quality assurance.

Product management and product marketing teams existed, but had no clearly defined responsibilities. Product marketing was delivering high-level requirements and product management was mainly detailing out these requirements in the form of specifications by consulting the specific developers. The main focus of product managers was to create sales configuration data and descriptions, providing release notes and building the bridge to marketing, sales and legal entities. Critical and relevant decisions regarding scope, etc. were made by the development managers. There was no separation between custom development and standard product development, which additionally led to fast changing priorities and a lack of clear defined milestones. This dynamic environment caused the circumstance that the finally implemented features and functionalities had nothing to do with the initial specifications done by product management.

Due to a missing portfolio alignment there were multiple implementations solving the same problem in different ways, which led to increased TCO on the customer side and an unclear portfolio messaging to the sales group.

Due to unclear product decision responsibilities, there was a series of meetings discussing feature and architecture requests of customers, characterized by a lack of clear decisions. If a new or existing customer was asking about a specific feature, the realization of this feature was dependent on the relationship of the dedicated sales person to the development manager. A clear product strategy was missing for

Fig. 1 Initial situation

several products. As a result, a roadmap discussion with customers was quite difficult and unsatisfying for all involved parties.

Beside all these negative aspects, it has to be emphasized that overall the software was successful in the market. The reason for this was mainly that the customers have been served in a rather flexible and pragmatic way. However, the disadvantage of this flexible and pragmatic approach was that the predictability of time, budget, architecture and committed features was rather low.

3   The Introduction Project

To improve the entire situation and to establish a more industrialized and scalable approach, it was decided to run a realignment project. The project was under the sponsorship of the board. Furthermore, a monthly status update within the board meeting was carried out to track the progress of the project. The goals of the project were defined in the very beginning with clear measurements, as depicted in Fig. 2:

To get a clear understanding of the problem and ensure the execution afterwards, the heads of the different software and hardware units (Banking software, Banking hardware, Retail software, Retail hardware) were appointed as project leads. To get a common view between the two industry specific areas, the alignment of the hardware and software processes in banking and retail represented an additional challenge. The creation of customer solutions requires a combination of hardware

Fig. 2 Objectives of the introduction project

and software components. Therefore, it is necessary to do a joint planning and coordination between both disciplines. The development has to take place in parallel to achieve the challenging time-to-market demands for the customers. We will focus in the following primarily on the software related findings. Furthermore, we will underline the cross points between software and hardware to finally build holistic solutions, consisting of both areas.

It was obvious, that to achieve the goals and remove the identified pain points, the changes had to be fundamental. The result was a completely new defined operating model, which consisted of three key elements:

1. Setup a new R&D organization to support project oriented product development and capture synergies.
2. Fundamentally change of the existing line driven to a development project driven R&D (see Fig. 3).
3. Foster entrepreneurship through introduction of dedicated product managers.

In order to setup a new R&D organization with project oriented-product development support and synergy effects, the following procedures were implemented: First, R&D was organized in product oriented competency centers. Second, a new CTO organization for technology and process excellence was introduced. To enable the change from line driven to a development project driven R&D, the project team introduced several improvements: The new role of project leads with development budget and resource responsibility was established. The existing line responsibility for development activities was shifted to project lead responsibility.

Fig. 3 From line to project organization

Furthermore, a new project oriented common development process (with a harmonized milestone system across all R&D units) was implemented. Finally, to address the missing entrepreneurship and the unclear product responsibility the following changes have been implemented by the project team:

- Separation of product management ("what do we want to develop") from product development ("how do we want to develop").
- Introduce strengthened role of product management, which is independent from development, having the end-2-end product responsibility through the whole product lifecycle and the full R&D budget responsibility.

To achieve independency from development, it was decided, that product management will be established in the form of a separate unit. This unit is reporting to the corresponding global heads of Software and Hardware. As a consequence, the development units have a reporting line to the global head. At the same time the product managers have a reporting line to the same senior manager as well. This ensured independency between product management and development by organizational design (see Fig. 4 below). Additionally, it was ensured that the global head has end-2-end product and service responsibility including product management, R&D and business services.

In the following we will primarily focus on the discussion of the changes which were carried out in the product management area. The main goal was to determine a responsible person, who manages the entire product life cycle of a certain product or product area. This person was established as the product entrepreneur. In order to

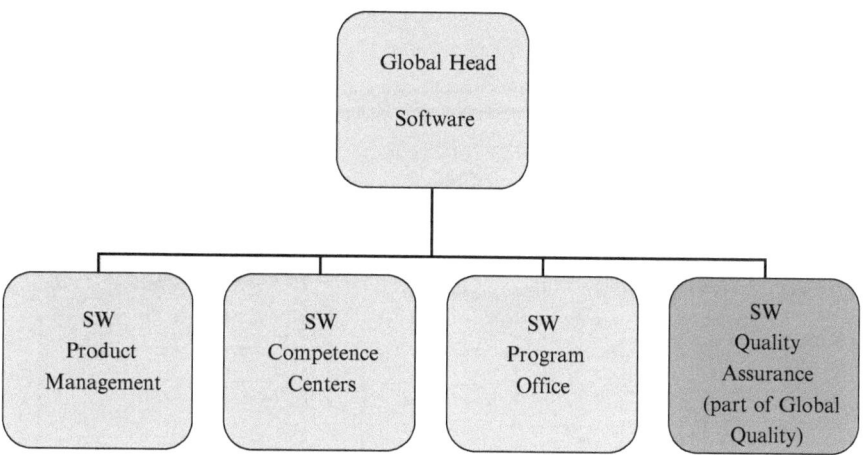

Fig. 4 Organization structure software development and product management

achieve this goal, the role of a product manager was redefined. The main tasks and responsibilities assigned to this role were the following:

- Identify growth potential in respective business segment, develop product strategy based on market, customer and competitor analysis in line with portfolio and solution strategy
- Translate market requirements into business requirements as a basis for new product developments and set up/align respective business plans
- Prepare development project jointly with R&D including functional specification, project plan and resource plan
- Launch development projects for dedicated products and review/approve development projects at achieved milestones
- Initiate market launch with Global Marketing (incl. communication, sales support, etc.)
- Management of product lifecycle including product phase-out.

The team was aware of the fact that the product manager has to be empowered to bring life to the defined role and to achieve the required goals. This led to the definition of enabling elements, supporting the extended responsibilities of the new product managers. The product manager

- Owns the product development budget based on portfolio decisions of a joint portfolio board,
- Is responsible for the milestones, which are covering product definition and post development phases and
- Has decision power for milestone release during development phase of new common milestone process

In order to clarify the role of the product manager (in the cross-divisional setup) and to set the defined responsibilities, the project team defined the interfaces to the major roles of the associated organizational units like development and product marketing. The most important counterparts of the product manager role were the

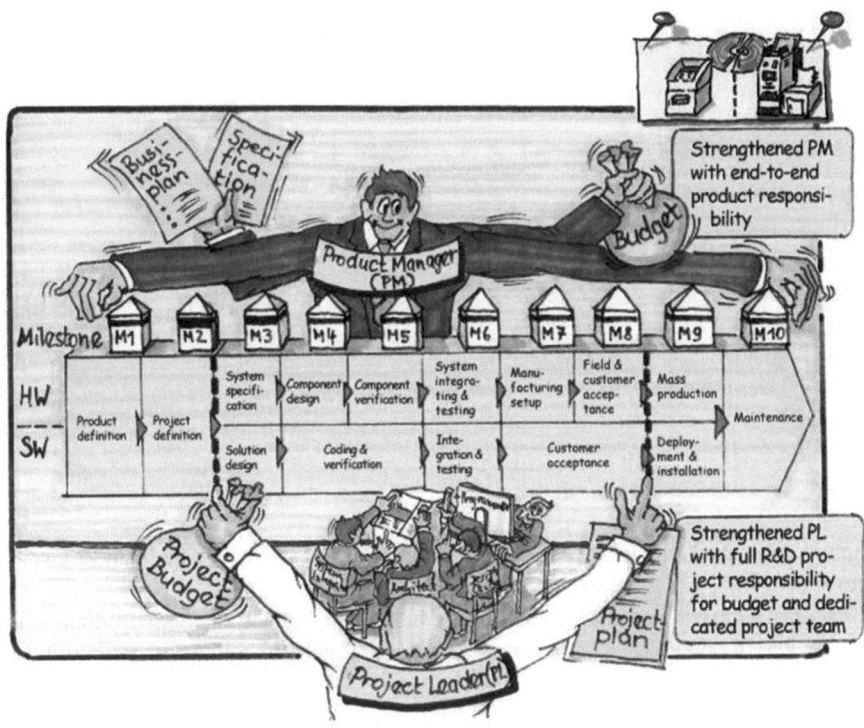

Fig. 5 Overall approach product management for software and hardware development

project manager role on the development side and the solution marketer role within the marketing organization. Performing market analysis, carrying out portfolio and solution strategy as well as management and definition of a go-to-market strategy are the responsibilities of the solution marketer. The corresponding tasks of the project manager are managing the execution of development projects, maintenance projects and customization projects within strategic customer development projects.

As mentioned before, Wincor Nixdorf is providing solutions which can consist of both software and hardware components. The most challenging projects are new product developments with a tight integration between both areas. In this case, the product managers have to work hand-in-hand and the development process has to be aligned. Due to that reason, the project team tried to establish a process, which in principle can work in parallel for both areas as depicted in Fig. 5. A principle idea was that the entire company should use the same terminology when it comes to projects, e.g. have a common understanding regarding the terms milestone, specific deliverables, roles and responsibilities. For both areas, the concept of overall product responsibility and budget ownership has been established. Product managers are leading the product definition milestones (M1 and M2) and are reviewing the product development milestones (M3–M8), which are under the responsibility of the project lead. To ensure final decisions in combined hardware-software projects, a so called Lead PM, is defined, who has the ultimate decision in escalation cases. This Lead PM is expected to work closely with the individual software and hardware PMs to ensure successful project execution.

The new setup was tested in four dedicated projects, which covered all four involved areas (software/hardware as well as banking/retail industry). The focus was to check the developed model on new product development and continuous improvement. One project was selected to test the new model for the development of a software solution without hardware dependency as well as the development of a tightly coupled software-hardware solution. With this selection all special cases of work were covered to evaluate the new model and detect gaps as early as possible. The outcomes of these pilot projects were the following: the business requirements, functional specification and architectural design had a scope and quality, which overachieved the expectations by far. It was possible to create test cases from early beginning and detail these after reviewing the design documents. The product definition took much longer than in the past and the executives were very nervous about the time spent to this. But the result was positive: These projects did have a change request rate which was only 30 % compared to the projects in the past. The stringent milestone reviews pushed the team to deliver all requested artifacts, because a clear supplier-customer relation was defined by every artifact. Further-more, it became clear, which kind of secondary costs were created by focusing on hardware requirements only and not looking at effects on the software side. By introducing a complete business case and product managers fighting for profitabil-ity of their areas a new dimension of constructive discussions was started. All of the pilot projects were finished in time, scope and budget, but failed some of the intermediate milestones because of learning effects on all sides.

4   Challenges, Changes and Achievements in the First Year

After defining the overall process, structure and responsibilities of the product management, marketing and development organization, the new model has to show the new approach in real life. It was obvious, that new tools, meetings, escalation paths have to be established to support the SW product management approach. In the center of these tools the market requirements document, the functional specification document and the architecture design documents had to be reviewed and adapted to the new process. Additionally a combined portfolio meeting had to be established to align the hardware, software development in coordination with service offerings required.

The portfolio meeting was divided in two segments. A companywide portfolio and roadmap meeting was introduced to align the company strategy with the dedicated product roadmaps. In this meeting the overall budget distribution on a high level was done based on strategic goals, roadmaps and business cases of the product managers. The scope was a budget distribution for the upcoming year. The second meeting was an operation based portfolio alignment meeting between hardware, software and services. This meeting had a monthly period and was intended to discuss the current and upcoming projects. For both meetings a framework had to be worked out to ensure comparable presentations and provide decision proposals.

For the operative product management work frameworks and tools had to work out and introduce. The market requirements document (related to the Milestone M1) had to include a market segmentation, a description of the market problem and a possible solution, a holistic business case and a competitive analysis. Marketing have to work closely with the product managers to get this document ready. The sales people have to give an indication about the sellable amount in the next years to give the management an indication about a possible ROI. In the beginning the M1 milestone was defined for all projects including the continuous improvement releases. Over time it was decided, that this kind of work should be done for new products. For the existing products a combined M1/M2 milestone was defined to reduce the necessary work. The M2 milestone itself had to define the necessary functionality, the project plan and more detailed effort estimation. In the combined M1/M2 milestone an updated business case and a review on the market requirements and competitive landscape was provided in extension to the central documents of the M2 milestone. This led to a more realistic project approach. Another kind of tool extension was introduced to the effort estimation within M2 milestone.

Additionally a classification of projects based on overall efforts was introduced. The reason for this was that the senior managers could not participate in all milestone meetings. Furthermore the effort to evaluate all checklist points for all projects was a huge undertaking. As a result four project categories were introduced, which had a relation to the participation list of a milestone meeting and the amount of milestone checklist topic to be covered.

The last point was to ensure the sustainability of the new model and align all departments to this goal. The mindset shift was a challenging undertaking, which required senior management support.

The overall achievement of the first year was a very high transparency of the projects and future product developments, a better strategic fit of the approved developments and a new quality of specification documents. A dedicated ROI transparency of all products was achieved and the business perspective got a better quality as before. Furthermore a one voice approach for the product roadmaps and company strategy was achieved.

5   Experiences and Lessons Learned

5.1   Experiences of the Introduction Project and the First Year

The introduction of such a radical change in the R&D operating model resulted in a resistance behavior of the R&D organization. The major issue was that many employees of the company were now stressed to leave the comfort zone and join the journey in a constructive way. First task was to give holistic information to the whole organization about the reasons to change and the new model. The team decided to have a town hall meeting with board support and involve the middle management in this exercise. The model was presented and a half day was spent in workshops to cover the first hand feedback of the managers and discuss their issues as well as detected gaps in the model. To make it illustrative for the whole organization, focused cartoons have been created. At the beginning, intensive discussion specifically with the human resource department on the usefulness of such cartoons have taken place. The project team decided to go ahead with this kind of communication and finally it resulted in a pretty good feedback from development.

It was obvious, that the biggest resistance came from the former development managers, because their kingdom was cut to a project-oriented development model with clear specifications. They precisely questioned the whole concept, especially when something was not explained in detail. In this phase, we discovered that it is very crucial to make crystal clear, that the change is not an option. This needs a lot of direct communication, tight tracking of pilot projects, coaching of the new project leads and strong support of the new product managers by top management. In the pilot phase, a lot of time has spent to ensure, that the business requirements are defined, the business case is valid and the functional specification has a superior quality. It is fundamental to demonstrate the entire organization, that the new model moves the quality of product definition to a new level. For example, in one of our pilot projects we spent triple effort in the definition of the product. The positive effect of this was that development recognized that for the first time a detailed specification was available. Furthermore, this specification provided already a stable basis to start implementation without an initial discussion.

The next hurdle was to assign a predefined budget for the development projects. To set up a contract between the product manager and the project manager we used the concept of power workshops. As a part of the power workshop, effort estimation is carried out based on the input of different experts relying on function points. The whole workshop is executed in the form of a game, similar to poker. Participants in the power workshops are a product manager, a project manager, an architect, a solution marketer, a professional service consultant, a quality specialist and a pilot customer (if already available). We made very positive experiences with the power workshop concept; specifically the quality of the effort estimations was impressive.

The product manager has to lead and steer the necessary milestone reviews to get the product delivered in scope, time and quality. The product manager has to act as single point of contact for change requests and strategic questions about the product. A lot of communication has to be done to educate sales, top management and customers that new requests have to be channeled via his or her desk. We experienced that blocking the direct interaction is fundamental. This channeling of the outside establishes the authority and the support of developers, because they are recognizing the advantage to have clear priorities based on well-defined functional specifications.

There were also specific learning's in the project with regard to combined hardware and software component development. In the past, hardware was designed and constructed without looking on firmware compatibility or investments needed on the application software side. The company was mainly hardware driven and the focus was on hardware innovations as priority 1. This led to the need of realizing critical business cases on the software side, but the budget on the hardware design was already invested, so the software group had to swallow the bitter pill. As mentioned above, specific revenue and profitability goals have been assigned to all product managers. This approach had to be changed fundamentally, so that at the beginning all areas (hardware, software and service) had to provide an own business case to get a complete picture about the solution. This resulted in new discussions at the beginning about the value of a small piece of innovation in comparison to the related costs afterwards. This kind of discussions could not be solved in every case by itself, because of the different objectives of the individual product managers. There was a need to introduce an additional concept to overcome this issue. The decision was to define a lead product manager to have a final decision in such cases. This lead product manager had to evaluate the different requests and to come up with a best solution with regards to the overall company goals. The milestone reviews also included the project lead and product manager from the other discipline to recognize early indicators.

During the first year it was very hard to get all necessary participants behind the concept of the milestone meetings. Since it was not possible to book the senior manager to all of the necessary meetings a project classification was introduced based on the importance of the development project. This adaptation was necessary and for the success very important.

The creation of the business cases was a big challenge, because the competitive data was not available at the fingertips and the necessary sales commitments was not in the DNA of the company so far. It was a combined effort of the controlling department, the marketing guys, the product managers and the sales people enforced by the senior management to bring this important decision instrument to a new level.

The next improvement area was the creation of the specification documents and the derived architecture and design documents. The quality, the documentation approach and the methodology was very different. Often the description of the non-functional requirements did not exist. To get a new quality of the specification documents a requirements management project was introduced. In this project an UML-based methodology was decided in combination with a controlled language especially for the non-functional requirements. To improve the usability of the software a UI design guide was created and the product managers were responsible for the creation of UI proposals in cooperation with the available UI design experts. Concerning the limited number of the available UI design experts, a prioritization of the projects were necessary to manage the support of these experts. For other projects a UI framework was defined to ensure UI consistency and provide a necessary usability.

A big discussion was the responsibility of the maintenance efforts and the testing efforts. In the beginning these budgets were assigned to the product managers as well. During the first year the assignment of the maintenance budget were redirected to the development managers. It was necessary to ensure architectural rework, hot fixes and technological improvements of the software. A related discussion was the budget for the development of application platform components and reuse components. The individual product manager was not willing to invest for such kind of additional development effort. To cover such kind of necessary development a central budget was created to ensure these developments.

5.2   Lessons Learned of the Introduction Project and the First Year

The overall lessons learned in the product management introduction project at Wincor-Nixdorf can be summarized through the following key items:
- Communicate, communicate and communicate
- Take new ways of communication like posters, feedback sessions with executives, special editions of internal newsletters etc.
- Be clear, that the new model is not an option
- Select strong product managers and give them senior management support
- Carry out face-to-face meetings on a regularly basis with the people who are losing some of their former power
- Make sure that the product definition of the first pilots are extraordinarily good
- Block all direct approaches to development for requirements definition
- Give the product manager budget responsibility to enable the new responsibilities
- Clarify who has the overall product responsibility and communicate this to the organization
- Define the interfaces and responsibilities between product management, marketing and development in the form of detailed role descriptions.
- Use visual signs to demonstrate that the product responsibility has changed by rearrangement of management meetings, introducing of portfolio board meetings etc.
- Be prepared and open to adapt the model for improvements
- Develop common framework and tools to ensure document and project consistency
- Plan central budgets to ensure creation of platform and reuse components
- Make sure, that the senior managers are attending the necessary milestone meetings. If this is a problem, then adapt the model by introducing a project classification based on project importance
- Focus on common methodology for specification documents
- Align all involved departments to the new model and ensure senior management support
- Do not forget to inform all necessary departments on a global base like sales, marketing and service departments on a global base

6   Summary

The paper provided a detailed description and a qualitative analysis of the experiences and lessons learned by the product management introduction project carried out in a banking & retail IT solutions company. The initial situation was characterized by a low predictability of time, budget, architecture and committed features. The introduction project fundamentally changed the overall operational model and strengthened the product management role. The new setup was first successfully evaluated within four pilot projects.

The most relevant experiences made in the overall introduction project together with the four pilot projects are:

(1) invest significant time in communication using different forms (visual, face-to-face, workshops, . . .), (2) establish strong and empowered product managements and ensure providing superior quality deliverables in the first pilot projects, and (3) ensure explicit specification of all involved roles (product management, development, marketing).

In the first year the project is only partly finished. There is a need to invest in the creation of necessary tools and frameworks to support the new model. These frameworks span from the yearly strategy and budget decision the operational project and strategy alignment meetings and the definition of the necessary documents of the product definition and development execution based on the specifics of your company. It is valuable to define common methodologies for the most important documents. The creation of a central budget is helpful to cover costs for creation of platform or reuse components. The establishment of cross-functional teams created a new spirit and quality, but often you are not able to staff all project teams in this combination. In this case plan for the most important projects and guide the others with guidelines. The senior management support has to be ensured and the company on a global base has to be informed about the new model and the necessary changes on all levels of the company.

Acknowledgements We would like to thank the consulting company McKinsey, who guided the introduction project from an external perspective.

References

Condon, D. (2002). *Inside the minds: Software product management: Managing software development from idea to product to marketing to sales*. Boston: Aspatore Books.

Ebert, C. (2007). The impacts of software product management. *Journal of Systems and Software, 80*(6), 850–861.

Ebert, C. (2009). Software product management. *Crosstalk, 22*, 15–19.

Gorchels, L. (2000). *The product manager's handbook: The complete product management resource*. New York: McGraw-Hill Professional.

Kilpi, T. (1998). Improving software product management process: Implementation of a product support system. *Proceedings of the thirty-first Hawaii international conference on system sciences, 1998* (Vol. 6, pp. 3–12). Kohala Coast, Hawaii: USA.

Kittlaus, H. B., & Clough, P. N. (2009). *Software product management and pricing: Key success factors for software organizations*. Berlin/Heidelberg: Springer.

Pragmatic Marketing, Inc. (2012). Pragmatic marketing framework. Retrieved April 17, 2012, http://www.pragmaticmarketing.com/pragmatic-marketing-framework

van de Weerd, I., Brinkkemper, S., Nieuwenhuis, R., Versendaal, J., & Bijlsma, L. (2006). Towards a reference framework for software product management. *14th IEEE international conference on requirements engineering* (pp. 319–322). Luxemburg.

Weerd, I., Bekkers, W., & Brinkkemper, S. (2010). Developing a maturity matrix for software product management. *Software Business, 51*, 76–89.

Xu, L., & Brinkkemper, S. (2007). Concepts of product software. *European Journal of Information Systems, 16*(5), 531–541.

Intertwining Lean and Design Thinking: Software Product Development from Empathy to Shipment

Tobias Hildenbrand and Johannes Meyer

Abstract

A few years back, everybody in the industry seemed to be talking about how "Lean Thinking" can improve software development. Best practices emerged, books were written and Lean Thinking, associated with agile process frameworks became somewhat of a standard work culture in software development. Now that many people are actually practicing lean and agile development, they have started to wonder about something called "Design Thinking". When we coach development teams in a large software company, we're frequently being asked whether Design Thinking is the next big thing substituting lean software development. After having guided several teams through successful projects, our verdict is: Design Thinking is not Lean's heir; in fact the two schools can be intertwined in many ways and complement each other very well. As we will elaborate in this case study, they share some integral core values and goals, and can therefore be applied in the same project without corrupting each other. As a proof of concept, we combined and utilized the underlying set of methods in order to explore a yet relatively unknown and unusual domain for SAP business applications: Software for professional sailors and their coaches that helps them to optimize their training experience and competitive performance.

1 Introduction: Related Work and Research Objective

Before we get into the actual sailing case study, it is important to note that SAP, world market leader in business software for large enterprises, has started a broad initiative to educate teams in Design Thinking, not only in development but across

T. Hildenbrand (✉)
SAP AG, Walldorf, Germany
e-mail: tobias.hildenbrand@sap.com

J. Meyer
Hasso-Plattner-Institut Academy GmbH, Potsdam, Germany
e-mail: johannes.meyer@hpi-academy.de

A. Maedche et al. (eds.), *Software for People*, Management for Professionals,
DOI 10.1007/978-3-642-31371-4_13, © Springer-Verlag Berlin Heidelberg 2012

all business areas. The work culture we describe is not restricted to this project, but is currently being broadly adopted in the company. Why would the teams that already practice lean and agile development for several years (Schnitter and Mackert 2011) need additional values, practices and another set of tools to do their job?

Let us be frank here from the beginning: developing business software is becoming more and more challenging. Together with the transforming requirements of business customers in different industries, products have to be in a constant cycle of innovation and adapt to ever new environments (Smith and Reinertsen 1992). Operating in such an environment, a steady flow of good ideas is the only justification for a business software company to flourish (Reinertsen 1997, 2009). Such a company therefore needs a structured framework not only on *how* it turns ideas into sellable products, but also on *how to come up with* those ideas in the first place. Design Thinking is such a framework, intended to increase the likelihood and reliability of innovations developed in teams (Brown 2009; Martin 2009).

Lean Thinking, on the other hand, has proven to make teams and organizations more efficient and transparent for almost 20 years, if you take *Scrum* as an exemplary process framework (Schwaber 1995; Sutherland and Schwaber 2011). However, Scrum assumes that teams already start with a "product vision" and a "product backlog" without a clear picture as to where that vision will come from (Highsmith 2009; Pichler 2010). On the enterprise level, Lean Thinking tells us to "focus on customer value" (Womack and Jones 1990, 2003), but besides a basic definition of "value", i.e. "what the customer is willing to pay for", Lean Thinking does not provide according guiding principles on how to find out what is actually valuable to the customer.

Besides pressure for innovation (Martin 2009), there are other good reasons why both Lean and Design Thinking make particular sense together and have their respective niche in the business software domain: *First of all*, business software projects for large enterprises can get rather bulky, delivering complex products with the help of many different teams (Larman and Vodde 2008). Without frameworks like Scrum and the ability to scale beyond single teams, it's almost certain that resources will be wasted, especially because software is not as transparent as other products (Leffingwell 2011). *Moreover*, developers in business software companies are often not actual users of their own products. Instead, they are expected to deliver something that their – often very IT-skilled – customers would not be able to build at the same price; however, most often without being experts for their customers' respective business domain and business processes. Hence, *empathy* is needed to take the famous walk in the customers' shoes and discover potentials for innovative applications. Once these opportunities have been discovered, it's not enough if they are just desirable to the customer (Pichler 2010): To be reasonable as a product, they also have to be viable in terms of business value, i.e. generate revenue for the software company, and feasible to be developed in the first place. Hence, an innovative and successful software product has to be desirable, viable, and feasible at the same time (Meinel and Leifer 2011). Design Thinking has successfully proven to help teams and organizations balance these "three spaces of innovation" for products, services, and customer experiences (Brown 2009).

It is therefore no surprise that both thinking schools share a fundamental set of core values and commonalities: *First*, both recommend forming and empowering interdisciplinary or so-called "cross-functional" teams (Schwaber 1995; Kelley 2008; Brown 2009; Blau et al. 2011b). This means that a team contains all skills required to address a certain market or customer need and control is decentralized as far as possible (Reinertsen 2009; Sutherland and Schwaber 2011). *Second*, both are about taking an economic perspective on product development, i.e. taking business value, viability, and revenue streams into account when managing the overall product portfolio and prioritizing requirements for particular products (Brown 2009; Reinertsen 2009). *Third*, the development process leverages on fast feedback cycles and gaining additional insights for further iterations. The principle of inspecting and adapting both product and process is inherent to lean and agile development (Reinertsen 2009; Sutherland and Schwaber 2011). In the same vein, Design Thinking suggests early, regular, and cheap prototyping to "deliver fast results and generate useful feedback" (Brown 2009, p. 87; Ries 2011).

Besides these and other inherent commonalities, another reason why Lean and Design Thinking don't collide is that they focus on different challenges and aspects in a development project lifecycle: While Lean Thinking and agile practices help organizations to *build and ship products right*, meaning e.g. in time and in quality, Design Thinking focuses on *building the right product* in the first place. Hence, it can help teams to understand the full context of a problem space from the perspectives of potential users and relevant stakeholders. Building on this understanding, teams can develop a product vision and derive requirements for what the product could actually do for the users within their respective context. Lean Thinking and agile methods, such as Scrum, Extreme Programming (XP, Beck 1999; Beck et al. 2001; Hildenbrand et al. 2008), and Clean Code (Martin 2008), for instance, provide the process framework for development organizations as well as concrete engineering principles to efficiently bring the product vision to life as shippable software (Chow and Cao 2008; cp. Fig. 1).

It is thus understandable that business software companies are particularly interested in introducing practices that ensure continuous and reliable innovation through empathy and streamline development processes with minimal waste. Nevertheless we are at the start of this journey and Design Thinking is just now spreading from consultancies into in-house product development teams, just like Lean Thinking spread from manufacturing into the software industry via agile practices a few years ago (Poppendieck 2002; Poppendieck and Poppendieck 2003; Larman and Vodde 2008).

Research Objective: Based on the commonalities and possibly conflicting areas inherent to software development as outlined above, our case study intends to shed light on how to leverage Lean and Design Thinking in order to *build the right software right* in one practical project setting. In particular, we investigate the underlying research question of *how to come up with an innovative product vision and derive requirements in a yet unknown domain*.

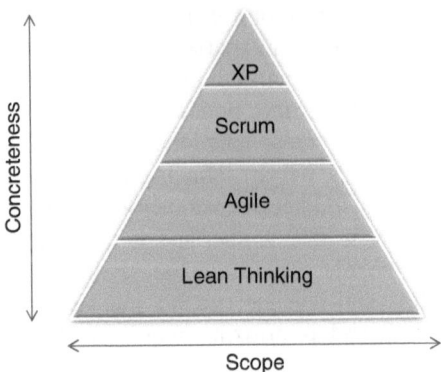

Fig. 1 From lean thinking to concrete software engineering techniques

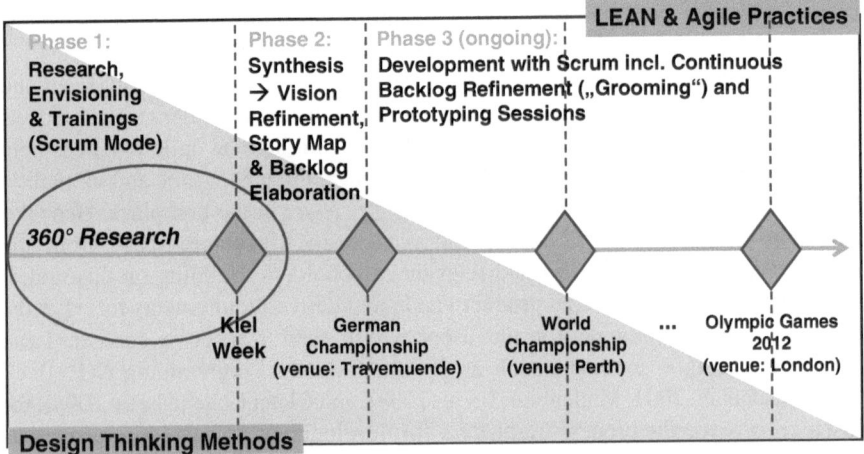

Fig. 2 Integrated approach for sailing team Germany project at SAP

Methodologically, this work follows a design science approach (Hevner et al. 2004). In doing so, our main "artifact" is the team-based process from the initial challenge or "project brief" (cf. Brown 2009) to a first working and potentially shippable software increment that users can apply and assess in their environment (Schwaber 1995; see also approach in Fig. 2). Hence, we later evaluate the *usefulness* of our process by customer adoption, development team satisfaction, and other types of feedback. Our case study therefore serves as observational design evaluation for the integrated approach described in Sect. 3.1 and Fig. 2 in particular (Hevner et al. 2004, p. 86). The constituents of this process are based on a combination of Lean and Design Thinking principles and practices. Moreover, we also evaluate the process from an internal team perspective, i.e. team learning and satisfaction as well as the "fun factor" within our development team. Our evaluation approach is based on a *single case study* setting within SAP as the organizational context (Eisenhardt 1989; Yin 2008, 2011) and we derive an initial set of conclusions under the particular contingencies of this case as a first step towards an integrated theory of efficient and effective software product development with a combination of Lean and Design Thinking principles and practices (Van de Ven and Drazin 1985).

The rest of this book chapter is structured as follows: the following Sect. 2 presents a brief overview of the case study setting and the respective customer, i.e. SAP's Sailing Program for Audi Sailing Team Germany. Section 3 then describes the process as set of practices that we designed, adapted, and intertwined for this particular team and setting. Section 4 will evaluate and discuss our methodological approach based on observations from the case study, while Sect. 5 will draw conclusions for software product development and provide an outlook on future development projects applying our approach and upcoming research programs in our pipeline.

2   SAP'S Sailing Program and Sailing Team Germany

As of 2011, SAP is sponsoring *Audi Sailing Team Germany* (STG), a recent initiative geared at promoting athletic sailing and building a common organizational structure between Germany's many diverse and clustered sailing clubs. As Marcus Baur, former Olympic sailor and co-head of STG, points out in an interview: "Sailing Team Germany has come together to achieve the goal of making Germany one of the best sailing nations in the world again" (STG 2011).

When analyzing the domain, many people underestimate that sailing is a highly strategic sport. In the majority of boat classes, it is not so much physical fitness, but experienced judgment of weather, water conditions and venues that make teams win. It is finding the adequate trim settings, being on the right side of the venue and anticipating events before they actually occur.

SAP as a software vendor chose to support STG's ambitious goal with software. Besides the classical support of a sponsor, SAP is particularly interested in showcasing its technology and ways of working by building software that provides true value to the sport. In an initial analysis of what SAP technology could do for the sailing domain, one of several emerging challenges was *How might we improve knowledge transfer among sailors and coaches so they can benefit from each other's experience and improve performance?* According to Marcus Baur, a fast knowledge transfer from experienced to younger sailors would offer a powerful and sustainable competitive advantage for the German sailing team towards the Olympic Games in London in 2012 and beyond (STG 2011).

You can call it lucky or not that the team that was selected to work on this challenge had not been in contact with the sailing domain before. The team included five developers, one Scrum Master, one Product Owner, as well as several part-time experts e.g. for user interface design, mobile applications, and Java platform services. From the beginning it was clear that there was a lot of learning to do before the team would get to a solid idea of what their product should do and what their impact on the users' daily experience should be.

On the other hand, starting a project without any assumptions gave us as coaches the chance to also intertwine our respective experience from both Lean and Design Thinking. This way, we developed a custom-made, integrated approach that was supposed to help the team get up to speed with sailing and build shippable software eventually. To be able to do so, they first needed to understand the sailors' problems, come up with an innovative product vision and derive high-level requirements for this yet unknown domain.

3   Intertwining Lean and Design Thinking

This section presents the integrated process and its application as part of the case study. In the overview, the different phases and objectives of the project are described along with the respective methods, practices, and techniques from Lean and Design Thinking.

3.1   Our Overall Approach

Lean software product development (Larman and Vodde 2008; Reinertsen 2009; Larman and Vodde 2010; Leffingwell 2011) has been adopted as a standard approach in SAP development for almost 3 years starting in 2009 (Schnitter and Mackert 2011; Blau et al. 2011a).

SAP's change template for this transition included (1) Lean Thinking principles as a basis (Womack and Jones 2003), (2) agile principles from the Agile Manifesto (Beck et al. 2001), (3) standard agile process frameworks such as Scrum (Sutherland and Schwaber 2011) and Kanban (Anderson 2010), as well as (4) well-established agile engineering techniques, e.g. from XP and Clean Code (Beck 1999; Martin 2009). The latter is seen as critical success factor in most Agile projects and missing link to the actual software "shop floor", i.e. the development teams, in large-scale Lean implementations (Chow and Cao 2008).

Figure 1 shows how Lean, agile principles, Scrum as a process framework, and agile engineering techniques such as XP can build upon and complement each other within SAP's overall "Lean Development Model" to enable successful software projects (Chow and Cao 2008):

Taken together, this new approach SAP is taking can be summarized for particular lines of business or bigger solutions as follows: instead of a large group spending a long time building a big piece of software, many smaller teams spend a short time (2–4 week iterations) building small pieces of software, while integrating regularly to see the whole (cp. also Kniberg 2007).

SAP's lean development approach, as described above, however, does not directly tell you how to come up with an innovative product vision and a good product backlog that includes the relevant requirements as "user stories"

Table 1 Overlapping terminology in lean and design thinking

Lean thinking and agile practices	Design thinking
Requirement	User need
Persona	Persona
Usage sequence	As-is scenario
Product vision	Solution
Epic (i.e. a coarse-grained user story)	To-be scenario
Product backlog item, e.g. as user story	Solution idea, prototype, implementation

(Leffingwell 2011), ordered according to customer value or other criteria (Sutherland and Schwaber 2011).

When we started to design a suitable approach to achieve this for our sailing project, it turned out to be necessary to synchronize on some of the terminology that Lean and Design Thinking use. As a result of this discussion, we came across overlaps for the following descriptions:

Table 1 contrasts selected terminology from our perspective: what Lean thinking calls requirements (Reinertsen 2009; Leffingwell 2011), may be what Design Thinking understands as "needs" coming out of a research phase. In both worlds, a persona embodies an archetypical user or user category (Patton 2008; Brown 2009). However, agile methods for requirements engineering (Hildenbrand et al. 2008) such as story mapping usually do not accurately distinguish as-is and to-be descriptions while Design Thinking clearly separates the problem space (as-is scenario) and the solution space (to-be scenario, see Meinel and Leifer 2011, for instance).

Moreover, lean and agile practices such as Scrum suggest decomposing the "solution idea" or "prototype" (Brown 2009) into a "product backlog" consisting of "backlog items" (Sutherland and Schwaber 2011) to answer the question what it actually takes to "bring the product to life" (Pichler 2010). Backlog items can be described as requirements from a user perspective in the form of so-called "user stories" (Cohn 2004). Larger, coarse-grained user stories are often called "epics" (Leffingwell 2011) and correspond to the to-be scenarios used in Design Thinking projects, e.g. prototyped with storyboards (Kelley 2001; Brown 2009).

After synchronizing on language and terminology, we derived our development approach based on the goals and boundary conditions given in the STG project. For instance, the team already decided to visit Kiel Week in June 2011 to meet the sailors and a preliminary shipment of useable software was planned for the German Championships in Travemuende in September 2011.

Figure 2 shows how we planned the transition from Design Thinking-driven user research to lean and agile development practices in later phases of the project. Our intention was to allow for an initial phase in which the team would not "think code" yet but just concentrate on the user:

While this visualization may suggest that agile practices played no role at the beginning of the project that is not the case: In fact, before our first project milestone, Kiel Week in June 2011, the team also maintained a backlog of things to develop and prepare, e.g. interview guides, appointments, and other logistics, with the "sprint goal" of preparing the user- and venue research (Sutherland and Schwaber 2011). Despite not developing any software yet, we used a Scrum-like process to learn as a team, get the most important things done prior to Kiel and make efficient use of the time at the sailing event. With the input gathered during these preparations and at the actual event, we then wanted to agree on our product vision and derive the "real backlog" in order to start continuous development and backlog refinement activities (cp. Fig. 2). That is, later on we wanted to run the project in a rather "standard lean and agile mode", as it was familiar to the team from previous development projects at SAP.

However, we think the process shown in Fig. 2 is only one of many possible ways in which a combination and intertwining of Lean and Design Thinking practices can be realized. In our particular case, it helped us to manage the transition from zero sailing domain knowledge to actually building shippable software for professional sailors and their coaches.

As indicated in Fig. 2, we therefore define three major phases: *Phase 1* includes user research, envisioning, and training of the team. In *Phase 2*, our goal was to merge all the findings from Phase 1 and come out with a stable product vision and a first set of requirements as user stories in the team's product backlog. *Phase 3* would then cover the actual coding and continuous feedback loops with stakeholders.

3.2   User Research, Envisioning, and Trainings (Phase 1)

Since the development team, including the product owner, did not have much experience in the sailing domain, we guided them through research to build up empathy for the potential users and a basic understanding of the domain. Classical *Design Thinking* (Meinel and Leifer 2011) suggests "observation" as the first diverging phase in an innovation project. In our software development domain, this has been extended to "360° Research", referring to observation and interviews with users plus secondary sources like analysts and thought leaders, competitors, analogous and adjacent domains.

In the sailing case, this meant that the team actually talked to sailors and coaches in their natural environment and observed their current behaviors, scrutinized existing "tools" (both on paper and electronic ones) and analyzed their goals and feelings. Secondly, they looked at sailing competitions and similar domains such as show jumping, formula one, and gliding, to name just a few. Third, they informed themselves and plunged into the sailing domain by analyzing books and articles, as well as computer-based sailing simulators.

To get some real-world and direct user experience, the team went to Kiel Week, one of Germany's biggest annual sailing events. Within this week, 15 interviews with various sailors, coaches, and other experts were scheduled and conducted by sub-teams of two members of the team including the developers, product owner, Scrum master, etc. Moreover, we reserved time for the observation of race

Table 2 Overall workshop agenda for synthesis, vision, and backlog elaboration (phase 2)

Workshop Day 1	Workshop Day 2	Workshop Day 3
Synthesis: storytelling and clustering of observations	**Product vision**: statement	**Recap**: Lean/agile development, Scrum and Kanban
Point-of-view: personas for expected users	**Story map**: usage sequence, personas, epics (backbone)	**Overview** of concrete *agile software engineering practices*
Ideation and **prototyping**	**User story writing** in pairs	**Working model** and charter, **tool support** required
Vision: product box	**Story map review**, prioritization and "slicing" of map	**Review** of overall workshop results with Marcus (STG)

preparations and actual regattas at the venue site. Last but not least, a full immersion into the topic was achieved by actually sailing as a team in Kiel.

Researching openly, without a direct objective for the product design, was also lots of fun for the team and within an impressively short time, they grew both together as a team, and into experts in their new domain.

3.3   Synthesis, Vision, and Backlog Elaboration (Phase 2)

Our clothes still soaked with salt water, we returned from Kiel to SAP Walldorf and started synthesizing what we had learned so far as a team. As part of our overall process (see Fig. 2), us coaches suggested conducting a 3-day workshop to develop the product vision, derive a backlog and start development team work. Table 2. summarizes the overall workshop agenda:

Workshop Day 1 – Back in the office, we applied Design Thinking practices such as time-boxed synthesis of key statements by our potential users. Each of the interviews was reported by the respective interviewers from the team in a round of so-called "storytelling"; information about user needs, pain points, and other potential insights was put on **post-its** (see Fig. 3).

In our setup, **storytelling** allowed six minutes per research area and no discussions, with questions being parked on a designated parking lot flip chart. That way, each team member was able to absorb the insights from all other interviews, including the ones they had not attended themselves.

After collecting about 250 of these data points, we clustered them into topic groups. We selected "silent clustering" for efficiency reasons, i.e. the participants put their share of the data points on a pin board and placed related ones close to each other. The overall arrangement could be changed by everyone until the clusters converge. With the highlights of about 20 clusters in mind (the clusters we found included "audio/video support", "trimming", and "tracking the boats", for instance), we developed our first two **personas** as stereotypical users: Tina the professional sailor and Thomas, a coach. The persona descriptions included their age, profession, boat class, background, motivation, and pain points. Design Thinking recommends this synthesis to get from diverging into converging mode and make empathy possible through focused formats.

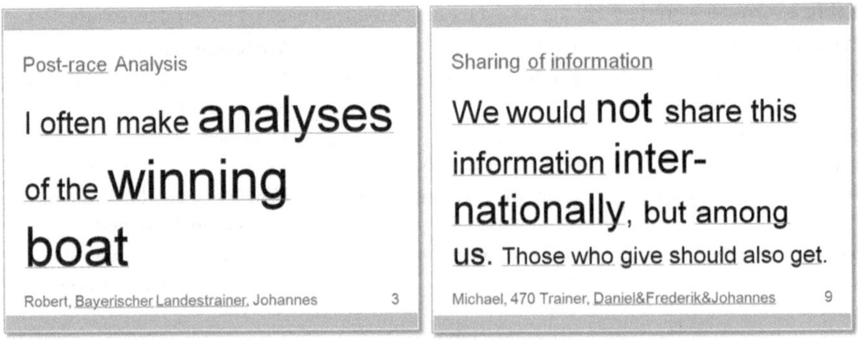

Post-race Analysis	Sharing of information
I often make **analyses** of the **winning boat**	We would **not** share this information **internationally**, but among us. Those who give should also get.
Robert, Bayerischer Landestrainer, Johannes 3	Michael, 470 Trainer, Daniel&Frederik&Johannes 9

Fig. 3 Example observations from storytelling in synthesis phase of workshop day 1

With these "flesh-and-blood" users and lots of fresh impressions from Kiel in mind, we were ready to switch on the "solution engine" and finally start to think about solution ideas to address some of the users' problems. Within three intense days in the field (2 days interviews, 1 day processing), the team had "build up a deep understanding of the sailing domain from a user perspective", as they mentioned in one of the later retrospective meetings. Now they were able to make the right decisions on the product features most useful and desirable to their personas.

With a structured view on needs and pain points, the first ideas started to spark and the team went into their first ideation session where they developed rough drafts of screens and to-be usage scenarios (cp. Table 1) the user could possibly go through in the future.

Figure 4 depicts an example of how a sailor could use our software on a mobile tablet device to record and share their experience after sailing while receiving post-race physiotherapy:

This "educated brain dump" was also a perfect warm-up for developing the product vision in the form of a sneak preview software package (called a "vision box", Highsmith 2009) with a product name, unique selling propositions, and some key features on it. We concluded day 1 with a first rough overall product vision in the form of the vision box and a brief vision statement:

> Sail Better provides easy access to training, trim, and venue data from various sources, allows you to log your own experience and learn from others – fostering collaboration between coaches and sailors to optimize your sailing performance

Workshop Day 2 – with our common product vision and personas already in place, we had an ideal starting point for developing our first product backlog. At this point some great ideas were on the table, but the team including product owner was not even close to having requirements as concrete backlog items to start development yet. Our agile tool of choice to get a full end-to-end picture of the users' processes and possible backlog items was thus a **user story map** (Patton 2008, see outline and data model in Fig. 5; cp. also terminology in Table 1):

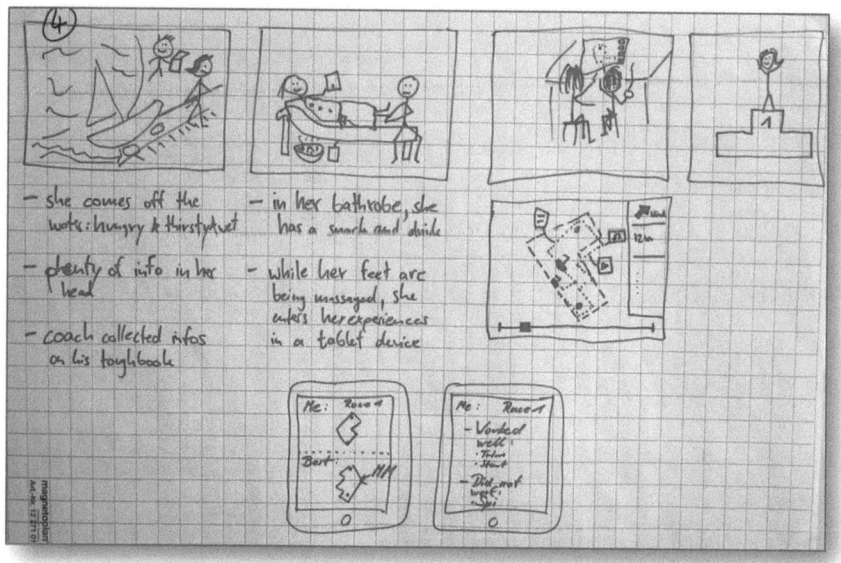

Fig. 4 Example of an early paper prototype for an experience with a mobile application

Fed by the ideas that had come up as prototypes in our day 1 ideation session and based on all the newly acquired knowledge about the daily lives of the user roles, it proved to be surprisingly easy for the team to first come up with an overarching usage sequence for sailors and coaches along the course of one season (i.e. one calendar year), and then fill this "backbone" with insight-based epics and user stories (Patton 2008; Leffingwell 2011). As the product owner put it:

> The team was so well warmed up, that we could write the user stories and immediately fill the story map as basis for our product backlog. This made my job a lot easier at this point in time.

Later, the map served as central reference for the product owner, customers and the team to see what the overall product is supposed to look like, what the current progress to plan is in terms of user stories implemented and remaining work as well as which ideas they want to implement next for which part of the user's daily conduct. Particular user stories are then pulled for sprint planning priority-wise and broken down into smaller stories to fit the sprints (Sutherland and Schwaber 2011; see also Sect. 3.4 and Table 3 for the team's concrete approach to working with user stories and done criteria along sprints).

Workshop Day 3 – on our last workshop day, we focused on *how* the team wants to work with the backlog. After having compiled and ordered a decent set of user stories, i.e. after having an actual backlog, we needed to discuss our **working model** as a team. To facilitate this, we presented and recapitulated existing lean and agile good practices to the team and decided afterwards which approach we start

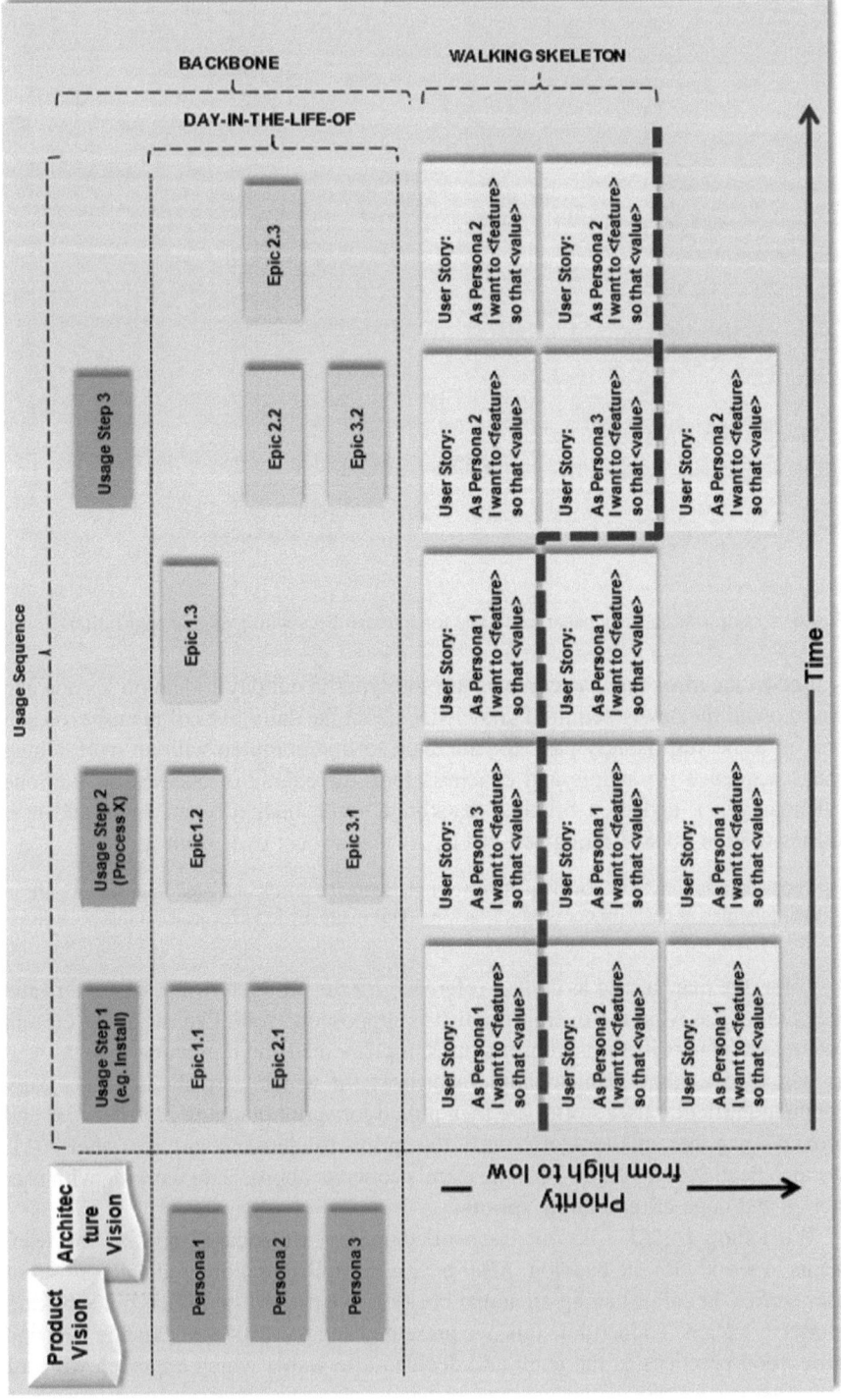

Fig. 5 Constituents and methodology of a user story map (Based on Patton 2008)

Table 3 Three-level approach of implementing user stories to get feedback

Artifact	Description and done criteria
1. Working software	User story fully deployed and integrated into on-demand application so that it can be tested in a browser on different devices
2. Hi-Fi prototype	Digital representation of relevant screen including the application's HTML5 UI design (in Visio or PowerPoint format)
3. Lo-Fi prototype	Paper prototype to communicate the basic idea, data fields, application workflow, etc., e.g. wireframes on A4 paper or comic-style user stories

with, and what our concrete "team parameters" for the Sail Better project would be, e.g. sprint length, time for daily scrum meetings, done criteria for user stories, etc. After discussing Scrum and Kanban as possible process frameworks and highlighting some proven agile engineering practices at SAP, we put the major parameters of our collaboration model such as initial sprint length, time for daily stand-up meetings, time boxes for backlog grooming and retrospectives, etc. on a team charter, "signed it with blood" (only in the figurative sense), and copied them to our team wiki. The team also decided to conduct continuous ideation and prototyping sessions for particular user stories. That is, the team iterates and ideates on certain aspects of the solution that are not yet so well understood as part of our development sprints (also called "spikes" in agile development, cf. Leffingwell 2011). We time-boxed these sessions to 1–2 h maximum and used paper prototyping as primary low fidelity tool to communicate about ideas and get feedback (see Sect. 3.4 and Table 3 in particular).

As a summary of post-Kiel workshop results, we had a clear product vision and backlog which was validated and aligned with our customer, STG. The team had agreed on a working model and our story map helped us to constantly maintain and overview of our requirements and continuously refine the features. Especially the personas (Tina and Thomas) keep us focused on our end users and facilitated communication within the team:

> Hey Chris, do you think Tina would find this radio button intuitive?

Paper prototypes and other cheap artifacts enabled us to continuously receive fast feedback from customers and colleagues right from the beginning and reduced risk tremendously.

One major problem we were facing was the fact that two developers had to go back to Palo Alto (USA) and work from there most of the time. That meant we needed to find suitable meeting times for both locations, had to get a sound station, figure out how to ensure transparency on major decisions and updates also electronically, etc. The main part of the team in Walldorf, however, used the artifacts from Kiel to "decorate" their shared office space and added lots of face-to-face collaboration tools, e.g. whiteboards, a projector, stand-up tables, loads of post-its as well as movable walls. Hence, the team room fosters communication (in terms of quality and frequency) and collaboration by full overall transparency and visual management. You would also often find pairs of developers discussing in the nearby coffee corner.

3.4   Scrum-Based Development and Continuous Design (Phase 3)

Literally on day four, i.e. day one after the workshop described above, the team started elaborating the early prototypes and user stories while receiving continuous feedback by STG.

As indicated in Fig. 2, we planned to get into a regular lean and agile development mode after a first complete delivery of the software at the German Championships in Travemuende. Since we were applying agile methods right from the start (see Sect. 3.2), i.e. maintaining an ordered backlog, working in iterations, etc., the transition from a predominantly Design Thinking-driven working mode to business-as-usual Scrum was very smooth. However, we never stopped experimenting with Design Thinking methods and techniques during Sprints and the team actively requested moderated breakout sessions when they approached new and unclear user stories.

In order to realize regular feedback and gain as many additional insights as possible from our STG users, the team agreed on three-levels of user story completion and according done criteria (cf. Sutherland and Schwaber 2011 and Table 3): if the team could not deliver the story as working software within one sprint, they tried to at least come up with a prototype to evaluate with STG. Sometimes a low-fidelity prototype, e.g. wireframe on paper, was just enough to get feedback. High-fidelity prototypes created with the help of professional user interface (UI) designers and tools such as Visio and PowerPoint were also utilized to refine paper prototype and get additional feedback on the actual look and feel before implementing the screen in HTML5. When stories were deployed and integrated, the users from STG could immediately access the new functionality via the on-demand platform.

4   Evaluation and Discussion

As a result of implementing our process, the team managed to get from zero sailing expertise in June 2011 to a first "shipment" to their customer, Audi Sailing Team Germany, as part of the German Championships in Travemuende in September 2011, i.e. after about 3 months. The feedback on our initial backlog, first prototypes and first software release was very positive and constructive. Due to the fact that we had cheap paper prototypes very early, even during our first team workshop, and continuously evaluated, discarded and/or refined these artifacts, the team received constant feedback from Sailing Team Germany and thus began to "flow".

4.1   Evaluation of Development Process from Empathy to Shipment

After a first delivery of the software in September 2011 in Travemuende, Germany, we collected feedback from the development team, Scrum Master, Product Owner, and STG as customer: most importantly, our customer and the users from STG confirmed that what the team built within the given time frame of barely 3 months went far beyond their expectations (STG 2011):

SAP Sail Better helps us to optimize what we do and it also helps us to innovate.

The Sail Better software has been delivered as an on demand solution with HTML5 UI. Thus, user stories for sailors and coaches could be evaluated in a real-live user environment on the intended devices such as laptops and iPads. At the World Championships in Perth in November, an extended shipment with all major user stories was provided and evaluated by STG: The Sail Better software solution is deemed highly useful to improve the preparations for the Olympic Games in London in 2012 – or as one professional sailor put it in Perth last year (STG 2011):

It is a big advantage over all competitors that we race against [at the world championships].

STG was not only impressed by the software, but also by the methods that have been applied. The product owner (PO) also underlined that the user story map helped him a lot to communicate with both the customer and the development team. Moreover, the PO appreciated that the team was able to nail down the first set of relevant user stories based on their finding from research and the visit to Kiel. Compared to other agile projects, this meant a tremendous boost on the way to development start. PO, development team, and Scrum Master (cf. Sutherland and Schwaber 2011) emphasized that in general the development of the team from having no clue about sailing to being ready to develop after Kiel Week and the workshop was amazing.

Based on our findings and evaluation results, the body of knowledge in both Design Thinking and Lean software product development and our experience with the STG project, we found some first themes to be discussed. The team is generally very positive that the time taken "before actually coding" is deemed useful for their result. All in all, they also claimed that

More projects should have an explicit Lean and Design Thinking coach.

Besides this general evaluation of the process, three main "patterns" which we also observed at other projects at SAP have been reconfirmed as findings by our case study:

(1) The *story mapping* technique (Patton 2008) helped us to synthesize and leverage on the findings from user research and bring the "to-be perspective" from Design Thinking into our backlog. (2) Despite the tight time frame, it paid off to spend a considerable amount of time for better understanding the problem domain, concrete user needs and impediments in the development project, i.e. we *stopped to think* at defined points in time. (3) Ideation and prototyping sessions – both, at the outset and within the sprints – enabled us to get fast feedback from our users. Superficially, Lean Thinking might define this as waste, but creating tangible and visual results very early potentially saved us from creating even more waste in the course of the project (see example in Sect. 4.3).

4.2   Story Maps Can Bridge the Gap from Research to Backlog

Story Mapping proved to be a powerful tool to structure the features of a classical prototype into a backlog. Especially in software product development it is important to consider the full life- or usage cycle of a product, and story maps can help raise awareness for details in the sequence. The team and especially the product owner confirmed the story map to be a useful reference in sprint planning and prioritization.

Story maps are structured and rather unemotional: because they follow the user's "Day in a Life" though, they can connect to Design Thinking much better than a classical backlog representation as a flat list. The reuse of the synthesized personas and thereby research data can help the team to empathize with the respective user stories.

Nevertheless our process applied in the STG case study had its biggest weakness at the point where the user story took over the results of our prototyping and product vision exercises. There is one interesting pitfall that has to be analyzed in more detail: As an innovation method, Design Thinking makes a strong point to differentiate between as-is and to-be scenarios and processes from a user perspective. While in "classical" agile requirements engineering (cf. Leffingwell 2011), these two points of reference are often the same in order to support the current process, Design Thinking has the very aim of disrupting the status quo with a true innovation.

For the team in our STG case, this "little" difference turned out to be difficult. Their feedback was that it was unclear what exactly should go on the story map. While they were eager to reuse the artifacts they had developed in the Design Thinking steps, there were two different sources they could draw from: The research data that described as-is processes and the future scenarios described in the prototypes. However, in agile development, there is only one map.

Our impression is that story mapping can be used for both, but with a clear distinction. A story map that assembles an overview of the current process can be a possible research artifact, but not automatically a basis for an innovative product and the respective backlog. If the story map is supposed to feed the backlog, it has to emerge from the usage scenario of the future solution. To make this transition possible, the respective prototypes themselves must already have a strong emphasis on the process (mockups are not enough), on the way they will influence the user's daily conduct in the future. On the other hand, it may help to enrich the story map to create more empathy. The use of visuals and pictures, for example, may be a way to improve the logical connection between prototypes and the story map. If we put descriptions of usage processes into the prototype and emotions into our story maps, they are likely to work even better.

4.3   Take Your Time, Stop to Think

Design Thinking suggests to spent sufficient time for observing and conducting user research to better understand the underlying problem space, customer needs, and develop true empathy for future users. This enables teams and organizations to build products that are desirable, feasible, and viable. Moreover, iteration in Design Thinking accepts the fact that a complete restart might be required due to insightful feedback from users (Brown 2009; Rics 2011).

Lean Thinking, on the other hand, reserves time to analyze which processes directly contribute to customer value, which ones are non-value-adding but nonetheless necessary, and which ones are deemed obvious waste. Retrospectives in Scrum (Derby and Schwaber 2006) and other methods, such as A3-based problem solving (Rother 2010) give guidelines on how to achieve continuous improvement, i.e. "sharpening the axe" efficiently and sustainably. In our STG project, for instance, we also conducted regular retrospectives in order to streamline the team processes.

Bottom line, both thinking schools reserve a reasonable amount of time for the implementation of their core values such as identifying value-adding activities and eliminating waste in recurring processes (in Lean Thinking) as well as developing empathy for user needs and pains by taking a user perspective and investing in exhaustive research and continuous prototyping (in Design Thinking). One could say that they both "stop to think", i.e. stop in order to think. In both cases, the time spent for thinking in these respects is well invested. The successful shipment of the "Sail Better" software to STG is one more proof point.

4.4   Innovation Needs Some Waste

"Waste" is a term from Lean Thinking and lean production systems coined at Toyota and Porsche, for instance. Waste denotes activities and processes that do not add direct value for the end customer in the sense that value is defined as "something the customer is willing to pay for" (Womack et al. 1990; Poppendieck 2002; Poppendieck and Poppendieck 2003; Womack and Jones 2003).

Innovation approaches such as Design Thinking, on the other hand, foster "real" brainstorming and the creation of ideas in large quantities. Many of these ideas might be discarded right away or later in the process based on relentless user feedback. That is, they literally end up in the "waste bin". Moreover, Design Thinking also suggests rapid and cheap prototyping to get feedback in order to "fail early and often" (Brown 2009, p. 87). Again, many of these prototypes will end up in the waste bin after they served their purpose of leveraging feedback on existing solution approaches or inspiring even better ideas.

Now, despite all the waste, can our two thinking schools intertwine to solve problems for the software industry that neither one could on its own? We think so, especially in standard software development processes. Just imagine this simple example:

A development team combines Design Thinking and Scrum. They spend a serious amount of time for user research, brainstorming, ideation, paper prototypes, etc. – similar to our team developing "Sail Better" for STG. Let us say 20 percent of their ideas make it into the final product which becomes a blockbuster – i.e. in Lean Thinking terms, ideation inferred 80 percent waste. On the other hand, another team does it the "textbook agile way" with some requirements workshops, user story writing, and backlog grooming. They realize 80 percent of the initial backlog, but the product completely fails on the market despite efficient development processes.

In Lean Thinking terms, the latter implies close to 100 % waste, since no customer is willing to pay for the software eventually (see also the "Lean Startup" approach by Ries 2011).

5   Conclusion and Outlook

To conclude, let's summarize again *why* the combination of the two thinking schools is so promising and *how* it helps software development teams to come up with an innovative product vision and derive requirements in a yet unknown domain:

While *Lean Thinking* and agile practices are meant to help us building products right, i.e. in-time, in-quality, etc., *Design Thinking* can help us to build the right product based on a valid customer problem in the first place. Both thinking schools address responding to desire at the customer side and working efficiently as a team, however with different emphasis: a lean development project, for example, expects the agile team and the product owner in particular, to already have a product vision ready. But where does that vision come from? Design Thinking, on the other hand, provides various methods to build empathy with end users and other inspiration sources for developing a solution idea or product vision as well as prototypes for what the product should actually do for the end user. But after that, it lacks a clear framework of the roles, artifacts, tools, and necessary steps that can take the vision from prototype to a shippable product.

In our concrete case, the STG project, we learned that understanding and developing empathy for the customers' context and experience enables the team to elaborate and choose the right backlog items and user stories to be developed. This process is mainly driven by Design Thinking practices. Iterative development and thus fast feedback reduces project risk and ensures efficient delivery and shipment of the software. The development and delivery process of Sail Better is mainly based on common Lean and Agile practices.

Besides the positive feedback from the team and the customers on both the approach and the solution, three main findings evolved from our case study: (1) *User story maps* can serve as a tool to bridge the gap from the empathy and insights gained with Design Thinking practices and the backlog to build the solution, (2) both thinking schools suggest to reserve a substantial amount of project time, i.e. stop to think, for implementing their core values, such as developing empathy by means of observation, user research, etc. as well as eliminating waste by reflecting the value-add created by particular processes, obvious waste, and according analysis and improvement activities. (3) Innovation and great solutions do not come for free and it may require a little "waste" due to scoping and prototyping from a Lean perspective in order to gain fast feedback and succeed eventually. Moreover, several core values of the two thinking schools are almost identical and hence facilitate intertwining the respective methods and techniques: e.g. cross-functional or multi-disciplinary teams working in iterations, continuous and fast feedback loops ("inspect and adapt") as well as a clear focus on customer value and desire.

Our future research on Lean and Design Thinking will include a multi-case study across 10–50 so-called "early adopter" projects at SAP that implement Lean and Design Thinking. In order to come closer to an integrated theory of both efficient and innovative software product development with Lean and Design Thinking principles and practices we need to better understand the contingencies in different project settings (Van de Ven 1985). Particular process design challenges include the smooth and efficient information and artifact flow from divergent and convergent thinking in iterative problem scoping and solution development. As we already experienced in the STG project, a clear distinction but smooth transition from as-is to to-be scenarios is critical to maintain this information flow. Another research trajectory revolves around scaling and embedding Design Thinking in a larger lean and agile enterprise software development setting. By this overall research agenda we try to address that managing the transition from traditional waterfall-like development and scaling reliable innovation and efficient delivery for up to 100 development teams working on one complex solution for various customer segments will be one of the major challenges in the software industry.

Acknowledgements We have to thank: Stefan Lacher, Jochen Guertler and his Innovation Center team, as well as Marcus Baur as main representative for Sailing Team Germany.

References

Anderson, D. J. (2010). *Kanban*. Sequim, WA: Blue Hole Press.

Beck, K. (1999). Embracing change with extreme programming. *Computer, 32*(10), 70–77.

Beck, K., Beedle, M., Bennekum, A. V., Cockburn, A., Cunningham, W., Fowler, M., et al. (2001). Agile manifesto.

Blau, B., & Hildenbrand, T. (2011b). Product line engineering in large-scale lean and agile software product development environments – Towards a hybrid approach to decentral control and managed reuse. *Presented at the 6th international conference on availability, reliability and security*, Vienna.

Blau, B., Hildenbrand, T., Xu, Y., & Fassunge, M. G. (2011a). Incentives and performance in large-scale lean software development – An agent-based simulation approach. *Presented at the 6th international conference on evaluation of novel approaches to software engineering (ENASE 2011)*, Beijing.

Brown, T. (2009). *Change by design: How design thinking transforms organizations and inspires innovation*. Harper Business.

Chow, T., & Cao, D. B. (2008). A survey study of critical success factors in agile software projects. *Journal of Systems and Software, 81*(6), 961–971.

Cohn, M. (2004). *User stories applied: For agile software development*. Boston: Addison-Wesley Professional.

Derby, E., Larsen, D., & Schwaber, K. (2006). *Agile retrospectives: Making good teams great*. Raleigh: Pragmatic Bookshelf.

Eisenhardt, K. M. (1989). Building theories from case study research. *Academy of Management Review, 14*(4), 532–550.

Hevner, A., March, S., Park, J., & Ram, S. (2004). Design science in information systems research. *MIS Quarterly, 28*(1), 75–105.

Highsmith, J. A., & Highsmith, J. (2009). *Agile project management: Creating innovative products*. Boston: Addison-Wesley Professional.

Hildenbrand, T., Geisser, M., Kude, T., Bruch, D., & Acker, T. (2008). Agile methodologies for distributed collaborative development of enterprise applications. *International conference on complex, intelligent and software intensive systems. CISIS 2008* (pp. 540–545), Barcelona.

Kelley, T. (2001). *The art of innovation*. London: Profile Books Ltd.

Kelley, T. (2008). *The ten faces of innovation*. London: Profile Books Ltd.

Kniberg, H. (2007). Scrum and XP from the Trenches. *InfoQ Enterprise Software Development Series*.

Larman, C., & Vodde, B. (2008). *Scaling lean & agile development: Thinking and organizational tools for large-scale Scrum*. Boston: Addison-Wesley Professional.

Larman, C., & Vodde, B. (2010). *Practices for scaling lean and agile development: Large, multisite, and offshore product development with large-scale scrum*. Addison-Wesley Professional. Upper Saddle River, NJ: USA

Leffingwell, D. (2011). Agile Software Requirements: Lean Requirements Practices for Teams, Programs, and the Enterprise. Addison-Wesley Professional. Upper Saddle River, NJ: USA.

Martin, R. C. (2008). *Clean code: A handbook of agile software craftsmanship*. Upper Saddle River: Prentice Hall.

Martin, R. L. (2009). *The design of business: Why design thinking is the next competitive advantage*. Harvard Business School Press. Boston: USA.

Meinel, C., & Leifer, L. (2011). *Design thinking: Understand – improve – apply*. Berlin/Heidelberg: Springer.

Patton, J. (2008). The new backlog. AgileProductDesign.com.

Pichler, R. (2010). *Agile product management with scrum: Creating products that customers love*. Amsterdam: Addison-Wesley Professional.

Poppendieck, M. (2002). Principles of lean thinking. *OOPSLA Onward*.

Poppendieck, M., & Poppendieck, T. (2003). *Lean software development: An agile toolkit*. Upper Saddle River: Addison-Wesley Professional.

Reinertsen, D. G. (1997). *Managing the design factory: A product developer's toolkit*. New York: Free Press.

Reinertsen, D. G. (2009). *The principles of product development flow: Second generation lean product development*. Redondo Beach, CA: Celeritas Publishing.

Ries E. (2011). *The lean startup: How constant innovation creates radically successful businesses*. Crown Publishing Group. London: UK.

Rother, M., & MyiLibrary. (2010). *Toyota kata: managing people for improvement, adaptiveness, and superior results*. New York: McGraw Hill.

Sailing Team Germany Uses. (2011). *SAP Sail Better*. youtube.com.

Schnitter, J., & Mackert, O. (2011). Large-scale agile software development at SAP AG. *Evaluation of Novel Approaches to Software Engineering, 230*, 209–220. doi:10.1007/978-3-642-23391-3_15

Schwaber, K., et al. (1995). Scrum development process. In *OOPSLA business object design and implementation workshop* (Vol. 27, pp. 10–19). Austin: TX.

Smith, P. G., & Reinertsen, D. G. (1992). Shortening the product development cycle. *Research Technology Management, 35*(3), 44–49.

Sutherland, J., & Schwaber, J. (2011). *Scrum Guide*, http://www.Scrum.org/scrumguides/ (cit. 2011).

Van de Ven, A. H., & Drazin, R. (1985). The concept of fit in contingency theory. *Research in Organizational Behavior, 7*(3), 333–365.

Womack, J. P., Jones, D. T. & Daniel, R. (1990). *The machine that changed the world.* Free Press. New York: USA.

Womack, J. P., & Jones, D. T. (2003). *Lean thinking: Banish waste and create wealth in your corporation.* New York: Simon and Schuster.

Yin, R. K. (2008). *Case study research: Design and methods* (Vol. 4). Thousand Oaks: Sage publications, Inc.

Yin, R. K. (2011). *Applications of case study research* (Vol. 34). Thousand Oaks: Sage Publications, Inc.

The Relationship Between Scrum and Release Planning Activities: An Exploratory Case Study

Michail Theuns, Kevin Vlaanderen, and Sjaak Brinkkemper

Abstract

In modern product software development settings, it becomes increasingly important to deal with rapid changes in scope, large numbers of users, and regular releases. These circumstances are ideal for an agile development method such as Scrum to prove its value. However, the implications that Scrum has on software product management (SPM) processes have not been investigated in detail. In this paper, we provide more insight into the link between release planning processes and Scrum, by performing a case study at a large Dutch social network provider. The results show an evolutionary approach to the implementation of Scrum, and the relation between several Scrum concepts and SPM capabilities. The findings presented in this paper contribute to more insight into the link between Scrum and SPM and can be of help to product software organizations that employ the Scrum development method.

1 Introduction

In contrast to traditional software packages tailored to satisfy one specific customer, today's software market shows a variety of product software packages that are aimed to serve an entire market with many customers (Regnell and Brinkkemper 2005). Because product software is released for an entire market instead of for just one customer, the development and management of product software is more complex. For example, while a customer-specific software package has to deal with a limited number of requirements coming from just one customer, product

M. Theuns • K. Vlaanderen (✉) • S. Brinkkemper
Utrecht University - Department of Information and Computing Sciences, Utrecht, the Netherlands
e-mail: m.theuns@uu.nl; k.vlaanderen@uu.nl; s.brinkkemper@uu.nl

A. Maedche et al. (eds.), *Software for People*, Management for Professionals,
DOI 10.1007/978-3-642-31371-4_14, © Springer-Verlag Berlin Heidelberg 2012

software has to deal with both an increasing amount of internal and external stakeholders (Ebert 2007), a large amount of requirements and often a much higher release frequency (Weerd et al. 2006).

These circumstances form an ideal environment for agile software development methods. Agile software development methods such as DSDM (Stapleton 1997), Extreme Programming (Beck 1999) and Scrum (Schwaber 1995) enable software companies to dynamically respond to changes in both development environment and target environment (Schwaber 1995). The benefits of agile software development already gained a lot of attention in scientific literature (Dingsøyr et al. 2006; Fitzgerald et al. 2006; Mann and Maurer 2005) and even the applicability of agile principles to the domain of software product management (SPM) gained some attention recently (Vlaanderen et al. 2011), although more research should reveal its applicability to other areas as well (Maglyas et al. 2011). However, the effects or implications of the implementation of agile development methods for a company's SPM processes haven't been investigated in detail yet. In this paper, we describe the implementation of Scrum at a large Dutch online social network provider. Using the situational assessment method (Bekkers et al. 2010), we identify the steps that were taken during the Scrum implementation and the effects it had on the company's SPM processes. The scope of the changes to the SPM processes at the case company is too large to present in this paper entirely. For this reason, we limit our results to the effects of Scrum on the release planning processes. Release planning is often concerned with large amounts of requirements and a high release frequency (Weerd et al. 2006), making it a critical task in the process of developing a successful product. The results can help companies on the verge of implementing an agile development method by providing guidance on how to prepare their SPM processes to facilitate a smooth and successful implementation. In addition, the results form a valuable addition to the knowledge infrastructure (Weerd et al. 2006; Vlaanderen et al. 2011) that is being developed to support product managers in improving their SPM processes.

The remainder of this paper is structured as follows. In the following section, we describe the research approach followed during this project. In Sect. 3, we position our work within existing scientific literature, after which we present our case study results in Sect. 4. We analyze the results in Sect. 5, where we link Scrum elements to release planning capabilities. We conclude with a discussion of our research in Sect. 6, and some pointers towards open research areas in Sect. 7.

2 Case Study Research Design

2.1 Research Question

This research aims at elaborating the relation between Scrum concepts and release planning processes. This information can be of value to companies that struggle with the interaction between agile release planning and the management of software products. By presenting the link between Scrum concepts and (in this case) release planning processes, and the growth in maturity that can be expected when implementing Scrum concepts, companies are given a handhold that shows which release planning capabilities can be implemented by the introduction to Scrum, allowing them to focus on implementing other software product management capabilities. To guide this research, the following main research question is answered throughout this paper:

> How are release planning capabilities related to the activities and concepts within the Scrum development method?

As acknowledged by Levy and Ellis (2006), building a solid theoretical foundation that is based on high quality resources enables researcher to better explain as well as understand the problems under investigation. Hence, we first focus on providing the reader with a clear description of software product management in general and release planning in particular. Furthermore, since this paper aims at discovering the relation between Scrum concepts and release planning processes, we will explain the concept of the Scrum development method and the elements associated with it. The next two subsections explain how we gathered and analyzed our data at the case company.

2.2   Data Gathering

Because we want to examine a phenomenon in its natural setting by gathering information from one or more entities (Benbasat et al. 1987), this research is set up as a case study. The case study is performed at a large Dutch online social network provider, which is explained in more detail in Sect. 4. Several methods for data collection during case studies are described in literature (Yin 2009). For our research, we initially conduct semi-structured interviews with four employees that were actively involved in improving the SPM processes and the implementation of Scrum. In order to obtain a clear and correct understanding of the evolution of the release planning processes at the case company as they implemented Scrum, we interviewed a developer, two product managers, and the head of product (also a member of the company board). The interviews were done in retrospect, meaning that the process improvements that are subject to this research were already implemented at the time of the interviews. However, all of the interviewees have been employed at the case company for at least 3 years, so they were involved in the process improvements from the beginning. This allowed us to gain a complete and correct picture of both operational and strategic processes, and the effects the implementation of Scrum had on these processes. To guide the interviews, a predefined questionnaire was used to ensure we would gather all the data needed to determine the maturity of the release planning processes over time, as we will describe in the next section. The one and a half hour interviews were semi-structured, because they are both well suited for the reconstruction of the process changes, as well as for the exploration of the perceptions and opinions of respondents regarding complex and sometimes sensitive issues. In addition, they enable probing for more information and clarification of answers (Barribal and While 1994). By comparing and contrasting the interview data from several interviewees, along with several related documents, we obtained a complete and correct overview of the evolution of SocialComp's Scrum and SPM processes over time.

2.3   Data Analysis

We first describe the implementation of Scrum, based on what we learned during the interviews. Next, we use the situational assessment method (Bekkers et al. 2010; Bekkers and Spruit 2010) to create four maturity matrices that illustrate the state of the software product management processes at different points in time. The situational assessment method was designed to aid product managers in improving their software product management practices. The maturity matrices present all of the important practices (called capabilities) related to the management of software products in a best practice order for implementation. Each capability is associated with a certain level of maturity, making the maturity matrices a convenient technique to visualize which capabilities are implemented in an organization and which capabilities should ideally be implemented. By comparing the four maturity matrices, we can identify the process improvements that were implemented over a period of 3 years, and thus reveal the evolution of the case company's software product management processes.

Next, we extend the situational assessment method by following a similar approach as used by Weerd, Brinkkemper and Versendaal (2010) and model the release planning processes in process-deliverable diagrams. A process-deliverable diagram consists of a process-side (based on UML activity diagrams) and a deliverable-side (based on UML class diagrams), and can be used to design and analyze the meta-models of methods, revealing both the activities and artifacts of a certain process (Weerd and Brinkkemper 2008). By modeling a snapshot of a process in retrospect and comparing it to a snapshot of the same process in a later point in time, we can identify the process steps or method increments that led to the process's current state. This provides us with much more detail about the release planning processes, and the improvements that were implemented over time. A method increment is basically any adaption in order to improve the overall performance of the method of subject (Weerd et al. 2007).

The result is four maturity matrices and four process-deliverable diagrams of the release planning processes, associated with four distinct points in time. We then compare these 'snapshots' of the software product management processes with the information we gathered about the implementation of Scrum. By analyzing which Scrum elements, and which software product management capabilities were implemented at different points in time, we can reveal the relation between the implementation of various Scrum elements and the evolution of the release planning processes.

3   Related Literature

3.1   Software Product Management

In order to create a profitable software product, software vendors have to take into account all the market requirements coming from the target market. As software products get bigger and more complex, proper management of these software products has become of critical value to the success of the software products (Ebert 2007; Weerd et al. 2006). This led to a new field of research called software product management, which can be defined as "the discipline that governs a product (or solution or service) over its whole lifecycle, from its inception to the market/ customer delivery, in order to generate the biggest possible value to the business" (Ebert 2007). Although software product management has many similarities with product management in other sectors, managing software products is usually more complex due to higher release frequencies, difficulties tracking changes in the design of the software products and the fact that product managers often have little authority over the development department (Weerd et al. 2006). To aid companies in improving their software product management practices, a reference framework called the SPM Competence Model has been developed (Weerd et al. 2006; Bekkers et al. 2010).

The SPM Competence Model (Fig. 1) presents an overview of all the aspects that are important to software product management, including the relevant external and internal stakeholders. The model addresses 15 focus areas, divided over 4 main business functions.

On a strategic level, the software product manager is responsible for managing the product portfolio, by developing product strategies, making decisions about product lifecycles and establishing partnerships with other companies in the software's ecosystem (Jansen, Finkelstein, and Brinkkemper, 2009). The goal of the portfolio management function is to maximize the products' value, spread risks and align with the company's strategy (Cooper et al. 2001).

On a more tactical level, the software product manager is concerned with translating the product strategy into a comprehensive roadmap which forecasts and plans future development steps in terms of release contents, time-to-market and stakeholders involved (Vähäniitty et al. 2002). Hence, the product planning function is mainly concerned with gathering information about a software product (line) and processing this information into product roadmaps that illustrate the ipcoming product releases over a time frame of approximately 3–5 years (Regnell and Brinkkemper 2005), and the use of resources, elements, and their structural relationships in that period (Vähäniitty et al. 2002).

Based on the roadmap, it is the software product manager's task to determine the set of requirements for the next release while keeping in mind all stakeholder demands, effectively managing scope changes to prevent delays and ultimately launch the release to the market. This is done in the release planning function, which comprises the process of selecting an optimal subset of requirements through the prioritization of requirements in accordance with all relevant stakeholders

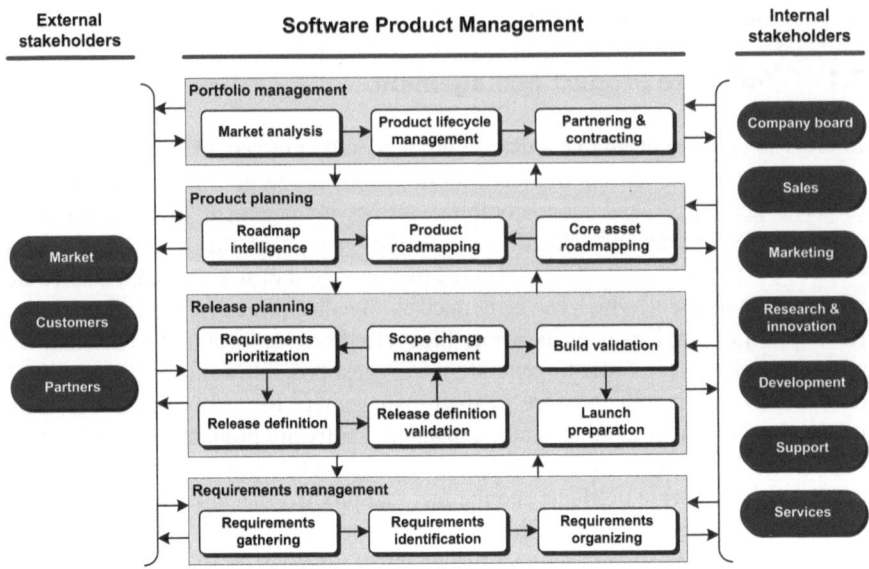

Fig. 1 SPM Competence Model (Bekkers et al. 2010)

(Carlshamre 2002) in order to plan, manage and launch a new release (Bekkers et al. 2010). The release plan contains a detailed description of the requirements to be included in the next release, a planning to ensure the release can be delivered on time, as well as various important technical, resource, budget, and risk constraints (Ruhe and Saliu 2005).

Since a release consists of a multitude of requirements, varying in size and quality, and coming from both internal and external stakeholders, the software product manager is also responsible for effectively managing all requirements. Requirements management encompasses all the activities involved in discovering, documenting, organizing and managing the large volumes of requirements of a software product (Sommerville 2007), the complex dependencies between the requirements (Carlshamre et al. 2001) and the involvement of all the stakeholders (Berander and Andrews 2005). It ensures that requirements are efficiently elicited from all relevant stakeholders (Browne and Rogich 2001), and organized in such a way that they are comprehensible for the development teams.

Each focus area represents a strongly coherent group of predefined goals (also called capabilities) that need to be achieved to reach the maturity levels with which they are associated (Bekkers et al. 2010). To measure the maturity of an organization's SPM processes, a situational assessment method was developed (Bekkers et al. 2010). This situational assessment method employs a capability maturity matrix to determine which capabilities are implemented in an organization and which capabilities should ideally be implemented. A comparison between the current and optimal situation results in an overview of the problem areas that need improvement in order to reach a higher maturity level.

3.2   Scrum

The goal of Scrum is to deliver as much quality software functionality as possible within a series of short time-boxed sprints (Sutherland 2001). Scrum has several distinctive characteristics. The product backlog is a prioritized, non-exhaustive list of functionality to be developed. Usually, product backlog items are not yet well-defined requirements, but rather express functionality in the form of a short description of the feature, defined using the terminology and context of the customer, also referred to as user stories. The product backlog is prioritized by the product owner, so that during the sprint planning meeting, a team of developers can easily pick the top priority items and commit to completing them within the next sprint. The list of top priority features to be developed during the next sprint is called the sprint backlog. During a sprint, the items to be developed are set and cannot change. This helps the development team to remain focused on the goal of the sprint. During a sprint, a storyboard is used to track progress on each sprint backlog item by categorizing them with respect to their status. Furthermore, daily Scrum meetings during which the completed tasks, the work remaining, and any obstacles encountered are discussed help the stakeholders to get an excellent understanding of the sprint progress (Rising and Janoff 2000).

Embedding Scrum within the context of a product software company is not a trivial task. This is recognized by several authors, including one of the founders of the Agile Alliance (Nerur et al. 2005). While agile methodologies can provide significant advantages to a software producing company, there are many challenges that can inhibit a successful move from traditional software development approaches to an agile environment, such as developer resistance, changes in decision making, and the need for increased customer involvement (Boehm and Turner 2005; Moe et al. 2008). Several Scrum implementations have been described in literature. For example, Sutherland (2001) reports on the introduction of Scrum into five different organizations with different technologies. In all five organizations, Scrum improved communication and de-livery of working functionality. Rising and Janoff (2000) describe the experiences three different development teams had with Scrum. The paper acknowledges similar benefits as described by Dingsøyr et al. (2006) and by Mann and Maurer (2005), such as improved customer satisfaction and more flexibility and transparency in the development process. Scrum also proved to be useful in a global, distributed software development environment (Hansen and Baggesen 2009). By employing an virtual task board during online Scrum meetings and moving Product Owners back and forth between the cross-continental locations, they were able to increase code quality and improve trust and understanding between members of distributed development teams, although resource estimation can be a tedious task (Dingsøyr et al. 2006).

Due to the perceived benefits of agile development methods such as Scrum, researchers are now also investigating the applicability of agile principles to other domains. For example, Towill and Christopher (2010) describe the combination of lean and agile principles in supply chain management, while Vlaanderen et al. (2011) apply Scrum principles to SPM to create a regular heartbeat in the SPM process in support of the development process.

4   Case Study Results

4.1   Case Company Introduction

SocialComp was founded in 2004 on the premise of providing a platform through which people could connect and discuss about their everyday lives. Already after 10 months, they reached one million members internationally, with over 80 million page views per month just from the Netherlands. This rapid growth required for several organizational changes. A CEO was appointed to lead the company at corporate level, and several product managers were hired to manage the development department, which grew from only 1 developer in 2004 to over 30 in 2008. After 2008, the number of developers gradually grew to 36, the reason for this declined pace of growth being their high hiring standards and an overall shortage of highly educated developers in the Dutch labor market.

The 36 developers were divided over development teams of approximately 10 developers per team, each team being directed by a product manager. However, despite having appointed a new CEO, the founders stayed actively involved in the development of the social platform. The product managers were often hampered in their work due to conflicting ideas between them and the founders, who were used to address developers directly instead of growing through a layer of product managers. This caused a chaotic working environment, since development teams were often ad hoc assigned to new development projects by the founders, before they could finish their work in progress. During this stage, there was no formal prioritization method in place to determine which projects to develop first. In fact, even a basic process to structurally gather, identify and organize requirements was missing. Prioritization was mainly done according to managers' gut feeling. To make things more complicated, the development teams worked according to the waterfall development model. However, the ever changing requirements made it difficult to finish a phase of the waterfall model since designs often had to be modified to accommodate new requirements. This caused a lot of stress and confusion amongst developers and product managers.

4.2   Implementation of Scrum and Software Product Management

Once the social network grew to be such a large service (over 11 million members in 2011 internationally with over six billion page views per day), the large amount of requirements and the lack of structure of the development department became serious threats to productivity. Therefore, they started searching for alternatives practices to increase productivity and reduce waste of time and resources. Based on the interview results, we could identify four phases in the overall improvement process and the implementation of Scrum and software product management. As described in Sect. 4.1, software product management encompasses many focus areas and capabilities. These focus areas and capabilities are shown in Table 1.

Table 1 Focus areas and capabilities for the release planning domain

Requirements prioritization	Release definition	Launch preparation
RP:A Int. stakeholder involvement	RD:A Basic req. selection	LP:A Internal communication
RP:B Prioritization methodology	RD:B Standardization	LP:B Formal approval
RP:C Customer involvement	RD:C Internal communication	LP:C External communication
RP:D Cost/revenue consideration	RD:D Advanced req. selection	LP:D Training
RP:E Partner involvement	RD:E Multiple releases	LP:E Launch impact analysis
		LP:F Sales & marketing support
Release definition validation	**Build validation**	**Scope change management**
RDV:A Internal validation	BV:A Internal validation	SCM:A Event notification
RDV:B Formal approval	BV:B External validation	SCM:B Milestone monitoring
RDV:C Business case	BV:C Certification	SCM:C Impact analysis
		SCM:D Scope change handling

We chose to only include the changes of the release planning processes in this paper because of two reasons. The main reason is that release planning has many similarities to Scrum and is therefore affected more by the implementation of Scrum than other software product management processes. The second reason is that we wanted to keep this section as concise as possible.

During the first phase (depicted in Table 2 Reference source not found. in the lighter shaded boxes), some capabilities were already implemented, but Scrum and software product management weren't implemented officially yet. Around fall 2010, they began experimenting with Scrum, mainly because of positive prior experiences among some employees. They began by cutting up the fairly large development teams into smaller, independent teams consisting of a maximum of six developers and a product manager, who was assigned the role of product owner. Although the product owners consulted the various stakeholders to determine which set of requirements to develop next, the product owners were now the only ones to direct their development teams. This required the organization to improve its internal communication about the contents of upcoming releases in order to maintain stakeholder satisfaction. This is reflected in Table 2 by 'release definition C' and 'release definition validation A'. 'Requirements prioritization D' shows that they started to take expected costs and revenues of requirements into account during prioritizing, although we could not ascribe this improvement to the implementation of Scrum.

Next, they introduced the 2-week sprints. At the beginning of each sprint cycle, the Product Owners would determine the requirements to be developed during the 2-week sprint during sprint planning meetings. Internal stakeholders were invited to attend the sprint planning meetings and voice their opinion about what to develop next, which is reflected by 'requirements prioritization A' in Table 3. During

Table 2 The evolution of the release planning processes during phases 1 and 2

Process \ Maturity	0	1	2	3	4	5	6	7	8	9	10
Release planning											
Requirements prioritization			A		B	C	D			E	
Release definition			A	B	C				D		E
Release definition validation					A			B		C	
Scope change management			A			B		C		D	
Build validation					A			B		C	
Launch preparation		A		B		C	D		E		F

Table 3 The evolution of the release planning processes during phases 2 and 3

Process \ Maturity	0	1	2	3	4	5	6	7	8	9	10
Release planning											
Requirements prioritization			A		B	C	D			E	
Release definition			A	B	C				D		E
Release definition validation					A			B		C	
Scope change management				A		B		C		D	
Build validation					A			B		C	
Launch preparation		A		B		C	D		E		F

sprints, the set of requirements to be developed is frozen, so it is very important that a set of requirements is chosen that can be delivered when the sprint ends. This is reflected in Table 3 by the implementation of 'release definition A', which means that constraints concerning engineering capacity were taken into account during requirements selection for the next release. Furthermore, the time-boxed nature of Scrum sprints (i.e. the start and end dates are set and do not change) required them to get a much better grip on the development process by monitoring milestones and keeping track of the remaining work. The disorganized funnel was gradually replaced by a structured, prioritized product backlog. This made planning which requirements to develop during the next sprint much easier. In consultation with the Product Owners, development teams could pick a set of requirements from the top of the product backlog, based on the estimated time needed to complete the various requirements. This resulted in several sprint backlogs, for each of the development teams. They introduced a planning board on which the development teams could adjust their sprint backlog items by marking requirements that are completed and estimating the time needed to complete remaining requirements. A burn down chart was introduced to give an overview of the sprint progress. In Table 3, these improvements are reflected by 'scope change management B', which represents the process of milestone monitoring. They also introduced daily standup meetings

Table 4 The evolution of the release planning processes during phases 3 and 4

Process \ Maturity	0	1	2	3	4	5	6	7	8	9	10
Release planning											
Requirements prioritization			A		B	C	D			E	
Release definition			A	B	C				D		E
Release definition validation					A			B		C	
Scope change management				A		B		C		D	
Build validation					A			B		C	
Launch preparation		A		B		C	D		E		F

of approximately 15 min, in which team members were asked to discuss what they did the day before, what they plan on doing today and what obstacles may have occurred. This helped them to gain better understanding of the work that has been done and the work that still remains. Finally, the introduction of demo meetings at the end of each sprint allowed for stakeholder involvement during the validation of the built functionality ('build validation B'). In this case, partner companies were even allowed the opportunity to test functionality before it was released to the public. Table 4 shows the fourth phase of the improvement process, which represents the current state at the case company. Two more improvements could be identified recently. Although the implementation of Scrum already contributed to the improvement of their requirements prioritization process, it was formalized during this phase with the introduction of Scrum's planning poker. Everyone in the organization, whether he is a developer, a product manager or a member of the board, now knows how to voice his opinion about the contents of upcoming releases without hampering the development process. This was not yet the case in the third phase, which is why we included 'requirements prioritization B' in Table 4. Furthermore, the contents of the release definition (i.e. the sprint backlog) became more structured by adding aspects such as the time path and needed capacity. This can also be attributed to the formalization process, and is reflected by 'release definition B' in Table 4

5 Analysis

Since Scrum was largely implemented during the transition from phase 2 to phase 3, we decided to take a closer look into the actual changes that occurred during the transition and to visualize the release planning evolution in the PDD depicted in Fig. 2. The left-hand side of the PDD shows activities performed during the method (based on a UML activity diagram), whereas the right-hand side of the PDD shows the concepts delivered by the activities (based on a UML class diagram). According to the modeling conventions used by Weerd, Brinkkemper and Versendaal (2007),

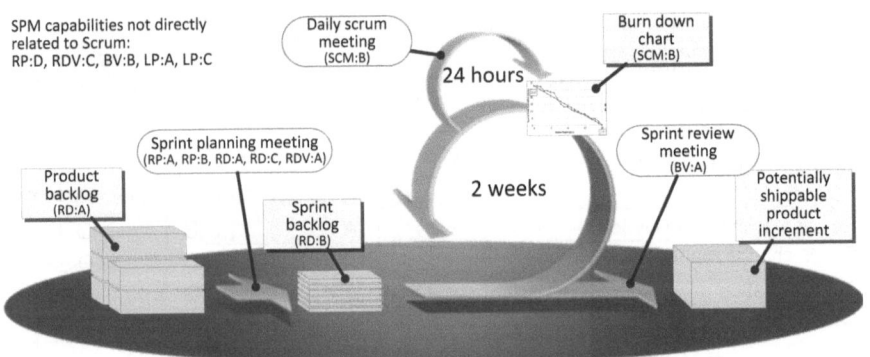

Fig. 2 Revealing the method increments of the release planning process (from phase 2 to 3)

we used gray markings to visualize the method increments that were inserted, whereas the shadings exhibit deleted parts. Note that the gray marked areas correspond with the darker shaded boxes in Table 3.

Based on our observations, we could relate several SPM capabilities implemented at SocialComp to Scrum concepts (see Fig. 3). The shadowed boxes represent Scrum concepts such as the product and sprint backlogs, the burn down chart and the product increment the sprint delivers. The rounded boxes symbolize Scrum activities such as the various Scrum meetings. It provides a simple overview of the capabilities for which Scrum concepts and activities can account.

As described earlier, sprints are time-boxed events. Hence, it is important to choose a set of requirements that can be completed during one sprint. Before the process improvements started, developers were often hampered in their work by intervening requirements coming from the management team. The implementation of the product backlog required them to estimate the time and resources required for each backlog item, which is why we associated 'release definition A' with the implementation of the product backlogs. As sprints came closer, more detailed information was added to the backlog items, and sprint backlog items became more standardized. Hence, we can say that the introduction of sprint backlogs is associated with the implementation of 'release definition B' which stands for standardization of release contents.

The sprint planning meetings could be associated with multiple capabilities. Whereas the management team was used to address developers directly, passing by the product managers, the sprint planning meetings created a place to discuss the contents of upcoming releases and sprints. It allowed internal stakeholders to voice their opinion about which requirements to develop ('requirements prioritization A'; 'release definition A'), without hampering the development process. Since the internal stakeholders were involved in the process of selecting and prioritizing requirements, 'release definition validation A' was automatically covered. Naturally, the implementation of the sprint planning meetings improved internal communication ('release definition C') greatly.

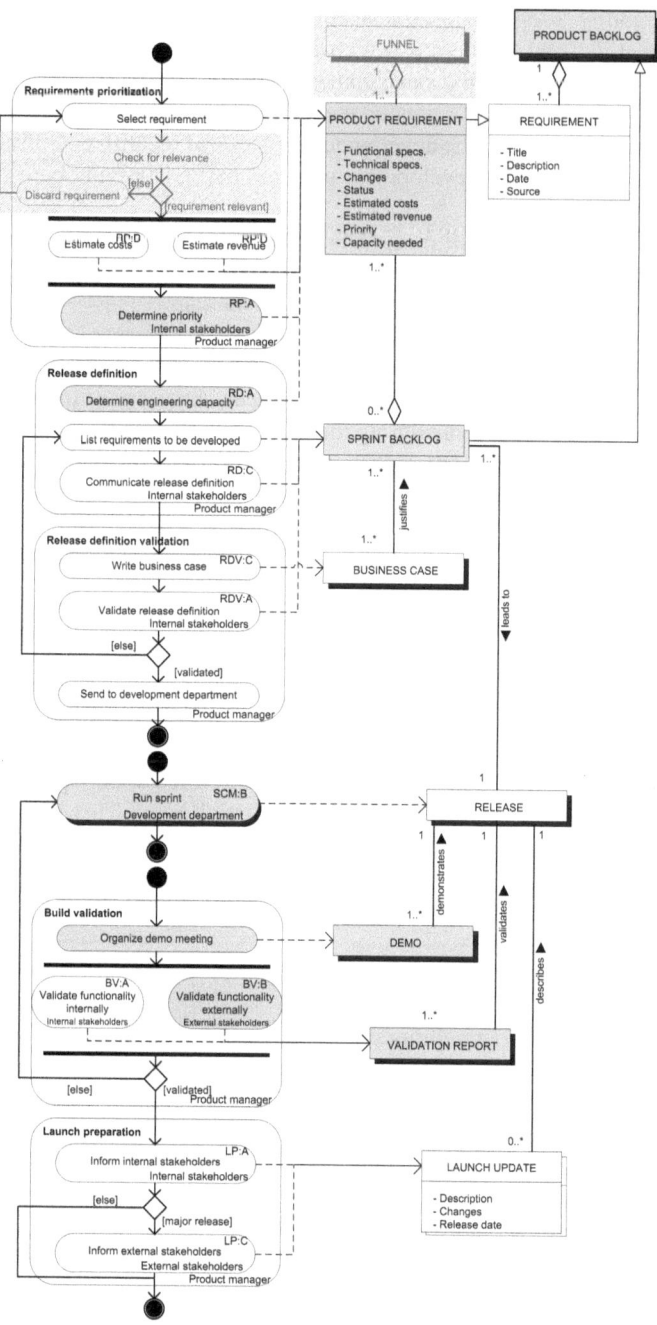

Fig. 3 Relating the SPM capabilities to Scrum concepts

The capability 'scope change management B' was associated with both the daily standup meetings and the burn down chart. The capability reflects the process of monitoring milestones in the development process, which is exactly what they gained from introducing daily standup meetings and the burn down chart. It allowed them to get a better grip on the development process, to identify possible difficulties early on, and monitor the development progress by updating the burn down chart when a task is finished.

'Build validation A' could be associated with the introduction of sprint review meetings, during which the development teams would demonstrate built functionality to the product managers and the management team.

Note that of all the release planning capabilities implemented, five could not be associated with the implementation of Scrum. For example, 'requirements prioritization D' was implemented in phase 2, which means they started to take prospected costs and revenues into account during the prioritization process. There is no Scrum element that prescribes cost/revenue consideration, and it was mainly caused by a change of management. The same holds for the business plan that was introduced to justify for each release plan ('release definition C'). Both were improvements imposed by the new management, who wanted to base their decisions on financial figures rather than on their gut feeling.

Furthermore, allowing partner companies, e.g. companies with a branded marketing campaign on the social network site, to test new functionality before going live ('build validation B') was a way of improving customer satisfaction rather than something prescribed by Scrum. Lastly, SocialComp has always communicated about upcoming releases. Internal (e.g. management or the sales department) and external (e.g. the users) stakeholders were kept informed about upcoming releases and new functionality ever since the start of SocialComp. This is also visible in Table 2, where 'launch preparation A' and 'launch preparation C' were already implemented in the first phase.

6 Discussion and Limitations

Although we used the four validity criteria as described in (Yin 2009) to ensure the quality and reliability of our work., it should be noted that this research is subject to some limitations. The findings presented in this paper are based on information regarding the SPM processes at one case company, posing a threat to the external validity. The external validity entails the possibility to generalize the research findings, so validating our findings at other web companies that recently implemented Scrum should eliminate this threat. Furthermore, although we also modeled the other business functions, we only studied the release planning processes in detail. Consequently, we only identified the relations between Scrum elements and release planning processes. In order to get a more comprehensive view of the relation between Scrum and SPM, future research should include the business functions requirements management, product roadmapping and portfolio management as well.

The construct validity, which concerns the operationalization and correct measurement of the concepts being studied, is safeguarded by validating the maturity matrices and PDDs that were created based on the data collected during the interviews in a second round of interviews. The internal validity concerns the completeness of concepts and the consistency between concepts. This is partly satisfied because we double-checked our information gathered and partly because we were able to link Scrum concepts to SPM capabilities. It should be noted though, that these links should be validated in follow-up research to completely satisfy internal validity. Furthermore, the case study report was reviewed by peer-researchers to ensure a reliable research approach. The empirical validity concerns the reproducibility of the research and is preserved by following a case study protocol. Furthermore, the interview results can be reproduced easily because we based the interviews on the situational assessment method (Bekkers et al. 2010).

Finally, the situational assessment method employs a questionnaire and a maturity model to determine the capabilities implemented in an organization and to reveal the areas that need improvement. We noticed during interviewing, that some of the capabilities are not applicable to agile software companies with a very informal organizational culture (for example, capabilities that prolong decision-making because all stakeholders have to get involved). By extending the situational assessment method with PDDs, we gain more insight in the actual processes and the associated capabilities. By modeling the processes, we were able to determine SocialComp's SPM maturity more accurately. Furthermore, the method offers a way to translate the maturity matrix to PDDs by adding information regarding the implemented capabilities to the activities depicted in the PDDs. A difficulty associated with the model-driven assessment method is that it is often challenging to get a correct picture of the entire process, since processes can be very complex with multiple concurrent activities and related concepts. While PDDs provide more detail about a certain process, areas that need improvement are not as conspicuous as in the maturity matrix. Furthermore, revealing method increments in PDDs is somewhat cumbersome, because the approach officially dictates that deleted and adapted activities or concepts should still be modeled.

7   Conclusions and Further Research

In this paper, we have described the results from a case study performed at a large, Dutch social network provider. We have gathered data regarding the implementation of Scrum, and the linkage between Scrum concepts and SPM capabilities. This data has been used to provide more insight into the effects of Scrum on SPM, and the co-evolution of Scrum and SPM when Scrum is implemented in an incremental manner.

The research presented in this paper forms yet a step towards a knowledge infrastructure that helps product managers in incrementally improving the SPM processes in their organizations. As noted by Vlaanderen et al. (2010), in order to establish a successful product software knowledge infrastructure, it is important to determine how certain methods in the SPM domain can change, what method increments are commonly found in practice and how method fragments can be analyzed. This research forms an addition to the existing knowledge base on method increments found in practice.

We are convinced that case study descriptions such as the one presented in this paper are a valuable addition to both scientific as well as the industrial software engineering field. However, in order to make such descriptions more concise and better comparable, we are in need of a more structured approach of modeling increments. Such an approach should be able to reflect changes in the process in relation to organization's contextual factors. Moreover, this research further matures the scientific literature on Scrum and release planning by revealing the link between the two. Providing insight into the association between Scrum concepts and the implementation of SPM capabilities can be of vital help to companies that want to implement either or both, as it provides insight into the maturity levels that can be expected.

References

Barribal, K. L., & While, A. (1994). Collecting data using a semi-structured interview: A discussion paper. *Journal of Advanced Nursing, 19*(2), 328–335. doi:10.1111/j.1365-2648.1994.tb01088.x.

Beck, K. (1999). *Extreme programming explained: Embrace change.* Boston: Addison-Wesley.

Bekkers, W. & Spruit, M. (2010). The situational assessment method put to the test: Improvements based on case studies. *Proceedings of the 4th international workshop on software product management, Sydney* (pp. 7–16). doi: 10.1109/IWSPM.2010.5623871

Bekkers, W., Spruit, M., Weerd, I. van de, Vliet, R. van, & Mahieu, A. (2010). A situational assessment method for software product management. *Proceedings of the 18th European conference on information systems, Pretoria* (pp. 22–34). Retrieved from http://dblp.uni-trier.de/db/conf/ecis/ecis2010.html

Bekkers, W., van de Weerd, I., Spruit, M., & Brinkkemper, S. (2010). A framework for process improvement in software product management. In A. Riel, R. O'Connor, S. Tichkiewitch, & R. Messnarz (Eds.), *Systems, software and services process improvement* (pp. 1–12). Berlin/Heidelberg: Springer. doi:10.1007/978-3-642-15666-3_1.

Benbasat, I., Goldstein, D. K., & Mead, M. (1987). The case study research strategy in studies of information systems. *MIS Quarterly, 11*(3), 369–386. doi:10.2307/248684.

Berander, P., & Andrews, A. (2005). Requirements prioritization. In A. Aurum & C. Wohlin (Eds.), *Engineering and managing software requirements* (pp. 69–94). Berlin/Heidelberg: Springer.

Boehm, B., & Turner, R. (2005). Management challenges to implementing agile processes in traditional development organizations. *IEEE Software, 22*(5), 30–39. doi:10.1109/MS.2005.129.

Browne, G. J., & Rogich, M. B. (2001). An Empirical Investigation of User Requirements Elicitation: Comparing the Effectiveness of Prompting Techniques. Journal of Management Information Systems, 17(4), 223–249.

Carlshamre, P. (2002). Release planning in market-driven software product development: Provoking an understanding. *Requirements Engineering, 7*(3), 139–151. doi:10.1007/s007660200010.

Carlshamre, P., Sandahl, K., Lindvall, M., Regnell, B., & Natt och Dag, J. (2001). An industrial survey of requirements interdependencies in software product release planning. *Proceedings of the 5th IEEE international symposium on requirements engineering, Toronto* (pp. 84–91). doi: 10.1109/ISRE.2001.948547

Cooper, R. G., Edgett, S. J., & Kleinschmidt, E. J. (2001). Portfolio Management for New Product Development: Results of an Industry Practices Study. *R&D Management, 31*(4).

Dingsøyr, T., Hanssen, G. K., Dybå, T., Anker, G., & Nygaard, J. O. (2006). Developing software with scrum in a small cross-organizational project. In I. Richardson, P. Runeson, & R. Messnarz (Eds.), *Lecture notes in computer science* (Software process improvement, Vol. 4257, pp. 5–15). Berlin/Heidelberg: Springer. doi:10.1007/11908562_2.

Ebert, C. (2007). The impacts of software product management. *Journal of Systems and Software, 80*(6), 850–861. doi:10.1016/j.jss.2006.09.017.

Fitzgerald, B., Hartnett, G., & Conboy, K. (2006). Customising agile methods to software practices at Intel Shannon. *European Journal of Information Systems, 15*(2), 200–213. doi:10.1057/palgrave.ejis.3000605.

Hansen, M. T., & Baggesen, H. (2009). From CMMI and isolation to scrum, agile, lean and collaboration. *Proceedings of the agile conference, Chicago* (pp. 283–288). doi: 10.1109/AGILE.2009.18

Jansen, S., Finkelstein, A., & Brinkkemper, S. (2009). A sense of community: A research agenda for software ecosystems. International Conference on Software Engineering (pp. 187–190). IEEE.

Levy, Y., & Ellis, T. J. (2006). A systems approach to conduct an effective literature review in support of information systems research. *Informing Science, 9*(1), 181–212. Retrieved from http://www.informingscience.us/icarus/journals/informingscij

Maglyas, A., Nikula, U., & Smolander, K. (2011). What do we know about software product management?. A systematic mapping study. *Proceedings of the 5th international workshop on software product management, Trento* (pp. 26–35). doi: 10.1109/IWSPM.2011.6046201

Mann, C., & Maurer, F. (2005). A case study on the impact of Scrum on overtime and customer satisfaction. *Proceedings of the agile development conference, Denver* (pp. 70–79). doi: 10.1109/ADC.2005.1

Moe, N. B., Dingsøyr, T., & Dybå, T. (2008). Understanding self-organizing teams in agile software development. *Proceedings of the 19th Australian conference on software engineering, Perth* (pp. 76–85). doi: 10.1109/ASWEC.2008.4483195

Nerur, S., Mahapatra, R., & Mangalaraj, G. (2005). Challenges of migrating to agile methodologies. *Communications of the ACM – Adaptive Complex Enterprises, 48*(5), 72–78. doi:10.1145/1060710.1060712.

Regnell, B., & Brinkkemper, S. (2005). Market-driven requirements engineering for software products. In A. Aurum & C. Wohlin (Eds.), *Engineering and managing software requirements* (pp. 287–308). Berlin/Heidelberg: Springer.

Rising, L., & Janoff, N. S. (2000). The scrum software development process for small teams. *IEEE Software, 17*(4), 26–32. doi:10.1109/52.854065.

Ruhe, G., & Saliu, M. O. (2005). Supporting software release planning decisions for evolving systems. *Proceedings of the 29th annual IEEE/NASA software engineering workshop, Greenbelt* (pp. 14–26). doi: 10.1109/SEW.2005.42

Schwaber, K. (1995). SCRUM development process. *Proceedings of the conference on object-oriented programming systems, languages, and applications, workshop on business object design and implementation* (pp. 117–134).

Sommerville, I. (2007). *Software engineering* (8th ed.). Boston: Addison-Wesley.

Stapleton, J. (1997). *DSDM: Dynamic systems development method.* Boston: Addison-Wesley.

Sutherland, J. (2001). Agile can scale: Inventing and reinventing scrum in five companies. *Cutter IT Journal, 14*(12), 5–11. Retrieved from http://www.cutter.com/itjournal.html

Towill, D., & Christopher, M. (2010). The supply chain strategy conundrum: To be lean or agile or to be lean and agile? *International Journal of Logistics Research and Applications, 5*(3), 299–309. doi:10.1080/1367556021000026736.

Vähäniitty, J., Lassenius, C., & Rautiainen, K. (2002). An Approach to Product Roadmapping in Small Software Product Businesses. *Conference Notes of the 7th European Conference on Software Quality* (pp. 12–13). Helsinki: Finland.

van de Weerd, I., & Brinkkemper, S. (2008). Meta-modeling for situation analysis and design methods. In M. R. Syed & S. N. Syed (Eds.), *Handbook of research on modern systems analysis and design technologies and applications* (pp. 38–58). Hershey: Idea Group Publishing.

van de Weerd, I., Brinkkemper, S., & Versendaal, J. (2007). Concepts for incremental method evolution: Empirical exploration and validation in requirements management. In J. Krogstie, A. Opdahl, & G. Sindre (Eds.), *Lecture notes in computer science* (Advanced information systems engineering, Vol. 4495, pp. 469–484). Berlin/Heidelberg: Springer.

van de Weerd, I., Brinkkemper, S., & Versendaal, S. (2010). Incremental method evolution in global software product management: A retrospective case study. *Information and Software Technology, 52*(7), 720–732. doi:10.1016/j.infsof.2010.03.002.

Vlaanderen, K., Weerd, I. van de, & Brinkkemper, S. (2010). Model-driven assessment in software product management. *Proceedings of the 3rd international workshop on software product management, Sydney* (pp. 17–25). doi: 10.1109/IWSPM.2010.5623868

Vlaanderen, K., Jansen, S., Brinkkemper, S., & Jaspers, E. (2011). The agile requirements refinery: Applying scrum principles to software product management. *Information and Software Technology, 53*(1), 58–70. doi:10.1016/j.infsof.2010.08.004.

Vlaanderen, K., Weerd, I. van de, & Brinkkemper, S. (2011). The online method engine: From process assessment to method execution. *Proceedings of the IFIP WG 8.1 working conference on method engineering, Paris* (pp. 108–122).

Weerd, I. van de, Brinkkemper, S., Nieuwenhuis, R., Versendaal, J., & Bijlsma, L. (2006). On the creation of a reference framework for software product management: Validation and tool support. *Proceedings of the 1st international workshop on software product management, Minneapolis/St. Paul* (pp. 3–12). doi: 10.1109/IWSPM.2006.6

Weerd, I. van de, Versendaal, J., & Brinkkemper, S. (2006). A product software knowledge infrastructure for situational capability maturation: Vision and case studies in product management. *Proceedings of the 12th working conference on requirements engineering: Foundation for software quality* (pp. 97–112). Luxemburg: Luxemburg

Yin, R. K. (2009). *Case study research: Design and methods* (4th ed.). London: Sage Publications.

Lessons Learned in the Development of a CRM SaaS Solution

Markus Bauer

Abstract

Software as a Service (SaaS) solutions have gained a significant momentum in the past few years. They promise to vastly simplify the long way from identifying the need for a new software system until its successful operation at a customer. Essentially, SaaS solutions have to face two potentially conflicting requirements: On one hand, customers expect that the software they use in the cloud can be customized smoothly to solve their specific business needs and requirements. On the other hand, they need to exploit the economy of scale principle by employing an architecture that handles all customers uniformly. This article examines these and a number of other requirements to SaaS systems and will shed some light on architectural concepts addressing these requirements. It illustrates some of the concepts with examples from a Java based SaaS solution for customer relationship management (CRM) and provides some lessons learned gained during the development and the first few years of offering the product on the market.

1 Introduction

Software that runs in the cloud has gained significant attraction in the past few years. As defined by the US National Institute of Standards and Technologies (NIST), cloud computing is "a model for enabling ubiquitous, convenient, on-demand network access to a shared pool of configurable computing resources (e.g. networks, servers, storage, applications and services) that can be rapidly provisioned and released with minimal management effort or service provider interaction" (Mell and Grance 2011). In more detail, cloud solutions have five essential characteristics:

M. Bauer
CAS Software AG, Karlsruhe, Germany
e-mail: markus.bauer@cas.de

A. Maedche et al. (eds.), *Software for People*, Management for Professionals,
DOI 10.1007/978-3-642-31371-4_15, © Springer-Verlag Berlin Heidelberg 2012

1. They are provided in an *on-demand self-service* oriented manner, so a costumer can unilaterally consume computing capabilities such as server time, network storage or application usage, without requiring human interaction with the service provider.
2. They are *available over the network* and accessible *through standard mechanisms*. This usually implies that the solutions can be used anytime and anywhere using a number of different client platforms, such as desktop computers, notebooks, tablets, mobile phones.
3. The provider's *computing resources are pooled to serve multiple costumers using a multi-tenant model*. Physical and virtual resources are dynamically assigned and reassigned according to customers demand. Examples of such resources include storage, processing time, memory, or network bandwidth.
4. Capabilities offered by the solution can be *elastically* provisioned and released to *scale rapidly with demand*. To the customer, capabilities often appear unlimited and can be consumed in any quantity at any time.
5. *Resource usage is metered* at some level of abstraction appropriate to the type of solution or service (e.g. storage, processing, bandwidth, or active user accounts). Typically resource usage is charged on a pay-per-use basis.

There are three basic service models for cloud offerings:

- *Software as a Service (SaaS):* The capability provided to the customer is to use the provider's application running on a cloud infrastructure. The applications are accessible from various client devices such as desktop computers, notebooks, tablets, mobile phones or just using a programmatic interface (API).
- *Platform as a Service (PaaS):* The capability provided to the customer is to deploy onto the cloud infrastructure customer-created or acquired applications created using programming languages, libraries, services and tools supported by the provider.
- *Infrastructure as a Service (IaaS):* The capability provided to the customer is to provision processing, storage, networks and other fundamental computing resources where the customer is able to deploy and run arbitrary software which may include operating systems and applications.

Figure 1 illustrates the distribution of responsibilities between the provider and the customer for these three service models and compares them with conventional IT solutions.

1.1   Why SaaS?

In the SaaS model, the provider hosts software applications and the associated data on central servers at the provider's location, and the provider also supports the hardware and software with a dedicated support staff. This relieves the customer from the responsibility for supporting the software and for purchasing and maintaining server hardware for it. In essence, the provider cares for all maintenance tasks that are typically required when running software applications, including tasks like providing backups for the data,...

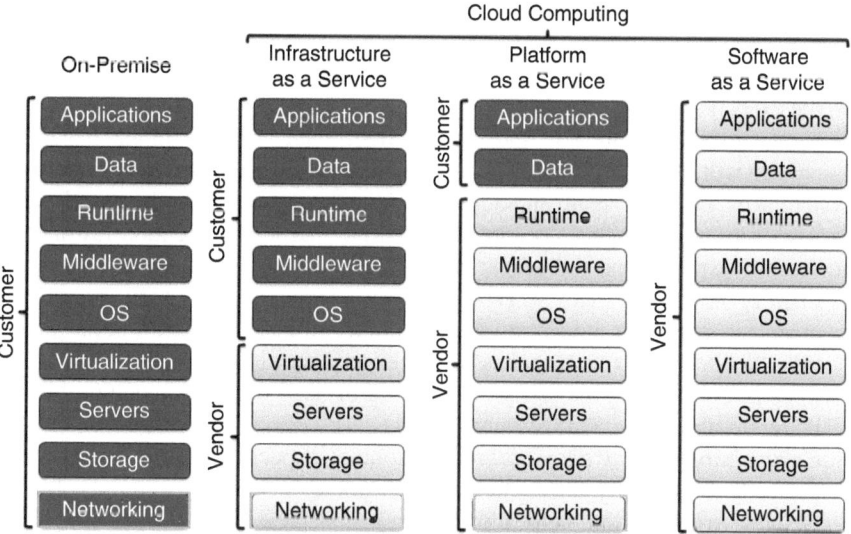

Fig. 1 Distribution of responsibilities for on-premise and cloud computing models

The provider or software vendor, on the other hand, has to provide all these tasks instead. However, the provider can vastly benefit from the principle of *economy of scale*. A SaaS vendor can serve a potentially large number of customers using one single consolidated environment. For example, a SaaS application installed in a load-balanced farm of five servers may be able to support 50 medium-sized customers. This means one customer would only be responsible for a tenth of a server. A similar application installed on-premise might require each customer to dedicate an entire server to the application – perhaps even more than one, if load balancing and high availability are concerns (Chong and Carraro 2006). A similar calculation might yield for trained staff that monitors and – in case of problems – troubleshoots the systems. These effects lead to substantial cost savings over traditional models. Given fair pricing models, both customers and vendors will benefit from these cost savings.

The aforementioned reduced operating costs per customer also allows vendors to address new markets by benefitting from selling to the *long tail* (Anderson 2004): smaller, niche customers that might have been inaccessible to traditional solution vendors due to high costs and the complexity of the IT systems involved with the traditional solutions can suddenly be targeted as well – provided that the SaaS solution can be tailored towards those niche customers.

In addition, customers may benefit from the fact that SaaS usually employs a *pay-per-use* model. Customers do not have to do a high initial investment in hardware and software, instead they are typically paying monthly or yearly fees depending on the number of user licenses they need and/or on the resources they consume. Especially for smaller customers, this simplifies the planning phase needed when introducing a new software solution drastically.

1.2   Customer Expectations

The pay-per-use model typically employed with SaaS solutions also has an impact on the expectations that customers associate with them. A software system does not represent an asset (which in the case of traditional software might have been associated with the acquisition costs of the software) anymore, instead, the software system is expected to create an additional value for the customer's enterprise.

As a consequence, SaaS vendors have to pay particular attention towards the customers' expectations and needs:

- *Ease of use, quick way of getting started:* Since SaaS systems promise an effortless start with a new software solution (no installation, no initial investment), customers expect that hassle-free experience also when starting to use the system. Considering the self-service nature of SaaS offerings, good usability is therefore a must for SaaS systems.
- *Customizability and extensibility:* Customers expect that a software system perfectly is perfectly adaptable to the customer's needs, his well-established business processes and helps him getting his business done.
- *Ubiquitous Access:* More and more customers want to benefit from the advantage that SaaS solutions are transparently available over the Internet in a way that they can work with these solutions anytime with almost any device they choose, be it with desktop computers in the office or at home, or with tablets or smart phones when being on the road.
- *High availability, good performance:* In many cases, customers entrust business critical data and processes with a SaaS solution. In these cases customers depend on that the system is available to them anywhere and anytime with good performance.
- *High security:* Customers decide on giving business critical data out of their hands into the cloud. Any doubts concerning security is fatal for the acceptance of SaaS solutions.
- *Interoperability with existing solutions:* As almost any business system has to exchange data with other systems, the same applies also to SaaS solutions. In many cases traditional on-premise systems have to interoperate with systems in the cloud and vice versa.

2   Example: SaaS CRM CAS PIA

To illustrate some of the concepts discussed in this chapter, we use examples from CAS PIA, a SaaS solution for contact management and customer relationship management (CRM) targeted to small and medium sized customers. It is available as pay-per-use software (depending on the number of users needed and various add-on features). Users can access the software via web browsers or native clients for most mobile platforms (e.g. iOS devices like the iPhone or iPad, Android tablets or phones).

It offers features relevant to the target customer group, such as a sophisticated address management, a campaign management including mass mailing capabilities, features for organizing the sales pipeline including opportunity management, workgroup features like calendaring, task scheduling and document management (Fig. 2).

3   Architecture

Most SaaS systems make use of a *layered architecture*. In the layered architecture (Buschmann et al. 1996), a system is decomposed into several distinct layers or *tiers* that can be developed, maintained and (often) deployed independently from each other:

- The *presentation layer* focuses on interacting with the user through a graphical user interface. It displays data and collects user input and commands. In most SaaS systems parts of the presentation layer run in a web browser or on mobile devices (in the form of native clients).
- The application layer or *business logic layer* provides operations that implement the processes and operations that the software solution provides.
- The *data layer* encapsulates the storage and provides access to the persistent data of the solution. In most cases this layer makes use of a database management system. Even though non-relational database technologies are getting more widespread with cloud solutions, most SaaS systems are still built using relational database technologies.

The SaaS paradigm imposes a number of specific requirements to that generic architecture. The following sections will discuss a number of these requirements and will provide some insight on architectural concepts addressing these requirements.

3.1   Meta Data Driven Architecture

In essence, SaaS solutions have to address two potentially conflicting requirements: On one hand they need to leverage the *economy of scale* principle (see Sect. 1.1) by employing a consolidated architecture that handles all customers uniformly, on the other hand customers demand that the software they use can be tailored to meet their specific requirements and match with their highly-individual business and the processes they work with.

Typically customers will want to customize a SaaS enterprise application on all three layers:

- *User interface:* Many customers will want to adapt the user interface to match with their corporate branding, i.e. adapt rather simple things like logos, colors and fonts, or to better reflect their internal nomenclature. In many cases customers will also like the ability to modify the layout and ordering of the presented information in order to put an emphasis on business critical information and hide less important information.
- *Business logic:* To optimally support customers implementing their daily business using the SaaS solution, a number of basic rules in the business logic layer

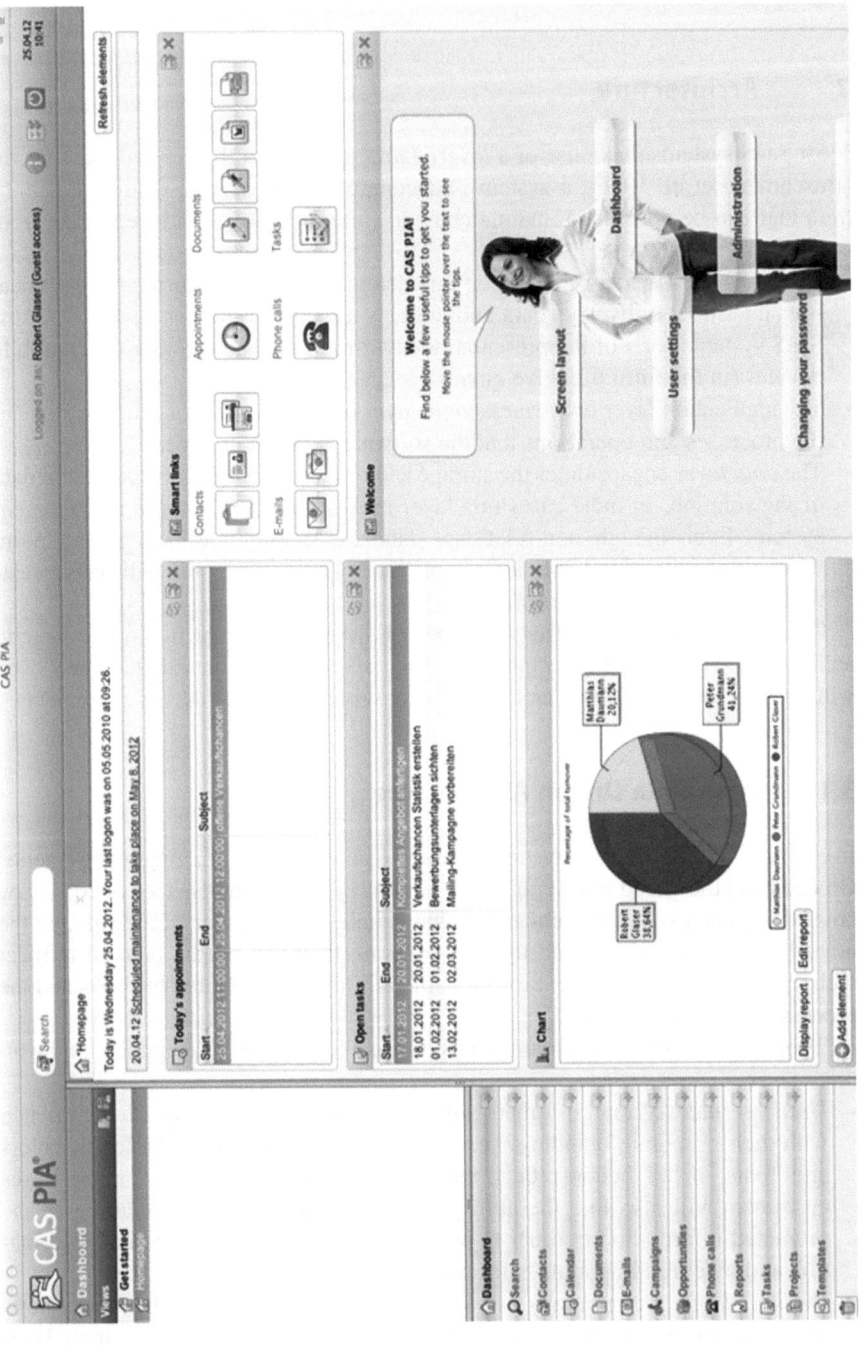

Fig. 2 Example screenshot from CAS PIA

must be customizable in order to cope with the specific requirements at the customer's site. A typical example from the CRM domain could be the rules that are used to evaluate the rating or potential of a customer. For one company such a rating might strongly depend on the yearly turnover with that customer, whereas another company might prefer to make that rating dependent on the number of sold licenses (in case of a software company) or the overall value of profitable insurance contracts (in case of an insurance company).

- *Data model extensions:* In many cases the data models shipped with the SaaS solution are meant to provide a good start for the majority of customers. In practice, many customers will find that they might want to store additional information in the system. In these cases extensions of the data model using custom fields for each customer are needed. Custom fields require that the underlying data models can be extended appropriately (see also Sect. 3.2). In many cases this will also require changes on the user interface level (the newly added custom fields have to be displayed in a suitable place) and on the business logic level (the custom fields may be involved in some of the business rules the customer wants to employ).

In traditional software systems, many of these customizations have been implemented by extending the system with customer specific code. In SaaS scenarios, where a key paradigm is that one consolidated codebase works for all customers, this approach is less suitable.

Instead, vendors try to implement generic mechanisms on all software layers that interpret customer specific configurations and use these to instantiate data models, business rules and workflows, as well as user interfaces specifically tailored towards the individual customers needs. In the literature, such an approach is often called *metadata driven* (Hicks et al. 1998), because these configurations contain models that define how the user data is structured, displayed and processed.

For PIA, this approach is shown in Fig. 3. For example, arbitrary new data objects containing fields of different standard types can be defined and configured using an XML-based data definition. Such a definition allows setting a number of different properties for these fields, e.g. names and labels, lengths for string fields, precision settings for number fields, but also more complex properties such as validation rules to ensure data consistency. On the user interface level, the structure and contents of data forms is also defined by an XML-based UI definition. Using appropriate tool support, consultants or even customers themselves can rearrange or extend portions of the standard PIA forms, e.g. to show or modify the custom data objects and fields introduced by customized data model definitions.

3.2   Multi-Tenancy

Multi-tenancy is the capability of a software system to serve multiple customers or *tenants* (which in turn comprise multiple users) from a single consolidated software system. As discussed above, a key to multi-tenancy on the application level is a

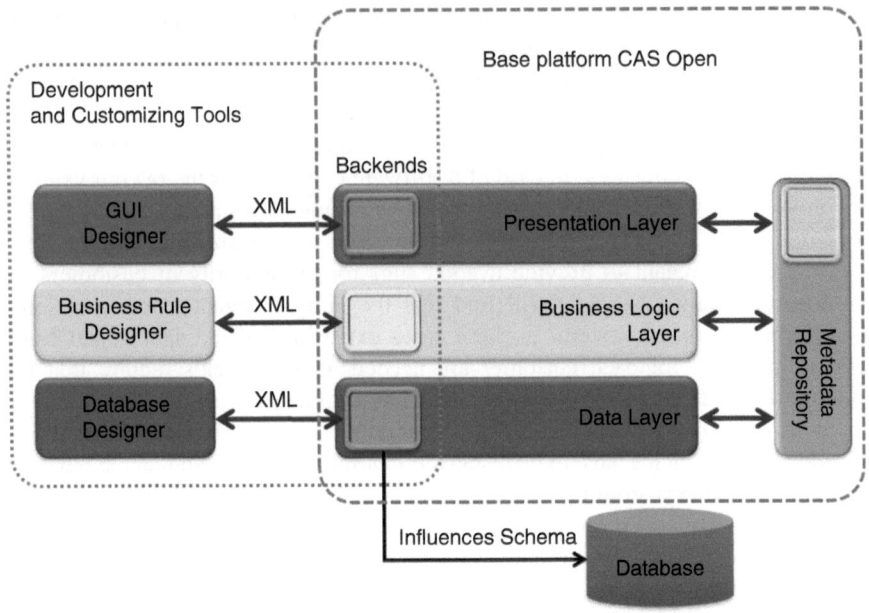

Fig. 3 Customization based on metadata

metadata based approach which allows for a great degree of tenant specific customization.

A key concern on the data layer level is the isolation of tenant specific data and the mapping of tenant structures to database schemas in such a way that individual customizations of the data models for each tenant are still possible.

The literature discusses different approaches for achieving multi-tenancy on the data layer:

- *One database per tenant:* Each of the tenants is mapped onto a separate physical database for storing the data.
- *One schema per tenant:* Each of the tenants is mapped into separate logical unit, often called *schema*, within a single physical database.
- *A shared database:* All tenants are stored in the same physical database and schema, but their information is separated using primary keys which are allocated as part of the database design and all the information is kept within the same physical tables.

The first two approaches have advantages with respect to tenancy isolation and data model flexibility. The data associated with each tenant is kept logically (or even physically) isolated from other tenants' data. Straightforward database techniques can be used for customizing the data models for each tenant individually. The shared-database approach on the other hand has an advantage concerning hosting costs – it is likely that less database server resources are required in this case. However, introducing flexible, tenant specific data models is tricky. There are a number of solutions for this problem (e.g. adding a preset number of data fields that tenants can use flexibly to store custom information (Chong and Carraro 2006), storing tenant specific custom fields in a linked, separate key-value table or employing huge generic data tables with metadata tables to ensure type-safety and pivot tables for optimized querying (Salesforce 2009)).

PIA employs a one-schema-per-tenant approach and is able to host some 1,000 tenants per MySQL database server instance.

3.3   Scalability

For any enterprise software, coming up with a scalable software architecture is a major concern. For SaaS enterprise systems, this is even more critical. The software will be used by thousands of users in parallel, namely the expected average number of concurrent users per customer multiplied by the number of customers having licensed the software.

There are different ways to achieve scalability. One way is to *scale-up* the system, i.e. to move the software to more powerful servers (i.e. more processing power, more RAM, more and faster storage,...) when the need arises. This is more or less straightforward from the software architecture's perspective, however it has serious drawbacks: the older hardware becomes useless, migration to the new hardware might be cumbersome, and scaling down is impossible.

For SaaS software, a *scale-out* strategy is much more suitable. A scale-out strategy means that the workload of the system can be distributed among several servers (often referred to by a farm).

As an example for a scale-out capable architecture, Fig. 4 depicts the deployment architecture of CAS PIA. A load balancer distributes the workload (i.e. requests issued by the clients) onto a number of application servers, which in turn make use of a number of database servers.

In this architecture, each of the application servers runs an identical instance of the application. To allow for such an architecture, a number of architectural rules need to be fulfilled (Chong and Carraro 2006):

- The application logic should be designed to operate in a *stateless way*, i.e. all user and session data should either be stored either on the client side, or in a distributed store that is accessible to any application instance. This allows that a user may interact with any of the application servers transparently, even within a single session – without even knowing it. In some cases this cannot be achieved, then a session- or IP-stable load balancing strategy is still an alternative.
- Any time and resource consuming operations should be implemented *asynchronously*. Long running operations (e.g. some complex database queries) can then run in the background while foreground resources can be dedicated towards new user transactions.
- Limited resources such as threads, network and database connections should be managed using *resource pools*. This allows for better resource management and utilization and reduces the overhead for initializing and destroying such resources.

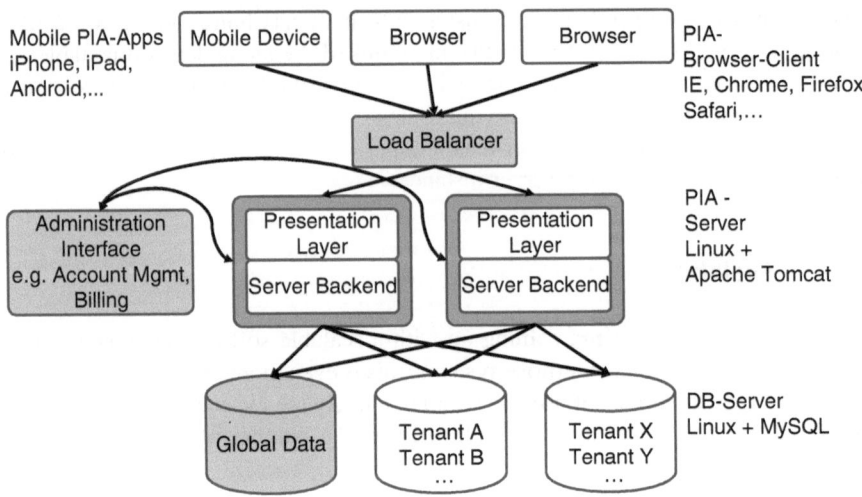

Fig. 4 Deployment architecture

- Database operations should be written in a way to maximize concurrency and minimize locking. Often it helps to distinguish between read-only and read-write transactions.
  A scaling-out architecture has a number of advantages:
- Instead of using expensive high-end servers, standard and cheap of-the-shelf servers can be used. To increase flexibility and ease maintenance in practice, often a number of virtual machines spread among different physical servers are used in such a scenario. In addition, a monitoring and control unit might be employed to dynamically add or remove these machines to the load-balancing cluster, providing a simple means for ensuring elasticity.
- A scale-out architecture is prepared for higher availability. Since many instances of the same application server are deployed anyway, the architecture has a good amount of redundancy built in.
  Scalability on the database layer will eventually require a partitioning of data among several database servers (Roy 2008). One advantage of the one-schema-per-tenant approach described above is, that the set of tenants can be easily partitioned into subsets that can be distributed onto a number of database servers. A global schema helps routing the requests to the corresponding server instance.

3.4   Technical Architecture and Infrastructure

Most software systems rely on a sound technical infrastructure. Since runtime requirements like high-availability, scalability and performance are of particular importance for SaaS systems, it is advisable to employ well-proven hardware and software components when building up the technical architecture. Choosing well-

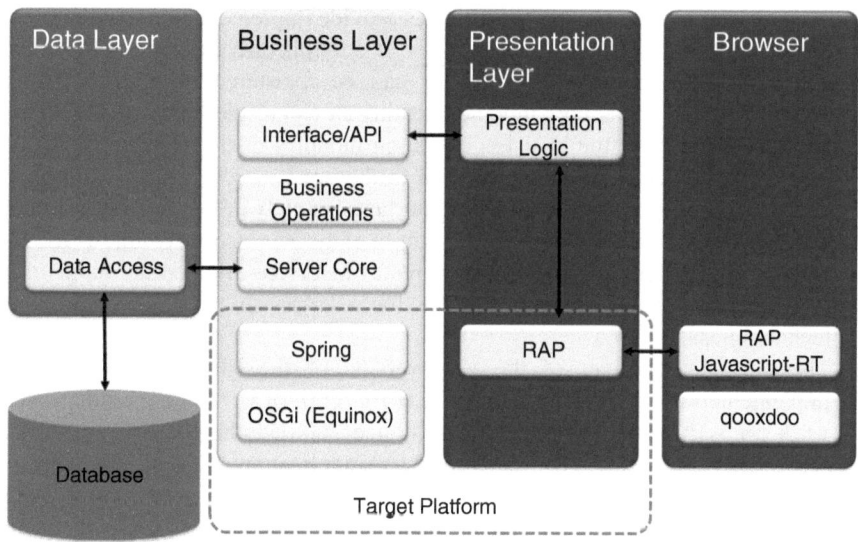

Fig. 5 Logical and technical architecture of PIA

established components helps ensuring a good basic quality but it also helps when deploying and operating the solution – this way, it is much more likely to find dedicated staff with existing know-how in computing centers or service providers.

Figure 4 illustrates the basic infrastructure for a PIA deployment. It consists of a farm of standard *Linux*-based PC-Servers that operate either as *Java* application servers based on *Apache Tomcat* or as database servers using *MySQL*. As mentioned previously these servers might also be provided in the form of virtual machines in some modern, scalable virtualization infrastructure.

Figure 5 provides a more detailed view on the software architecture of the application servers implemented using a *Java* technology stack. In PIA an *OSGi* run-time (McAffer et al. 2010) is used to provide an infrastructure for deploying and running independent software modules. Working with that OSGi run-time is structured and simplified using the well-proven *Spring* framework (Johnson et al. 2005; Walls 2009), which manages the different application modules and their dependencies.

- The *server core* module makes use of the data access module to manage generic (extensible) data objects. It also is responsible for enforcing a strict security policy by providing and verifying security contexts (e.g. based on user and tenant credentials).
- The *data access* module encapsulates database specifics. It enforces tenant isolation and implements a powerful permission system, thereby strictly controlling the access to the data stored in the databases. As a clean interface, it provides a database and platform neutral simplified SQL-like language for data access including a number of helper functions to simplify the access of more complex data structures.

- A number of *business operation* modules provide implementations for the CRM related features in PIA as well as a set of administrative functions (user and account management). New modules can be registered using mechanisms provided by the server core module, creating an extensible platform.
- Any operation from the business operation modules or the server core with a publically defined interface is exposed to the presentation layer (and to other clients, see Sect. 3.6) via a number of interfaces, namely in-process method calls, RMI and SOAP-style web services. A subset of those is also accessible as REST-style web services. This way, PIA provides a service-oriented an *application programming interface (API)* suitable for a large variety of use cases and technologies.
- The presentation layer of the web version of the PIA GUI is currently implemented using the *Eclipse Rich Ajax Platform (RAP)*, a server-side framework for AJAX-style user interfaces (Lange 2008). Eclipse RAP promotes a server-side development approach for AJAX applications. In RAP, basically all user interface controls have a server-side representation in Java, a lifecycle infrastructure is responsible for exchanging messages and synchronizing the status with JavaScript counterparts of the UI controls running in the users browser. A PIA specific generic *presentation logic* module provides generic user interface functionality like reusable controls, the application frame, configurable list and form views (based on metadata, see Sect. 3.1).
- In many modules, proven libraries are used to simplify the implementation. The data layer might illustrate this: it makes have use of *Ehcache* libraries and the *Spring SQL templates*.

3.5   Security

Security and safe operation of a SaaS system is a very important topic. SaaS systems might be seen as an attractive prey to attackers because they operate on the data of many customers and organizations. In general, the literature provides a huge set of methods and tools to help building secure web applications – the OWASP project for example provides a good starting point (OWASP 2012).

With respect to SaaS systems, two things are of particular importance

- *Isolation of tenants.* Users from one tenant should *never* be able to access data from other tenants. Isolation of tenant data is a concept, which should be embedded deeply into the application architecture. In PIA for example, any operation is strictly associated with a security context, which is always evaluated and enforced when eventually accessing tenant data from the database.
- *Safe data access paths crossing subsystem boundaries.* It has been a good practice to use subsystem boundaries also as a bulkhead to contain the impact of security flaws. Each subsystem interface should therefore ensure that it only allows sane, flawless interactions. An example might be a routine in the data layer that checks all incoming SQL expressions for syntactic and semantic sanity

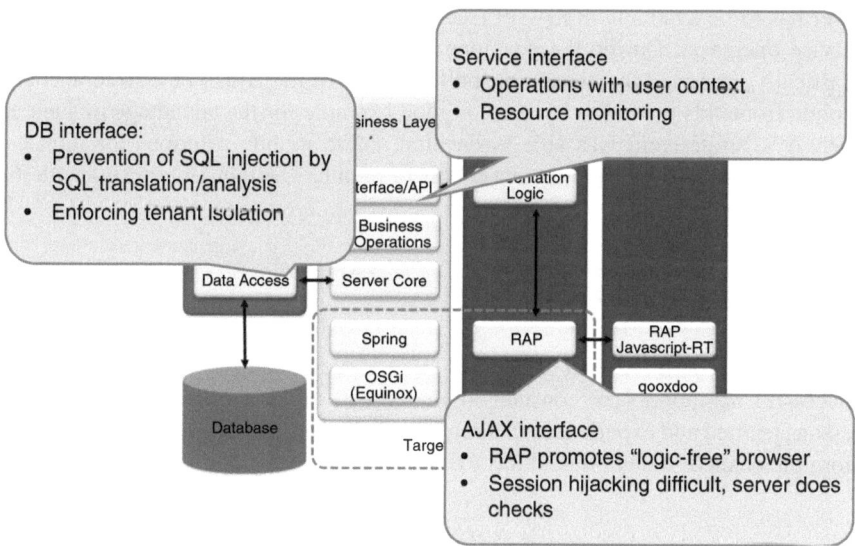

Fig. 6 Security provisions at subsystem boundaries

to avoid SQL injection. Similar measures should be designed for service interfaces and for AJAX-style user interfaces when validating user input.[1]

Figure 6 indicates some of the security provisions made in the PIA architecture.

3.6   Design Towards APIs

An important requirement for SaaS systems is that they are interoperable with existing solutions, even if these solutions are conventionally deployed on-premise. Another concern of many customers is that they want to have some flexible access to their data stored in the cloud systems. Many customers are reluctant to accept the concept of storing their data in silos without having a good method of accessing it.

The key to address these requirements is to provide good, powerful and easy to use APIs that adhere to defined and well-established standards. Many SaaS solutions provide SOAP- or REST-style web service interfaces to access their data or functions.

In the future, the power and expressiveness of such APIs will be a distinguishing feature of SaaS solutions. Although they are good guidelines on API design (see for example Tulach 2008), a good API design cannot easily be enforced. However, a simple trick may improve APIs a lot: *"Eat your own food"*, i.e. force yourself to use your own APIs. In PIA, for example, any function that is used by the presentation

---

[1] Validating user input should actually be implemented both on the client side (for providing quick user feedback) and on the server side (for keeping things secure).

layer has to be available in its API (see Sect. 3.4) and must be available as a web service operation. During the development of PIA it could be observed that this drastically improved the cleanness and the power of the API. The development of mobile frontends proved to be another good example for the advantage of such an API. A separate team was able to develop native mobile solutions for iOS and Android devices independently in a couple of months – without interfering with the core development team.

4 Lessons Learned

Looking back on more than 3 years of initial development and almost 4 years of successful operation (and constant improvement) of PIA, there are a number of lessons learned and experiences that might be helpful for vendors that like to benefit from the chances a SaaS model has to offer.

4.1 Customers Expect an Easy Start

Customers have already taken in the message: a SaaS solution may simplify the introduction of a new software system. This raises expectations concerning the usability of the software. Customers expect an easy start. The software is readily available on the Internet and can immediately be used (after registering, often even in a free trial phase). This means that most customers are not willing to spend a lot of time reading user manuals or view training materials.

In consequence, a good SaaS solution should be easy to learn while a user is already doing his first steps with the software. Frequently used features and features that many users might look for at the very beginning must be easy to find and to use. Using familiar user interface concepts can help here a lot. However, beginners are likely turn into advanced users if they like the product, so more complex and powerful functions still need to be present in the software and features relevant to daily users (such as keyboard shortcuts) should not be omitted.

PIA, as an example, uses a screen layout often employed e-mail clients, a software category almost everybody in PIA's target audience has used previously: It uses a navigation area (with folders) on the left part of the screen and a content area with lists or forms on the right part of the screen. Functions are organized in toolbars that are immediately familiar for users in PIA's target audience – people in small or medium sized enterprises that are already using *ribbons* in Microsoft's Office products (Fig. 7).

For PIA, usability tests have been used to optimize the user interface of the solutions. Using an early prerelease version of the system, more than 50 users from the expected target group with different experience levels have been closely observed while they were working with the software. They were asked to perform simple, but typical tasks, such as creating and modifying customer contacts, scheduling appointments, assign tasks to co-workers or composing an electronic

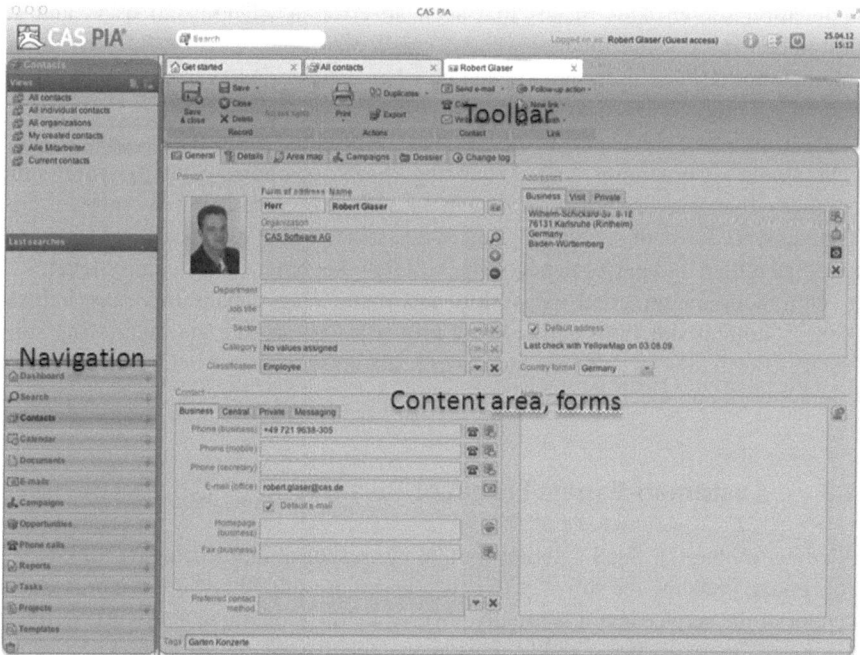

Fig. 7 PIA screen layout

mailing to a list of example customers. In many cases, the results were surprising and helpful and lead to the improvement of the user interface. In some cases improvements were as simple as adapting the terminology used in the software, in some cases processes were completely redesigned to better reflect the users' expectations.

Even after product launch, closely monitoring the customer base will provide a lot of insights. Customers of PIA make use of a number of support channels, such as phone or e-mail support. All support requests are recorded in a ticketing system. A structured evaluation of these tickets provides an invaluable means for identifying usability problems or weak spots in the feature sets. As an example, it became clear after a very short time after product launch, that importing existing customer data into PIA was a major obstacle for many customers: the feature was present in PIA but difficult to use and not powerful enough for many users. The feature was therefore improved a lot in later releases of PIA.

4.2   Quality Is Important

Apart from the external quality (offering a good, easy to use and powerful feature set), the internal quality or *implementation quality* of a SaaS solution is equally important. Consider a critical error (that eventually results in a crash) in an application server. This means that such an error is affecting all users and all customers in the same time. Similarly, small performance issues, in some cases tolerable for a single user, quickly add up when considering a larger customer base and a large number of concurrent active users.

It is therefore advisable to install quality oriented software processes when developing, maintaining and enhancing SaaS solutions. Quality improving practices like test driven development or pair programming may support this. Tool support for both source code level assessments and run-time level tests, e.g. automated load and performance tests, will help keeping a good quality level.

During operation good measuring and monitoring capabilities may help to identify critical situations early. Many proven solutions like the monitoring suite *Nagios* (Barth 2008) can be extended with custom sensors that can closely monitor critical resources specific to the SaaS solution.

4.3   Customers Expect Frequent Releases

A key advantage of SaaS solutions is that the responsibility (including all hassles) concerning updating the software to new releases are shifted towards the provider or vendor of the service and it is usually covered by the monthly or yearly subscription fee. From the experience with PIA, customers quickly get used to this commodity and are more eagerly expecting new releases with more and better features than it used to be the case with on-premise solutions. This will require a release-often strategy on the vendor's side and development processes that help reducing costs for assembling, stabilizing and "shipping" a new version. Experience shows, that agile methods like *Scrum* (Pichler 2008) help achieving these goals.

4.4   Offering SaaS Solutions Calls for Changes at the Vendor

Section 1.1 has argued that offering a SaaS solution may attract new customer segments. The experience from PIA underpins this, a number of small-sized companies have decided to subscribe to a SaaS CRM solution that had most likely never bought the traditional on-premise CRM solution the company is also offering. The new type of costumers and the lack of extensive projects usually associated with the introduction of business software calls for a number of changes in how a vendor interfaces with his customers:

A larger number of smaller customers will want to receive support, training and in some cases even consulting on how to best use the software and on how to better organize their business processes. For larger scale traditional software installations such services could easily be embedded and financially aligned with the introduction and customizing process for the software. For smaller customers on a tight IT budget, self-service mechanisms like online tutorials, web-based seminars, FAQ or support forums seem much more appropriate. Similarly, billing processes need to be adjusted to reflect the self-service nature of SaaS offerings. Customers will pay smaller amounts on a regular basis, in many cases using credit cards or similar payment methods.

It takes time to prepare a vendor's organization to accommodate these new customer interaction methods and processes.

4.5   Customers Still Ask for Some Personal Contact

The experience of PIA shows, that the new customer segments, i.e. small and medium enterprises that make up a bulk of the well-known German *Mittelstand*, still need to build confidence when entrusting their data and their business to a SaaS solution and its vendor. Internal experiments have shown that customers who have made some personal contact with the vendor, even on phone, are more likely to subscribe to the service than those who have just joined the free trail phase.

5   Summary

SaaS offerings provide chances for both customers and vendors. Customers benefit from a cost-effective, easy and risk-free way to introduce new software systems. Vendors may address completely new customer groups that might have been out of reach with traditional on-premise solutions due to high costs.

A good user interface design and suitable software architecture is required to make SaaS software successful for both customers and vendors. A well-thought architecture can leverage the principle of economy of scale for both the vendor and the customer without affecting the customer's need for highly customizable and tailored solutions.

For many customers, switching to a SaaS solution is still a matter of trust. Many customers are still reluctant to entrust their data and businesses to the cloud. It is desirable and likely that this will improve over time. A number of measures will help here: good user-friendly and flexible solutions will attract more and more customers, well-proven architectures will hopefully prove that software in the cloud is not less reliable and safe than traditional on-premise software.

References

Anderson, C. (2004). The long tail. In *Wired Magazine*. Issue 12.10 (pp. 170–177). New York: Conde Nast Publications.

Barth, W. (2008). *Nagios: System and network monitoring*. San Francisco: No Starch Press.

Buschmann, F., Meunier, R., Rohnert, H., Sommerlad, P., & Stal, M. (1996). *Pattern-oriented software architecture* (A system of patterns, Vol. 1). Chichester: Wiley.

Chong, F., & Carraro, G. (2006). *Architecture strategies for catching the long tail.*: MSDN Library, Microsoft Corporation.

Hicks, D.L., Tochtermann K., Rose, T., & Eich, S. (1998). Using metadata to support customization. In: Metadata'99: Proceedings of the Third IEEE Computer Society Metadata Conference, Bethesda, Maryland, USA, April 5-6, 1999.

Johnson, R., Höller, J., Arendsen, A., Risberg, T., & Sampaleanu, C. (2005). *Professional Java development with the spring-framework*. Indianapolis: Wiley.

Lange, F. (2008). *Eclipse rich ajax platform: Bringing rich client to the web*. Berkeley: Apress.

McAffer, J., Paul, W., & Archer, S. (2010). *OSGi and equinox: Creating highly modular Java Systems*. Upper Saddle River: Addison-Wesley Professional.

Mell, P., & Grance, T. (2011). *The NIST definition of cloud computing*. NIST Special Publication 800-145 (pp. 2–3). Gaithersburg, Maryland: National Institute of Standards and Technology.

OWASP Project. (2012). The open web application security project. https://www.owasp.org.

Pichler, R. (2008). *Agile product management with scrum: Creating products that customers love*. Upper Saddle River: Addison-Wesley.

Roy, R. (2008). Shard – A database design. http://technoroy.blogspot.de/2008/07/shard-database-design.html.

Salesforce. (2009). The force.com multitenant architecture. Whitepaper. Salesforce.com, http://www.developerforce.com/media/ForcedotcomBookLibrary/Force.com_Multi-tenancy_WP_101508.pdf.

Tulach, J. (2008). *Practical API design: Confessions of a Java framework architect*. Berkeley: Apress.

Walls, G. (2009). *Modular Java with OSGi and spring*. Raleigh: Pragmatic Bookshelf.

About the Authors

Dr. Markus Bauer leads the development of SaaS solutions and the underlying platforms at CAS Software AG, Germany. He has more than 15 years of working experience on software architecture and design – both as a researcher and a practitioner. Before joining CAS, he lead the software engineering research group at FZI Forschungszentrum Informatik, Karlsruhe, and received a Ph.D. in Computer Science from the University of Karlsruhe in 2005.

A. Maedche et al. (eds.), *Software for People*, Management for Professionals,
DOI 10.1007/978-3-642-31371-4, © Springer-Verlag Berlin Heidelberg 2012

Achim Botzenhardt is Research Associate and PhD Student at the Chair of Information Systems IV - Enterprise Systems (ERIS) at the University of Mannheim. He studied Business Informatics at the University of Mannheim with specialization in international management, marketing, and e-commerce. His specific research interest is cross-functional integration of product management and product design in software development.

Prof. Dr. Sjaak Brinkkemper is Full Professor of organization and information at the Department of Information and Computing Sciences of Utrecht University, The Netherlands. He leads a group of about 35 researchers specialized in the methodology of product software development, implementation and alignment, and entrepreneurship in software ecosystems.

Johannes Britsch studied business administration at the University of with intercultural qualification Japanese at the University of Mannheim and Heidelberg. Beside Japanese culture and language, he specialized in marketing and international management. Since June 2010 Johannes Britsch is external Ph.D. student at the Institute for SME Research and assistant of the executive director of CAS Software AG, Karlsruhe

Clemens N. Buss holds a M.Sc. in Complex Systems, having studied in Gothenburg and Rehovot, Israel and attended the HPI School of Design Thinking. He is pursuing a Ph.D. in physics at the Max-Planck-Institute in Göttingen. He is a co-founder of inventedhere.

Katrin Dribbisch works as a Research Associate at the Social Science Research Center Berlin (WZB). She studied political science and design thinking in Berlin, Potsdam and Warsaw and is a co-founder of inventedhere and Service Design Berlin. She is planning to pursue a Ph.D. in the field of design thinking and public sector innovation.

Dr. Samuel A. Fricker is Assistant Professor for Software Product Management and Requirements Engineering at the School of Computing, Blekinge Institute of Technology. He is Chairperson of the International Software Product Management, ISPMA e.V.

Rainer Grau is Director and Partner of Zühlke. In the role as distinguished consultant he is responsible to drive the knowledge areas innovation, product management, business analysis, requirements engineering, lean management and agility for customers and in his company. He is second chair of the International Requirements Engineering Board IREB and founding board member of the International Software Product Management Association ISPMA and is engaged as adjunct professor at several universities in Switzerland teaching Scrum, Lean Management und Requirements Engineering and as mentor in the bachelor and master programs.

Martin Groß works as consultant for user interface development with Microsoft and IBM technologies at DATEV eG. Among his main topics interaction design, usability, user centred design and user interface patterns, he is doing a lot of research in the field of innovative user interfaces for business software. He develops design studies and teaches DATEV developers.

Lennart Hennigs is a Product Designer at Deutsche Telekom AG and has worked in the field of User Centered Design and User Experience for more than 10 years. He studied Computer Science and Philosophy at the University of Paderborn.

Dr. Tobias Hildenbrand conducted his doctoral studies on requirements engineering ("Traceability in Distributed Collaborative Software Development") at the University of Mannheim and the University of California, Irvine, between 2004 and 2008. After working as an assistant professor in Mannheim, he joined SAP's development organization in 2009. After program management responsibility for the global rollout of lean and agile software development at SAP, Tobias Hildenbrand is currently driving the implementation of lean development and Design Thinking in SAP's 11 strategic investment areas. In doing so, he acts as agile requirements engineering consultant and Design Thinking coach for various development projects and product teams. Tobias is also involved in related research and teaching activities together with the University of Mannheim, Karlsruhe Institute of Technology, Hasso-Plattner-Institute and SAP Research.

Felix Kahrau studied Business Engineering at Karlsruhe Institute of Technology (KIT) and Lappeenranta University of Technology (LUT, Finland) with specialization in organization, entrepreneurship und applied computer science. Since November 2009 he is a Research Assistant at the Chair of Information Systems IV – Enterprise Systems (ERIS), University of Mannheim. His research interest focuses on design of activity management systems and their application in enterprise context.

Hans-Bernd Kittlaus is the Owner and CEO of InnoTivum Consulting (www. innotivum.com) and works as consultant, interim manager and trainer for software organizations in the areas of software product management, SaaS, IT strategy, business process management and software development. Before he was Director of SIZ GmbH, Bonn, Germany (German Savings Banks Organization) and Head of Software Product Management and Development units of IBM. He has published numerous articles and books, a.o. "Software Product Management and Pricing – Key Success Factors for All Software Organizations", Springer, 2009. He is Diplom-Informatiker, certified PRINCE2 Practitioner, ISPMA Certified Software Product Manager, founding board member of ISPMA (International Software Product Management Association e.V.), and member of ACM and GI.

Kira Krämer studied business administration and design thinking in Berlin, Potsdam and Sydney. She is engaged in research about social entrepreneurship and networks and is also a co-founder of Six Innovations and inventedhere.

Peter LoBue graduated from Temple University with a B.Sc. in Mathematics and Computer Science and attended the HPI School of Design Thinking. He works as a Consultant for experience design at NTT Data. He is also a co-founder of Six Innovations and inventedhere.

Prof. Dr. Alexander Maedche is Full Professor and Chairperson of the Chair of Information Systems IV, Enterprise Systems (ERIS) at the Business School and managing director of the Institute of Enterprise Systems (InES), both at the University of Mannheim. He studied business engineering and received a Ph.D. (Dr. rer. pol.) from the University of Karlsruhe. After his Ph.D., he worked 3 years at the Research Center for Computer Science (FZI) at the University Karlsruhe as head of a research group for knowledge-based systems. In the time frame of 2003–2009 he worked in the industry in various management positions. One important focus of his current work is researching software development processes with specific emphasis on product management and product design.

Hendrik Meth studied Business Informatics at the University of Mannheim and the City University of New York. After graduation, he worked as an IT Consultant and Project Manager in the Automotive Industry. Since June 2010 he is a Research Assistant at the Institute for Enterprise Systems (InES), University of Mannheim. His research interest focuses on the integration of user-centered design and requirements engineering with a methodological emphasis on design science research.

Johannes Meyer is a Design Thinking evangelist, coach and practitioner. He received an M.A. in cultural studies with a research focus on power relations & popular culture in social media. He worked as a teacher in Ski Lanka, in online startups and user research. After studying Design Thinking at the Hasso Plattner Institute in Potsdam, Johannes became an internal innovation consultant at SAP, co-designing applications for the banking, accounting and retail industry. He is now the General Program Manager of the HPI Academy and its learning track for professionals. In this function, he designs and conducts workshops and consulting formats in the field of Design Thinking, innovation and IT.

Ludwig Neer is software enthusiast and was born in Budapest. He studied business engineering with specialization in computer science in Karlsruhe and already operated as an entrepreneur from the second semester on. In 1986 he co-founded with Martin Hubschneider the CAS-Software AG. For the success of the company he retired his academic studies. Today Ludwig Neer is Head of Research and Technology of the CAS Software AG, which employs more than 220 employees.

Achim Oberg is a Research Assistant at the Institute for SME Research of Prof. Woywode at the University of Mannheim. After studying business informatics at the University of Mannheim and St. Gallen he researched the application of organization-theoretical concepts to analyze information systems within and between enterprises.

Kostanija (Conny) Petrovic is Manager Consumer Insight at the Nokia's Location & Commerce unit, where she helps product teams to innovate their products and services based on user feedback. She has previous experience in User Research and User Experience Design and Innovation Research, working at SAP AG, Open Text and the Technische Universität München respectively. She is the president of the German UPA, a professional association for Usability and User Experience Professionals.

Dr. Marcus Plach is a founder and Managing Director of ERGOSIGN GmbH, a specialised provider of user interface design services. After studying Psychology at the University of Regensburg, he was admitted to the Cognitive Science program at the Saarland University in Saarbrücken where he earned a Ph.D. in Cognitive Science. Besides his managerial commitments at ERGOSIGN, Marcus Plach is driving the optimization of design processes. As a lead consultant he coaches clients introducing user-centered design methods. He accounts for strategic development and corporate communications of ERGOSIGN.

Stefanie Pötzsch joined DATEV eG in 2011 and is part of the technology guideline project team. Previously, she worked as Research Assistant at Technische Universität Dresden and was involved in different European projects in the field of data privacy and user behavior, usability and user interface design.

Maik Schacht has studied business administration at Mannheim's University of cooperative education. Since his graduation 12 years ago, he gained practical experiences in various fields of duties such as content management or e-commerce. Now, Maik Schacht is Senior Innovation Manager of the IT provider within a large German chemical company.

Silvia Schacht is Ph.D. student at the Chair of Information Systems IV – Enterprise Systems (ERIS), University of Mannheim. Since 2 years she researches on modern technologies adapted in enterprise systems to improve knowledge management and employees' motivation.

Florian Scheiber studied business administration at the University of Mannheim with specialization in organization, marketing and psychology. Since September 2008 he is a Research Assistant at the Chair of SMEs and Entrepreneurship of Prof. Woywode at the University of Mannheim. In spring 2011 Mr. Scheiber was guest researcher at Stanford University for 3 months. Floran Scheibers research focus is diffusion and adaption of organizational practices as well as structuration of organizational fields.

Dr. Christian Schloegel is Global Head for Software Development and Product Management at Wincor Nixdorf. He introduced a dedicated Software Product Management at Wincor Nixdorf and established a central architecture approach to introduce a software product line. In the past he held different management positions at SAP AG including establishment of a central architecture group and was responsible as Senior Vice President Software Product Management.

Sebastian C. Scholz is User Experience Director at ERGOSIGN, a specialised provider of user interface design service. Besides heading the company's Munich's office, he helps clients in the enterprise, industry and medical sector to develop competitive user experience strategies. Practicing and preaching user centered design since the mid-nineties he has the most fun doing scoping and analysis internationally, which bridges two of his favourite research and publishing topics: Understanding and subsequently shaping corporate design strategies as well as intercultural design aspects.

Ulf Schubert is Head of User Experience Design and Standards at DATEV eG in Nuremberg. He is responsible for user centered design and the user experience design of DATEV software. Before that, he worked as user experience consultant und user experience designer for different companies including SirValUse Consulting in Hamburg. He publishes his experiences and knowledge at his User Experience Blog (www.ux-blog.de).

Abraham Taherivand studied information systems and design thinking in Stuttgart and Potsdam. He is a Partner and Co-founder of several startups based in Germany and is currently working as a project manager in the area of free and open knowledge.

Michail Theuns is a student enrolled in the Master of Business Informatics at Utrecht University. In his research, he studies the implementation of SPM in companies leveraging the product-service system business model. His research interests include SPM and global software development.

Kevin Vlaanderen is currently employed as a Researcher at Utrecht University. His research interests focus on the domains of software product management, software process improvement, method engineering, and agile software development. He is an active reviewer for several scientific conferences, and a personal member of the International Software Product Management Board (ISPMA).

Prof. Dr. Dieter Wallach is a Professor of Human-Computer Interaction and Usability Engineering at the Computer Science and Microsystems Technology Department of the University of Applied Sciences in Kaiserslautern. After studying Psychology, Computer Science and Information Science at the Saarland University in Saarbrücken he earned a Ph.D. in Cognitive Science before working as a Postdoctoral Associate at the Carnegie Mellon University in Pittsburgh, USA and the University of Basle, Switzerland. Dieter Wallach was offered professorships for New Media, Social Aspects of Software Engineering and Psychological Ergonomics. Besides his academic life he is also a Founder and Managing Director of ERGOSIGN, a specialised provider of user interface design services.

Anja M. Wölbling studied business administration and design thinking in Potsdam. She is a co-founder of Six Innovations and inventedhere and conducts research on the impact of design thinking on organizations and the implementation of ideas.

Prof. Dr. Michael Woywode is heading the Institute for SME Research at the University of Mannheim. Michael Woywode received his Ph.D. in Economics and habilitated in Business Administration at the University of Mannheim. He stayed 2 years as guest researcher at Stanford University and was Chairperson for international management at RWTH Aachen. Since September 2009 Michael Woywode is Chairperson of Chair of SMEs and Entrepreneurship and Director of the Institute for SME Research at the University of Mannheim. His scientific work has been published in various international journals.

Dominika Wruk studied business administration at the University of Mannheim and at the Ecole de Management in Bordeaux with specialization in logistics, Industrial Management and international management. Since June 2008 she is a Research Assistant at the Chair of SMEs and Entrepreneurship of Prof. Woywode at the University of Mannheim. In fall 2011 Mrs. Wruk was guest researcher at Stanford University for 3 months.